AF594794

Library of America, a nonprofit organization, champions our nation's cultural heritage by publishing America's greatest writing in authoritative new editions and providing resources for readers to explore this rich, living legacy.

IN CONGRESS, JULY 4, 1776.

The unanimous Declaration of the thirteen united States of America

The earliest extant photograph (1883) of the engrossed Declaration of Independence.

THE LIVING DECLARATION

A Biography of America's Founding Text

TED WIDMER

Foreword By Gordon S. Wood

LIBRARY OF AMERICA

THE LIVING DECLARATION
A BIOGRAPHY OF AMERICA'S FOUNDING TEXT BY TED WIDMER

Published in the United States by Library of America,
14 East 60th Street, New York, NY 10022.
Visit our website at www.loa.org

Frontispiece: The earliest extant photo of the engrossed Declaration of Independence. From a "Negative taken by the Publisher July 25, 1883, from the Original Parchment in the Library of the Department of State." (Washington, D.C.: A. G. Gedney, 1883.) Courtesy of Library of Congress, Prints & Photographs Division.

This paper meets the requirements of
ANSI/NISO Z39.48–1992 (Permanence of Paper).

Distributed to the trade in the United States
by Penguin Random House Inc.
and in Canada by Penguin Random House Canada Ltd.

The authorized representative in the EU for product safety and compliance
is eucomply OÜ, Pärnu mnt 139b-14, 11317 Tallinn, Estonia.
hello@eucompliancepartner.com

Library of Congress Control Number: 2026935476
ISBN 978–1–59853–844–1

1 3 5 7 9 10 8 6 4 2

Printed in the United States of America

The Living Declaration
is published with generous support from

LES LEVI

**DAVID BRUCE SMITH,
GRATEFUL AMERICAN FOUNDATION**

and

**THE NATIONAL ENDOWMENT
FOR THE HUMANITIES**

CONTENTS

THE DECLARATION OF INDEPENDENCE

GORDON S. WOOD

To be an American is not to be someone, but to believe in something. And the something that Americans most readily believe in can be found in the Declaration of Independence. By itself it makes the United States a nation.

The United States has not been a nation in any traditional meaning of the term, that is, a political body composed of a people with a common ancestry or cultural heritage. There is no American ethnicity that corresponds to the state called the United States, and there was no such distinctive ethnicity even in 1776 when the United States was created. Although the first sentence of the Declaration of Independence holds out the promise of Americans becoming "one people," at the end of the text the members of the Continental Congress could only mutually pledge "to each other" their lives, their fortunes, and their sacred honor. There was nothing else but themselves they could dedicate themselves to—no patria, no fatherland, no nation as yet.

Even at the time of the founding America already had a diverse society. In addition to seven hundred thousand people of African descent and tens of thousands of native Indians, nearly all the peoples of Western Europe were represented in the country. In the census of 1790 only 60 percent of the white population of well over three million could claim English ancestry. The rest were composed of a variety of ethnicities—Germans, Scots, Irish, Scotch-Irish, Dutch, and several others.

For eighteenth-century enlightened reformers, ethnic diversity and multiculturalism were not good things. The revolutionary leaders' idea of a modern nation, shared by enlightened British, French, and German eighteenth-century thinkers as well, was one that, as David Ramsay said, was composed of "a homogeneous people," a society that was not broken up by differences of dialects, ethnicity, religion, and local customs.

Thus many of the revolutionary leaders were desperate to think of themselves as a homogeneous people. John Jay lived in New York, the most diverse city in the country, and was himself three-eighths French and five-eighths Dutch with no English ancestry whatsoever. Nevertheless, in *Federalist* No. 2 Jay had the nerve to declare that "Providence has been pleased to give this one connected country to one united people—a people descended from the same ancestors, speaking the same language, professing the same religion, attached to the same principles of government, [and] very similar in their manners and customs."

Jay's statement was based on hope, not reality. Many other revolutionary leaders had little of his confidence in America's homogeneity and instead wondered whether America could ever be a real, honest-to-goodness nation. John Adams certainly had his doubts. In America, he said, there was nothing like "the patria of the Romans, the Fatherland of the Dutch, or the Patrie of the French." All he could see was an appalling diversity of religious denominations and ethnicities. At one point he counted at least twenty different religious sects in the United States. "We are such a Hotch potch of people," he concluded, "such an omnium gatherum of English, Irish, German, Dutch, Sweedes, French, &c. that it is difficult to give a name to the Country, characteristic of the people."

In the aftermath of the War of 1812, the rematch with Great Britain that some Americans called the second War of Independence, Secretary of the Treasury Albert Gallatin, himself a Swiss immigrant, thought that the people had become "more American; they feel and act more as a nation; and I hope that the permanency of the Union is thereby better secured." The war had the effect of diminishing the country's sense of being English. The war tied Englishness exclusively to a Federalist Party that was on its last legs and about to disappear.

Yet immigration from Europe continued, and the country was even more ethnically diverse and farther away than ever from being a traditional nation. Hezekiah Niles, the most important journalist of the early nineteenth century, saw the problem and offered a new solution to the establishing of "a NATIONAL CHARACTER" for Americans. Despite the victory over Britain in the War of 1812, Niles knew that eliminating the old English habits of mind would never be enough to make America a real nation. If we were to have a new nation, Niles declared in a public appeal in 1817 addressed to the two former Republican presidents Thomas Jefferson and James Madison, we needed new principles, new ideas, new ways of thinking. "We seek a new revolution," he said, "not less important, perhaps, in its consequences than that of 1776—a revolution in letters; a shaking off of the fetters of the mind." To do this, he said, "we should begin with the establishment of first principles," principles that were close at hand in Jefferson's Declaration of Independence. Thus, the Declaration, said Niles, "shall be the base of all the rest—the *common reference* in cases of doubt and difficulty."

It was Abraham Lincoln who decisively developed Niles's insight and argued for the unifying importance of the Revolution and the Founders to all Americans. When Lincoln declared in 1859 "all honor to Jefferson," he paid homage to the Founder who he knew could explain why the United States was one nation, and why it should remain so. Half the American people, said Lincoln, had no direct blood connection to the revolutionaries of 1776. These German, Irish, French, and Scandinavian citizens either had come from Europe themselves or their ancestors had, and they had settled in America, "finding themselves our equals in all things." Although these immigrants may have had no actual connection in blood with the revolutionary generation that could make them feel part of the rest of the nation, they had, said Lincoln, "that old Declaration of Independence" with its expression of the moral principle of equality to draw upon. This principle, which was "applicable to all men and all times," made all these different peoples one with the Founders, "as though they were blood of the blood, and flesh of the flesh of the men who wrote that Declaration." This emphasis on liberty and equality, Lincoln said, shifting images, was "the electric cord . . . that links the hearts of patriotic and liberty-loving men together, that will link those patriotic hearts as long as the love of freedom exists in the minds of men throughout the world."

In Jefferson's Declaration Lincoln found a solution to the great problem of American identity: how the great variety of individuals in America with all their diverse ethnicities, races, and religions could be brought together into a single nation. As Lincoln grasped better than anyone ever has, the Revolution and its Declaration of Independence offered us a set of beliefs that through the generations has supplied a bond that holds together the most diverse nation that history has ever known.

Since now the whole world is in the United States, nothing but the ideals coming out of the Revolution and their subsequent rich and contentious history can turn such an assortment of different individuals into the "one people" that the Declaration says we are. That is why, as Ted Widmer shows so powerfully in this book, the Declaration of Independence is the most important document in American history.

INTRODUCTION

TED WIDMER

"The Declaration of Independence makes a difference."

—Herman Melville to Evert Duyckinck, March 28, 1849

This book tells the story of our ongoing relationship with the most important American state paper ever written, and one of the great documents of world history. It examines the Declaration of Independence in close detail, not just its words but the actual parchment on which the words are written.

Now in the care of the National Archives, that parchment holds a special place in the hearts of Americans. It is very secure, in a titanium vault that is lowered into an underground crypt each evening. But nothing about the Declaration's history is static. It was born in a time of ferment, with British warships bearing down on New York to suppress a rebellion that had already gone on too long, in the opinion of His Britannic Majesty, King George III. During the war, it was frequently moved and sequestered, to protect it from invading armies. Since then, it has survived other hardships, including a series of relocations between temporary capitals, another British invasion (in 1814), and at least five different homes in Washington. In the immediate aftermath of Pearl Harbor, it was again spirited away, this time to impregnable Fort Knox, in Kentucky.

The stresses of these emergency measures, along with the ravages of time, have altered the appearance of the Declaration. Like the American people, it has changed over the years. That includes the way we think about it; each generation has found new ways of reading the text, and new ways to apply its wisdom to the here and now.

In short, it is far from a dead letter. Careful study by archivists has established an unusual fact about the Declaration. It moves in its case, expanding and contracting, almost as if it is breathing. Befitting a parchment made from animal skin, and written with an ink derived from trees, it responds to the atmosphere around it. In other words, the Declaration comes from the same source—"Nature and . . . Nature's God"—that it describes. Like all artifacts created from living things, it adapts to its surroundings. In a sense, it *does* breathe.

That is not unlike the arguments in the text itself, still stretching out after all these years. Lincoln once said that the Declaration had been written for the "future use" of Americans, and that it would continue to ripen over time, ultimately extending to "all people of all colors everywhere." He acted on that belief, finding antislavery arguments in the text that might have come as a surprise to Thomas Jefferson, its primary author. At times, Lincoln's reverence for the Declaration bordered on the supernatural. As we shall see, when he visited Independence Hall in 1861, on his way to his inauguration, he mentioned the "breathings" he could hear, emanating from the building where the founding text had been debated and approved.

In all of these ways, the Declaration feels more alive than most historical documents. That is the idea behind *The Living Declaration*. America's founding text continues to send out powerful signals, 250 years after it was created. It speaks to Americans across the political spectrum, and it speaks to millions of non-Americans as well. Around the world, disenfranchised peoples look to it for sustenance. It breathes new life, every day, into the ideas that it articulates.

It is ancient by some measures—a quarter of a millennium, the same age that our oldest animal, a giant tortoise, can live to. But it will always be evergreen, as long as governments continue to disappoint their peoples, and those peoples, quite naturally, seek out the words to express a longing for something better.

The 39 Steps

At the same time, the Declaration can be daunting. To approach its most famous version today requires some effort, beginning with a climb of

Figure 1: *Fourth of July banners adorn the National Archives Building in Washington, D.C.*

thirty-nine steps from the street level of Pennsylvania Avenue, toward the massive doors that served, for decades, as the main entrance of the National Archives. The number of steps bears no relation to the Hitchcock thriller of the same name; it derives instead from an architect's decision to honor the thirty-nine signers of the Constitution. Still, it could have been worse: The Declaration had fifty-six signers.

Once inside the darkened rotunda, a visitor must navigate long lines and unsmiling security guards, before being allowed, briefly, to stand before the Declaration and the other "Charters of Freedom" (the Constitution and the Bill of Rights). It is a humbling experience, by design. The enormity of the Rotunda and the impressive size of the formal encasement, holding the charters, behind bulletproof glass, create a feeling of awe. There is a distinctly religious feeling, enhanced by the cathedral-like setting of the room, with its low lighting, its seventy-five-foot ceiling, and the sound of people whispering in hushed tones. The charters are kept in a "Freedom Shrine," a word used since the "Enshrinement Ceremony" of 1952. "Shrine," historically, has meant a place where holy objects are stored, like a reliquary, or the Ark of the Covenant.

Indeed, there are signs that the Ark of the Covenant may have entered into the thinking of the architect. Behind the shrine, there are words chiseled into the wall, almost as if these were the stone tablets bearing the Ten Commandments, brought down from Mount Sinai by Moses. The feeling of human insignificance is not diminished by the fact that the Declaration, with its badly faded ink, has become nearly impossible to read. After a few moments of squinting at the parchment, in a vain effort to penetrate its inscrutable mysteries, the visitor is asked to keep the line moving.

The designers of the shrine were well-intentioned; they wanted us to feel reverence before a document that is sacred to millions. But reverence can get in the way of understanding. The purpose of this book is to adjust the lighting, to make it easier to read the Declaration again.

Through a wide range of selections, we will look closely at the words of the original document (including those that were deleted) and follow the story of how these words have spoken to us, in different ways, across our history. We will explore the Declaration's antecedents, its creation in the summer of 1776, and the myriad ways in which we have lived with it ever since.

This latter part is important. We have been responding to the Declaration for a long time. These responses constitute the heart of the book. Many voices will be included, befitting a cacophonous democracy. They come from the Right, the Left, and all stations in between.

The Declaration of Independence is many things: a political statement, announcing the formation of a new government; an impassioned Enlightenment argument for universal human rights; and a legal document of sorts, almost a warrant, a catalogue of twenty-seven offenses committed by a king who was not likely to respond well to such an unflinching assault on his dignity.

For all of these reasons, it can be a challenging document, not easily simplified. Pauline Maier titled her indispensable book about the Declaration *American Scripture*—an apt phrase for a text that we read with Talmudic reverence. Maier was alert to the Declaration's many internal contradictions. It drew from foreign sources, including British ones, as it argued for America's independence from Britain. It repeated well-known phrases and concepts, many of which were conservative, even as it created a radically new approach to government. It expressed reverence for "Nature's God," the "Creator," and "divine Providence," but in a studiously understated way that avoided the more pious phrasings routinely cited in European state documents. Its primary author, Thomas Jefferson, was a staunch advocate for a "wall of separation between church and state."

It will always be important to listen to the Founders. They created the document collectively, but did not always speak with one voice. Even as it was coming into existence, the Declaration meant different things to different people, a pattern that has remained consistent.

It is equally important to hear from the many Americans who did *not* feel embraced by the Declaration's promises, despite Lincoln's assurances that all peoples would eventually get there. The long struggle to extend the Declaration's writ provides an important theme of the book. The story is better for being contested.

Americans have debated the meanings of the Declaration, sometimes bitterly, ever since Jefferson finished his first draft. His sentences grew in relevance in the approach to the Civil War, when they exposed America's failings during a searing debate over slavery. They grew some more in the twentieth century, with Americans pressing to extend the Declaration's promises at home and around the world.

As Lincoln predicted, the Declaration would prove a "hard nut to crack" for any would-be despots, because it so clearly articulates the values that define our democracy (despite the fact the Declaration does not use that word). To this day, efforts to reframe our system of government inevitably bump up against these values. They remain powerful; yet they were much debated at the time, and have been debated ever since. Perhaps for that reason, Lincoln called the Declaration a "proposition," as if democracy were not entirely a settled matter. During the Civil War, it took sacrifice and hard work to convert the proposition into a fact. That was the thrust of Lincoln's speech at Gettysburg. It will surely require more work in the future, and many hard choices. A keener understanding of the Declaration is a logical place to begin.

What Is the Declaration of Independence?

Let's start, then, with a simple question. What exactly is the Declaration of Independence? The answer is not as straightforward as we might expect. Richard Henry Lee, who proposed independence in Congress, once called it "the Thing." In a letter to Thomas Jefferson, on July 21, 1776, he wrote, "the *Thing* is in its nature so good, that no Cookery can spoil the Dish for the palates of Freemen."

John Adams, Jefferson's friend and occasional rival, had a different view. He participated in the writing of the text, as a member of the drafting committee, and as an editor of Jefferson's first draft. But his perspective on the Declaration was decidedly more nuanced, especially in later decades, as the document became more famous, and enhanced Jefferson's reputation at the expense of his own.

In those years, Adams dismissed the Declaration as "a Theatrical Show" and a "Stage Effect," of some fleeting interest, but far less important than the actual vote for independence. To Adams, the Declaration was like a marquee poster, calling attention to the performance, but nothing like the main event. There is a tension between the views of Adams and Jefferson that has never been entirely resolved. Which was more important? Independence, the thing itself? Or the document that described independence so sublimely?

The Founders were empirically minded men; indeed, they defined the Declaration as a statement of facts ("Let facts be submitted to a candid world"). So here are some facts: the Declaration is a document that—first and foremost—declares independence. It asserts that a new country has come into existence. It gives a name to that country. It gives a date too. In all of these ways, it resembles a birth certificate for the United States of America.

But the facts do not tell the whole story. It is much more than a birth certificate. It is a philosophical statement, asserting the capacity of human beings to govern themselves. It is a diplomatic overture to other nations—because a declaration of independence creates a new country, with a need for recognition. And it is a resounding expression of collective purpose—of confederation—as a people were girding themselves for war, against another people to whom they were closely related.

For all of these reasons, the Declaration rewards close study.

The Engrossed Declaration

For most of us, when we think of the Declaration of Independence we think of a specific artifact. It is the parchment on display at the National Archives, seen by more than a million people a year. It is the star of the film *National Treasure*. Even though it is very famous, the "original" Declaration still holds surprises. As a parchment, it was created from an animal's skin—a calf, likely,

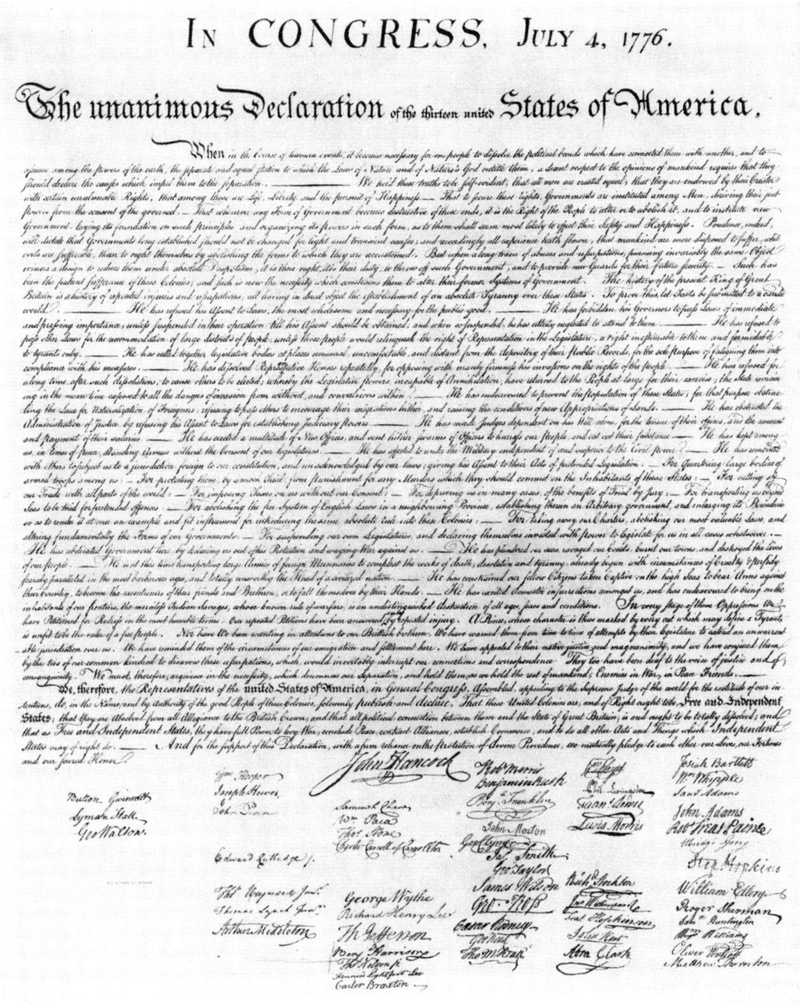

IN CONGRESS, JULY 4, 1776.

The unanimous Declaration of the thirteen united States of America,

Figure 2: *A facsimile of the engrossed version of the Declaration of Independence.*

but possibly a sheep or a goat. Microscopic analysis has revealed scars that were on the animal's skin. The parchment is 24¼ by 29¾ inches, containing 1,320 words (1,337 if you include the title). If you add the signers' names, the word count climbs to 1,458. They are written out in iron gall ink, the conventional ink for an important public document. It is an ink made from tannic acids (made from oak gall-nuts, a kind of tree growth made by wasps), a binding agent (derived from gum Arabic, a tree sap), and iron compounds.

But this document did not exist on July 4, 1776, the date that is inscribed so prominently at the top. It was "engrossed," or prepared for a formal signing, after an order by the Continental Congress, on July 19, to create a more durable version of the document that was lying before Congress as it declared independence. That assignment went to a scribe with good handwriting, Timothy Matlack. If not quite a signer himself, Matlack contributed meaningfully as a calligrapher whose artistry enhanced the argument. His skill at writing out the words helped those words to reach people, legibly, as they came in ever-greater numbers to see the document that gave birth to their country. He made two small mistakes in his transcription, inadvertently adding to the sense that the Declaration was (and remains) a work in progress. After he had finished his task, the engrossed Declaration was signed by most of the delegates, a month after the vote for independence, on August 2.

But again, there is more to the story. A few states had changed their delegations between early July and early August, with the result that the signers of August 2 were not identical to the men who voted for independence a month earlier. Some who voted for independence in July were no longer in Philadelphia; some who weren't in Congress on July 4 signed it a month later. A member of the five-person drafting committee, Robert Livingston, never signed it at all. One delegate, George Read, actually voted *against* independence in July, but still signed the engrossed Declaration in August. Several delegates signed after August 2 (Jefferson called them "post-signers").

The Dunlap Broadside

There is another version of the Declaration that was issued closer to July 4. Its importance can hardly be overstated.

One of the first acts of the newly independent nation was to announce the fact of its existence. And so, on July 4, Congress ordered that the Declaration that it had just approved be "authenticated and printed," and that the committee that had prepared the Declaration be responsible for printing it. Or as Congress instructed, to "superintend & correct the press."

Accordingly, a manuscript copy of the Declaration was taken to the Market Street print shop of John Dunlap, an Irish immigrant, probably on the night of

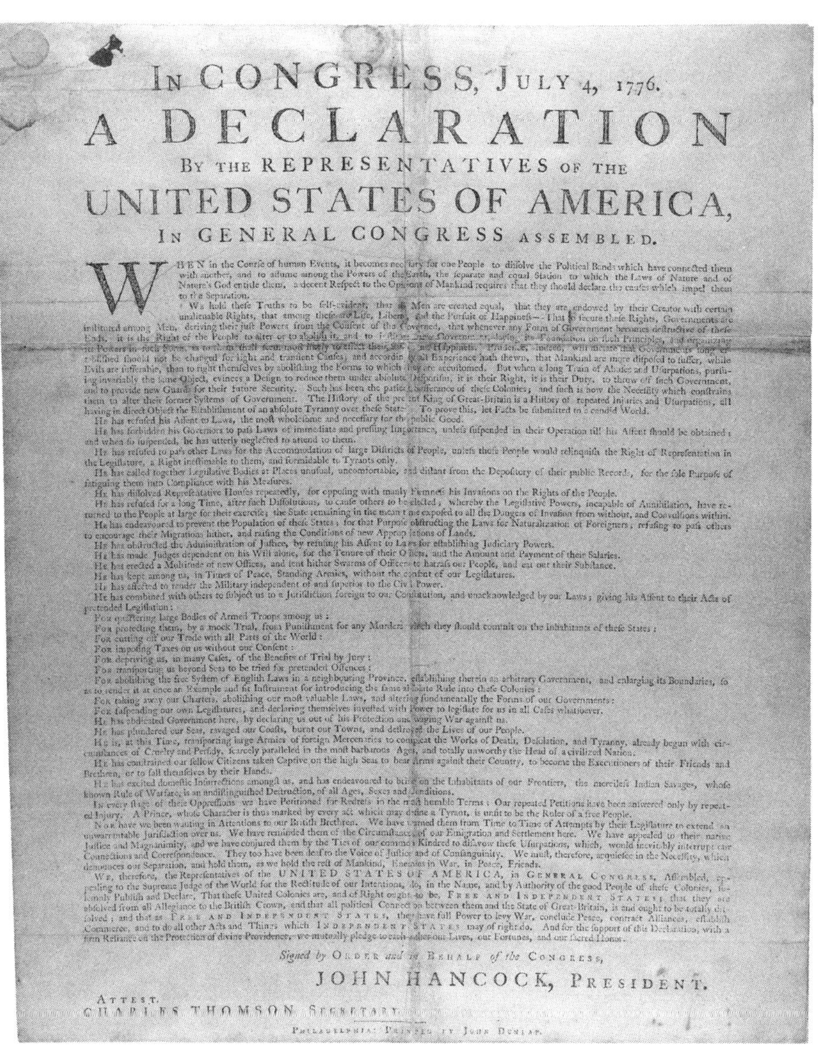

IN CONGRESS, JULY 4, 1776.

A DECLARATION

BY THE REPRESENTATIVES OF THE

UNITED STATES OF AMERICA,

IN GENERAL CONGRESS ASSEMBLED.

WHEN in the Course of human Events, it becomes necessary for one People to dissolve the Political Bands which have connected them with another, and to assume among the Powers of the Earth, the separate and equal Station to which the Laws of Nature and of Nature's God entitle them, a decent Respect to the Opinions of Mankind requires that they should declare the causes which impel them to the Separation.

We hold these Truths to be self-evident, that all Men are created equal, that they are endowed by their Creator with certain unalienable Rights, that among these are Life, Liberty, and the Pursuit of Happiness—That to secure these Rights, Governments are instituted among Men, deriving their just Powers from the Consent of the Governed, that whenever any Form of Government becomes destructive of these Ends, it is the Right of the People to alter or to abolish it, and to institute new Government, laying its Foundation on such Principles, and organizing its Powers in such Form, as to them shall seem most likely to effect their Safety and Happiness. Prudence, indeed, will dictate that Governments long established should not be changed for light and transient Causes; and accordingly all Experience hath shewn, that Mankind are more disposed to suffer, while Evils are sufferable, than to right themselves by abolishing the Forms to which they are accustomed. But when a long Train of Abuses and Usurpations, pursuing invariably the same Object, evinces a Design to reduce them under absolute Despotism, it is their Right, it is their Duty, to throw off such Government, and to provide new Guards for their future Security. Such has been the patient Sufferance of these Colonies; and such is now the Necessity which constrains them to alter their former Systems of Government. The History of the present King of Great-Britain is a History of repeated Injuries and Usurpations, all having in direct Object the Establishment of an absolute Tyranny over these States. To prove this, let Facts be submitted to a candid World.

He has refused his Assent to Laws, the most wholesome and necessary for the public Good.

He has forbidden his Governors to pass Laws of immediate and pressing Importance, unless suspended in their Operation till his Assent should be obtained; and when so suspended, he has utterly neglected to attend to them.

He has refused to pass other Laws for the Accommodation of large Districts of People, unless those People would relinquish the Right of Representation in the Legislature, a Right inestimable to them, and formidable to Tyrants only.

He has called together Legislative Bodies at Places unusual, uncomfortable, and distant from the Depository of their public Records, for the sole Purpose of fatiguing them into Compliance with his Measures.

He has dissolved Representative Houses repeatedly, for opposing with manly Firmness his Invasions on the Rights of the People.

He has refused for a long Time, after such Dissolutions, to cause others to be elected; whereby the Legislative Powers, incapable of Annihilation, have returned to the People at large for their exercise; the State remaining in the mean time exposed to all the Dangers of Invasion from without, and Convulsions within.

He has endeavoured to prevent the Population of these States; for that Purpose obstructing the Laws for Naturalization of Foreigners; refusing to pass others to encourage their Migrations hither, and raising the Conditions of new Appropriations of Lands.

He has obstructed the Administration of Justice, by refusing his Assent to Laws for establishing Judiciary Powers.

He has made Judges dependent on his Will alone, for the Tenure of their Offices, and the Amount and Payment of their Salaries.

He has erected a Multitude of new Offices, and sent hither Swarms of Officers to harrass our People, and eat out their Substance.

He has kept among us, in Times of Peace, Standing Armies, without the consent of our Legislatures.

He has affected to render the Military independent of and superior to the Civil Power.

He has combined with others to subject us to a Jurisdiction foreign to our Constitution, and unacknowledged by our Laws; giving his Assent to their Acts of pretended Legislation:

For quartering large Bodies of Armed Troops among us:

For protecting them, by a mock Trial, from Punishment for any Murders which they should commit on the Inhabitants of these States:

For cutting off our Trade with all Parts of the World:

For imposing Taxes on us without our Consent:

For depriving us, in many Cases, of the Benefits of Trial by Jury:

For transporting us beyond Seas to be tried for pretended Offences:

For abolishing the free System of English Laws in a neighbouring Province, establishing therein an arbitrary Government, and enlarging its Boundaries, so as to render it at once an Example and fit Instrument for introducing the same absolute Rule into these Colonies:

For taking away our Charters, abolishing our most valuable Laws, and altering fundamentally the Forms of our Governments:

For suspending our own Legislatures, and declaring themselves invested with Power to legislate for us in all Cases whatsoever.

He has abdicated Government here, by declaring us out of his Protection and waging War against us.

He has plundered our Seas, ravaged our Coasts, burnt our Towns, and destroyed the Lives of our People.

He is, at this Time, transporting large Armies of foreign Mercenaries to compleat the Works of Death, Desolation, and Tyranny, already begun with circumstances of Cruelty and Perfidy, scarcely paralleled in the most barbarous Ages, and totally unworthy the Head of a civilized Nation.

He has constrained our fellow Citizens taken Captive on the high Seas to bear Arms against their Country, to become the Executioners of their Friends and Brethren, or to fall themselves by their Hands.

He has excited domestic Insurrections amongst us, and has endeavoured to bring on the Inhabitants of our Frontiers, the merciless Indian Savages, whose known Rule of Warfare, is an undistinguished Destruction, of all Ages, Sexes and Conditions.

In every stage of these Oppressions we have Petitioned for Redress in the most humble Terms: Our repeated Petitions have been answered only by repeated Injury. A Prince, whose Character is thus marked by every act which may define a Tyrant, is unfit to be the Ruler of a free People.

Nor have we been wanting in Attentions to our British Brethren. We have warned them from Time to Time of Attempts by their Legislature to extend an unwarrantable Jurisdiction over us. We have reminded them of the Circumstances of our Emigration and Settlement here. We have appealed to their native Justice and Magnanimity, and we have conjured them by the Ties of our common Kindred to disavow these Usurpations, which, would inevitably interrupt our Connections and Correspondence. They too have been deaf to the Voice of Justice and of Consanguinity. We must, therefore, acquiesce in the Necessity, which denounces our Separation, and hold them, as we hold the rest of Mankind, Enemies in War, in Peace, Friends.

We, therefore, the Representatives of the UNITED STATES OF AMERICA, in GENERAL CONGRESS, Assembled, appealing to the Supreme Judge of the World for the Rectitude of our Intentions, do, in the Name, and by Authority of the good People of these Colonies, solemnly Publish and Declare, That these United Colonies are, and of Right ought to be, FREE AND INDEPENDENT STATES; that they are absolved from all Allegiance to the British Crown, and that all political Connection between them and the State of Great-Britain, is and ought to be totally dissolved; and that as FREE AND INDEPENDENT STATES, they have full Power to levy War, conclude Peace, contract Alliances, establish Commerce, and to do all other Acts and Things which INDEPENDENT STATES may of right do. And for the support of this Declaration, with a firm Reliance on the Protection of divine Providence, we mutually pledge to each other our Lives, our Fortunes, and our sacred Honor.

Signed by ORDER *and in* BEHALF *of the* CONGRESS,

JOHN HANCOCK, PRESIDENT.

ATTEST.

CHARLES THOMSON, SECRETARY.

PHILADELPHIA: PRINTED BY JOHN DUNLAP.

Figure 3: *The Dunlap Broadside.*

July 4. It was presumably written in Jefferson's hand, and it may have been carried by his hand as well. One would expect the nervous author to be in Dunlap's shop, watching every word carefully, like a hawk protecting its chicks. As any parent knows, it is important to get the details right when announcing a birth.

Franklin and Adams may have been there as well; they too were parents in their way. It is charming to imagine America's greatest printer "superintending" the process by busying about the press, tightening its clamps, and aligning the paper. In every way they could, these ink-splattered geniuses willed the document, and by extension the republic, into existence. We will never know for sure, but as Franklin might have appreciated: print the legend.

There is evidence that it was done quickly, and in excitement. Watermarks were reversed, and some copies look as if they were folded before the ink could dry. Bits of punctuation float around from one copy to another. "We were all in haste," John Adams later recalled in an 1822 letter to Timothy Pickering.

But in spite of the hurry, the result was an artifact for the ages. The Dunlap Broadside was a handsome production, set in Caslon type, easily readable. The early known copies were 11¾ inches by 17 inches. But they are not uniform; there are intriguing variations. A copy sold by Sotheby's in 1993 was larger (19¾ inches by 15¾ inches). A single extant copy is on vellum.

The Congress then ordered that "copies of the declaration be sent to the several assemblies, conventions and committees, or councils of safety, and to the several commanding officers of the continental troops; that it be proclaimed in each of the United States, and at the head of the army."

Already, this was beginning to happen on July 5, as John Hancock, the president of the Continental Congress, sent the first copies around the country. This was part of a strategy of distribution that was nearly as important as the writing itself. The Declaration calls attention to the fact, claiming that it will "publish" as well as "declare" independence.

"Declaring" turned out to be an act of speaking, as well as printing. Appropriately, many Americans first heard of their country's independence through a public reading, or some other democratic ritual, as the people of America's towns and villages gathered to hear the news. Hancock had asked that the Declaration be proclaimed "in such a Mode, as that the People may be universally informed of it."

In Philadelphia, the Declaration was read aloud on July 8, from a wooden stage that had been built seven years earlier, in 1769, to observe an astronomical phenomenon, the Transit of Venus. Following the reading, the Royal Arms were taken down from a room inside Independence Hall (not so named until the 1820s), and thrown into a bonfire.

One of the more dramatic readings occurred in New York, where George Washington ordered it read to the troops on the evening of July 9. They had gathered on the parade grounds in lower Manhattan, where they were anxiously expecting the imminent arrival of the British fleet. The soldiers were so moved by Washington's short speech, and the words of the Declaration itself, that they caused pandemonium, toppling a statue of George III that would later be melted into 42,088 musket balls.

In addition to the printings and readings, delegates sent broadsides back home to their constituents, as John Adams did to Mary Palmer, on July 5, adding, "It compleats a Revolution, which will make as good a Figure in the History of Mankind, as any that has preceded it." It is intriguing that he used the word "compleats," since the Declaration was as much a beginning as an end. But as Adams understood better than most, it was indeed a "revolution" to get Americans to think of themselves as a new nation.

That revolution accelerated in the weeks that followed, as the words flew around the land. The Declaration was soon reprinted in nineteen other broadsides and in at least twenty-nine newspapers, including Dunlap's papers in Philadelphia and Baltimore. Perhaps as many as two hundred Dunlap Broadsides were printed; twenty-six are known to exist today, including three in British repositories. No copies were sent to King George III, the principal target of the Declaration. No matter: he would soon respond by labeling it "treason," pure and simple.

Figure 4: *Mary Katharine Goddard's image graces the cover of her Baltimore Almanack for 1783.*

The Dunlap Broadside differed in a few meaningful ways from the engrossed Declaration, not least in having a different title. It published only two signatures, those of John Hancock, the president of the Continental Congress, and Charles Thomson, the secretary of Congress (who did not sign the engrossed Declaration). But these two printed signatures were all the more meaningful for the danger that Hancock and Thomson faced.

The engrossed Declaration would list all of the signers; but their names were kept secret until January 18, 1777, when a second broadside of the Declaration was printed, listing all of them. This edition holds real interest, for it added yet another new name, that of the woman, Mary Katharine Goddard, who printed it. Based in Baltimore (where Congress had fled), Goddard came from a family of printers, and had already published other tracts in support of independence, including Thomas Paine's *Common Sense.* She presumably had access to the engrossed Declaration while she carefully transcribed the signatures. She added her own name in a printer's note, near the bottom of the sheet, almost as if she were signing it. Perhaps she was.

In a sense, Mary Katharine Goddard embodied the forceful sentiment that Abigail Adams had expressed to her husband John, urging him to "remember the ladies" as he and his fellow Founders built a new order with a promise of equal rights for all. Goddard did not ask for any special treatment. But because of her skill and intelligence, she was ready to print a most important Declaration when asked.

Who Wrote the Declaration?

Most schoolchildren can identify Thomas Jefferson as author of the Declaration, and they are not wrong. But "draftsman" might be a more accurate term, for Jefferson's brief included accepting instructions before, during, and after the writing of his early drafts.

The Continental Congress appointed a Committee of Five on June 11, 1776, including John Adams, Thomas Jefferson, Benjamin Franklin, Robert Livingston, and Roger Sherman. Their charge was to draft the official document that would express the resolve of Congress—and by extension, the American people—as they were taking this perilous and portentous step.

As John Adams later told the story, the Committee held several meetings, and defined "the Articles of which the Declaration was to consist." It then asked Adams and Jefferson to write a suitable draft, or as Adams wrote, to clothe these thoughts "in a proper Dress." In his letter to Pickering, Adams claimed that Jefferson urged him to write the document, at first. But Adams demurred, citing several reasons, including his feeling that he had become "obnoxious" in pressing so adamantly for independence, that a Southerner was more appropriate, and that Jefferson was well-suited to the task because of "the Elegance of his pen."

It should be noted that Jefferson did not remember the story quite the same way; he simply recalled accepting the assignment. He had arrived a month earlier, and found lodging on the second floor of a three-story house, owned by a German American bricklayer and his young family (see page 47). There he lived throughout the summer, along with an enslaved fourteen-year-old, Robert Hemmings (or Hemings), whom he brought with him from Monticello. If only we knew more of Hemmings (described as a "bright mulatto") and his perspective on the document that was coming into existence, so near to him, and so far.

Jefferson worked quickly, using a portable writing desk of his own design (now in the Smithsonian). Around June 21, he had a draft ready for his fellow committee members, and on June 28, he submitted an improved draft to Congress, where it was laid on a table for all to read. This is the moment portrayed in the well-known painting by John Trumbull.

Figure 5: *Artist John Trumbull depicts the Committee of Five presenting their Declaration to Congress.*

The image of Jefferson hunched over his desk fits the narrative of a writer of genius, churning out a great work from the depths of his imagination. It is an attractive image, and it was attractive to him as well. In later years, Jefferson was so content to be credited as the "author of the Declaration" that he had the phrase chiseled into his tombstone.

But the notion of solitary authorship does not entirely square with the story of a text—and a country—coming together from many points of origin. It began with verbal exchanges, within the Committee of Five.

It changed with edits from the committee (and from Adams and Franklin in particular), before going through another round of edits from Congress. It does not detract from Jefferson's achievement to acknowledge that these edits improved the Declaration.

This was in keeping with the intent of Congress, which did not want too much authorial independence. Instead, it hoped for a document that would express the aspirations of the American people in a language that all could understand. As Jefferson recalled near the end of his life, in 1825:

> This was the object of the Declaration of Independence. Not to find out new principles, or new arguments, never before thought of, not merely to say things which had never been said before; but to place before mankind the common sense of the subject, in terms so plain and firm as to command their assent, and to justify ourselves in the independent stand we are compelled to take. Neither aiming at originality of principle or sentiment, nor yet copied from any particular and previous writing, it was intended to be an expression of the American mind, and to give to that expression the proper tone and spirit called for by the occasion.

He certainly lived up to the Committee's expectations, delivering a work that has brilliantly stood the test of time. It is appropriately solemn, but at the same time, it is not overwritten. With spartan self-discipline, it generally avoids long words, and often achieves more by saying less. The adjectives—*decent, self-evident, equal, candid*—reflect the document itself, and its desire to communicate clearly, to as many people as possible, in the spirit of democracy. Unlike so much language written in the eighteenth century, the sentences are alive, not archaic at all.

Still, it was a difficult balancing act, which Jefferson handled adeptly. The Declaration speaks eternal truths, but it was composed in a precise time and place, full of thoughts that were specific to July 1776. In the first two paragraphs, Jefferson uses a soaring language to describe the rights that inhere in all human beings. But the bulk of the document is an angry philippic against George III for his refusal to uphold those rights. In a series of detailed accusations, departing from the universal generalities at the beginning, Jefferson lists the violations, like an irritable prosecutor.

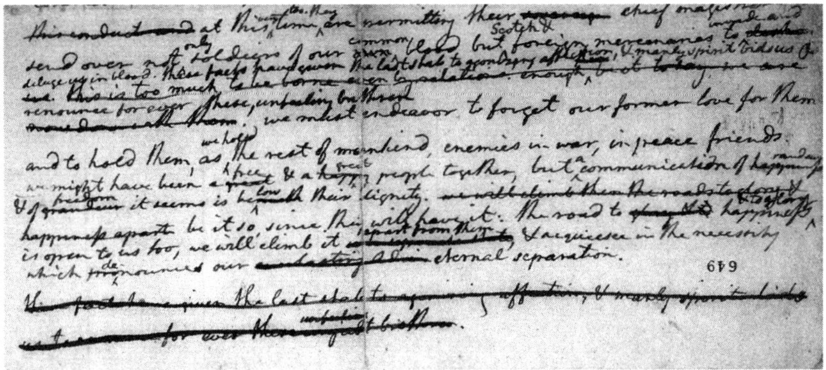

Figure 6: *A fragment from the earliest known draft of the Declaration of Independence, written by Thomas Jefferson in June 1776.*

This section of the Declaration is less well remembered, but it, too, shows literary artistry. Jefferson builds suspense by repeating "he has" at the front of each accusation. The verbs become more active (*plundered . . . ravaged . . . burnt . . . destroyed*) as the document pulls the reader, tidally, toward independence. In a language reminiscent of the Book of Exodus—familiar to nearly all Americans—Jefferson describes "swarms of officers" sent to "harass our people, and eat out their substance."

There were other threats as well, less easily ascribed to the King. As many scholars have noted, the sentences we love to quote, about equality, are belied by those that tacitly acknowledge slavery and the unsettled relations between the new nation and the older Indigenous nations, equally American, watching warily. Native peoples doubtless read these same words with skepticism—particularly the passage that denounces "merciless Indian savages." But despite these inconsistencies, or perhaps even because of them, the Declaration represented "the American mind" well, just as Jefferson and his editors hoped that it would.

Several extant manuscripts show the draft coming together. A small fragment from the earliest known draft describes the various abuses the Americans have endured at the hands of the King, and includes some language that was discarded by Jefferson in favor of the more elegant sentences to come.

Then, a most important document, called the "Rough Draft" of the Declaration, from a moment in June when Jefferson had revealed his first efforts to his fellow committee members, and they (Adams and Franklin)

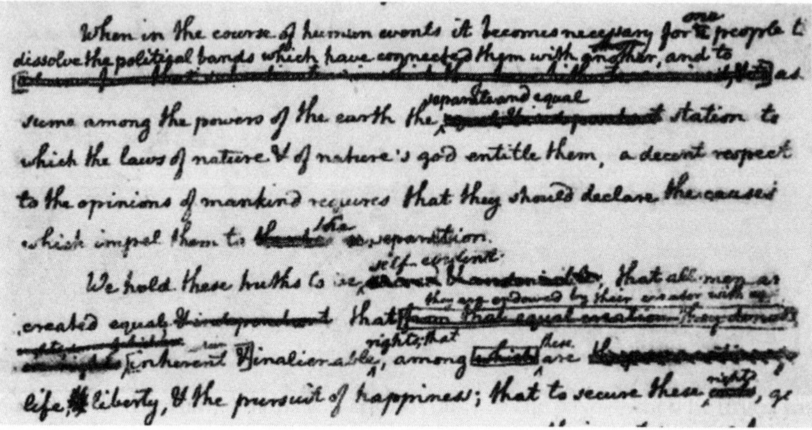

When in the course of human events it becomes necessary for one people to dissolve the political bands which have connected them with another, and to assume among the powers of the earth the separate and equal station to which the laws of nature & of nature's god entitle them, a decent respect to the opinions of mankind requires that they should declare the causes which impel them to the separation.

We hold these truths to be self-evident; that all men are created equal; that they are endowed by their creator with inherent & inalienable rights; that among these are life, liberty, & the pursuit of happiness; that to secure these rights, go

Figure 7: *"Sacred and undeniable" become "self-evident" as the Committee of Five weighs in on Jefferson's draft.*

were adding their additions and deletions. A letter from Jefferson to Franklin on June 21 requests editorial guidance. On the same day, Franklin wrote to George Washington to inform him that "a Declaration of Independence is preparing."

Here can be seen some of the most critical improvements, including an all-important change from "we hold these truths to be sacred & undeniable" to "we hold these truths to be self-evident." "Self-evident" is written as a superscript, above the deleted words, with a caret indicating placement below. Some scholars have speculated that the edit came from Benjamin Franklin, and it is easy to imagine that a scientist would have been thinking about the nature of evidence. But there is no evidence to support the claim. It should be noted that John Locke used "self-evident" repeatedly in *An Essay Concerning Human Understanding.*

On July 2, Congress voted for independence. For the next two days, it debated the Declaration, before calling for another vote, on July 4. Shortly after a measure was made to deliver a shipment of flint to the American troops in New York, Congress ordered the Declaration read aloud, and then approved it.

This second vote was as important as the first. The Declaration was more than a postscript; it was an extraordinary testament, all that Congress had asked for, and more. It was an event unto itself. So momentous was the July 2 vote for independence that it needed a stirring defense, on July 4, before the tribunal of the world's peoples. In a language of plain common sense, it needed to persuade a disinterested observer that the cause was warranted, just, and based on truths that were obvious—another way of saying "self-evident." The Declaration admitted that "Governments long established should not be changed for light and transient causes." It then went on to argue for principles that were anything but transient; they have proven their worth for 250 years and counting.

That the Declaration was touched by so many authorial hands feels right. As lucid as Jefferson's sentences were, they were more authentic for the fact that the other delegates had contributed. As a result, the Declaration was—and remains—the considered expression of a people, speaking through their representatives, to the rest of humanity.

In short, there were many declarations of independence. An argument for democracy needed to survive a democratic writing process, and so it did, through deliberations in a committee, and then in Congress, before the near-simultaneous declarations of printers, newspaper editors, and town criers who shouted the news to the people. Together, the resolutions, the votes, the broadsides, the readings, and the engrossed Declaration added up to a collective act of transcendent importance. They created a country, based on an idea, written out with great care.

As the Founders understood, they were composing a document that brought together many constituent parts. Despite Jefferson's pride of authorship, it is fitting that the first person is never used. The emphasis throughout is on the second-person plural, the all-inclusive "We" that defines so many of the charter documents, including the Constitution, which begins with "We the People." "We" appears sixteen times in Jefferson's original draft, and eleven times in the final version.

The Declaration concluded with a resonant promise, very distant from the "Royal We." Instead, the Founders affirmed a "Democratic We" that represented a genuine solidarity, forged in the face of imminent danger: "we mutually pledge to each other our Lives, our Fortunes and our sacred Honor." This was no longer thirteen separate British colonies; it was the United States of America.

The Living Declaration

This book, though, is about more than the writing of the Declaration, in all of its variants. It also examines the persistent impact of its words, and the long afterlife of a text whose meaning has shifted over time. "Each age will have to reconsider it," Robert Frost wrote in a poem, "The Black Cottage," that touched on these themes. And so we have. In five parts, covering 250 years, this volume offers a biography of sorts, describing the way that Americans and others have absorbed the Declaration, celebrated its anniversaries, and applied its leveling energies to other forms of injustice, of which the world has never been in short supply.

Simply declaring independence did not mean that independence existed in the eyes of the world. It would take years of fighting, and thousands of deaths, before Great Britain officially recognized the United States in the Treaty of Paris in 1783. Suddenly there was an immense new country in the world, organized around different principles than any society in Europe, Asia, or Africa. It would take time to fit this unwieldy constellation of thirteen states into the planetary orbit of nations—the so-called powers of the earth, as the Declaration phrases it.

But steadily, Americans found their footing on the world stage. As they did so, the words of the Declaration attracted renewed interest. At first, it was seen as a document that merely accomplished its stated purpose, and announced that all ties were severed between the former colonies and Great Britain. Along the way, it did so much more. As the Declaration asserted the reasons that Americans wanted to live in a country of their own, it also offered a novel theory of self-government, arguing that power flowed from the bottom up, from the people to their leaders. It did this in a calm language, without invective. It also added a daring claim that people were in some sense "equal," endowed with a braidery of human rights, including "Life, Liberty and the pursuit of Happiness." They also wielded an important right to "alter or to abolish" a government that failed to respect these rights.

To most people around the world, these truths were far from self-evident, and they remain opaque in many places to this day. In 1776, governments ruled from the top down, through force. No nation had ever been invented with a proclamation of rights, or with the idea that governments derive their powers from a thin abstraction called "the consent of the governed." Nations had never been invented on the basis of an "idea" at all. They had simply evolved, after centuries of fighting between warlords, into domination by monarchs who asserted a divine right to rule.

The United States would be different. By achieving independence, Americans had furnished a proof of concept, to go along with their theory. The belief in popular sovereignty, so clearly articulated in the Declaration's opening paragraphs, would evolve into a kind of "American creed," as the Swedish sociologist Gunnar Myrdal phrased it, in the middle decades of the twentieth century, at a time when Europeans were trying to understand how the United States had become so powerful. In no other country does a founding document hold the same sort of emotional sway.

Of course, there have always been glaring inconsistencies, beginning with the fact that the Declaration's soaring lines about equality were penned by a Virginia slaveowner. In 1776, Jefferson completed a census of the "Number of souls in my family." He counted 117 in all, including his personal family, his free workers, and eighty-three slaves. One of them, a child of about three years, was Sally Hemings, with whom Jefferson would eventually have several children, all enslaved.

But Jefferson's words had a power all their own, even if they did not do much to describe the squalid realities of life at Monticello. In the decades that followed, they began to resonate in new ways, to an ever-expanding radius of readers. It did not happen overnight; even in the 1780s, after independence, there was not a great deal of attention paid to the words that began the Declaration so promisingly. They never attracted the close textual commentary that accompanied the writing of the Constitution, eleven years after the Declaration.

Still, there were important exceptions, such as Lemuel Haynes, an African American veteran of the early battles of the Revolution, who glimpsed the possibilities within the Declaration, far ahead of most of his peers, and wrote an essay in response (see pp. 66–69). In the decades that followed, others joined in. During the political struggles of the first party system, partisans of Thomas Jefferson often found it advantageous to promote his authorship of the Declaration, as proof of his democratic credentials.

For a time, these struggles drove apart Jefferson and Adams, who was given far less credit for his own prodigious contributions to independence. But in old age, the two Argonauts reconciled, happily, and wrote long letters that shed considerable light on the summer of 1776. When they died on the same day, fifty years later, and that day happened to be July 4, Americans were stunned. The creed deepened, and the words began to take on an aura.

That was apparent in the reverential language one reader, a rail-thin country boy in Indiana, always used to describe the Declaration. In the titanic struggle over slavery that resulted in the Civil War, the Declaration played a central role, showing how relevant it remained. It could plausibly be used to argue for equality, as Abraham Lincoln did, or for the right to secede, as Jefferson Davis did.

But in every sense, Lincoln's reading was deeper. In a telling note that he wrote to himself (see page 159), just after his election, he borrowed from the Bible to describe the Declaration as an "apple of gold," surrounded by a "picture of silver," by which he meant the Constitution. Both were valuable, but for Lincoln, the "apple of gold," and the central idea of equality, was the idea that defined America.

In the years that followed Lincoln's triumph, it became more and more difficult to enlist the Declaration on the side of privilege. The Civil War and new constitutional amendments gave his vision a seemingly unassailable moral and legal standing. As the United States grew into an increasingly complex and diverse society, other groups demanded that the Declaration's promises extend to them. Feminists, labor leaders, and immigrant activists all sought to claim the document in new ways, and in so doing, stretched it out some more. The Declaration provides an essential through line in our history as a people, and in the larger story of the struggle for human freedom.

A Hard-Bought Thing

In his old age, John Adams fretted about the ability of the young to understand what he and his generation had been through. In a letter to Jefferson, he reminded his former adversary—now, again, his friend—that the surest way to maintain democracy was simply to remember the story of how it began.

That this would not always be easy, Adams well understood; democracy's opponents would always try to make the study of the past more difficult than it needs to be. As he wrote, "Arbitrary power, wherever it has resided, has never failed to destroy all the records Memorials and Histories of former times which it did not like and to corrupt or interpolate such as it was cunning enough to preserve or to tolerate."

The best antidote, of course, has always been simple—to read, and to reread. And to read deeply, not just a few words appearing fleetingly on a screen, before vanishing.

From the beginning, the Founders encouraged us to do just that. Today John Hancock is most famous for his outsized signature on the engrossed

Declaration, but he well understood the importance of remembering what had happened. In a letter accompanying the Goddard edition of the Declaration, sent to each of the thirteen states, he wrote: "As there is not a more distinguished Event in the History of America, than the Declaration of her Independence—nor any, that in all probability will so much excite the Attention of future Ages, it is highly proper, that the Memory of that Transaction, together with the Causes that gave Rise to it, should be preserved in the most careful Manner that can be devised."

Many modern readers have felt the same way. A 1958 textbook, *Adventures in American Literature*, offered advice that still resonates:

> A state paper as difficult and important as the Declaration of Independence cannot be read in the casual, offhand manner with which we read narrative. It demands slow, attentive, careful reading of the kind a lawyer applies to a legal document. You must think about each sentence and be sure you understand exactly what is meant, phrase by phrase.
>
> Perhaps the full meaning of this important document can best be obtained by cooperative class study. Let each student read a sentence from the Declaration, following his reading by a precise restatement of the whole thought of that sentence in his own words. Such an intensive study will make the Declaration much more meaningful to you. The satisfactory reading of prose filled with important ideas is, like freedom, a hard-bought thing.

If we imagine ourselves again standing before the Freedom Shrine at the National Archives, we might ask why the Declaration, a document that accomplished its primary aim centuries ago, is presented on an equal footing with the Constitution, the legal charter whose sentences continue to shape our lives on a daily basis. It is difficult to weigh the significance of the various founding documents in relation to each other. They are all essential. We live under the rules prescribed by the Constitution, while believing in the truths articulated by the Declaration. They balance each other.

But by at least one measure, the Declaration is preeminent. In case of a nuclear attack, government officials long ago decided to give top priority to the Declaration. It is regarded as the single most valuable artifact in the possession of the United States of America, and in a sense, the key to understanding it all. Although the plans are secret, some details have leaked about how the U.S. government would respond in the event of a catastrophic new war. In all likelihood, the Declaration would be spirited away to an enormous underground complex, beneath Mount Weather, near Berryville, Virginia, sixty miles to the west of Washington. There it would live alongside top government officials, including the president, the cabinet, and the Supreme Court (Congress appears to be on its own).

That is precisely how Lincoln thought of the relationship between the Declaration and the Constitution. They are both critical, but the idea is more important than the rules. The apple of gold is framed by the picture of silver. That is the equipoise the Founders carefully designed, and bequeathed to us for safekeeping.

Before we embark, let us attend to the text itself, here in the final engrossed version.

The Declaration of Independence

July 4, 1776

IN CONGRESS, JULY 4, 1776
THE UNANIMOUS DECLARATION OF THE THIRTEEN UNITED STATES OF AMERICA,

When in the Course of human events, it becomes necessary for one people to dissolve the political bands which have connected them with another, and to assume among the powers of the earth, the separate and equal station to which the Laws of Nature and of Nature's God entitle them, a decent respect to the opinions of mankind requires that they should declare the causes which impel them to the separation.

We hold these truths to be self-evident, that all men are created equal, that they are endowed by their Creator with certain unalienable Rights, that among these are Life, Liberty and the pursuit of Happiness.—That to secure these rights, Governments are instituted among Men, deriving their just powers from the consent of the governed,—That whenever any Form of Government becomes destructive of these ends, it is the Right of the People to alter or to abolish it, and to institute new Government, laying its foundation on such principles and organizing its powers in such form, as to them shall seem most likely to effect their Safety and Happiness. Prudence, indeed, will dictate that Governments long established should not be changed for light and transient causes; and accordingly all experience hath shewn, that mankind are more disposed to suffer, while evils are sufferable, than to right themselves by abolishing the forms to which they are accustomed. But when a long train of abuses and usurpations, pursuing invariably the same Object evinces a design to reduce them under absolute Despotism, it is their right, it is their duty, to throw off such Government, and to provide new Guards for their future security.—Such has been the patient sufferance of these Colonies; and such is now the necessity which constrains them to alter their former Systems of Government. The history of the present King of Great Britain is a history of repeated injuries and usurpations, all having in direct object the establishment of an absolute Tyranny over these States. To prove this, let Facts be submitted to a candid world.

He has refused his Assent to Laws, the most wholesome and necessary for the public good.

He has forbidden his Governors to pass Laws of immediate and pressing importance, unless suspended in their operation till his Assent should be obtained; and when so suspended, he has utterly neglected to attend to them.

He has refused to pass other Laws for the accommodation of large districts of people, unless those people would relinquish the right of Representation in the Legislature, a right inestimable to them and formidable to tyrants only.

He has called together legislative bodies at places unusual, uncomfortable, and distant from the depository of their public Records, for the sole purpose of fatiguing them into compliance with his measures.

He has dissolved Representative Houses repeatedly, for opposing with manly firmness his invasions on the rights of the people.

He has refused for a long time, after such dissolutions, to cause others to be elected; whereby the Legislative powers, incapable of Annihilation, have returned to the People at large for their exercise; the State remaining in the mean time exposed to all the dangers of invasion from without, and convulsions within.

He has endeavoured to prevent the population of these States; for that purpose obstructing the Laws for Naturalization of Foreigners; refusing to pass others to encourage their migrations hither, and raising the conditions of new Appropriations of Lands.

He has obstructed the Administration of Justice, by refusing his Assent to Laws for establishing Judiciary powers.

He has made Judges dependent on his Will alone, for the tenure of their offices, and the amount and payment of their salaries.

He has erected a multitude of New Offices, and sent hither swarms of Officers to harrass our people, and eat out their substance.

He has kept among us, in times of peace, Standing Armies without the Consent of our legislatures.

He has affected to render the Military independent of and superior to the Civil power.

He has combined with others to subject us to a jurisdiction foreign to our constitution, and unacknowledged by our laws; giving his Assent to their Acts of pretended Legislation:

For Quartering large bodies of armed troops among us:

For protecting them, by a mock Trial, from punishment for any Murders which they should commit on the Inhabitants of these States:

For cutting off our Trade with all parts of the world:

For imposing Taxes on us without our Consent:

For depriving us in many cases, of the benefits of Trial by Jury:

For transporting us beyond Seas to be tried for pretended offences:

For abolishing the free System of English Laws in a neighbouring Province, establishing therein an Arbitrary government, and enlarging its Boundaries so as to render it at once an example and fit instrument for introducing the same absolute rule into these Colonies:

For taking away our Charters, abolishing our most valuable Laws, and altering fundamentally the Forms of our Governments:

For suspending our own Legislatures, and declaring themselves invested with power to legislate for us in all cases whatsoever.

He has abdicated Government here, by declaring us out of his Protection and waging War against us.

He has plundered our seas, ravaged our Coasts, burnt our towns, and destroyed the lives of our people.

He is at this time transporting large Armies of foreign Mercenaries to compleat the works of death, desolation and tyranny, already begun with circumstances of Cruelty & perfidy scarcely paralleled in the most barbarous ages, and totally unworthy the Head of a civilized nation.

He has constrained our fellow Citizens taken Captive on the high Seas to bear Arms against their Country, to become the executioners of their friends and Brethren, or to fall themselves by their Hands.

He has excited domestic insurrections amongst us, and has endeavoured to bring on the inhabitants of our frontiers, the merciless Indian Savages, whose known rule of warfare, is an undistinguished destruction of all ages, sexes and conditions.

In every stage of these Oppressions We have Petitioned for Redress in the most humble terms: Our repeated Petitions have been answered only by repeated injury. A Prince, whose character is thus marked by every act which may define a Tyrant, is unfit to be the ruler of a free people.

Nor have We been wanting in attentions to our Brittish brethren. We have warned them from time to time of attempts by their legislature to extend an unwarrantable jurisdiction over us. We have reminded them of the circumstances of our emigration and settlement here. We have appealed to their native justice and magnanimity, and we have conjured them by the ties of our common kindred to disavow these usurpations, which, would inevitably interrupt our connections and correspondence. They too have been deaf to the voice of justice and of consanguinity. We must, therefore, acquiesce in the necessity, which denounces our Separation, and hold them, as we hold the rest of mankind, Enemies in War, in Peace Friends.

We, therefore, the Representatives of the united States of America, in General Congress, Assembled, appealing to the Supreme Judge of the world for the rectitude of our intentions, do, in the Name, and by Authority of the good People of these Colonies, solemnly publish and declare, That these United Colonies are, and of Right ought to be Free and Independent States; that they are Absolved from all Allegiance to the British Crown, and that all political connection between them and the State of Great Britain, is and ought to be totally dissolved; and that as Free and Independent States, they have full Power to levy War, conclude Peace, contract Alliances, establish Commerce, and to do all other Acts and Things which Independent States may of right do. And for the support of this Declaration, with a firm reliance on the protection of divine Providence, we mutually pledge to each other our Lives, our Fortunes and our sacred Honor.

JOHN HANCOCK

[MASSACHUSETTS]

Button Gwinnett
Lyman Hall
George Walton
[GEORGIA]

William Hooper
Joseph Hewes
John Penn
[NORTH CAROLINA]

Edward Rutledge
Thomas Heyward, Jr.
Thomas Lynch, Jr.
Arthur Middleton
[SOUTH CAROLINA]

Samuel Chase
William Paca
Thomas Stone
Charles Carroll of Carrollton
[MARYLAND]

George Wythe
Richard Henry Lee
Thomas Jefferson
Benjamin Harrison
Thomas Nelson, Jr.
Francis Lightfoot Lee
Carter Braxton
[VIRGINIA]

Robert Morris
Benjamin Rush
Benjamin Franklin
John Morton
George Clymer
James Smith
George Taylor
James Wilson
George Ross
[PENNSYLVANIA]

Cesar Rodney
George Read
Thomas McKean
[DELAWARE]

William Floyd
Philip Livingston
Francis Lewis
Lewis Morris
[NEW YORK]

Richard Stockton
John Witherspoon
Francis Hopkinson
John Hart
Abraham Clark
[NEW JERSEY]

Josiah Bartlett
William Whipple
[NEW HAMPSHIRE]

Samuel Adams
John Adams
Robert Treat Paine
Elbridge Gerry
[MASSACHUSETTS]

Stephen Hopkins
William Ellery
[RHODE ISLAND]

Roger Sherman
Samuel Huntington
William Williams
Oliver Wolcott
[CONNECTICUT]

Matthew Thornton
[NEW HAMPSHIRE]

These words are at once familiar and startling. But what do they mean? Do we understand them in the same way the Founders did? How has each generation reckoned with them? These are the questions that drive this book. Jurists and legal scholars often speak of a "living Constitution," suggesting a text that must be continually reread to acknowledge the evolving imperatives of our national life. In the same way, the Declaration of Independence remains intensely alive.

The Living Declaration tells the story of a text through texts, those that set the stage for the Declaration, and those that were in turn influenced and inspired by it. There is value in immersing ourselves in these writings, attending to the ways in which language recurs and reverberates and evolves. These texts speak to many audiences at once. Each was the product of a specific historical moment, directed in most cases to now long-vanished readers. (There are notes in the back of the book that identify quotes and illuminate obscure references.) But by addressing timeless themes about the purpose of a nation, they echo across the centuries. They speak to us, and they talk to each other as well, in a conversation that will never end.

The voices gathered here are impassioned, and though often at odds, all are united in the belief that the Declaration reveals something crucial about the American people and the struggle for human freedom. As we mark the nation's 250th anniversary, it's worth listening to them to see what they have to say about who we have been, who we are, and who we might yet become.

THE LIVING DECLARATION

PART I

WHEN IN THE COURSE OF HUMAN EVENTS 1689–1776

Why do we have a Declaration of Independence, and why does it make universal claims about human rights?

Often seen as the beginning of one story—that of the United States of America—the Declaration of Independence also marked the ending of another, that of British America. It was the culmination of a long debate about the nature of the British Empire, and the rights of Americans within it.

To many, that ending did not feel inevitable. The concept of independence would have struck most Americans as unthinkable, even two years previous. But in the spring of 1775, long-simmering tensions exploded into violence around Boston, where British troops occupied a tense city. The skirmishes at Lexington and Concord, in April, alarmed Americans around the country, and when a pitched engagement was fought at Bunker Hill, in June, the battle lines were drawn.

In the early years of the debate, American anger was largely directed at Parliament, where Americans were unrepresented, despite a growing number of taxes and revenue schemes directed at them. But in the fall of 1775, after Bunker Hill, the British monarch, King George III, thrust himself into the argument with a series of harsh speeches and actions, declaring that the American colonies were "out of his protection," and effectively on their own. It would have been difficult to come up with a more persuasive argument for independence.

The cause quickened in the early months of 1776, and matured in late spring. With the arrival of summer, all of the pieces were in place for a momentous decision, and the creation of an extraordinary political text to justify it.

But the Declaration of Independence did more than simply proclaim the birth of a new nation; at times the Founders even went beyond that, to suggest that a new era was beginning as well. The Great Seal of the United States claims as much, asserting that "a new order for the ages" (*Novus Ordo Seclorum*) was launched on July 4, 1776. Many Americans were prepared to believe it; the very thought launched a thousand Fourth of July orations, as aspirational as the fireworks that were usually propelled into the heavens as soon as the speeches were finished and the wind died down.

At the same time, the Declaration also drew on deep wellsprings, tying the Founders to the past. As they navigated their course toward independence, they were strengthened by their familiarity with earlier writers. Not surprisingly, many of these writers were English. Among the contradictions of the latter stages of the imperial debate was the pride Americans felt in their English "birthright," even as they sought, ultimately, to sever their bonds with the mother country. By that word, they usually meant their understanding of the broad set of freedoms that had been shaped by centuries of English tradition, including the Magna Carta, the Common Law, habeas corpus, and the various ways in which Parliament had established limits on the "divine right of kings" in the seventeenth century.

Figure 8: *The future English monarchs William of Orange, the "Protector of Liberty," and his wife, Mary, the eldest daughter of the deposed king, are presented with the terms of Parliament's remarkable revolution.*

A key text in that tradition was the English Declaration of Right, drafted by Parliament in 1689, at a delicate moment, as English leaders were orchestrating the ouster of an unpopular king, James II, and the arrival of his daughter, Mary, and her husband, William, Prince of Orange, as the new monarchs (Mary II and William III, usually known as William and Mary).

Framed by the legacy of generations of sectarian conflict, these complex maneuvers, collectively known as the Glorious Revolution, led to a happy balance that preserved a royal succession, while making it clear that future monarchs would be Protestant and would refrain from acting without parliamentary consent. The Declaration of Right was read to William and Mary, who agreed to abide by its claims. Later, on February 13, 1689, its various "rights and liberties" were enacted by Parliament and became known as the English Bill of Rights. These remain a vital part of the British "constitution," which is not a single document, but a set of understandings about the rights of subjects, the structure of government, and the limits of royal power.

The Declaration of Right begins with a catalogue of thirteen grievances, citing all the ways in which James II had overstepped his authority, including the maintenance of standing armies, and the denial of trial by jury (both of which would be echoed in the Declaration of Independence). It also adds thirteen clauses, defining the powers that monarchs would be required to share with Parliament in the years ahead.

Eight decades later, these thirteen grievances and clauses were of high interest to the thirteen American colonies. The Declaration of Right offered a vivid precedent to another people, distant, but still English in their way, seeking again to check an abuse of power. Ironically, it was Parliament itself, not the King, that now seemed to threaten the balance of the British constitution. As revolutionary as it was, the Declaration of Independence never wavered from a fundamentally conservative hope, to perpetuate "the free spirit of English laws."

An Act declareing the Rights and Liberties of the Subject and Setleing the Succession of the Crowne [English Declaration of Right]

February 13, 1689

WHEREAS the Lords Spirituall and Temporall and Commons assembled at Westminster lawfully fully and freely representing all the Estates of the People of this Realme did upon the thirteenth day of February in the yeare of our Lord one thousand six hundred eighty eight present unto their Majesties then called and known by the Names and Stile of William and Mary Prince and Princesse of Orange being present in their proper Persons a certaine

Declaration in Writeing made by the said Lords and Commons in the Words following viz

Whereas the late King James the Second by the Assistance of diverse evill Councellors Judges and Ministers imployed by him did endeavour to subvert and extirpate the Protestant Religion and the Lawes and Liberties of this Kingdome

By Assumeing and Exerciseing a Power of Dispensing with and Suspending of Lawes and the Execution of Lawes without Consent of Parlyament.

By Committing and Prosecuting diverse Worthy Prelates for humbly Petitioning to be excused from Concurring to the said Assumed Power.

By issueing and causeing to be executed a Commission under the Great Seale for Erecting a Court called The Court of Commissioners for Ecclesiasticall Causes.

By Levying Money for and to the Use of the Crowne by pretence of Prerogative for other time and in other manner then the same was granted by Parlyament.

By raising and keeping a Standing Army within this Kingdome in time of Peace without Consent of Parlyament and Quartering Soldiers contrary to Law.

By causing severall good Subjects being Protestants to be disarmed at the same time when Papists were both Armed and Imployed contrary to Law.

By Violating the Freedome of Election of Members to serve in Parlyament.

By Prosecutions in the Court of Kings Bench for Matters and Causes congizable onely in Parlyament and by diverse other Arbitrary and Illegall Courses.

And whereas of late yeares Partiall Corrupt and Unqualifyed Persons have beene returned and served on Juryes in Tryalls and particularly diverse Jurors in Tryalls for High Treason which were not Freeholders,

And excessive Baile hath beene required of Persons committed in Criminall Cases to elude the Benefitt of the Lawes made for the Liberty of the Subjects.

And excessive Fines have beene imposed.

And illegall and cruell Punishments inflicted.

And severall Grants and Promises made of Fines and Forfeitures before any Conviction or Judgement against the Persons upon whome the same were to be levyed.

All which are utterly and directly contrary to the knowne Lawes and Statutes and Freedome of this Realme.

And whereas the said late King James the Second haveing Abdicated the Government and the Throne being thereby Vacant His Hignesse the Prince of Orange (whome it hath pleased Almighty God to make the glorious Instrument of Delivering this Kingdome from Popery and Arbitrary Power) did (by the Advice of the Lords Spirituall and Temporall and diverse principall Persons of the Commons) cause Letters to be written to the Lords Spirituall and Temporall being Protestants and other Letters to the severall Countyes Cityes Universities Burroughs and Cinque Ports for the Choosing of such Persons to represent them as were of right to be sent to Parlyament to meete and sitt at Westminster upon the two and twentyeth day of January in this Yeare one thousand six hundred eighty and eight in order to such an Establishment as that their Religion Lawes and Liberties might not againe be in danger of being Subverted, Upon which Letters Elections haveing beene accordingly made.

And thereupon the said Lords Spirituall and Temporall and Commons pursuant to their respective Letters and Elections being now assembled in a full and free Representative of this Nation takeing into their most serious Consideration the best meanes for attaining the Ends aforesaid Doe in the first place (as their Auncestors in like Case have usually done) for the Vindicating and Asserting their auntient Rights and Liberties, Declare

That the pretended Power of Suspending of Laws or the Execution of Laws by Regall Authority without Consent of Parlyament is illegall.

That the pretended Power of Suspending of Laws or the Execution of Laws by Regall Authority as it hath beene assumed and exercised of late is illegall.

That the Commission for erecting the late Court of Commissioners for Ecclesiasticall Causes and all other Commissions and Courts of like nature are Illegall and Pernicious.

That levying Money for or to the Use of the Crowne by pretence of Prerogative without Grant of Parlyament for longer time or in other manner then the same is or shall be granted is Illegall.

That it is the Right of the Subjects to petition the King and all Commitments and Prosecutions for such Petitioning are Illegall.

That the raising or keeping a standing Army within the Kingdome in time of Peace unlesse it be with Consent of Parlyament is against Law.

That the Subjects which are Protestants may have Arms for their Defence suitable to their Conditions and as allowed by Law.

That Election of Members of Parlyament ought to be free.

That the Freedome of Speech and Debates or Proceedings in Parlyament ought not to be impeached or questioned in any Court or Place out of Parlyament.

That excessive Baile ought not to be required nor excessive Fines imposed nor cruell and unusuall Punishments inflicted.

That Jurors ought to be duely impannelled and returned and Jurors which passe upon Men in Trialls for High Treason ought to be Freeholders.

That all Grants and Promises of Fines and Forfeitures of particular persons before Conviction are illegall and void.

And that for Redresse of all Grievances and for the amending strengthening and preserveing of the Lawes Parlyaments ought to be held frequently.

And they doe Claime Demand and Insist upon all and singular the Premises as their undoubted Rights and Liberties and that noe Declarations Judgements Doeings or Proceedings to the Prejudice of the People in any of the said Premisses ought in any wise to be drawne hereafter into Consequence or Example. To which Demand of their Rights they are particularly encouraged by the Declaration of his Highnesse the Prince of Orange as being the onely meanes for obtaining a full Redresse and Remedy therein. Haveing therefore an intire Confidence That his said Highnesse the Prince of Orange will perfect the Deliverance soe farr advanced by him and will still preserve them from the Violation of their Rights which they have here asserted and from all other Attempts upon their Religion Rights and Liberties. The said Lords Spirituall and Temporall and Commons assembled at Westminster doe Resolve That William and Mary Prince and Princesse of Orange be and be declared King and Queene of England France and Ireland and the Dominions thereunto belonging to hold the Crowne and Royall Dignity of the said Kingdomes and Dominions to them....

One of the most lasting legacies of the Glorious Revolution was John Locke's *Two Treatises of Government*. Though it was published anonymously in 1689, it had in fact been written eight years earlier, during the crisis provoked by the prospect of James II's accession to the throne. A physician and philosopher, Locke lent his pen to the cause of the so-called Country Party, which had sought to exclude James from the succession as a Catholic. When the House of Commons put forth an Exclusion Bill in 1681, it was voted down in the House of Lords, and James assumed the throne. Many of the bill's supporters fled the country; Locke spent more than half a decade in exile in the Netherlands prior to the Glorious Revolution.

The first of the *Two Treatises* refuted the divine right of kings; the second explored the nature of civil society, defined certain rights as natural, and offered reasons that governments based on consent were more likely to survive than authoritarian states. Its full title was *An Essay Concerning the True Original Extent and End of Civil Government.* For publication Locke gave his essays a new introduction that situated their arguments in the radically altered circumstances of 1689, making it appear that they were written in response to them.

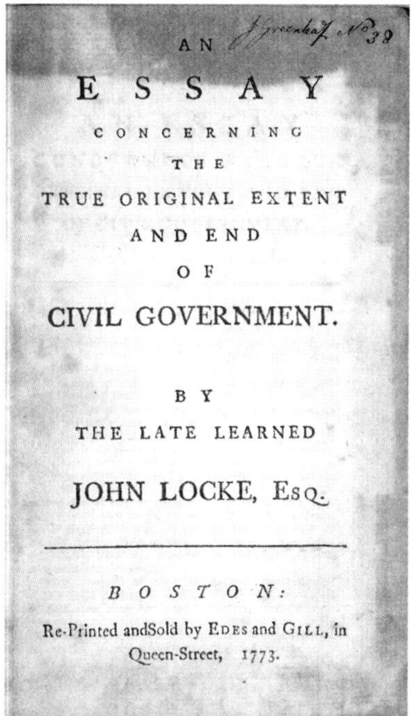

AN
ESSAY
CONCERNING
THE
TRUE ORIGINAL EXTENT
AND END
OF
CIVIL GOVERNMENT.

BY
THE LATE LEARNED
JOHN LOCKE, Esq.

BOSTON:
Re-Printed and Sold by EDES and GILL, in
Queen-Street, 1773.

Figure 9: *The first American publication of Locke's most famous work was issued at a crucial moment in the imperial crisis by Boston printers Benjamin Edes and John Gill, who were leaders in the colonial capital's patriot movement.*

Locke's work was enormously influential in America. In a sense, he too was an American framer of sorts, having contributed substantially to the *Fundamental Constitutions of Carolina* (1669), a document that envisioned a semi-feudal society in the American Southeast. It was ahead of its time in affording religious freedom, but differed markedly from his more idealistic work, in providing protections for slavery and hereditary titles (which he may have inserted at the behest of his employers, the colony's proprietors).

When writing in defense of Parliament's rights, he was more visionary, and the second of his *Two Treatises* was important in reassuring Americans that they were correct to reject tyranny and demand what Locke called "the consent of the people." Like that concept, which Jefferson would call "the consent of the governed," many other of his ideas found their way into the Declaration of Independence. "Nature's God" can be traced to Locke's interest in a state of nature in which people enjoy "original liberty" and "perfect freedom." The "self-evident truth" that "all men are created equal" derives from Locke's assertion that "it is evident that all human beings . . . are equal amongst themselves." Elsewhere he warns a people to be alert to "a long train of abuses" by their leaders, another resonant phrase.

The first American edition of Locke's work was published in Boston in 1773, just as the imperial debate was entering a decisive new phase. This was not a coincidence. New Englanders had been skeptical of royal overreach since their ancestors fled the persecutions of Charles I in the seventeenth century. By 1773, Boston had become a tinderbox, and Locke's work again inspired Americans to demand the rights that he had articulated almost a century earlier. From their perspective, it was they who were mindful of a tradition of civil liberties that had allowed Britons to flourish on both sides of the Atlantic. The British, on the other hand, were in danger of forgetting their own heritage, and surrendering to what Locke calls "the boundless will of tyranny." Like the hero of Homer's *Odyssey*, whom Locke invokes in this passage, Americans were determined to defend themselves.

An Essay Concerning the True Original Extent and End of Civil Government. By the Late Learned John Locke, Esq.

Boston: Re-Printed and sold by Edes and Gill,
in Queen-Street, 1773.

. . . . The reason why men enter into society, is the preservation of their property; and the end why they chuse and authorize a legislative, is, that there may be laws made and rules set, as guards and fences to the properties of all the members of the society, to limit the power, and moderate the dominion, of every part and member of the society: for since it can never be supposed to be the will of the society, that the legislative should have a power to destroy that which every one designs to secure, by entering into society, and for which the people submitted themselves to legislators of their own making; whenever the *legislators endeavour to take away, and destroy the property of the people,* or to reduce them to slavery under arbitrary power, they put themselves into a state of war with the people, who are thereupon absolved from any farther obedience, and are left to the common refuge, which God hath provided for all men, against force and violence. Whensoever therefore the *legislative* shall transgress this fundamental rule of society; and either by ambition, fear, folly or corruption, *endeavour to grasp* themselves, *or put into the hands of any other, an absolute power* over the lives, liberties, and estates of the people; by this breach of trust they *forfeit the power* the people had put into their hands for quite contrary ends, and it devolves to the people, who have a right to resume their original liberty, and, by the establishment of a new legislative, (such as they shall think fit) provide for their own safety and security, which is the end for which they are in society. What I have said here concerning the legislative in general, holds true, also concerning the supreme executor, who having a double trust put in him, both to have a part in the legislative, and the supreme execution of the law, acts against both, when he goes about to set up his own arbitrary will as the law of the society. He *acts* also *contrary to his trust,* when he either employs the force, treasure, and offices of the society, to corrupt the *representatives,* and gain them to his purposes; or openly pre-engages the *electors,* and prescribes to their choice, such, whom he has, by sollicitations, threats, promises, or otherwise, won to his designs; and employs them to bring in such, who have promised before-hand what to vote, and what to enact. Thus to regulate candidates and electors, and new-model the ways of election, what is it but to cut up the government by the roots, and poison the very fountain of public security? for the people having reserved to themselves the choice of their *representatives,* as the fence to their properties, could do it for no other end, but that they might always be freely chosen, and so chosen, freely act, and advise, as the necessity of the commonwealth, and the public good should, upon examination, and mature debate, be judged to require. This, those who give their votes before they hear the debate, and have weighed the reasons on all sides, are not capable of doing. To prepare such an assembly as this, and endeavour to set up the declared abettors of his own will, for the true *representatives* of the people, and the law-makers of the society, is certainly as great a *breach of trust*, and as perfect a declaration of a design to subvert the government, as is possible to be met with. To which, if one shall add rewards and punishments visibly employed to the same end, and all the arts of perverted law made use of, to take off and destroy all that stand in the way of such a design, and will not comply and consent to betray the liberties of their country, it will be past doubt what is doing. What power they ought to have in the society, who thus employ it contrary to the trust went along with it in its first institution, is easy to determine; and one cannot but see, that he, who has once attempted any such thing as this, cannot any longer be trusted.

To this perhaps it will be said, that the people being ignorant, and always discontented, to lay the foundation of government in the unsteady opinion and uncertain humour of the people, is to expose it to certain ruin; and *no government will be able long to subsist*, if the people may set up a new legislative, whenever they take offence at the old one. To this I answer, Quite the contrary. People are not so easily got out of their old forms, as some are apt to suggest. They are hardly to be prevailed with to amend the acknowledged faults in the frame they have been accustomed to. And if there be any original defects, or adventitious ones introduced by time or corruption; it is not an easy thing to get them changed, even when all the world sees there is an opportunity for it. This slowness and aversion in the people to quit their old constitutions, has, in the many revolutions which have been seen in this kingdom, in this and former ages, still kept us to, or, after some interval of fruitless attempts, still brought us back again to our old legislative of king, lords and commons: and whatever provocations have made the crown be taken from some of our princes heads, they never carried the people so far as to place it in another line.

But it will be said, this *hypothesis* lays a *ferment for* frequent *rebellion*. To which I answer,

First, No more than any other *hypothesis*: for when the people are made miserable, and find themselves *exposed to the ill usage of arbitrary power*, cry up their governors, as much as you will, for sons of *Jupiter*; let them be sacred and divine, descended, or authorized from heaven; give them out for whom or what you please, the same will happen. *The people generally ill treated*, and contrary to right, will be ready upon any occasion to ease themselves of a burden that sits heavy upon them. They will wish and seek for the opportunity, which in the change, weakness and accidents of human affairs, seldom delays long to offer itself. He must have lived but a little while in the world, who has not seen examples of this in his time; and he must have read very little, who cannot produce examples of it in all sorts of governments in the world.

Secondly, I answer, such *revolutions happen* not upon every little mismanagement in public affairs. *Great mistakes* in the ruling part, many wrong and inconvenient laws, and all the *slips* of human frailty, will be *born by the people* without mutiny or murmur. But if a long train of abuses, prevarications and artifices, all tending the same way, make the design visible to the people, and they cannot but feel what they lie under, and see whither they are going; it is not to be wondered, that they should then rouze themselves, and endeavour to put the rule into such hands which may secure to them the ends for which government was at first erected; and without which, ancient names, and specious forms, are so far from being better, that they are much worse, than the state of nature, or pure anarchy; the inconveniencies being all as great and as near, but the remedy farther off and more difficult.

Thirdly, I answer, that *this doctrine* of a power in the people of providing for their safety a-new, by a new legislative, when their legislators have acted contrary to their trust, by invading their property, is *the best fence against rebellion*, and the probablest means to hinder it: for *rebellion* being an opposition, not to persons, but authority, which is founded only in the constitutions and laws of the government; those, whoever they be, who by force break through, and by force justify their violation of them, are truly and properly *rebels*: for when men, by entering into society and civil government, have excluded force, and introduced laws for the preservation of property, peace, and unity amongst themselves, those who set up force again in opposition to the laws, do *rebellare*, that is, bring back again the state of war, and are properly rebels: which they who are in power, (by the pretence they have to authority, the temptation of force they have in their hands, and the flattery of those about them) being likeliest to do; the properest way to prevent the evil, is to shew them the danger and injustice of it, who are under the greatest temptation to run into it.

In both the fore-mentioned cases, when either the legislative is changed, or the legislators act contrary to the end for which they were constituted; those who are guilty are *guilty of rebellion*: for if any one by force takes away the established legislative of any society, and the laws by them made, pursuant to their trust, he thereby takes away the umpirage, which every one had consented to, for a peaceable decision of all their controversies, and a bar to the state of war amongst them. They, who remove, or change the legislative, take away this decisive power, which no body can have, but by the appointment and consent of the people; and so destroying the authority which the people did, and no body else can set up, and introducing a power which the people hath not authorized, they actually *introduce a state of war*, which is that of force without authority: and thus, by removing the legislative established by the society, (in whose decisions the people acquiesced and united, as to that of their own will) they untie the knot, and *expose the people a-new to the state of war*. And if those, who by force take away the legislative, are *rebels*, the *legislators* themselves, as has been shewn, can be no less esteemed so; when they, who were set up for the protection, and preservation of the people, their liberties and properties, shall by force invade and endeavour to take them away; and so they putting themselves into a state of war with those who made them the protectors and guardians of their peace, are properly, and with the greatest aggravation, *rebellantes*, rebels.

But if they, who say *it lays a foundation for rebellion*, mean that it may occasion civil wars, or intestine broils, to tell the people they are absolved from obedience when illegal attempts are made upon their liberties or properties, and may oppose the unlawful violence of those who were their magistrates, when they invade their properties contrary to the trust put in them; and that therefore this doctrine is not to be allowed, being so destructive to the peace of the world: they may as well say, upon the same ground, that honest men may not oppose robbers or pirates, because this may occasion disorder or bloodshed. If any *mischief* come in such cases, it is not to be charged upon him who defends his own right, but *on him that invades* his neighbours. If the innocent honest man must quietly quit all he has, for peace sake, to him who will lay violent hands upon it, I desire it may be considered, what a kind of peace there will be in the world, which consists only in violence and rapine; and which is to be maintained only for the benefit of robbers and oppressors. Who would not think it an admirable peace betwixt the mighty and the mean, when the lamb, without resistance, yielded his throat to be torn by the imperious wolf? *Polyphemus*'s den gives us a perfect pattern of such a peace, and such a government, wherein *Ulysses* and his companions had nothing to do, but quietly to suffer themselves to be devoured. And no doubt *Ulysses*, who was a prudent man, preached up *passive obedience*, and exhorted them to a quiet submission, by representing to them of what concernment peace was to mankind; and by shewing the inconveniences might happen, if they should offer to resist *Polyphemus*, who had now the power over them.

The end of government is the good of mankind; and which is *best for mankind*, that the people should be always exposed to the boundless will of tyranny, or that the rulers should be sometimes liable to be opposed, when they grow exorbitant in the use of their power, and employ it for the destruction, and not the preservation of the properties of their people?

Nor let any one say, that mischief can arise from hence, as often as it shall please a busy head, or turbulent spirit to desire the alteration of the government. It is true, such men may stir whenever they please; but it will be only to their just ruin and perdition: for till the mischief be grown general, and the ill designs of the rulers become visible or their attempts sensible to the greater part, the people who are more disposed to suffer than right themselves by resistance, are not apt to stir. The examples of particular injustice, or oppression of here and there an unfortunate man, moves them not. But if they universally have a persuasion, grounded upon manifest evidence, that designs are carrying on against their liberties and the general course and tendency of things cannot but give them strong suspicions of the evil intention of their governors who is to be blamed for it? Who can help it, if they, who might avoid it, bring themselves into this suspicion? Are the people to be blamed, if they have the sense of rational creatures, and can think of things no otherwise than as they find and feel them? And is it not rather *their fault*, who put things into such a posture, that they would not have them thought to be as they are? I grant, that the pride, ambition, and turbulency of private men have sometimes caused great disorders in common-wealths, and factions have been fatal to states and kingdoms. But whether *the mischief* hath *oftener* begun *in the peoples wantonness*, and a desire to cast off the lawful authority of their rulers, or *in the rulers insolence*, and endeavours to get and exercise an arbitrary power over their people; whether oppression, or disobedience, gave the first rise to the disorder, I leave it to impartial history to determine. This I am sure, whoever, either ruler or subject, by force goes about to invade the rights of either prince or people, and lays the foundation for *overturning* the constitution, and frame of *any just government*, is highly guilty of the greatest crime, I think, a man is capable of, being to answer for all those mischiefs of blood, rapine and desolation, which the breaking to pieces of governments bring on a country. And he who does it, is justly to be esteemed the common enemy and pest of mankind, and is to be treated accordingly. . . .

A year later, in 1774, American grievances remained unaddressed, and the situation was becoming more serious. In response to the Boston Tea Party (December 16, 1773), Parliament issued a set of harsh punitive measures, collectively known as the Coercive Acts (more colorfully called "the Intolerable Acts" in America). Under the acts, the port of Boston was closed until "peace and obedience to the laws" could be restored, and all damages paid for the destroyed tea. Massachusetts lost most of the powers of self-government it had enjoyed under its 1691 charter, which was itself another legacy of the Glorious Revolution.

Other measures, like the Administration of Justice Act (which allowed trials for British officials to be moved to Halifax, where the British admiralty was based, or to Britain) and the Quartering Act (which allowed the housing of troops in private homes), extended the Crown's retaliation to the colonies as a whole. Still another parliamentary statute, the Quebec Act, passed at the same time, was greeted with equal hostility. Its extension of certain rights to Catholic French Canadians struck many Anglo Americans as another sign of a larger plot to strip them of their rights, and resonated with a people who keenly remembered the religious tensions of the seventeenth century.

***Figure 10:** Jefferson's contribution to the great pamphlet debate was to turn the focus squarely onto the British monarch, George III, laying the groundwork for the final rupture.*

By any measure, the Intolerable Acts badly backfired, stiffening opposition in Massachusetts and arousing the sympathies of Americans from New Hampshire to the Carolinas. From September 5 to October 26, 1774, delegates from twelve colonies met in Philadelphia, calling themselves the Continental Congress.

Thomas Jefferson, a young and relatively unknown member of the House of Burgesses, Virginia's colonial legislature, had been unable to attend the special convention that elected the Old Dominion's delegates to the Continental Congress. Instead, he prepared instructions for them, urging the delegation to take a strong stand in defense of American rights. Apparently without his knowledge, the instructions were printed in Williamsburg, the colonial capital, as a short pamphlet—the instant media of the era.

A Summary View of the Rights of British America was noticed by the delegates, both for its eloquence and its deep learning. Jefferson did not advocate independence, claiming of Great Britain, "It is neither our wish, nor our interest, to separate from her." But he also wrote with a firm command of American history, and a distinct pride in his people, who merely wished to assert "their rights, as derived from the laws of nature, and not as the gift of their chief magistrate." Several of his phrases would be repeated two years later, including a reference to the lives and fortunes of the delegates, and a paragraph denouncing slavery, which was included in Jefferson's first draft of the Declaration, but removed from the final document. His focus on King George III signaled an important shift away from earlier arguments targeted at Parliament.

Thomas Jefferson, *A Summary View of the Rights of British America, &c.*

August 1774

RESOLVED, that it be an instruction to the said deputies, when assembled in general congress with the deputies from the other states of British America, to propose to the said congress that an humble and dutiful address be presented to his majesty, begging leave to lay before him, as chief magistrate of the British empire, the united complaints of his majesty's subjects in America; complaints which are excited by many unwarrantable encroachments and usurpations, attempted to be made by the legislature of one part of the empire, upon those rights which God and the laws have given equally and independently to all. To represent to his majesty that these his states have often individually made humble application to his imperial throne to obtain, through its intervention, some redress of their injured rights, to none of which was ever even an answer condescended; humbly to hope that this their joint address, penned in the language of truth, and divested of those expressions of servility which would persuade his majesty that we are asking favours, and not rights, shall obtain from his majesty a more respectful acceptance. And this his majesty will think we have reason to expect when he reflects that he is no more than the chief officer of the people, appointed by the laws, and circumscribed with definite powers, to assist in working the great machine of government, erected for their use, and consequently subject to their superintendance. And in order that these our rights, as well as the invasions of them, may be laid more fully before his majesty, to take a view of them from the origin and first settlement of these countries.

To remind him that our ancestors, before their emigration to America, were the free inhabitants of the British dominions in Europe, and possessed a right which nature has given to all men, of departing from the country in which chance, not choice, has placed them, of going in quest of new habitations, and of there establishing new societies, under such laws and regulations as to them shall seem most likely to promote public happiness. That their Saxon ancestors had, under this universal law, in like manner left their native wilds and woods in the north of Europe, had possessed themselves of the island of Britain, then less charged with inhabitants, and had established there that system of laws which has so long been the glory and protection of that country. Nor was ever any claim of superiority or dependence asserted over them by that mother country from which they had migrated; and were such a claim made, it is believed that his majesty's subjects in Great Britain have too firm a feeling of the rights derived to them from their ancestors, to bow down the sovereignty of their state before such visionary pretensions. And it is thought that no circumstance has occurred to distinguish materially the British from the Saxon emigration. America was conquered, and her settlements made, and firmly established, at the expence of individuals, and not of the British public. Their own blood was spilt in acquiring lands for their settlement, their own fortunes expended in making that settlement effectual; for themselves they fought, for themselves they conquered, and for themselves alone they have right to hold. Not a shilling was ever issued from the public treasures of his majesty, or his ancestors, for their assistance, till of very late times, after the colonies had become established on a firm and permanent footing. That then, indeed, having become valuable to Great Britain for her commercial purposes, his parliament was pleased to lend them assistance against an enemy, who would fain have drawn to herself the benefits of their commerce, to the great aggrandizement of herself, and danger of Great Britain. Such assistance, and in such circumstances, they had often before given to Portugal, and other allied states, with whom they carry on a commercial intercourse; yet these states never supposed, that by calling in her aid, they thereby submitted themselves to her sovereignty. Had such terms been proposed, they would have rejected them with disdain, and trusted for better to the moderation of their enemies, or to a vigorous exertion of their own force. We do not, however, mean to under-rate those aids, which to us were doubtless valuable, on whatever principles granted; but we would shew that they cannot give a title to that authority which the British parliament would arrogate over us, and that they may amply be repaid by our giving to the inhabitants of Great Britain such exclusive privileges in trade as may be advantageous to them, and at the same time not too restrictive to ourselves. That settlements having been thus effected in the wilds of America, the emigrants thought proper to adopt that system of laws under which they had hitherto lived in the mother country, and to continue their union with her by submitting themselves to the same common sovereign, who was thereby made the central link connecting the several parts of the empire thus newly multiplied. . . .

That these are our grievances which we have thus laid before his majesty, with that freedom of language and sentiment which becomes a free people claiming their rights, as derived from the laws of nature, and not as the gift of their chief magistrate: Let those flatter who fear; it is not an American art. To give praise which is not due might be well from the venal, but would ill beseem those who are asserting the rights of human nature. They know, and will therefore say, that kings are the servants, not the proprietors of the people. Open your breast, sire, to liberal and expanded thought. Let not the name of George the third be a blot in the page of history. You are surrounded by British counsellors, but remember that they are parties. You have no ministers for American affairs, because you have none taken from among us, nor amenable to the laws on which they are to give you advice. It behoves you, therefore, to think and to act for yourself and your people. The great principles of right and wrong are legible to every reader; to pursue them requires not the aid of many counsellors. The whole art of government consists in the art of being honest. Only aim to do your duty, and mankind will give you credit where you fail. No longer persevere in sacrificing the rights of one part of the empire to the inordinate desires of another; but deal out to all equal and impartial right. Let no act be passed by any one legislature which may infringe on the rights and liberties of another. This is the important post in which fortune has placed you, holding the balance of a great, if a well poised empire. This, sire, is the advice of your great American council, on the observance of which may perhaps depend your felicity and future fame, and the preservation of that harmony which alone can continue both to Great Britain and America the reciprocal advantages of their connection. It is neither our wish, nor our interest, to separate from her. We are willing, on our part, to sacrifice every thing which reason can ask to the restoration of that tranquillity for which all must wish. On their part, let them be ready to establish union and a generous plan. Let them name their terms, but let them be just. Accept of every commercial preference it is in our power to give for such things as we can raise for their use, or they make for ours. But let them not think to exclude us from going to other markets to dispose of those commodities which they cannot use, or to supply those wants which they cannot supply. Still less let it be proposed that our properties within our own territories shall be taxed or regulated by any power on earth but our own. The God who gave us life gave us liberty at the same time; the hand of force may destroy, but cannot disjoin them. This, sire, is our last, our determined resolution; and that you will be pleased to interpose with that efficacy which your earnest endeavours may ensure to procure redress of these our great grievances, to quiet the minds of your subjects in British America, against any apprehensions of future encroachment, to establish fraternal love and harmony through the whole empire, and that these may continue to the latest ages of time, is the fervent prayer of all British America!

Less than two weeks after it convened, the First Continental Congress endorsed the Suffolk County Resolves, which had recently been adopted by a convention in Massachusetts, and which declared that the Coercive Acts were due no obedience. The Suffolk Resolves further called for the formation of a provincial assembly free from imperial control, for the nonpayment of taxes, for a boycott of British imports, and, most portentously, for weekly militia training. A little more than two weeks later, on October 5, a unified Congress (the abbreviation N.C.D. is short for *nemine contradicente*, Latin for "unanimously") issued its own Declaration and Resolves that formally protested against the "unconstitutional" expansion of British rule, including new taxes and new courts. In addition,

***Figure 11:** The Continental Congress convened to respond to the British ministry's imposition of the Coercive Act's onto Massachusetts, likened here to an imperial jail cell.*

the document asserted important Lockean rights, including "life, liberty, and property," the right of representation, the right of assembly, and other rights consistent with "English liberty." Moderating its bold tone, the Declaration and Resolves also expressed a nostalgic hope that by addressing American claims, the British government might restore the mutual respect that had served for decades as the basis of "happiness and prosperity" in the empire.

Declaration and Resolves of the First Continental Congress

October 14, 1774

Whereas, since the close of the last war, the British parliament claiming a power of right to bind the people of America, by statute in all cases whatsoever, hath in some acts expressly imposed taxes on them, and in others under various presences, but in fact for the purpose of raising a revenue, hath imposed rates and duties payable in these colonies, established a board of commissioners with unconstitutional powers, and extended the jurisdiction of courts of admiralty, not only for collecting the said duties, but for the trial of causes merely arising within the body of a county.

And whereas in consequence of other statutes, judges, who before held only estates at will in their offices, have been made dependant on the crown alone for their salaries, and standing armies kept in time of peace. And it has lately been resolved in parliament, that by force of a statute made in the thirty-fifth year of the reign of King Henry the Eighth, colonists may be transported to England, and tried there upon accusations for treasons and misprisions, or concealment of treasons committed in the colonies; and by a late statute, such trials have been directed in cases therein mentioned.

And whereas in the last session of parliament, three statutes were made: one intituled, "An act to discontinue in such manner, and for such time as are therein mentioned, the landing and discharging, lading or shipping of goods, wares and merchandize, at the town, and within the harbour of Boston, in the province of Massachusetts-Bay, in North-America." Another intituled, "An act for the better regulating the government of the province of the Massachusetts-Bay, in New-England." And another intituled, "An act for the impartial administration of justice, in the cases of persons questioned for any act done by them in the execution of the law, or for the suppression of riots and tumults, in the province of the Massachusetts-Bay, in New-England." And another statute was then made, "for making more effectual provision for the government of the province of Quebec, &c." All which statutes are impolitic, unjust and cruel, as well as unconstitutional, and most dangerous and destructive of American rights.

And whereas, assemblies have been frequently dissolved, contrary to the rights of the people, when they attempted to deliberate on grievances; and their dutiful, humble, loyal, and reasonable petitions to the crown for redress, have been repeatedly treated with contempt by his Majesty's ministers of state.

The good people of the several colonies of New-Hampshire, Massachusett's-Bay, Rhode-Island and Providence plantations, Connecticut, New-York, New-Jersey, Pennsylvania, New-Castle, Kent and Sussex on Delaware, Maryland, Virginia, North-Carolina, and South-Carolina, justly alarmed at these arbitrary proceedings of parliament and administration, have severally elected, constituted, and appointed deputies to meet and sit in general congress in the city of Philadelphia, in order to obtain such establishment, as that their religion, laws, and liberties may not be subverted: Whereupon the deputies so appointed being now assembled, in a full and free representation of these colonies, taking into their most serious consideration the best means of attaining the ends aforesaid, do in the first place, as Englishmen their ancestors in like cases have usually done, for asserting and vindicating their rights and liberties, DECLARE,

That the inhabitants of the English colonies in North-America, by the immutable laws of nature, the principles of the English constitution, and the several charters or compacts, have the following RIGHTS.—

Resolved, N.C.D. 1. That they are entitled to life, liberty, and property; and they have never ceded to any sovereign power whatever, a right to dispose of either without their consent.

Resolved, N.C.D. 2. That our ancestors, who first settled these colonies, were at the time of their emigration from the mother country, entitled to all the rights, liberties, and immunities of free and natural born subjects, within the realm of England.

Resolved, N.C.D. 3. That by such emigration they by no means forfeited, surrendered, or lost any of those rights, but that they were, and their descendants now are, entitled to the exercise and enjoyment of all such of them, as their local and other circumstances enable them to exercise and enjoy.

Resolved, 4. That the foundation of English liberty and of all free government, is a right in the people to participate in their legislative council: and as the English colonists are not represented, and from their local and other circumstances cannot properly be represented in the British parliament, they are entitled to a free and exclusive power of legislation in their several provincial Legislatures, where their right of representation can alone be preserved, in all cases of taxation and internal polity, subject only to the negative of their sovereign, in such manner as has been heretofore used and accustomed: But from the necessity of the case, and a regard to the mutual interests of both countries, we chearfully consent to the operation of such acts of the British parliament, as are bona fide, restrained to the regulation of our external commerce, for the purpose of securing the commercial advantages of the whole empire to the mother country, and the commercial benefits of its respective members, excluding every idea of taxation internal or external, for raising a revenue on the subjects in America without their consent.

Resolved, N.C.D. 5. That the respective colonies are entitled to the common law of England, and more especially to the great and inestimable privilege of being tried by their peers of the vicinage, according to the course of that law.

Resolved, 6. That they are entitled to the benefit of such of the English statutes, as existed at the time of their colonization; and which they have, by experience, respectively found to be applicable to their several local and other circumstances.

Resolved, N.C.D. 7. That these, his Majesty's colonies, are likewise entitled to all the immunities and privileges granted and confirmed to them by royal charters, or secured by their several codes of provincial laws.

Resolved, N.C.D. 8. That they have a right peaceably to assemble, consider of their grievances, and petition the King; and that all prosecutions, prohibitory proclamations, and commitments for the same, are illegal.

Resolved, N.C.D. 9. That the keeping a standing army in these colonies, in times of peace, without the consent of the legislature of that colony in which such army is kept, is against law.

Resolved, N.C.D. 10. It is indispensibly necessary to good government, and rendered essential by the English constitution, that the constituent branches of the legislature be independant of each other; that, therefore, the exercise of legislative power in several colonies, by a council appointed, during pleasure, by the crown, is unconstitutional, dangerous, and destructive to the freedom of American legislation.

All and each of which, the aforesaid deputies in behalf of themselves, and their constituents, do claim, demand, and insist on, as their indubitable rights and liberties; which cannot be legally taken from them, altered or abridged by any power whatever, without their own consent, by their representatives in their several provincial legislatures.

In the course of our inquiry, we find many infringements and violations of the foregoing rights; which, from an ardent desire that harmony and mutual intercourse of affection and interest may be restored, we pass over for the present, and proceed to state such acts and measures as have been adopted since the last war, which demonstrate a system formed to enslave America.

Resolved, N.C.D. That the following acts of parliament are infringements and violations of the rights of the colonists; and that the repeal of them is essentially necessary, in order to restore harmony between Great Britain and the American colonies, viz.

The several acts of 4 Geo. III. ch. 15. and ch. 34.—5 Geo. III. ch. 25.—6 Geo. III. ch. 52.—7 Geo. III. ch. 41. and ch. 46.—8 Geo. III. ch. 22. which impose duties for the purpose of raising a revenue in America, extend the powers of the admiralty courts beyond their ancient limits, deprive the American subject of trial by jury, authorise the judges certificate to indemnify the prosecutor from damages, that he might otherwise be liable to, requiring oppressive security from a claimant of ships and goods seized, before he shall be allowed to defend his property, and are subversive of American rights.

Also 12 Geo. III. ch. 24. intituled "An act for the better securing his Majesty's dock-yards, magazines, ships, ammunition and stores." Which declares a new offence in America, and deprives the American subject of a constitutional trial by jury of the vicinage, by authorizing the trial of any person charged with the committing any offence described in the said act out of the realm, to be indicted and tried for the same in any shire or county within the realm.

Also the three acts passed in the last session of parliament, for stopping the port and blocking up the harbour of Boston, for altering the charter and government of Massachusetts Bay, and that which is intituled, "An act for the better administration of justice, &c."

Also the act passed in the same session for establishing the Roman catholic religion in the province of Quebec, abolishing the equitable system of English laws, and erecting a tyranny there, to the great danger, from so total a dissimilarity of religion, law and government to the neighbouring British colonies, by the assistance of whose blood and treasure the said country was conquered from France.

Also the act passed in the same session for the better providing suitable quarters for officers and soldiers in his Majesty's service in North-America.

Also, that the keeping a standing army in several of these colonies, in time of peace, without the consent of the legislature of that colony in which such army is kept, is against law.

To these grievous acts and measures Americans cannot submit; but, in hopes their fellow-subjects in Great Britain will, on a revision of them, restore us to that state, in which both countries found happiness and prosperity, we have for the present only resolved to pursue the following peaceable measures; 1. To enter into a non-importation, non-consumption, and non-exportation agreement or association. 2. To prepare an Address to the people of Great Britain, and a Memorial to the inhabitants of British America. And, 3. To prepare a loyal Address to his Majesty; agreeable to Resolutions already entered into.

In the spring of 1775, what had been a war of words became a war of arms. The bloody engagements at Lexington and Concord in April and at Bunker Hill in June led the recently convened Second Continental Congress to issue a major statement of resolve, published on July 6.

As its title suggests, the *Declaration . . . Setting forth the Causes and Necessity of their taking up Arms* states that Americans were quite willing to fight for their rights. It was written by new member Thomas Jefferson and veteran delegate John Dickinson, an unlikely but constructive pairing. Jefferson was one of the younger and more radical members of Congress. Dickinson, by contrast, was an established older presence, who had led the patriot cause a decade earlier, first in opposition to the Stamp Act in 1765, and then with his influential pamphlet series, *Letters from a Farmer in Pennsylvania* (1767–68). By 1775, however, he had become Congress's leading voice of caution, urging conciliation at every opportunity. While this latest declaration denounced British policy and asserted American pride ("Our cause is just. Our union is perfect."), it did not contemplate a formal separation. But in their strong language, including their desire to place their cause before "the opinion of mankind," the Americans were inching closer.

***Figure 12:** The fighting at Lexington and Concord on April 19, 1775, radically altered the terms of the imperial crisis, forcing many to consider the possibility of a permanent break.*

A Declaration by the Representatives of the United Colonies of North-America . . . Setting forth the Causes and Necessity of their taking up Arms.

July 6, 1775

If it was possible for men, who exercise their reason to believe, that the Divine Author of our existence intended a part of the human race to hold an absolute property in, and an unbounded power over others, marked out by his infinite goodness and wisdom, as the objects of a legal domination, never rightfully resistible, however severe and oppressive, the Inhabitants of these Colonies might at least require from the Parliament of Great-Britain, some evidence, that this dreadful authority over them has been granted to that body. But a reverence for our great Creator, principles of humanity, and the dictates of common sense, must convince all those who reflect upon the subject, that government was instituted to promote the welfare of mankind, and ought to be administered for the attainment of that end. The legislature of Great-Britain, however, stimulated by an inordinate passion for a power not only unjustifiable, but which they know to be peculiarly reprobated by the very constitution of that kingdom, and desperate of success in any mode of contest, where regard should be had to truth, law, or right, have at length, deserting those, attempted to effect their cruel and impolitic purpose of enslaving these Colonies by violence, and have thereby rendered it necessary for us to close with their last Appeal from Reason to Arms.—Yet, however blinded that assembly may be, by their intemperate rage for unlimited domination, so to slight justice and the opinion of mankind, we esteem ourselves bound by obligations of respect to the rest of the world, to make known the justice of our cause.

Our forefathers, inhabitants of the island of Great-Britain, left their native land, to seek on these shores a residence for civil and religious freedom. At the expence of their blood, at the hazard of their fortunes, without the least charge to the country from which they removed, by unceasing labor and an unconquerable spirit, they effected settlements in the distant and inhospitable wilds of America, then filled with numerous and warlike nations of barbarians.—Societies or governments, vested with perfect legislatures, were formed under charters from the crown, and an harmonious intercourse was established between the colonies and the kingdom from which they derived their origin. The mutual benefits of this union became in a short time so extraordinary as to excite astonishment. It is universally confessed that the amazing increase of the wealth, strength and navigation of the realm, arose from this source; and the minister who so wisely and successfully directed the measures of Great-Britain in the late war, publicly declared, that these colonies enabled her to triumph over her enemies.—Towards the conclusion of that war, it pleased our sovereign to make a change in his counsels.—From that fatal moment, the affairs of the British empire began to fall into confusion, and gradually sliding from the summit of glorious prosperity to which they had been advanced by the virtues and abilities of one man, are at length distracted by the convulsions, that now shake it to its deepest foundations.—The new ministry finding the brave foes of Britain, though frequently defeated, yet still contending, took up the unfortunate idea of granting them a hasty peace, and of then subduing her faithful friends.

These devoted colonies were judged to be in such a state, as to present victories without bloodshed, and all the easy emoluments of statuteable plunder.—The uninterrupted tenor of their peaceable and respectful behavior from the beginning of colonization, their dutiful, zealous and useful services during the war, though so recently and amply acknowledged in the most honorable manner by his Majesty, by the late king, and by Parliament, could not save them from the meditated innovations.—Parliament was influenced to adopt the pernicious project, and assuming a new power over them, have in the course of eleven years given such decisive specimens of the spirit and consequences attending this power, as to leave no doubt concerning the effects of acquiescence under it. They have undertaken to give and grant our money without our consent, though we have ever exercised an exclusive right to dispose of our own property; statutes have been passed for extending the jurisdiction of courts of Admiralty and Vice-Admiralty beyond their ancient limits; for depriving us of the accustomed and inestimable privilege of trial by jury in cases affecting both life and property; for suspending the legislature of one of the colonies; for interdicting all commerce of another; and for altering fundamentally the form of government established by charter, and secured by acts of its own legislature solemnly confirmed by the crown; for exempting the "murderers" of colonists from legal trial, and in effect, from punishment; for erecting in a neighbouring province, acquired by the joint arms of Great-Britain and America, a despotism dangerous to our very existence; and for quartering soldiers upon the colonists in time of profound peace. It has also been resolved in parliament, that colonists charged with committing certain offences, shall be transported to England to be tried.

But why should we enumerate our injuries in detail? . . .

Our cause is just. Our union is perfect. Our internal resources are great, and if necessary, foreign assistance is undoubtedly attainable.—We gratefully acknowledge, as signal instances of the Divine favour towards us, that his Providence would not permit us to be called into this severe controversy, until we were grown up to our present strength, had been previously exercised in warlike operations, and possessed of the means of defending ourselves.—With hearts fortified with these animating reflections, we most solemnly, before GOD and the world declare, that, exerting the utmost energy of those powers, which our beneficent Creator hath graciously bestowed upon us, the arms we have been compelled by our enemies to assume, we will, in defiance of every hazard, with unabating firmness and perseverance, employ for the preservation of our liberties, being with one mind resolved, to dye Free-men rather than to live Slaves.

Lest this declaration should disquiet the minds of our friends and fellow subjects in any part of the empire, we assure them, that we mean not to dissolve that Union which has so long and so happily subsisted between us, and which we sincerely wish to see restored.—Necessity has not yet driven us into that desperate measure, or induced us to excite any other nation to war against them.—We have not raised armies with ambitious designs of separating from Great-Britain, and establishing independent states.—We fight not for glory or for conquest. We exhibit to mankind the remarkable spectacle of a people attacked by unprovoked enemies, without any imputation, or even suspicion, of offence. They boast of their privileges and civilization, and yet proffer no milder conditions than servitude or death.—

In our own native land, in defence of the freedom that is our birthright, and which we ever enjoyed till the late violation of it—for the protection of our property, acquired solely by the honest industry of our fore-fathers and ourselves, against violence actually offered, we have taken up arms. We shall lay them down when hostilities shall cease on the part of the aggressors, and all danger of their being renewed shall be removed, and not before.

With an humble confidence in the mercies of the supreme and impartial Judge and Ruler of the universe, we most devoutly implore his divine goodness to conduct us happily through this great conflict, to dispose our adversaries to reconciliation on reasonable terms, and thereby to relieve the empire from the calamities of civil war.

Congress's declaration in defense of taking up arms had premised its arguments on "a reverence for our great Creator, principles of humanity, and the dictates of common sense." None of that seemed to impress the King; on November 9, 1775, the news reached Philadelphia that George III had rejected the conciliatory Olive Branch Petition that Congress had extended and formally pronounced the colonies to be in a state of rebellion.

Less than a month later, Congress disavowed its allegiance to Parliament, leaving only the tie to the King as the last ligament of empire. That tie was fatally weakened on January 10, 1776, when an anonymous forty-seven-page pamphlet, titled *Common Sense*, was published in Philadelphia. Its author, Thomas Paine, was a recent English immigrant who had arrived a little over a year earlier, in November 1774. Though it would be difficult to call Paine a Founder in the traditional sense, his tract caught the public's mood perfectly and proved to be wildly popular.

Figure 13: *Englishman Thomas Paine had been in the colonies for only fourteen months when he wrote* Common Sense, *the incendiary pamphlet that did more than any other to advance the push for independence from the British Crown.*

Unlike most pamphleteers to that point, Paine had no qualms about arguing for independence. In a populist language, he demolished the theory of the divine right of kings and wondered aloud if any country had ever benefited from its "crowned ruffians." In America, he argued proudly, "the law is king," and not the other way around. *Common Sense* did not do much to instruct Americans how to build a government of their own, except urging them to write a "Continental Charter" that would resemble the Magna Carta. John Adams felt that Paine was "better at tearing down than building up." But in shaping public opinion toward independence, this bold pamphlet played an essential role in the drama of 1776.

Thomas Paine, *Common Sense, Addressed to the Inhabitants of America, . . . A New Edition, with Several Additions in the Body of Work.*

February 1776

SOME writers have so confounded society with government, as to leave little or no distinction between them; whereas they are not only different, but have different origins. Society is produced by our wants, and government by our wickedness; the former promotes our happiness *positively* by uniting our affections, the latter *negatively* by restraining our vices. The one encourages intercourse, the other creates distinctions. The first is a patron, the last a punisher.

Society in every state is a blessing, but government even in its best state is but a necessary evil; in its worst state an intolerable one; for when we suffer, or are exposed to the same miseries by a *government*, which we might expect in a country *without government*, our calamity is heightened by reflecting that we furnish the means by which we suffer. Government, like dress, is the badge of lost innocence; the palaces of kings are built on the ruins of the bowers of paradise. For were the impulses of conscience clear, uniform, and irresistibly obeyed, man would need no other lawgiver; but that not being the case, he finds it necessary to surrender up a part of his property to furnish means for the protection of the rest; and this he is induced to do by the same prudence which in every other case advises him out of two evils to choose the least. *Wherefore*, security being the true design and end of government, it unanswerably follows that whatever *form* thereof appears most likely to ensure it to us, with the least expence and greatest benefit, is preferable to all others.

In order to gain a clear and just idea of the design and end of government, let us suppose a small number of persons settled in some sequestered part of the earth, unconnected with the rest, they will then represent the first peopling of any country, or of the world. In this state of natural liberty, society will be their first thought. A thousand motives will excite them thereto, the strength of one man is so unequal to his wants, and his mind so unfitted for perpetual solitude, that he is soon obliged to seek assistance and relief of another, who in his turn requires the same. Four or five united would be able to raise a tolerable dwelling in the midst of a wilderness, but *one* man might labour out the common period of life without accomplishing any thing; when he had felled his timber he could not remove it, nor erect it after it was removed; hunger in the mean time would urge him from his work, and every different want call him a different way. Disease, nay even misfortune would be death, for though neither might be mortal, yet either would disable him from living, and reduce him to a state in which he might rather be said to perish than to die.

Thus necessity, like a gravitating power, would soon form our newly arrived emigrants into society, the reciprocal blessings of which, would supersede, and render the obligations of law and government unnecessary while they remained perfectly just to each other; but as nothing but heaven is impregnable to vice, it will unavoidably happen, that in proportion as they surmount the first difficulties of emigration, which bound them together in a common cause, they will begin to relax in their duty and attachment to each other; and this remissness, will point out the necessity, of establishing some form of government to supply the defect of moral virtue.

Some convenient tree will afford them a State-House, under the branches of which, the whole colony may assemble to deliberate on public matters. It is more than probable that their first laws will have the title only of REGULATIONS, and be enforced by no other penalty than public disesteem. In this first parliament every man, by natural right, will have a seat.

But as the colony increases, the public concerns will increase likewise, and the distance at which the members may be separated, will render it too inconvenient for all of them to meet on every occasion as at first, when their number was small, their habitations near, and the public concerns few and trifling. This will point out the convenience of their consenting to leave the legislative part to be managed by a select number chosen from the whole body, who are supposed to have the same concerns at stake which those have who appointed them, and who will act in the same manner as the whole body would act were they present. If the colony continue increasing, it will become necessary to augment the number of the representatives, and that the interest of every part of the colony may be attended to, it will be found best to divide the whole into convenient parts, each part sending its proper number; and that the *elected* might never form to themselves an interest separate from the *electors*, prudence will point out the propriety of having elections often; because as the *elected* might by that means return and mix again with the general body of the *electors* in a few months, their fidelity to the public will be secured by the prudent reflexion of not making a rod for themselves. And as this frequent interchange will establish a common interest with every part of the community, they will mutually and naturally support each other, and on this (not on the unmeaning name of king) depends the *strength of government, and the happiness of the governed.*

Here then is the origin and rise of government; namely, a mode rendered necessary by the inability of moral virtue to govern the world; here too is the design and end of government, viz. freedom and security. And however our eyes may be dazzled with show, or our ears deceived by sound; however prejudice may warp our wills, or interest darken our understanding, the simple voice of nature and of reason will say, it is right.

I draw my idea of the form of government from a principle in nature, which no art can overturn, viz. that the more simple any thing is, the less liable it is to be disordered, and the easier repaired when disordered; and with this maxim in view, I offer a few remarks on the so much boasted constitution of England. That it was noble for the dark and slavish times in which it was erected, is granted. When the world was over run with tyranny the least remove therefrom was a glorious rescue. But that it is imperfect, subject to convulsions, and incapable of producing what it seems to promise, is easily demonstrated.

Absolute governments (tho' the disgrace of human nature) have this advantage with them, that they are simple; if the people suffer, they know the head from which their suffering springs, know likewise the remedy, and are not bewildered by a variety of causes and cures. But the constitution of England is so exceedingly complex, that the nation may suffer for years together without being able to discover in which part the fault lies, some will say in one and some in another, and every political physician will advise a different medicine.

I know it is difficult to get over local or long standing prejudices, yet if we will suffer ourselves to examine the component parts of the English constitution, we shall find them to be the base remains of two ancient tyrannies, compounded with some new republican materials. . . .

To Conclude, however strange it may appear to some, or however unwilling they may be to think so, matters not, but many strong and striking reasons may be given, to shew, that nothing can settle our affairs so expeditiously as an open and determined declaration for independance. Some of which are,

First.—It is the custom of nations, when any two are at war, for some other powers, not engaged in the quarrel, to step in as mediators, and bring about the preliminaries of a peace: but while America calls herself the Subject of Great-Britain, no power, however well disposed she may be, can offer her mediation. Wherefore, in our present state we may quarrel on for ever.

Secondly.—It is unreasonable to suppose, that France or Spain will give us any kind of assistance, if we mean only, to make use of that assistance for the purpose of repairing the breach, and strengthening the connection between Britain and America; because, those powers would be sufferers by the consequences.

Thirdly.—While we profess ourselves the subjects of Britain, we must, in the eye of foreign nations, be considered as rebels. The precedent is somewhat dangerous to *their peace*, for men to be in arms under the name of subjects; we, on the spot, can solve the paradox: but to unite resistance and subjection, requires an idea much too refined for common understanding.

Fourthly.—Were a manifesto to be published, and despatched to foreign courts, setting forth the miseries we have endured, and the peaceable methods we have ineffectually used for redress; declaring, at the same time, that not being able, any longer, to live happily or safely under the cruel disposition of the British court, we had been driven to the necessity of breaking off all connections with her; at the same time, assuring all such courts of our peaceable disposition towards them, and of our desire of entering into trade with them: Such a memorial would produce more good effects to this Continent, than if a ship were freighted with petitions to Britain.

Under our present denomination of British subjects, we can neither be received nor heard abroad: The custom of all courts is against us, and will be so, until, by an independance, we take rank with other nations.

These proceedings may at first appear strange and difficult; but, like all other steps which we have already passed over, will in a little time become familiar and agreeable; and, until an independance is declared, the Continent will feel itself like a man who continues putting off some unpleasant business from day to day, yet knows it must be done, hates to set about it, wishes it over, and is continually haunted with the thoughts of its necessity.

Figure 14: *Still a relatively obscure provincial lawyer when the portrait from which this engraving was taken was painted in 1766, by 1776 John Adams was the leading voice for independence in the Continental Congress. He was "our Colossus on the floor," recalled Jefferson.*

Throughout the colonies, in the winter and spring of 1776, the structures of imperial rule began to collapse. But as ad hoc assemblies improvised governing authority, many wondered about the sources of their legitimacy.

Few were thinking harder about the sinews of government than Massachusetts delegate John Adams, who had been reading deeply in his law and history books for years. In March, two North Carolina delegates asked him for advice on drafting a new form of government, and he responded with detailed letters. When George Wythe of Virginia saw them, he asked Adams for similar advice. Then Johnathan Dickinson Sergeant of New Jersey asked for a copy, and Adams responded with an enlarged version. Finally, when Richard Henry Lee of Virginia requested yet another master plan, Adams decided to put his various letters together in an anonymous pamphlet, first advertised for sale in Philadelphia on April 22.

Thoughts on Government proved to be essential, arriving at the perfect moment for a Congress veering toward independence, but unsure what lay on the other side of the void. It was an uplifting tract in many ways, including its assertion that a good government ought to promote "happiness," a word that Jefferson would repurpose meaningfully in the Declaration of Independence. A sensitive historian, Adams was comfortable in the past—when he urged his fellow delegates to build "an Empire of Laws, and not of men," he recalled a Whig phrase that can be traced back to James Harrington's *Oceana* (1656). But he was also a visionary, already imagining how a democracy would actually work. He wrote in measured tones about the branches of government, and their internal checks and balances, and reassured his fellow delegates that they would find a reasonable accommodation if they trusted each other. In a letter written that spring to John Penn, one of the two North Carolina delegates, parts of which are incorporated into the text below, he conveyed the thrill of the adventure, arguing, "It has been the Will of Heaven that We should be thrown into Existence at a Period when the greatest Philosophers and Lawgivers of Antiquity would have wished to live."

John Adams, *Thoughts on Government, Applicable to the Present State of the American Colonies*

April 1776

My dear Sir,

If I was equal to the task of forming a plan for the government of a colony, I should be flattered with your request, and very happy to comply with it; because as the divine science of politicks is the science of social happiness, and the blessings of society depend entirely on the constitutions of government, which are generally institutions that last for many generations, there can be no employment more agreeable to a benevolent mind, than a research after the best.

Pope flattered tyrants too much when he said,

"For forms of government let fools contest,
That which is best administered is best."

Nothing can be more fallacious than this: But poets read history to collect flowers not fruits—they attend to fanciful images, not the effects of social institutions. Nothing is more certain from the history of nations, and the nature of man, than that some forms of government are better fitted for being well administered than others.

We ought to consider, what is the end of government, before we determine which is the best form. Upon this point all speculative politicians will agree, that the happiness of society is the end of government, as Divines and moral Philosophers agree that the happiness of the individual is the end of man. From this principle it will follow, that the form of government, which communicates ease, comfort, security, or in one word happiness to the greatest number of persons, and in the greatest degree, is the best.

All sober enquiries after truth, ancient and modern, Pagan and Christian, have declared that the happiness of man, as well as his dignity consists in virtue. Confucius, Zoroaster, Socrates, Mahomet, not to mention authorities really sacred, have agreed in this.

If there is a form of government then, whose principle and foundation is virtue, will not every sober man acknowledge it better calculated to promote the general happiness than any other form?

Fear is the foundation of most governments; but is so sordid and brutal a passion, and renders men, in whose breasts it predominates, so stupid, and miserable, that Americans will not be likely to approve of any political institution which is founded on it.

Honor is truly sacred, but holds a lower rank in the scale of moral excellence than virtue. Indeed the former is but a part of the latter, and consequently has not equal pretensions to support a frame of government productive of human happiness.

The foundation of every government is some principle or passion in the minds of the people. The noblest principles and most generous affections in our nature then, have the fairest chance to support the noblest and most generous models of government.

A man must be indifferent to the sneers of modern Englishmen to mention in their company the names of Sidney, Harrington, Locke,

Milton, Nedham, Neville, Burnet, and Hoadley. No small fortitude is necessary to confess that one has read them. The wretched condition of this country, however, for ten or fifteen years past, has frequently reminded me of their principles and reasonings. They will convince any candid mind, that there is no good government but what is Republican. That the only valuable part of British constitution is so; because the very definition of a Republic, is "an Empire of Laws, and not of men." That, as a Republic is the best of governments, so that particular arrangement of the powers of society, or in other words that form of government, which is best contrived to secure an impartial and exact execution of the laws, is the best of Republics.

Of Republics, there is an inexhaustable variety, because the possible combinations of the powers of society, are capable of innumerable variations.

As good government, is an empire of laws, how shall your laws be made? In a large society, inhabiting an extensive country, it is impossible that the whole should assemble, to make laws: The first necessary step then, is, to depute power from the many, to a few of the most wise and good. But by what rules shall you chuse your Representatives? Agree upon the number and qualifications of persons, who shall have the benefit of choosing, or annex this priviledge to the inhabitants of a certain extent of ground.

The principal difficulty lies, and the greatest care should be employed in constituting this Representative Assembly. It should be in miniature, an exact portrait of the people at large. It should think feel, reason, and act like them. That it may be the interest of this Assembly to do strict justice at all times, it should be an equal representation, or in other words equal interest among the people should have equal interest in it. Great care should be taken to effect this, and to prevent unfair, partial, and corrupt elections. Such regulations, however, may be better made in times of greater tranquility than the present, and they will spring up of themselves naturally, when all the powers of government come to be in the hands of the people's friends. At present it will be safest to proceed in all established modes to which the people have been familiarised by habit. . . .

In the present exigency of American affairs, when by an act of Parliament we are put out of the royal protection, and consequently discharged from our allegiance; and it has become necessary to assume government for our immediate security, the Governor, Lieutenant-Governor, Secretary, Treasurer, Commissary, Attorney-General, should be chosen by joint Ballot, of both Houses. And these and all other elections, especially of Representatives, and Councillors, should be annual, there not being in the whole circle of the sciences, a maxim more infallible than this, "Where annual elections end, there slavery begins." . . .

A CONSTITUTION, founded on these principles, introduces knowledge among the People, and inspires them with a conscious dignity, becoming Freemen. A general emulation takes place, which causes good humour, sociability, good manners, and good morals to be general. That elevation of sentiment, inspired by such a government, makes the common people brave and enterprizing. That ambition which is inspired by it makes them sober, industrious and frugal. You find among them some elegance, perhaps, but more solidity; a little pleasure, but a great deal of business—some politeness, but more civility. If you compare such a country with the regions of domination, whether Monarchial or Aristocratical, you will fancy yourself in Arcadia or Elisium.

IF the Colonies should assume governments separately, they should be left entirely to their own choice of the forms, and if a Continental Constitution should be formed, it should be a Congress, containing a fair and adequate Representation of the Colonies, and its authority should sacredly be confined to these cases, viz. war, trade, disputes between Colony and Colony, the Post-Office, and the unappropriated lands of the Crown, as they used to be called.

THESE Colonies, under such forms of government, and in such a union, would be unconquerable by all the Monarchies of Europe.

YOU and I, my dear Friend, have been sent into life, at a time when the greatest law-givers of antiquity would have wished to have lived. How few of the human race have ever enjoyed an opportunity of making an election of government more than of air, soil, or climate, for themselves or their children. When! Before the present epocha, had three millions of people full power and a fair opportunity to form and establish the wisest and happiest government that human wisdom can contrive? . . .

Figure 15: Thomas Jefferson seen here in a likeness taken more than a decade after the independence summer, would come to jealously guard his role in the drafting of the Declaration.

By late spring 1776, events were moving quickly, especially in Virginia, the largest of the colonies. Thomas Jefferson had returned to Congress, somewhat reluctantly, in May. He would have preferred to be in Williamsburg, where Virginia's patriot leaders were framing a new government. Instead, he spent weeks laboring on a draft constitution, which he dispatched to Williamsburg in the care of fellow delegate George Wythe, his former law professor at the College of William and Mary, who was returning home. The Virginia Assembly would not adopt Jefferson's draft—they had nearly completed their work on another. But they were taken by his preamble, which was tantamount to a declaration of independence, and previewed the language soon to come in the real thing, particularly the catalogue of royal offenses. By introducing King George III as "George Guelf," using an old German name linked to the House of Hanover, Jefferson already shows his rising contempt for the monarchy, even before listing all the King's many misdeeds.

Thomas Jefferson, Preamble to the Virginia Constitution

[before June 13, 1776]

A Bill for new-modelling the form of Government and for establishing the Fundamental principles thereof in future.

Whereas George Guelf king of Great Britain and Ireland and Elector of Hanover, heretofore entrusted with the exercise of the kingly office in this government hath endeavored to pervert the same into a detestable and insupportable tyranny;

by putting his negative on laws the most wholesome & necessary for ye. public good;

by denying to his governors permission to pass laws of immediate & pressing importance, unless suspended in their operation for his assent, and, when so suspended, neglecting to attend to them for many years;

by refusing to pass certain other laws, unless the persons to be benefited by them would relinquish the inestimable right of representation in the legislature

by dissolving legislative assemblies repeatedly and continually for opposing with manly firmness his invasions on the rights of the people;

when dissolved, by refusing to call others for a long space of time, thereby leaving the political system without any legislative head;

by endeavoring to prevent the population of our country, & for that purpose obstructing the laws for the naturalization of foreigners & raising the conditions of new appropriations of lands;

by keeping among us, in times of peace, standing armies & ships of war;

by affecting to render the military independent of & superior to the civil power;

by combining with others to subject us to a foreign jurisdiction, giving his assent to their pretended acts of legislation

for quartering large bodies of troops among us;

for cutting off our trade with all parts of the world;

for imposing taxes on us without our consent;

for depriving us of the benefits of trial by jury;

for transporting us beyond seas to be tried for pretended offences; and

for suspending our own legislatures & declaring themselves invested with power to legislate for us in all cases whatsoever;

by plundering our seas, ravaging our coasts, burning our towns and destroying the lives of our people;

by inciting insurrections of our fellow subjects with the allurements of forfeiture & confiscation

by prompting our negroes to rise in arms among us; those very negroes whom by an inhuman use of his negative he hath refused us permission to exclude by law

by endeavoring to bring on the inhabitants of our frontiers the merciless Indian savages, whose known rule of warfare is an undistinguished destruction of all ages, sexes, & conditions of existence;

by transporting at this time a large army of foreign mercenaries to compleat the works of death, desolation, & tyranny already begun with circumstances of cruelty & perfidy so unworthy the head of a civilized nation;

by answering our repeated petitions for redress with a repetition of injuries;

and finally by abandoning the helm of government and declaring us out of his allegiance & protection;

by which several acts of misrule the said George Guelf has forfeited the kingly office and has rendered it necessary for the preservation of the people that he should be immediately deposed from the same, and divested of all it's privileges, powers, & prerogatives:

And forasmuch as the public liberty may be more certainly secured by abolishing an office which all experience hath shewn to be inveterately inimical thereto and it will thereupon become further necessary to re-establish such antient principles as are friendly to the rights of the people and to declare certain others which may co-operate with and fortify the same in future.

Be it therefore enacted by the authority of the people that the said George Guelf be, and he hereby is deposed from the kingly office within this government and absolutely divested of all it's rights, powers and prerogatives; and that he and his descendants and all persons claiming by or through him, and all other persons whatsoever shall be & for ever remain incapable of the same; and that the said office shall henceforth cease and never more either in name or substance be re-established within this colony. . . .

Figure 16: *Principally the work of lawyer George Mason, the Virginia Declaration of Rights anticipates much of the language Jefferson would deploy in the Declaration of Independence.*

On June 12, 1776, a constitutional convention in Williamsburg adopted a Virginia Declaration of Rights that would exert a considerable influence on the final shape and tone of the Declaration of Independence. Written in a tavern by George Mason, the Virginia Declaration begins with a ringing statement, owing plenty to John Locke, that "all men are by nature equally free and independent, and have certain inherent rights . . . namely, the enjoyment of life and liberty, with the means of acquiring and possessing property, and pursuing and obtaining happiness and safety."

That was hardly the only language in the Virginia Declaration that would be re-stated, usually in a simpler, more elegant way, in the Declaration of Independence. Another was the assertion that the people have an "unalienable" right to "alter or abolish" a government that no longer protects their liberties.

The Virginia Declaration of Rights was also a model for the Constitution and Bill of Rights, defining broad rights relating to justice (trial by jury), freedom of the press, a "well regulated militia," and "the exercise of religion, according to the dictates of conscience." (The latter clause was added by James Madison.)

Despite some anxiety in the Virginia Convention over whether Mason's language about equality might apply to slaves, the delegates approved his declaration, and Jefferson had yet another precedent to consider as he worked on a crucial declaration of his own in Philadelphia, with all of these words swirling in his head.

Virginia Declaration of Rights

June 12, 1776

Made by the Representatives of the good people of Virginia, assembled in full and free Convention; which rights do pertain to them, and their posterity, as the basis and foundation of Government.

FIRST, That all men are by nature equally free and independent, and have certain inherent rights, of which, when they enter into a state of society, they cannot, by any compact, deprive or divest their posterity; namely, the enjoyment of life and liberty, with the means of acquiring and possessing property, and pursuing and obtaining happiness and safety.

2d. That all power is vested in, and consequently derived from, the people; that magistrates are their trustees and servants, and at all times amenable to them.

3d. That government is, or ought to be instituted for the common benefit, protection and security, of the people, nation, or community, of all the various modes and forms of government that is best, which is capable of producing the greatest degree of happiness and safety, and is most effectually secured against the danger of maladministration; and that whenever any government shall be found inadequate or contrary to these purposes, a majority of the community hath an indubitable, unalienable, and indefeasible right, to perform, alter, or abolish it, in such manner as shall be judged most conducive to the public weal.

4th. That no man, or set of men, are intitled to exclusive or separate emoluments or privileges from the community, but in consideration of public services; which, not being descendible, neither ought the offices of magistrate, legislator, or judge, to be the hereditary.

5th. That the Legislative and Executive powers of the state should be separate and distinct from the judiciary; and that the members of the two first may be restrained from oppression, by feeling and participating the burthens of the people, they should at fixed periods, be reduced to a private station, return into that body from which they were originally taken, and the vacancies be supplied by frequent, certain, and regular elections, in which all, or any part of the former members, to be again eligible, or ineligible, as the laws shall direct.

6th. That elections of members to serve as representatives of the people, in Assembly, ought to be free, and that all men, having sufficient evidence of permanent common interest with, and attachment to, the community, have the right of suffrage, and cannot be taxed or deprived of their property for public uses without their own consent, or that of their representatives so elected, nor bound by any law to which they have not, in like manner, assented for the public good.

7th. That all power of suspending law, or the execution of laws, by any authority without consent of the representatives of the people, is injurious to their rights, and ought not to be exercised.

8th. That in all capital or criminal prosecutions, a man hath a right to demand the cause and nature of his accusation, to be confronted with the accusers and witnesses, to call for evidence in his favor, and to a speedy trial by an impartial jury of his vicinage, whithout whose unanimous consent he cannot be found guilty, nor can he be compelled to give evidence against himself; that no man be deprived of his liberty, except by the law of the land, or the judgment of his peers.

9th. That excessive bail ought not to be required, nor excessive fines imposed, nor cruel unusual punishments inflicted.

10th. The general warrants, whereby any officer or messenger may be commanded to search suspected places without evidence of a fact committed, or to seize any person or persons not named, or whose offense is not particularly described and supported by evidence, are grievous and oppressive, and ought not to be granted.

11th. That in controversies respecting property, and in suits between man and man, the ancient trial by jury is preferable to any other, and ought to be held sacred.

12th. That the freedom of the press is one of the great bulwarks of liberty, and can never be restrained but by dispotic governments.

13th. That a well regulated militia, composed of the body of the people trained to arms, is the proper, natural, and safe defence of a free state; that standing armies, in time of peace, should be avoided, as dangerous to liberty; and that, in all cases, the military should be under strict subordination to, and governed by, the civil power.

14th. That the people have a right to uniform government; and therefore, that no government separate from, or independent of the government of Virginia, ought to be erected or established within the limits thereof.

15th. That no free government, or the blessing of liberty, can be preserved to any people but by a firm adherence to justice, moderation, temperance, frugality, and virtue, and by frequent recurrence to fundimental principles.

16th. That religion, or the duty which we owe to our CREATOR, and the manner of discharging it, can be directed only by reason and conviction, not by force or violence, and therefore all men are equally entitled to the free exercise of religion, according to the dictates of conscience; and that it is the mutual duty of all to practice Christian forbearance, love, and charity, towards each other.

Figure 17: *An engraving depicting a contentious town hall meeting in* McFingal: A Modern Epic Poem, or, The Town-meeting, *by patriot poet John Trumbull, first serialized in the* Connecticut Courant *in 1775.*

As the Second Continental Congress and Virginia were barreling toward independence, the same effect could be discerned around the country—not quite a country yet—as local communities expressed sentiments of their own. Public opinion was an important force in the spring of 1776, as Loyalists gradually lost the argument (in part because many were leaving). Well before July 4, local governments were validating the desire to move past their dependence on the British Crown, so consistently hostile to American interests, and begin something new and better. On May 4, 1776, Rhode Island became the first colony to formally renounce its allegiance to the Crown. Six weeks later, on June 20, 1776, a town meeting in Natick, Massachusetts, expressed its rejection of the "glaring impropriety" of a distant government, three thousand miles away, still trying to control America's destiny. In Natick, the general feeling was that "the sooner" the break could come, the better.

Natick, Massachusetts Town Meeting Resolves

June 20, 1776

At a meeting of the town of *Natick, June* 20, 1776, legally warned, in consequence of a resolve of the late House of Representatives being laid before the Town, setting forth their sense of the obligations that lie upon every town in this Colony solemnly to engage to support with their lives and fortunes the honourable Continental Congress, should said Congress, for the safety of the Colonies, come into the measure of declaring themselves independent of the Kingdom of *Great Britain*, it was unanimously

Voted, That, in consideration of the many acts of the *British* Parliament, passed at divers sessions of the same, within about thirteen years past, relating to said Colonies, especially those within the two or three last years, by which every idea of moderation, justice, humanity, and Christianity are entirely laid aside, and those principles and measures adopted and pursued which would disgrace the most unenlightened and uncivilized tribe of aboriginal natives in the most interior parts of this extensive continent; and, also, in consequence of the glaring impropriety, incapacity, and fatal tendency, of any State whatever, at the distance of three thousand miles, to legislate for these Colonies, which at the same time are so numerous, so knowing, and capable of legislating; or to have a negative upon those laws which they, in their respective Assemblies, and by their united representation in General Congress, shall, from time to time, want and establish for themselves; and upon divers other considerations, which, for brevity's sake, we omit to mention,—we, the inhabitants of *Natick*, in town-meeting assembled, do hereby declare, agreeable to the tenor of the aforementioned resolve, that, should the honourable Continental Congress declare these *American* Colonies independent of the Kingdom of *Great Britain*, we will, with our lives and fortunes, join with the other inhabitants of this Colony, and with those of the other Colonies, in supporting them in such measure, which we look upon to be both important and necessary, and which, if we may be permitted to suggest our opinion, the sooner it is come into the fewer difficulties we shall have to contend with, and the grand objects of peace, liberty, and safety, will be more likely speedily to be restored and established in our once happy land.

In Philadelphia, the wheels were turning. On June 7, 1776, Virginia's Richard Henry Lee proposed a historic motion, seconded by John Adams, that the thirteen colonies were now "free and independent states."

Lee's motion was formally approved on July 2—the reason that Adams wrote to his wife, Abigail, in a letter of July 3, to predict that "The Second Day of July 1776, will be the most memorable Epocha, in the History of America," and likely to be celebrated with "Pomp and Parade with Shews, Games, Sports, Guns, Bells, Bonfires and Illuminations from one End of this Continent to the other from this Time forward forever more."

Figure 18: *A nineteenth-century watercolor of the Jacob Graff House, on the southwest corner of Seventh and Market Streets in Philadelphia, where Jefferson drafted the Declaration of Independence. It stands in rebuilt form today, a shrine to the nation's most momentous writing assignment.*

The document needed to declare this independence was also moving forward rapidly. On June 11, Adams had been tapped to serve on a five-member committee to draft the text explaining and defending independence to the world. The assignment of drafting the document went to Thomas Jefferson, who submitted an impressive first draft, written between June 11 and June 28. In the days that followed, the draft was laid on a table in Congress, which asked for eighty-six alterations. Jefferson later expressed his feeling that the text had been "mangled," but the edits improved the Declaration, and in its shorter form, it secured approval more easily.

Notable among the deletions was a paragraph alleging that King George had impeded American attempts to limit or abolish the slave trade; a dubious point given the fact that so many Americans, including Jefferson, were financially dependent upon slavery. It was a stretch to blame a distant monarch for a longstanding practice that Americans profited greatly from and had shown little interest in curbing, with a few exceptions here and there (including an antislavery tract addressed to Congress and published in 1776 by a Rhode Island minister, Samuel Hopkins). Wisely, Congress deleted an argument that seemed "oratorical"—not a term of praise—and at best, semi-sincere. It and the other edits are represented here, with underlining indicating cuts and additions included in the margins.

Jefferson's Draft of "A Declaration by the Representatives of the United States of America, in General Congress Assembled"

June 1776

When in the course of human events it becomes necessary for one people to dissolve the political bands which have connected them with another, and to assume among the powers of the earth the separate & equal station to which the laws of nature and of nature's God entitle them, a decent respect to the opinions of mankind requires that they should declare the causes which impel them to the separation.

We hold these truths to be self-evident: that all men are created equal; that they are endowed by their creator with <u>inherent and</u> inalien- certain
able rights; that among these are life, liberty, & the pursuit of happiness: that to secure these rights, governments are instituted among men, deriving their just powers from the consent of the governed; that whenever any form of government becomes destructive of these ends, it is the right of the people to alter or abolish it, & to institute new government, laying it's foundation on such principles, & organizing it's powers in such form, as to them shall seem most likely to effect their safety & happiness. Prudence indeed will dictate that governments long established should not be changed for light & transient causes; and accordingly all experience hath shown that mankind are more disposed to suffer while evils are sufferable,

than to right themselves by abolishing the forms to which they are accustomed. But when a long train of abuses & usurpations begun at a distinguished period and pursuing invariably the same object, evinces a design to reduce them under absolute despotism, it is their right, it is their duty to throw off such government, & to provide new guards for their future security. Such has been the patient sufferance of these colonies; & such is now the necessity which constrains them to expunge their former systems of government. The history of the present king of Great Britain is a history of unremitting injuries & usurpations, among which appears no solitary fact to contradict the uniform tenor of the rest but all have in direct object the establishment of an absolute tyranny over these states. To prove this let facts be submitted to a candid world for the truth of which we pledge a faith yet unsullied by falsehood.

repeated

He has refused his assent to laws the most wholesome & necessary for the public good.

He has forbidden his governors to pass laws of immediate & pressing importance, unless suspended in their operation till his assent should be obtained; & when so suspended, he has utterly neglected to attend to them.

He has refused to pass other laws for the accommodation of large districts of people, unless those people would relinquish the right of representation in the legislature, a right inestimable to them, & formidable to tyrants only.

He has called together legislative bodies at places unusual, uncomfortable, and distant from the depository of their public records, for the sole purpose of fatiguing them into compliance with his measures.

He has dissolved representative houses repeatedly & continually for opposing with manly firmness his invasions on the rights of the people.

He has refused for a long time after such dissolutions to cause others to be elected, whereby the legislative powers, incapable of annihilation, have returned to the people at large for their exercise, the state remaining in the meantime exposed to all the dangers of invasion from without & convulsions within.

He has endeavored to prevent the population of these states; for that purpose obstructing the laws for naturalization of foreigners, refusing to pass others to encourage their migrations hither, & raising the conditions of new appropriations of lands.

obstructed He has suffered the administration of justice totally to cease in by some of these states refusing his assent to laws for establishing judiciary powers.

He has made our judges dependant on his will alone, for the tenure of their offices, & the amount & paiment of their salaries.

He has erected a multitude of new offices by a self assumed power and sent hither swarms of new officers to harass our people and eat out their substance.

He has kept among us in times of peace standing armies and ships of war without the consent of our legislatures.

He has affected to render the military independent of, & superior to the civil power.

He has combined with others to subject us to a jurisdiction foreign to our constitutions & unacknowledged by our laws, giving his assent to their acts of pretended legislation for quartering large bodies of armed troops among us; for protecting them by a mock-trial from punishment for any murders which they should commit on the inhabitants of these states; for cutting off our trade with all parts of the world; for imposing taxes on us without our consent; for depriving us [ ] of the benefits of trial by jury; for transporting us beyond seas to be tried for pretended offences; for abolishing the free system of English laws in a neighboring province, establishing therein an arbitrary government, and enlarging it's boundaries, so as to render it at once an example and fit instrument for introducing the same absolute rule into these states; for taking away our charters, abolishing our most valuable laws, and altering fundamentally the forms of our governments; for suspending our own legislatures, & declaring themselves invested with power to legislate for us in all cases whatsoever.

in many cases

colonies

He has abdicated government here withdrawing his governors, and declaring us out of his allegiance & protection.

by declaring us out of his protection, and waging war against us.

He has plundered our seas, ravaged our coasts, burnt our towns, & destroyed the lives of our people.

He is at this time transporting large armies of foreign mercenaries to compleat the works of death, desolation & tyranny already begun with circumstances of cruelty and perfidy [ ] unworthy of the head of a civilized nation.

scarcely parallelled in the most barbarous ages, & totally

He has constrained our fellow citizens taken captive on the high seas to bear arms against their country, to become the executioners of their friends & brethren, or to fall themselves by their hands.

He has [ ] endeavored to bring on the inhabitants of our frontiers the merciless Indian savages, whose known rule of warfare is an undistinguished destruction of all ages, sexes, & conditions <u>of existence</u>.

excited domestic insurrection among us, & has

<u>He has incited treasonable insurrections of our fellow-citizens, with the allurements of forfeiture & confiscation of our property.</u>

<u>He has waged cruel war against human nature itself, violating it's most sacred rights of life and liberty in the persons of a distant people who have never offended him, captivating & carrying them into slavery in another hemisphere, or to incur miserable death in their transportation thither. This piratical warfare, the opprobium of INFIDEL powers, is the warfare of the CHRISTIAN king of Great Britain. Determined to keep open a market where MEN should be bought & sold, he has prostituted his negative for suppressing every legislative attempt to prohibit or to restrain this execrable commerce. And that this assemblage of horrors might want no fact of distinguished die, he is now exciting those very people to rise in arms among us, and to purchase that liberty of which he has deprived them, by murdering the people on whom he also obtruded them: thus paying off former crimes committed against the LIBERTIES of one people, with crimes which he urges them to commit against the LIVES of another.</u>

In every stage of these oppressions we have petitioned for redress in the most humble terms: our repeated petitions have been answered only by repeated injuries.

A prince whose character is thus marked by every act which may define a tyrant is unfit to be the ruler of a [ ] people <u>who mean to be free. Future ages will scarcely believe that the hardiness of one man adventured, within the short compass of twelve years only, to lay a foundation so broad & so undisguised for tyranny over a people fostered & fixed in principles of freedom</u>.

free

Nor have we been wanting in attentions to our British brethren. We have warned them from time to time of attempts by their legislature to extend <u>a</u> jurisdiction over <u>these our states</u>. We have reminded them of the circumstances of our emigration & settlement here, <u>no one of which could warrant so strange a pretension: that these were effected at the expense of our own blood & treasure, unassisted by the wealth or the</u>

an unwarrantable us

strength of Great Britain: that in constituting indeed our several forms of government, we had adopted one common king, thereby laying a foundation for perpetual league & amity with them: but that submission to their parliament was no part of our constitution, nor ever in idea, if history may be credited: and, we [ ] appealed to their native justice and magnanimity as well as to the ties of our common kindred to disavow these usurpations which were likely to interrupt our connection and correspondence. They too have been deaf to the voice of justice & of consanguinity, and when occasions have been given them, by the regular course of their laws, of removing from their councils the disturbers of our harmony, they have, by their free election, re-established them in power. At this very time too they are permitting their chief magistrate to send over not only soldiers of our common blood, but Scotch & foreign mercenaries to invade & destroy us. These facts have given the last stab to agonizing affection, and manly spirit bids us to renounce forever these unfeeling brethren. We must endeavor to forget our former love for them, and hold them as we hold the rest of mankind, enemies in war, in peace friends. We might have been a free and a great people together; but a communication of grandeur & of freedom it seems is below their dignity. Be it so, since they will have it. The road to happiness & to glory is open to us too. We will tread it apart from them, and acquiesce in the necessity which denounces our eternal separation [ ]!

have

and we have conjured them by

would inevitably

We must therefore

and hold them as we hold the rest of mankind, enemies in war, in peace friends.

We therefore the representatives of the United States of America in General Congress assembled do in the name & by authority of the good people of these states reject & renounce all allegiance & subjection to the kings of Great Britain & all others who may hereafter claim by, through or under them: we utterly dissolve all political connection which may have heretofore have subsisted between us & the people or parliament of Great Britain: & finally we do assert & declare

We therefore the representatives of the United States of America in General Congress assembled, appealing to the supreme judge of the world for the rectitude of our intentions, do in the name, & by the authority of the good people of these colonies, solemnly publish & declare that these united colonies are & of right ought to be free & independent states; that they are absolved from all allegiance to the British crown, and that all political connection between them & the state of these colonies to be free & independent states, & that as free & independent states, they have full power to levy war, conclude peace, contract alliances, establish commerce, & to do all other acts & things which independent states may of right do.

And for the support of this declaration we mutually pledge to each other our lives, our fortunes, & our sacred honor.

Great Britain is, & ought to be, totally dissolved; & that as free & independent states they have full power to levy war, conclude peace, contract alliances, establish commerce & to do all other acts & things which independant states may of right do.

And for the support of this declaration, with a firm reliance on the protection of divine providence we mutually pledge to each other our lives, our fortunes, & our sacred honor.

News of the Declaration spread quickly. John Hancock, the president of the Congress, sent word of the momentous event around the country, carried by couriers on fast horses. Thanks to Philadelphia printer John Dunlap, who stayed up late on the night of July 4 to print as many as two hundred broadsides, Americans were soon able to read the text for themselves, or at least hear it. In many places, the Declaration was read publicly; including, as we have seen, before the troops in New York City, by command of George Washington. That was in keeping with the desire of Congress, which *ordered* it to be read. One delegate, Christopher Marshall, insisted that it was important to literally *declare* the Declaration.

Within days, newspapers were reprinting the words of the Declaration. A few weeks later, Europeans could read them too, in newspapers of their own.

But the full measure of the Declaration took some time to appreciate. At first, its importance was understood to be the news that it announced—independence—and not so much the language used to announce it. That is the reason John Adams predicted that July 2, the day of the vote for independence, would become a great national holiday. The vote was the great achievement, a political victory of the highest consequence for those, like Adams, who had been tilling the soil. A nation was coming into existence, and Adams was not wrong to feel that the newborn was more important than the birth certificate. The arrival of the United States of America would forever alter

***Figure 19:** One of the earliest depictions of the Declaration being read publicly—"The Manner in which the American Colonies Declared themselves Independent"—from a history of England published in 1783.*

the balance of power in the world. As leading patriot John Jay said, "we have passed the Rubicon."

By contrast, July 4, the day the Declaration was approved by Congress, seemed less significant at first. As Adams put it, Jefferson's pretty language was "dress and ornament rather than Body, Soul or Substance." It was meaningful to lay the argument before a candid world, but the document could not compete with the much larger fact of the nation itself.

With the passage of time, however, it became clear that Jefferson had wrought a literary miracle with his elegant phrasing of the central ideas behind the resolution, the revolution, and America itself. Or, as an early historian wrote, somewhat melodramatically, "the glory of the act is overshadowed by the glory of its annunciation."

PART II

GOVERNMENTS ARE INSTITUTED 1776–1826

How important was the Declaration to Americans in the founding era? What did it mean to aspiring communities in other parts of the world?

From the beginning, Americans were naturally drawn to the Declaration of Independence and the date of July 4, written in large letters at the head of the document: "IN CONGRESS, JULY 4, 1776."

It felt like a birthday, and they celebrated accordingly, with each return of the date. Beginning in 1777, the *Pennsylvania Evening Post* reported, "Yesterday the 4th of July, being the anniversary of the Independence of the United States of America, was celebrated in this city with demonstrations of joy and festivity."

These annual rituals deepened with time, especially once independence became a reality and not merely an aspiration, after the Treaty of Paris was signed in 1783, formally ending the Revolutionary War. In theory, with independence a fait accompli, the document announcing it might have become something of an afterthought. Pauline Maier, one of our foremost historians of the Declaration, found that it was at first "forgotten almost entirely." There was little reason for most Americans to dwell on it as they turned their attention to the new texts needed to construct a durable working government. The Constitution and the Bill of Rights would lay a critical legal and political foundation that the Declaration lacked. Yet those documents, as substantial as they are, were less inspiring to read. Their bland formulations conveyed the dry business of state-building with all the excitement of an act of incorporation.

Thanks to its soaring preamble, the Declaration remained relevant even as the work of erecting new political structures dominated the attention of the Founders. The simple power of its language would ensure that it was not forgotten. With time, as new grievances arose over perceived inequalities, the Declaration would acquire a new relevance, particularly in its ringing phrases about human rights and the consent of the governed. They were read and remembered by all the groups who felt excluded from the new corridors of power, including farmers, workers, and immigrants. As Maier writes, the Declaration was eventually "elevated into something akin to holy writ, which made it a prize worth capturing on behalf of one cause after another."

Figure 20: *This political cartoon, engraved by Paul Revere in 1773, depicts Thomas Hutchinson as "The wicked Statesman, or the Traitor to his Country, at the Hour of DEATH."*

For one group of Americans, however, the Declaration was far from sacred. The text speaks with serene confidence of "one people," united in purpose. The truth was, of course, more complicated. The ringing unanimity expressed in the Declaration can sometimes blind us to the reality that the Revolution was also a civil war that tore American communities apart. Indeed, part of the document's purpose, like any revolutionary manifesto, was to suggest greater consensus than actually existed. Few Americans understood this tension more viscerally than Thomas Hutchinson, the last civilian governor of the Massachusetts Bay Colony, and one of the Declaration's sharpest early critics. Unlike many colonial viceroys, who had often had no real ties to the provinces they governed, Hutchinson was a native-born Bostonian, proud of his descent from an old Bay Colony family, and the author of a highly regarded *History of the Province of Massachusets-Bay*.

The Revolution was deeply personal for Hutchinson. As much as he loved his home, he was out of step with the historical moment, and enraged his fellow Bostonians with his supine willingness to toe the British line. A mob ransacked his fine Palladian mansion during the Stamp Act crisis in 1765, and things disintegrated further until he was replaced by a military governor in 1774.

Loyalist to the end, and now living bitterly in exile in London, Hutchinson obtained a copy of the Declaration in August 1776. (It would not have escaped his attention that July 4, 1776, was the same day he had recently received an honorary degree from Oxford.)

Hutchinson read the text carefully and noticed that several of its criticisms of the King in fact applied to his own actions. His feathers were easily ruffled, and he soon picked up his pen to refute this "most infamous Paper" and its "false and frivolous" reasoning in a pamphlet.

Taking the Declaration clause by clause, his critiques are sometimes devastating, as when he questions the justifications for "depriving more than an hundred thousand Africans of their rights to liberty, and the *pursuit of happiness*, and in some degree to their lives, if these rights are so absolutely unalienable."

But in other ways, Hutchinson is oblivious to the concerns of his fellow Americans, much as he had been while governor. The pamphlet's sycophantic tone, written as "A Letter to a Noble Lord," suggests little affinity for the democratic feeling that pulses through the Declaration. Stubbornly, he glosses over the many ways in which the British government had precipitated the imperial crisis, through acts of savage violence, parliamentary insults, and a supreme royal indifference. Strangely, for a historian of Massachusetts, Hutchinson insists that Americans were not a distinct people at all and could never receive permission to leave the empire without the assent of the King. With this dogged misreading of history, Hutchinson spectacularly fails to grasp the central insight of the Declaration: that a people may decide their fate for themselves.

Thomas Hutchinson, *Strictures Upon the Declaration of the Congress at Philadelphia. In a Letter to a Noble Lord, &c.*

October 15, 1776

MY LORD, The last time I had the honour of being in your Lordships company, you observed that you was utterly at a loss to what facts many parts of the Declaration of Independence published by the Philadelphia Congress referred, and that you wished they had been more particularly mentioned, that you might better judge of the grievances, alledged as special causes of the separation of the Colonies from the other parts of the Empire. This hint from your Lordship induced me to attempt a few Strictures upon the Declaration. Upon my first reading it, I thought there would have been more policy in leaving the World altogether ignorant of the motives to this Rebellion, than in offering such false and frivolous reasons in support of it; and I flatter myself, that before I have finished this letter, your Lordship will be of the same mind. . . .

They begin, my Lord, with a false hypothesis, That the Colonies are one *distinct people*, and the kingdom another, connected by *political* bands. The Colonies, *politically* considered, never were a *distinct* people from the kingdom. There never has been but one *political* band, and that was just the same before the first Colonists emigrated as it has been ever since, the Supreme Legislative Authority, which hath essential right, and is indispensably bound to keep all parts of the Empire entire, until there may be a separation consistent with the general good of the Empire, of which good, from the nature of government, this authority must be the sole judge. I should therefore be impertinent, if I attempted to shew in what case a *whole people* may be justified in rising up in oppugnation to the powers of government, altering or abolishing them, and substituting, in whole or in part, new powers in their stead; or in what sense all men are created equal; or how far life, liberty, and the *pursuit of happiness* may be said to be unalienable; only I could wish to ask the Delegates of Maryland, Virginia, and the Carolinas, how their Constituents justify the depriving more than an hundred thousand Africans of their rights to liberty, and *the pursuit of happiness*, and in some degree to their lives, if these rights are so absolutely unalienable; nor shall I attempt to confute the absurd notions of government, or to expose the equivocal or inconclusive expressions contained in this Declaration; but rather to shew the false representation made of the facts which are alledged to be the evidence of injuries and usurpations, and the special motives to Rebellion. There are many of them, with design, left obscure; for as soon as they are developed, instead of justifying, they rather aggravate the criminality of this Revolt.

The first in order, *He has refused his assent to laws the most wholesome and necessary for the public good*; is of so general a nature, that it is not possible to conjecture to what laws or to what Colonies it refers. I remember no laws which any Colony has been restrained from passing, so as to cause any complaint of grievance, except those for issuing a fraudulent paper-currency, and making it a legal tender; but this is a restraint which for many years past has been laid on Assemblies by an act of Parliament, since which such laws cannot have been offered to the King for his allowance. I therefore believe this to be a general charge, without any particulars to support it; fit enough to be placed at the head of a list of imaginary grievances.

The laws of England are or ought to be the laws of its Colonies. To prevent a deviation further than the local circumstances of any Colony may make necessary, all Colony laws are to be laid before the King; and if disallowed, they then become of no force. Rhode-Island, and Connecticut, claim by Charters, an exemption from this rule, and as their laws are never presented to the King, they are out of the question. Now if the King is to approve of all laws, or which is the same thing, of all which the people judge for the public good, for we are to presume they pass no other, this reserve in all Charters and Commissions is futile. This charge is still more inexcusable, because I am well informed, the disallowance of Colony laws has been much more frequent in preceding reigns, than in the present.

He has forbidden his Governors to pass laws of immediate and pressing importance, unless suspended in their operation till his assent should be obtained, and when so suspended, he has utterly neglected to attend them.

Laws, my Lord, are in force in the Colonies, as soon as a Governor has given his assent, and remain in force until the King's disallowance is signified. Some laws may have their full effect before the King's pleasure can be known. Some may injuriously affect the property of the subject; and some may be prejudicial to the prerogative of the Crown, and to the trade, manufactures and shipping of the kingdom. Governors have been instructed, long before the present or the last reign, not to consent to such laws, unless with a clause suspending their operations until the pleasure of the King shall be known. I am sure your Lordship will think that nothing is more reasonable.

In Massachuset's Bay, the Assembly would never pass a law with a suspending clause. To pass laws which must have their whole operation, or which must cause some irreparable mischief before the King's pleasure can be known, would be an usurpation of the People upon the Royal Prerogative: To cause the operation of such laws to be suspended until the King can signify his pleasure by force of instructions, similar to what has been given in all former Reigns, can never be charged as an usurpation upon the rights of the People.

I dare say, my Lord, that if there has ever been an instance of any laws lying longer than necessary before the King's pleasure has been signified, it has been owing to inattention in some of the servants of the Crown, and that upon proper application any grievance would have been immediately redressed. . . .

He has combined with others to subject us to a jurisdiction foreign to our Constitution and unacknowledged by our Laws; giving his assent to their pretended Acts of Legislation.

This is a strange way of defining the part which the Kings of England take in conjunction with the Lords and Commons in passing Acts of Parliament. But why is our present Sovereign to be distinguished from all his predecessors since Charles the Second? Even the Republic which they affect to copy after, and Oliver, their favourite, because an Usurper, *combined* against them also. And then, how can a jurisdiction submitted to for more than a century be *foreign* to their constitution? And is it not the grossest prevarication to say this jurisdiction is *unacknowledged* by their laws, when all Acts of Parliament which respect them, have at all times been their rule of law in all their judicial proceedings? If this is not enough; their own subordinate legislatures have repeatedly in addresses, and resolves, in the most express terms *acknowledged* the supremacy of Parliament; and so late as 1764, before the conductors of this Rebellion had settled their plan, the House of Representatives of the leading Colony made a public declaration in an address to their Governor, that, although they humbly apprehended they might propose their objections, to the late Act of Parliament for granting certain duties in the British Colonies and Plantations in America, yet they at the same time, *acknowledged* that it was their duty to yield obedience to it while it continued unrepealed.

If the jurisdiction of Parliament is foreign to their Constitution, what need of specifying instances, in which they have been subjected to it? Every Act must be an usurpation and injury. . . .

They have, my Lord, in their late address to the people of Great Britain, fully avowed these principles of Independence, by declaring they will pay no obedience to the laws of the Supreme Legislature; they have also pretended, that these laws were the mandates or edicts of the Ministers, not the acts of a constitutional legislative power, and have endeavoured to persuade such as they called their British Brethren, to justify the Rebellion begun in America; and from thence they expected a general convulsion in the Kingdom, and that measures to compel a submission would in this way be obstructed. These expectations failing, after they had gone too far in acts of Rebellion to hope for impunity, they were under the *necessity* of a separation, and of involving themselves, and all over whom they had usurped authority, in the distresses and horrors of war against that power from which they revolted, and against all who continued in their subjection and fidelity to it.

Gratitude, I am sensible, is seldom to be found in a community, but so sudden a revolt from the rest of the Empire, which had incurred so immense a debt, and with which it remains burdened, for the protection and defence of the Colonies, and at their most importunate request, is an instance of ingratitude no where to be parallelled.

Suffer me, my Lord, before I close this Letter, to observe, that though the professed reason for publishing the Declaration was a decent respect to the opinions of mankind, yet the real design was to reconcile the people of America to that Independence, which always before, they had been made to believe was not intended. This design has too well succeeded. The people have not observed the fallacy in reasoning from the *whole* to *part*; nor the absurdity of making the *governed* to be *governors*. From a disposition to receive willingly complaints against Rulers, facts misrepresented have passed without examining. Discerning men have concealed their sentiments, because under the present *free* government in America, no man may, by writing or speaking, contradict any part of this Declaration, without being deemed an enemy to his country, and exposed to the rage and fury of the populace.

I have the honour to be,
My LORD,
Your Lordship's most humble,
And most obedient servant.

To the Right Honourable
the E—— of—— }

London, October, 15*th*. 1776.

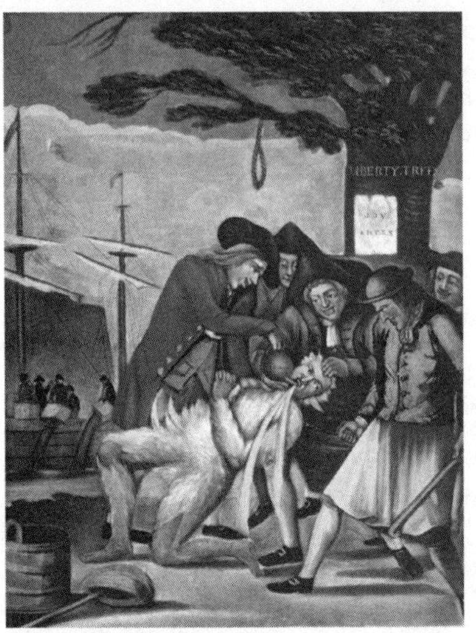

Figure 21: *"The Bostonians Paying the Excise-man, or Tarring and Feathering," a widely circulated British dramatization of the "oppression and tyranny" experienced by American Loyalists.*

As summer turned to fall, two different documents were drafted in New York, to show how many Americans wished to remain under royal protection. The first was a petition prepared on October 16, 1776, and signed by 948 prominent New Yorkers, stating their loyalty to King George III. A month later, on November 28, more than 700 Loyalists signed a second petition, avowing their fidelity to the Crown.

While reference to these documents can be found in the historical record, the originals were lost for nearly two centuries. Then in 1947, the second petition was located among the papers of a British official, Sir Henry Strachey, secretary of the King's Commissioners for Restoring Peace. The Strachey family generously released it, and it was purchased for the New-York Historical Society, which rebranded it, with some cheek, "a Declaration of Dependence."

Petition of 547 loyalists from New York City

November 28, 1776

To the Right Honorable Richard Viscount Howe, of the Kingdom of Ireland, and His Excellency The Honorable William Howe, Esquire, General of His Majesty's Forces in America, the King's Commissioners for restoring Peace in His Majesty's Colonies and Plantations in North America, &c. &c. &c.

May it please your excellencies.

Impressed with the most grateful sense of the Royal Clemency, manifested in your Proclamation of the 14th. of July last, whereby His Majesty hath been graciously pleased to declare, "That he is desirous to deliver His American subjects from the calamities of War, and other oppressions, which they now undergo:" and equally affected with sentiments of gratitude for that generous and humane attention to the happiness of these Colonies, which distinguishes your Excellencies subsequent Declaration, evincing your disposition "to confer with His Majesty's well affected subjects, upon the means of restoring the public Tranquility, and establishing a permanent union with every Colony as a part of the British Empire."

We whose names are hereunto subscribed, Inhabitants of the City and County of New-York, beg leave to inform your Excellencies: that altho most of us have subscribed a general Representation with many others of the Inhabitants; yet we wish that our conduct, in maintaining inviolate our loyalty to our Sovereign, against the strong tide of oppression and tyranny, which had almost overwhelmed this Land, may be marked by some line of distinction, which cannot well be drawn from the mode of Representation that has been adopted for the Inhabitants in general.

Influenced by this Principle, and from a regard to our peculiar Situation, we have humbly presumed to trouble your Excellencies with the second application; in which, we flatter ourselves, none participate but those who have ever, with unshaken fidelity, borne true Allegiance to His Majesty, and the most warm and affectionate attachment to his Person and Government. That, notwithstanding the tumult of the times, and the extreme difficulties and losses to which many of us have been exposed, we have always expressed, and do now give this Testimony of our Zeal to preserve and support the Constitutional Supremacy of Great Britain over the Colonies; and do most ardently wish for a speedy restoration of that union between them, which, while it subsisted, proved the unfailing source of their mutual happiness and prosperity.

We cannot help lamenting that the number of Subscribers to this Address is necessarily lessened, by the unhappy circumstance that many of our Fellow-Citizens, who have firmly adhered to their loyalty, have been driven from their Habitations, and others sent Prisoners into some of the neighbouring Colonies: and tho' it would have afforded us the highest satisfaction, could they have been present upon this occasion: yet we conceive it to be a duty we owe to ourselves and our posterity, whilst this testimony of our Allegiance can be supported by known and recent facts, to declare to your Excellencies; that so far from having given the least countenance or encouragement, to the most unnatural, unprovoked Rebellion, that ever disgraced the annals of Time; we have on the contrary, steadily and uniformly opposed it, in every stage of its rise and progress, at the risque of our Lives and Fortunes.

Figure 22: Lemuel Haynes, shown here in an 1837 engraving, was just twenty-three when he drafted his remarkable response to the Declaration of Independence.

Worlds away from Thomas Hutchinson's aristocratic exile, and the relative privilege of New York Loyalists, other less fortunate Americans were responding in their own way to the Declaration of Independence. Some were quick to see how easily Jefferson's language could be adapted to the cause of abolition, including a Philadelphia Quaker, Anthony Benezet, who warned Americans that slavery violated the spirit of the Declaration, and the Rhode Island legislature, which passed a law against slavery in 1783, specifically arguing that "all men are created equal." The Black leader James Forten heard the first public reading of the Declaration in Philadelphia on July 4, 1776, as a nine-year-old, and never forgot it, throughout a long and active life working against slavery. That included his authorship of an 1813 pamphlet, *Letters from a Man of Colour* . . . , that cited the Declaration. There were ironies upon ironies in the fact that the inspiring words came from the hand of a slaveowner, albeit one who periodically opposed the peculiar institution. Still, the convergence was often meaningful, as it was on July 4, 1799, the day that New Jersey chose to begin gradual emancipation.

One early reader of special sensitivity was Lemuel Haynes, the son of an interracial couple in Connecticut, who was raised as an indentured servant by another couple, in a small town (Granville) in western Massachusetts. They taught him to read and encouraged his education. At age twenty-one, he was freed of his obligations. On the day after Lexington and Concord, he marched with a group of volunteer Minutemen to Roxbury, on the outskirts of Boston, to join the other militia forces assembled there. After his military service, the young veteran returned to his religious studies. He would go on to become, in 1785, the first Black ordained minister in the United States, and enjoy a long and distinguished career as a minister to mostly white churches in Rutland, Vermont.

Two centuries later, a scholar named Ruth Bogin made an important discovery. In a Harvard library, she found an unpublished essay, probably from 1776, in which Haynes responded to the Declaration of Independence, arguing that its language about rights should also apply to African Americans, and particularly to the enslaved. Written across forty-six manuscript pages, the essay was titled "Liberty Further Extended: Or Free thoughts on the illegality of Slave-keeping; wherein those arguments that are used in its vindication are plainly confuted."

Haynes did not know who had written the Declaration, which he attributed simply to "Congress." But he was sufficiently moved by its language to begin his essay with a quotation of the lines that, for him, presented compelling evidence that this was a country for all Americans.

Lemuel Haynes, "Liberty Further Extended"

[Late 1776]

We hold these truths to be Self-Evident, that all men are created Equal, that they are Endowed By their Creator with Ceartain unalienable rights, that among these are Life, Liberty, and the pursuit of happyness.

Congress.

The Preface.

As *tyrony* had its Origin from the infernal regions: so it is the Deuty, and honner of Every son of freedom to repel her first motions. But while we are Engaged in the important struggle, it cannot Be tho't impertinent for us to turn one Eye into our own Breast, for a little moment, and See, whether thro' some inadvertency, or a self-contracted Spirit, we Do not find the monster Lurking in our own Bosom; that now while we are inspir'd with so noble a Spirit and Becoming Zeal, we may Be Disposed to tear her from us. If the following would produce such an Effect the auther should rejoice.

It is Evident, by ocular demonstration, that man by his Depravety, hath procured many Courupt habits which are detrimental to society; And altho' there is a way prescrib'd Whereby man may be reinstated into the favour of god, yet these courupt habits are Not Extirpated, nor can the subject of renovation Bost of perfection, 'till he Leaps into a state of immortal Existance. yet it hath pleas'd the majesty of Heaven to Exhibet his will to men, and Endow them With an intulect Which is susceptible of speculation; yet, as I observ'd before, man, in consequence of the fall is Liable to digressions. But to proceed,

Liberty, & freedom, is an innate principle, which is unmoveblу placed in the human Species; and to see a man aspire after it, is not Enigmatical, seeing he acts no ways incompatible with his own Nature; consequently, he that would infring upon a mans Liberty may reasonably Expect to meet with oposision, seeing the Defendant cannot Comply to Non-resistance, unless he Counter-acts the very Laws of nature.

Liberty is a Jewel which was handed Down to man from the cabinet of heaven, and is Coaeval with his Existance. And as it proceed from the Supreme Legislature of the univers, so it is he which hath a sole right to take away; therefore, he that would take away a mans Liberty assumes a prerogative that Belongs to another, and acts out of his own domain.

One man may bost a superorety above another in point of Natural previledg; yet if he can produse no convincive arguments in vindication of this preheminence his hypothesis is to Be Suspected. To affirm, that an Englishman has a right to his Liberty, is a truth which has Been so clearly Evinced, Especially of Late, that to spend time in illustrating this, would be But Superfluous tautology. But I query, whether Liberty is so contracted a principle as to be Confin'd to any nation under Heaven; nay, I think it not hyperbolical to affirm, that Even an affrican, has Equally as good a right to his Liberty in common with Englishmen.

I know that those that are concerned in the Slave-trade, Do pretend to Bring arguments in vindication of their practise; yet if we give them a candid Examination, we shall find them (Even those of the most cogent kind) to be Essencially Deficient. We live in a day wherein *Liberty* & *freedom* is the subject of many millions Concern; and the important Struggle hath alread caused great Effusion of Blood; men seem to manifest the most sanguine resolution not to Let their natural rights go without their Lives go with them; a resolution, one would think Every one that has the Least Love to his country, or futer posterity, would fully confide in, yet while we are so zelous to maintain, and foster our own invaded rights, it cannot be tho't impertinent for us Candidly to reflect on our own conduct, and I doubt not But that we shall find that subsisting in the midst of us, that may with propriety be stiled *Opression*, nay, much greater opression, than that which Englishmen seem so much to spurn at. I mean an oppression which they, themselves, impose upon others.

It is not my Business to Enquire into Every particular practise, that is practised in this Land, that may come under this Odeus Character; But, that I have in view, is humbly to offer som free thoughts, on the practise of *Slave-keeping*. Opression, is not spoken of, nor ranked in the sacred miracles, among the Least of those sins, that are the procureing Cause of those signal Judgments, which god is pleas'd to bring upon the Children of men. Therefore let us attend. I mean to write with freedom, yet with the greatest Submission.

And the main proposition, which I intend for some Breif illustration is this, Namely, That an *African*, or, in other terms, *that a Negro may Justly Chalenge, and has an undeniable right to his Liberty: Consequently, the practise of Slave-keeping, which so much abounds in this Land is illicit. . . .*

Figure 23: *A 1788 engraving of the 1787 emblem by English potter Josiah Wedgwood, this image became a symbol of the transatlantic abolition movement.*

On January 13, 1777, in Thomas Hutchinson's hometown of Boston, seven enslaved African Americans petitioned the new state government of Massachusetts for their freedom. Clearly, the Declaration had encouraged them to think about their situation in new ways. As Hutchinson understood, Jefferson's language about equality cut two ways, inspiring democratic aspirations around the world, while at the same time exposing the hypocrisy of a slave society that was not equal at all.

In this instance, the petitioners, including Prince Hall, a well-known leader of Boston's Black community, were arguing that the Declaration's promises ought to apply to all Americans. Throughout the petition are words ("unalienable") and phrases that signaled the unmistakable effect of Jefferson's language on the fledgling nation's most marginalized members. By 1783, after a series of court cases, the Massachusetts Supreme Court declared slavery inconsistent with the new state constitution (drafted by John Adams), and therefore illegal.

Lancaster Hill, Peter Bess, Brister Slenser, Prince Hall, and Others, "The Petition of a great number of Negroes who are detained in a state of Slavery"

January 13, 1777

To the Honorable Council & House of Representatives for the State of Massachusetts-Bay, in General Court assembled January 13th 1777—

The Petition of a great number of Negroes who are detained in a state of Slavery in the Bowels of a free & Christian Country Humbly Shewing—

That your Petitioners apprehend that they have, in common with all other Men, a natural & unalienable right to that freedom, which the great Parent of the Universe hath bestowed equally on all Mankind, & which they have never forfeited by any compact or agreement whatever—But they were unjustly dragged, by the cruel hand of Power, from their dearest friends, & some of them even torn from the embraces of their tender Parents—from a populous, pleasant & plentiful Country—& in Violation of the Laws of Nature & of Nation & in defiance of all the tender feelings of humanity, brought hither to be sold like Beasts of Burthen, & like them condemned to slavery for Life—Among a People professing the mild Religion of Jesus—A People not insensible of the sweets of rational freedom—Nor without spirit to resent the unjust endeavours of others to reduce them to a State of Bondage & Subjection—Your Honors need not to be informed that a Life of Slavery, like that of your petitioners, deprived of every social privilege, of every thing requisite to render Life even tolerable, is far worse than Non-Existence—In imitation of the laudable example of the good People of these States, your Petitioners have long & patiently waited the event of Petition after Petition by them presented to the Legislative Body of this State, & can not but with grief reflect that their success has been but too similar—They can not but express their astonishment, that it has never been considered, that every principle from which America has acted in the course of her unhappy difficulties with Great-Britain, pleads stronger than a thousand arguments in favor of your Petitioners—They therefore humbly beseech your Honors, to give this Petition its due weight & consideration, & cause an Act of the Legislature to be passed, whereby they may be restored to the enjoyment of that freedom which is the natural right of all Men—& their Children (who were born in this land of Liberty) may not be held as Slaves after they arrive at the age of twenty one years—So may the Inhabitants of this State (no longer chargeable with the inconsistency of acting, themselves, the part which they condemn & oppose in others) be prospered in their present glorious struggles for Liberty; & have those blessings secured to them by Heaven, of which benevolent minds can not wish to deprive their fellow Men.

And your Petitioners, as in Duty Bound shall ever pray.

Lancaster Hill
x Peter Bess
Brister Slenser
Prince Hall
his
Jack x Pierpont
mark
his
Nero x Funelo
mark
his
Newport x Sumner
mark
Job Lock

***Figure 24:** "Mr. de Lafayette, Commander of the Paris National Guard, Receives the City's Sword for the Defense of Liberty."*

If the Declaration's international reach was somewhat limited in its first decade, the French Revolution would help bring it wider notice. Many French *philosophes* had approved of the document. Writing of the United States, whose independence France had done so much to facilitate, Condorcet noted, "The act which declares its independence is a simple and sublime expression of those rights so sacred and so long forgotten." Mirabeau, similarly, wrote, "The sublime manifesto of the United States of America was very generally applauded."

The Marquis de Lafayette "had a particular affection for the Declaration" and was instrumental in the French National Assembly's adoption of the Declaration of the Rights of Man and of the Citizen on August 26, 1789, as the French Revolution was beginning. Indeed, Lafayette helped to draft an early version, with advice from Thomas Jefferson, then in Paris as U.S. minister.

Many sentences retained a Jeffersonian feel, including the first article, "Men are born and remain free and equal in rights." But in other places, the French Declaration vested confidence and political power in a centralized "Nation" to a degree that would have troubled most of the American Founders. There were other differences as well. Jefferson had premised his argument on the "self-evident" fact that Americans already possessed their rights, and that it was a mere matter of common sense to defend them. In France, by contrast, the concept of rights was far less well understood by a people long conditioned to autocratic rule, as the violent excesses of the French Revolution soon made clear to all but its most ardent defenders. Because of this the French Declaration reads more like a primer in the ways of liberty.

The Declaration of the Rights of Man and of the Citizen (Déclaration des droits de l'homme et du citoyen)

August 26, 1789

The representatives of the French People, formed into a National Assembly, considering ignorance, forgetfulness or contempt of the rights of man to be the only causes of public misfortunes and the corruption of Governments, have resolved to set forth, in a solemn Declaration, the natural, unalienable and sacred rights of man, to the end that this Declaration, constantly present to all members of the body politic, may remind them unceasingly of their rights and their duties; to the end that the acts of the legislative power and those of the executive power, since they may be continually compared with the aim of every political institution, may thereby be the more respected; to the end that the demands of the citizens, founded henceforth on simple and incontestable principles, may always be directed toward the maintenance of the Constitution and the happiness of all.

In consequence whereof, the National Assembly recognises and declares, in the presence and under the auspices of the Supreme Being, the following Rights of Man and of the Citizen.

Article first: Men are born and remain free and equal in rights. Social distinctions may be based only on considerations of the common good.

II. The aim of every political association is the preservation of the natural and imprescriptible rights of Man. These rights are Liberty, Property, Safety and Resistance to Oppression.

III. The principle of any Sovereignty lies primarily in the Nation. No corporate body, no individual may exercise any authority that does not expressly emanate from it.

IV. Liberty consists in being able to do anything that does not harm others: thus, the exercise of the natural rights of every man has no bounds other than those that ensure to the other members of society the enjoyment of these same rights. These bounds may be determined only by Law.

V. The Law has the right to forbid only those actions that are injurious to society. Nothing that is not forbidden by Law may be hindered, and no one may be compelled to do what the Law does not ordain.

VI. The Law is the expression of the general will. All citizens have the right to take part, personally or through their representatives, in its making. It must be the same for all, whether it protects or punishes. All citizens, being equal in its eyes, shall be equally eligible to all high offices, public positions and employments, according to their ability, and without other distinction than that of their virtues and talents.

VII. No man may be accused, arrested or detained except in the cases determined by the Law, and following the procedure that it has prescribed. Those who solicit, expedite, carry out, or cause to be carried out arbitrary orders must be punished; but any citizen summoned or apprehended by virtue of the Law, must give instant obedience; resistance makes him guilty.

VIII. The Law must prescribe only the punishments that are strictly and evidently necessary; and no one may be punished except by virtue of a Law drawn up and promulgated before the offense is committed, and legally applied.

IX. As every man is presumed innocent until he has been declared guilty, if it should be considered necessary to arrest him, any undue harshness that is not required to secure his person must be severely curbed by Law.

X. No one may be disturbed on account of his opinions, even religious ones, as long as the manifestation of such opinions does not interfere with the established Law and Order.

XI. The free communication of ideas and of opinions is one of the most precious rights of man. Any citizen may therefore speak, write and publish freely, except what is tantamount to the abuse of this liberty in the cases determined by Law.

XII. To guarantee the Rights of Man and of the Citizen a public force is necessary; this force is therefore established for the benefit of all, and not for the particular use of those to whom it is entrusted.

XIII. For the maintenance of the public force, and for administrative expenses, a general tax is indispensable; it must be equally distributed among all citizens, in proportion to their ability to pay.

XIV. All citizens have the right to ascertain, by themselves, or through their representatives, the need for a public tax, to consent to it freely, to watch over its use, and to determine its proportion, basis, collection and duration.

XV. Society has the right to ask a public official for an accounting of his administration.

XVI. Any society in which no provision is made for guaranteeing rights or for the separation of powers, has no Constitution.

XVII. Since the right to Property is inviolable and sacred, no one may be deprived thereof, unless public necessity, legally ascertained, obviously requires it, and just and prior indemnity has been paid.

Figure 25: *Samuel Adams, one of the early leaders of the protests against the Crown in Massachusetts and a signer of the Declaration of Independence, was newly elevated to the governorship of the Bay State at the time of this portrait.*

News of the outbreak of the French Revolution arrived at a volatile moment for Americans, just months after the hotly contested ratification of the Constitution and the establishment of the federal government in New York. Throughout the 1790s, it would remain an important fault line, dividing Americans into admirers and skeptics, and accelerating a trend toward political factions that was already underway. With time, these factions would coalesce into parties, with Federalists following George Washington, John Adams, and Alexander Hamilton (although Adams and Hamilton did not always agree), and Republicans following Thomas Jefferson and James Madison. Federalists were worried by disorder at home and abroad. Republicans were encouraged that democratic principles appeared to be on the march.

Setting a pattern that would be repeated throughout our history, the warring partisans looked to vindicate their views by appealing back to the Declaration. It was in this period that authorship of the Declaration, "our great American charter," as a Republican newspaper called it in 1792, began to be attributed more widely to "the immortal Jefferson." (As early as 1783, Yale's president, Ezra Stiles, had mentioned Jefferson as the author, in a sermon that praised the way he "poured the soul of the continent into the monumental act of Independence.") Jefferson's identification with the nation's founding charter strengthened the Republicans in their struggle to win control of Congress and the presidency.

Samuel Adams was a signer of the Declaration and had championed democratic aspirations from the earliest days of the Revolution. In 1794, as the new governor of Massachusetts, he extolled Jefferson's egalitarian vision to the state legislature. In this passage he quotes from the Declaration as well as the Massachusetts Constitution, written by his younger cousin, John.

Samuel Adams, Address to the Massachusetts Legislature

January 17, 1794

. . . The people of this Commonwealth, have heretofore been possessed of the intire sovereignty within and over their own territories. They were "not controulable by any other laws than those to which their constituted representative body gave their consent." This, I presume, was the case in every other State of the Union.—But, after the memorable declaration of their Independence was by solemn treaty, agreed to and ratified by the British King, the only power that could have any pretence to dispute it, they considered themselves decidedly free and independent of all other people. Having taken rank among nations, it was judged that their great affairs could not well be conducted under the direction of a number of distinct sovereignties. They therefore formed and adopted a Federal Constitution; by which certain powers of sovereignty are delegated and entrusted to such persons as they shall judge proper from time to time to elect; to be exercised conformably to, and within the restrictions of the said Constitution, for the purposes of strengthening and confirming the Union, and promoting the safety and happiness of the confederate Commonwealth. All powers not vested in Congress, remain in the separate States to be exercised according to their respective Constitutions.—Should not unremitting caution be used, least any degree of interference or infringement might take place, either on the rights of the Federal Government on the one side, or those of the several States on the other. Instances of this kind may happen; for infallibility is not the lot of any man or body of men, even the best of them on earth. The human mind in its present state, being very imperfect, is liable to a multitude of errors. Prejudice, that great source of error, often creeps in and takes possession of the hearts of honest men, without even their perceiving it themselves. Honest men will not feel themselves disgusted, when mistakes are pointed out to them with decency, candor and friendship, nor will they, when convinced of truth, think their own dignity degraded by correcting their own errors.

Among the objects of the Constitution of this Commonwealth, Liberty and Equality stand in a conspicuous light. It is the first article in our Declaration of rights, "all men are born free and equal, and have certain natural, essential and unalienable rights." In the supposed state of nature, all men are equally bound by the laws of nature, or to speak more properly, the laws of the Creator:—They are imprinted by the finger of God on the heart of man. Thou shall do no injury to thy neighbour, is the voice of nature and reason, and it is confirmed by written revelation. In the state of nature, every man hath an equal right by honest means to acquire property, and to enjoy it; in general, to pursue his own happiness, and none can consistently controul or interrupt him in the pursuit. But, so turbulent are the passions of some, and so selfish the feelings of others, that in such a state, there being no social compact, the weak cannot always be protected from the violence of the strong, nor the honest and unsuspecting from the arts and intrigues of the selfish and cunning. Hence it is easy to conceive, that men, naturally formed for society, were inclined to enter into mutual compact for the better security of their natural rights. In this state of society, the unalienable rights of nature are held sacred:—And each member is intitled to an equal share of all the social rights. No man can of right become possessed of a greater share: If any one usurps it, he so far becomes a tyrant; and when he can obtain sufficient strength, the people will feel the rod of a tyrant. Or, if this exclusive privilege can be supposed to be held in virtue of compact, it argues a very capital defect; and the people, when more enlightened, will alter their compact, and extinguish the very idea.

These opinions, I conceive to be conformable to the sentiments held up in our State Constitution. It is therein declared, that Government is instituted for the common good; not for the profit, honor or private interest of any one man, family, or class of men. And further, all the inhabitants of this Commonwealth, having such qualifications, as shall be established by their Constitution, have an equal right to elect or be elected for the public employments.

Before the formation of this Constitution, it had been affirmed as a self evident truth, in the declaration of Independence, very deliberately made by the Representatives of the United States of America in Congress assembled that, "all men are created equal, and are endowed by their Creator with certain unalienable rights." This declaration of Independence was received and ratified by all the States in the Union, and has never been disannulled. May we not from hence conclude, that the doctrine of Liberty and Equality is an article in the political creed of the United States.

Our Federal Constitution ordains that, no title of nobility shall be granted by the United States. The framers of that Constitution probably foresaw that such titles, vain and insignificant in themselves, might be in time, as they generally, and I believe always have been, the introductory to the absurd and unnatural claims of hereditary and exclusive privileges.

The Republic of France have also adopted the same principle, and laid it as the foundation of their Constitution. That nation having for many ages groaned under the exercise of the pretended right claimed by their Kings and Nobles, until their very feelings as men were become torpid, at length suddenly awoke, from their long slumber, abolished the usurpation, and placed every man upon the footing of equal rights. "All men are born free and equal in rights," if I mistake not, is their language.

From the quotations I have made, I think it appears, that the Constitutions referred to, different as they may be in forms, agree altogether in the most essential principles upon which legitimate governments are founded. I have said essential principles, because I conceive that without Liberty and Equality, there cannot exist that tranquillity of mind, which results from the assurance of every citizen, that his own personal safety and rights are secure:—This, I think is a sentiment of the celebrated Montesquieu; and it is the end and design of all free and lawful Governments. Such assurance, impressed upon the heart of each, would lead to the peace, order and happiness of all. For I should think, no man, in the exercise of his reason would be inclined in any instance to trespass upon the equal rights of citizens, knowing that if he should do it, he would weaken and risque the security of his own. Even different nations, having grounded their respective Constitutions upon the afore-mentioned principles, will shortly feel the happy effects of mutual friendship, mutual confidence and united strength. Indeed I cannot but be of opinion, that when those principles shall be rightly understood and universally established, the whole family and brotherhood of man will then nearly approach to, if not fully enjoy that state of peace and prosperity, which ancient Prophets and Sages have foretold. . . .

EQU [—105—]

Epit′omiſer, Epit′omiſt, *n.* one who abridges
E′poch or Ep′ocha, [ch as k] *n.* a point of time to date from (ode
Ep′ode, *n.* a ſtanza following the ſtrophe, poem,
Ep′opy or E′pos, *n.* an epic poem or its ſubject
Ep′ulary, *a.* relating or belonging to a feaſt, jolly
Epulátion, *n.* a feaſt, a banquet, jollity, joy
Epulot′ic, *a.* healing, cicatrizing, drying up ſores
Equabil′ity, *n.* equality, evenneſs, uniformity
E′quable, *a.* equal to itſelf, even, uniform, alike
E′quably, *ad.* equally, evenly, uniformly, ſteadily
E′qual, *a.* like another, even, uniform, ſame, juſt
E′qual, *n.* one who is of the ſame rank and age
E′qual, E′qualize, *v. t.* to make or become equal, portion out, compare, recompenſe (neſs
Equal′ity, *n.* likeneſs, evenneſs, uniformity, ſame-
E′qually, *ad.* of or on the ſame degree, impartially
Equanim′ity, *n.* evenneſs of mind, compoſure
Equan′imous, *a.* even, calm, cool, compoſed
Equátion, *n.* a bringing of things to an equality
Equãtor, *n.* a line dividing the globe into 2 equal
Equatórial, *a.* pertaining to the equator (parts
E″querry, *n.* one who has care of horſes, a ſtable
Equeſt′rian, *a.* appearing on horſeback, noble
Equian″gular, *a.* having equal or like angles
Equicrúral, *a.* having equal legs or ſides, iſoſceles
Equidis′tant, *a.* ſet or being at the ſame diſtance
Equidis′tantly, *ad.* at the ſame diſtance

Equiv′ocal
Equiv′ocat
Equivocáti
Equiv′ocat
E″quivoke
E′ra, *n.* an
Eradiátion
Erad′icate,
Eradicátion
Eráſe, *v. t.*
Eráſable, *a*
Eráſed, *pa.*
Eráſement
Eráſure, *n.*
Ere, *ad.* be
Er′ebus, *n.*
Erect′, *v.* to
Erect′, *a.* r
Erec′tion,
Erect′neſs,
Erelong′, *a*
Er′emit, *n.*
Eremit′ica
Erenow′ *a*
Erewhíle,
Erin″go, *n*
Er′melin,
white f

Figure 26: *In his first dictionary, the 1806* Compendious Dictionary of the English Language, *American lexicographer Noah Webster defined equality as "likeness, evenness, uniformity, sameness."*

The partisan strife of the 1790s culminated in the election of 1800, which saw Jefferson defeat the incumbent, John Adams, ushering the nation's first opposition party into power. The Federalists were suddenly thrust into the political wilderness. Opposition to Jefferson went hand in glove with disdain for the French Revolution and an increasingly jaundiced view of the natural rights theory that Republicans saw undergirding both revolutions. This necessarily implicated the Declaration. Noah Webster, the famed lexicographer, offered a case in point in his 1802 Fourth of July oration before the citizens of New Haven, Connecticut. Though a staunch Yankee and a meticulous grammarian, his equivocating definition of equality, developed here in a lengthy footnote to his speech, showed how fragile the core principle of the Declaration remained a generation after it was written. There were, as we shall see, many Southern voices quite willing to take up his skepticism toward the idea that "all men are created equal."

Noah Webster, *An Oration, Pronounced before the Citizens of New Haven, on the Anniversary of the Declaration of Independence*

July 4, 1802

. . . The eminent characters who have conducted the revolutions in England and America, have laid it down as a fundamental principle in government, that by nature all men are *free, independent,* and *equal;* and this principle, without definition or limitation, forms a main pillar of our constitutions.

If there were but a single man on earth, he certainly could have no masters, but the elements and the inflexible laws of nature. But political axioms, if not mere empty sounds, must have reference to a social state. How then, can men, exposed to each others power, and wanting each others aid, be *free* and *independent*? If one member of a society is free and independent, all the members must be equally so. In such a community, no restraint could exist, for this would destroy freedom and independence. But in such a state of things, the will of each individual would be his only rule of action, and his *will* would be supported by his *strength*. Force then would be the ultimate arbiter of right and wrong, and the wills of the weaker must bend to the power of the stronger. A society, therefore, existing in a state of nature, if such a state can be supposed in which there should be no law but individual wills, must necessarily be in perpetual anarchy or despotism. But no such state of society can exist. The very act of associating destroys the natural freedom and independence of each member of the society, anterior to any compact limiting their respective powers and rights; for it is a principle, resulting from the very nature of society, independent of any mutual agreement for the purpose, that one individual shall not exercise his own power to another's prejudice. Of course, by the very constitution of society, the will of each member is restrained by the laws of general utility, or common good, the details of which are to be regulated by the supreme power. Whatever may be the abstract reasoning of men on this subject, the practice has been, and by the nature of man, must continue to be, that the members of a state or body politic, hold all their rights subject to the direction and control of the sovereignty of the state. It is needless to discuss questions of natural right as distinct from a social state; for all rights are social, and subordinate to the supreme will of the whole society. Nor, without such a supreme controlling power over all the members of a state, can an individual possess and enjoy liberty. In the supposed state of nature, every man being free from the restraint of *law*, every man would be subject to the restraint of *force*, and of course would be a slave. Civil liberty, therefore, instead of being derived from *natural freedom* and *independence*, is the creature of society and government. Man is too feeble to protect himself, and unless he can protect himself, he is not free. But to secure protection, man must submit to the restraints of a sovereign power; subordination, therefore, is the very essence of civil liberty. Yet how often has the abstract, undefined proposition, that "all men are by nature free and independent," furnished the motive or the apology, for insurrection!

Equally fallacious is the doctrine of *equality*, of which much is said, and little understood. That one man in a state, has as good a right as another to his life, limbs, reputation and property, is a proposition that no man will dispute. Nor will it be denied that each member of a society, who has not forfeited his claims by misconduct, has an equal right to protection. But if by *equality*, writers understand an equal right to distinction, and influence; or if they understand an equal share of talents and bodily powers; in these senses, all men are *not* equal. Such an equality would be inconsistent with the whole economy of nature. In the animal and vegetable world, however strong the general resemblance in the individuals of a species, each is marked with a distinct character; and this diversity is one of the principal beauties of creation, and probably an important feature in the system. There are, and there must be, distinctions among men * * * they are established by nature, as well as by social relations. Age, talents, virtue, public services, the possession of office and certain natural relations, carry with them just claims to distinction, to influence and authority. Miserable, indeed, would be the condition of men, if the son could disengage himself from the authority of his father; the apprentice from the command of his master; and the citizen from the dominion of the law and the magistrate.*

* No doctrine has been less understood or more abused, than that of political *equality*. It is admitted that all men have an equal right to the enjoyment of their life, property and personal security; and it is the duty as it is the object, of government to protect every man in this enjoyment. The man who owns a single horse or cow, has as strong a claim to have that property protected, as the man who owns a ship or a thousand acres of land. So far the doctrine of *equal rights*, is vindicable. But that all men have an equal claim to distinction and authority, is contradicted by the opinions and practice of people in every country. Whatever absurdities men may write, publish and repeat, respecting natural and political equality; in practice, they are usually correct, and would always be so, if they could be left to act from their unbiassed sentiments. All men naturally respect age, experience, superior wisdom, virtue and talents * * * and when they are to make appointments, they pursue this natural sentiment, and select men who are best qualified for the places. If most men should be asked, are you qualified for the office of chief magistrate * * * of judge * * * of ambassador * * * of president of a college * * * of commander of a ship of war? They will acknowledge their unfitness * * * they abandon all claims to these distinctions. But the same men will maintain that they have all an *equal right* to suffrage; that is, to an *equal* influence in government. But all men are not equally competent to judge of proper characters to fill offices. This is however not the main objection to the principle. Government is chiefly concerned with the *rights of person* and *rights of property*. Personal rights are few, and are not subject to much difficulty or jealousy. All men are agreed in the *principle* of protecting *persons*, and differ very little in the *mode*. But the *rights of property*, which are numerous, and form nineteen twentieths of all the objects of government, are beyond measure intricate, and difficult to be regulated with justice. Now if all men have an equal right of suffrage, those who have *little* and those who have *no* property, have the power of making regulations respecting the property of others * * * that is, an equal right to control the property with those who own it. Thus, as property is *unequally* and suffrages *equally* divided, the principle of *equal* suffrage becomes the basis of *inequality of power*. And this principle, in some of our larger cities, actually gives a *majority of suffrages* to the men who possess not a *twentieth of the property*. Such is the fallacy of abstract propositions in political science! In truth, this principle of *equal suffrage* operates to produce extreme *inequality of rights*; a monstrous inversion of the natural order of society * * * a species of oppression that will ultimately produce a revolution.

Again * * * It is asserted as an axiom in politics, that the sovereign power resides in the *people*. Unfortunately our language does not, like the Roman, distinguish the *populus* from the *plebs*; the free citizens from those who have not the privilege of suffrage. But if we restrict the word *people* to the free citizens or electors, what act of sovereign power do they or can they exercise? They cannot assemble for debate; but sovereignty consists in the single will of a body acting together, deliberating, deciding, and capable of carrying its decrees into effect. Do the people possess this power?

To avoid this absurdity, some writers allege that sovereign power is *derived from* the people. This proposition is more correct. The people possess the right of electing agents or substitutes to meet and constitute the supreme power * * * and farther than this right of electing, which is exercised by a private act of each individual, the people cannot possibly have a share in the sovereign power. This right of election is certainly a precious right, and one which, if used with discretion, is the safety and glory of a free state; but the exercise of it cannot, with propriety, be denominated, an act of sovereignty. . . .

Equally absurd is the doctrine that the universal enjoyment of the right of suffrage, is the best security for free elections and a pure administration. The reverse is proved by all experience, to be the fact; that a liberal extension of the right of suffrage accelerates the growth of corruption, by multiplying the number of corruptible electors, and reducing the price of venal suffrages.

It has also been a received maxim, that a frequent rotation of officers, is among the means of guarding a state from the malpractices of the public agents. But this principle has been extended too far, and experience has compelled some of the states to recede from it in their revised constitutions. It has been found that a short and precarious tenure of offices, is the direct means of degrading them, and making them an object of desire only to worthless and incompetent men.

Such are the brilliant theories which have dazzled the founders of our states! Such the illusions by which the admirers of a republican government have been fascinated and misled! But it is the fate of man to be confounded by his own wisdom, and to see the elegant structures raised by his fancy, demolished by the rough hand of experiment. Nor is mortification the only evil to be expected from the falacy of political doctrines. Errors, wrought into constitutions, have a sanction that gives them high authority, which it requires a long period of time, and perhaps the experience of several public calamities, to destroy. . . .

Figure 27: *This frontispiece illustration from his 1805* Historical Account of the Empire of Hayti *depicts author Marcus Rainsford interviewing a veteran of the Haitian Revolution.*

The Declaration's relevance only deepened as other nations in the Western Hemisphere began to seek independence for themselves.

Haiti—formerly the French colony of Saint-Domingue—was a difficult case in point. An enormously profitable source of sugar and coffee for the French, Haiti had been subject to an unusually cruel and labor-intensive form of slavery. Inspired by the French Revolution, which had itself been influenced by the American Revolution, Haitians began a thirteen-year struggle for freedom in 1791. The brutally violent conflict finally resulted in the expulsion of the French, the abolition of slavery, and a determination by Haitians to forge a new path of their own.

On November 29, 1803, they issued the first of what would be two declarations of independence. Written by "an admirer of the work of Jefferson," it was a remarkably conciliatory text that seemed to appeal primarily to a foreign audience, or, in the parlance of the Declaration, "the opinions of mankind." This focus proved unsatisfactory to some of the revolutionaries, and on the first of January 1804, in the port city of Gonaïves, Haiti proclaimed its independence for a second time, in a text this time very much directed to the Haitian people themselves. (Long thought missing, an original copy of this declaration was discovered in 2010 by a Canadian researcher, Julia Gaffield, in the British National Archives.) With its understandable anger against the "barbarians" who had subjected Haiti to a particularly cruel form of colonial dominion, this second text is a far cry from the serene Enlightenment language of the American Declaration, whose author, so often a champion of the right to alter or abolish a government, would as president stubbornly refuse to extend diplomatic recognition to the Haitians. Southerners would continue to block recognition for more than a generation. Not until the administration of Abraham Lincoln, when secession effectively removed Southern opposition in Congress, would the United States finally enter into diplomatic relations with the Haitian Republic.

Haitian Declaration of Independence

November 29, 1803, and January 1, 1804

PROCLAMATION OF DESSALINES, CHRISTOPHE, AND CLERVAUX, CHIEFS OF ST. DOMINGO.

In the Name of the Black People, and Men of Color of St. Domingo:

The Independence of St. Domingo is proclaimed. Restored to our primitive dignity, we have asserted our rights; we swear never to yield them to any power on earth; the frightful veil of prejudice is torn to pieces, be it so for ever. Woe be to them who would dare, to put together its bloody tatters.

Oh! Landholders of St. Domingo, wandering in foreign countries, by proclaiming our independence, we do not forbid you, indiscriminately, from returning to your property; far be from us this unjust idea. We are not ignorant that there are some among you that have renounced their former errors, abjured the injustice of their exhorbitant pretensions, and acknowledged the lawfulness of the cause for which we have been spilling our blood these twelve years. Toward those men who do us justice, we will act as brothers; let them rely for ever on our esteem and friendship; let them return among us. The God who protects us, the God of Freemen, bids us to stretch out towards them our conquering arms. But as for those, who, intoxicated with foolish pride, interested slaves of a guilty pretension, are blinded so much as to believe themselves the essence of human nature, and assert that they are destined by heaven to be our masters and our tyrants, let them never come near the land of St. Domingo: if they come hither, they will only meet with chains or deportation; then let them stay where they are; tormented by their well-deserved misery, and the frowns of the just men whom they have too long mocked, let them still continue to move, unpitied and unnoticed by all.

We have sworn not to listen with clemency towards all those who would dare to speak to us of slavery; we will be inexorable, perhaps even cruel, towards all troops who, themselves forgetting the object for which they have not ceased fighting since 1780, should come from Europe to bring among us death and servitude. Nothing is too dear, and all means are lawful, to men from whom it is wished to tear the first of all blessings. Were they to cause rivers and torrents of blood to run; were they, in order to maintain their liberty, to conflagrate seven eighths of the globe, they are innocent before the tribunal of Providence, that never created men, to see them groaning under so harsh and shameful a servitude.

In the various commotions that took place, some inhabitants against whom we had not to complain, have been victims by the cruelty of a few soldiers or cultivators, too much blinded by the remembrance of their past sufferings to be able to distinguish the good and humane land-owners from those that were unfeeling and cruel, we lament with all feeling souls so deplorable an end, and declare to the world, whatever may be said to the contrary by wicked people, that the murders were committed contrary to the wishes of our hearts. It was impossible, especially in the crisis in which the colony was, to be able to prevent or stop those horrors. They who are in the least acquainted with history, know that a people, when assailed by civil dissentions, though they may be the most polished on earth, give themselves up to every species of excess, and the authority of the chiefs, at that time not firmly supported, in a time of revolution cannot punish all that are guilty, without meeting with new difficulties. But now a-days the Aurora of peace hails us, with the glimpse of a less stormy time; now that the calm of victory has succeeded to the trouble of a dreadful war, every thing in St. Domingo ought to assume a new face, and its government henceforward be that of justice.

Done at the Head-Quarters, Fort Dauphin, November 29, 1803.

(Signed)
Dessalines.
Christophe.
Clerveaux.

PROCLAMATION FOR A SOLEMN ABJURATION OF THE FRENCH NATION.

LIBERTY OR DEATH!—NATIVE ARMY, THE GENERAL IN CHIEF TO THE PEOPLE OF HAYTI.

CITIZENS,

It is not enough to have expelled from your country the barbarians who have for ages stained it with blood—it is not enough to have curbed the factions which, succeeding each other by turns, sported with a phantom of liberty which France exposed to their eyes. It is become necessary, by a last act of national authority, to ensure for ever the empire of liberty in the country which has given us birth. It is necessary to deprive an inhuman government, which has hitherto held our minds in a state of the most humiliating torpitude, of every hope of being enabled again to enslave us. Finally, it is necessary to live independent, or die. Independence or Death! Let these sacred words serve to rally us—let them be signals of battle, and of our re-union.

Citizens—Countrymen—I have assembled on this solemn day, those courageous chiefs, who, on the eve of receiving the last breath of expiring liberty, have lavished their blood to preserve it. These generals, who have conducted your struggles against tyranny, have not yet done. The French name still darkens our plains: every thing recals the remembrance of the cruelties of that barbarous people. Our laws, our customs, our cities, every thing bears the characteristic of the French.—Hearken to what I say!—the French still have a footing in our island! and you believe yourselves free and independent of that republic, which has fought all nations, it is true, but never conquered those who would be free! What! victims for fourteen years by credulity and forbearance! conquered not by French armies, but by the canting eloquence of the proclamations of their agents! When shall we be wearied with breathing the same air with them? What have we in common with that bloody-minded people? Their cruelties compared to our moderation—their colour to ours—the extension of seas which separate us—our avenging climate—all plainly tell us they are not our brethren; that they never will become such; and, if they find an asylum among us, they will still be the instigators of our troubles and of our divisions. Citizens, men, women, young and old, cast round your eyes on every part of this island; seek there your wives, your husbands, your brothers, your sisters—what did I say? seek your children—your children at the breast, what is become of them? I shudder to tell it—the *prey of vultures*. Instead of these interesting victims, the affrighted eye sees only their assassins—tigers still covered with their blood, and whose terrifying presence reproaches you for your insensibility, and your guilty tardiness to avenge them—what do you wait for, to appease their manes? Remember that you have wished your remains to be laid by the side of your fathers—When you have driven out tyranny—will you descend into their tombs, without having avenged them? No: their bones would repulse yours. And ye, invaluable men, intrepid Generals, who, insensible to private sufferings, have given new life to liberty, by lavishing your blood; know, that you have done nothing if you do not give to the nations a terrible, though just example, of the vengeance that ought to be exercised by a people proud of having recovered its liberty, and zealous of maintaining it. Let us intimidate those, who might dare to attempt depriving us of it again: let us begin with the French; let them shudder at approaching our shores, if not on account of the cruelties they have committed, at least at the terrible resolution we are going to make—To devote to death whatsoever native of France should soil with his sacrilegious footstep, this territory of liberty.

We have dared to be free—let us continue free by ourselves, and for ourselves; let us imitate the growing child; his own strength breaks his leading-strings, which become useless and troublesome to him in his walk. What are the people who have fought us? what people would reap the fruits of our labours? and what a dishonourable absurdity, to conquer to be slaves!

Slaves—leave to the French nation this odious epithet; they have conquered to be no longer free—let us walk in other footsteps; let us imitate other nations, who, carrying their solicitude into futurity, and dreading to leave posterity an example of cowardice, have preferred to be exterminated, rather than be erased from the list of free people. Let us, at the same time, take care, lest a spirit of proselytism should destroy the work—let our neighbours breathe in peace—let them live peaceably under the shield of those laws which they have framed for themselves; let us beware of becoming revolutionary fire-brands—of creating ourselves the legislators of the Antilles—of considering as a glory the disturbing the tranquility of the neighbouring islands; they have not been, like the one we inhabit, drenched with the innocent blood of the inhabitants—they have no vengeance to exercise against the authority that protects them; happy, never to have experienced the pestilence that has destroyed us, they must wish well to our posterity.

Peace with our neighbours, but accursed be the French name—eternal hatred to France: such are our principles.

Natives of Hayti—my happy destiny reserves me to be one day the centinel who is to guard the idol we now sacrifice to. I have grown old fighting for you, sometimes almost alone; and if I have been happy enough to deliver to you the sacred charge confided to me, recollect it is for you, at present, to preserve it. In fighting for your liberty, I have laboured for my own happiness: before it shall be consolidated by laws which shall ensure individual liberty, your chiefs whom I have assembled here, and myself, owe you this last proof of our devotedness.

Generals, and other chiefs, unite with me for the happiness of our country: the day is arrived—the day which will ever perpetuate our glory and our independence.

If there exist among you a lukewarm heart, let him retire, and shudder to pronounce the oath which is to unite us. Let us swear to the whole world, to posterity, to ourselves, to renounce France for ever, and to die, rather than live under its dominion—to fight till the last breath for the independence of our country.

And ye, people, too long unfortunate, witness the oath we now pronounce: recollect that it is upon your constancy and courage I depended when I first entered the career of liberty to fight despotism and tyranny, against which you have been struggling these last fourteen years; remember that I have sacrificed every thing to fly to your defence—parents, children, fortune, and am now only rich, in your liberty—that my name has become a horror to all friends of slavery, or despots; and tyrants only pronounce it, cursing the day that gave me birth; if ever you refuse or receive with murmuring the laws, which the protecting angel that watches over your destinies, shall dictate to me for your happiness, you will merit the fate of an ungrateful people. But away from me this frightful idea: You will be the guardians of the liberty you cherish, the support of the Chief who commands you.

Swear then to live free and independent, and to prefer death to every thing that would lead to replace you under the yoke; swear then to pursue for everlasting, the traitors, and enemies of your independence.

J. J. Dessalines.
Head-quarters, Gonaives, 1st Jan. 1804,
1st Year of Independence.

Haiti's fight for independence was unique in many ways, but it was far from the only such struggle in the New World. In 1808, after Napoleon Bonaparte invaded Spain and placed his brother Joseph on the throne, the Spanish Empire was thrown into chaos. In Venezuela, long-standing discontent with Spanish authority finally ripened on July 5, 1811. On that day, Venezuelan patriots issued a declaration, or as they styled it, an "act" of independence. In some ways, it was quite different from its American precursor. For one, it wore its religion on its sleeve, promising to defend "the holy Catholic and Apostolic Religion of Jesus Christ."

Figure 28: *A historical painting by Venezuelan artist Martín Tovar y Tovar captures the sense of excitement that accompanied that nation's declaration of independence.*

But in many other ways, it took up the language of the Declaration of Independence, placing faith in "the order of events" and "the purposes for which governments were established," while seeking "to take amongst the powers of the earth the place of equality which the Supreme Being and Nature assign to us." As if that were not close enough, a final passage bound the signers to "pledge our lives, fortunes, and the sacred tie of our national honour."

The question of whether to recognize the independence of Venezuela and the other Latin American republics that would soon break away from Spain's tottering empire roiled American politics for several years, ultimately leading in 1823 to the promulgation of the Monroe Doctrine, which declared the Western Hemisphere off-limits to future European colonization. Independence thus reinforced independence, as a world of empires began to transform into a world of nations.

Venezuelan Act of Independence.

July 5, 1811

In the Name of the All-powerful God,

WE the Representatives of the united Provinces of CARACAS, CUMANA, BARINAS, MARGARITA, BARCELONA, MERIDA, and TRUXILLO, forming the American Confederation of Venezuela, in the South Continent, in Congress assembled, considering the full and absolute possession of our Rights, which we recovered justly and legally from the 19th of April, 1810, in consequence of the occurrences in Bayona, and the occupation of the Spanish Throne by conquest, and the succession of a new Dynasty, constituted without our consent: are desirous, before we make use of those Rights, of which we have been deprived by force for more than three ages, but now restored to us by the political order of human events, to make known to the world the reasons which have emanated from these same occurrences, and which authorise us in the free use we are now about to make of our own Sovereignty.

We do not wish, nevertheless, to begin by alledging the rights inherent in every conquered country, to recover its state of property and independence; we generously forget the long series of ills, injuries, and privations, which the sad right of conquest has indistinctly caused, to all the descendants of the Discoverers, Conquerors, and Settlers of these Countries, plunged into a worse state by the very same cause that ought to have favoured them; and, drawing a veil over the 300 years of Spanish dominion in America, we will now only present to view the authentic and well-known facts, which ought to have wrested from one world, the right over the other, by the inversion, disorder, and conquest, that have already dissolved the Spanish Nation.

This disorder has increased the ills of America, by rendering void its claims and remonstrances, enabling the Governors of Spain to insult and oppress this part of the Nation, thus leaving it without the succour and guarantee of the Laws. . . .

In consequence of all these solid, public, and incontestable reasons of policy, which so powerfully urge the necessity of recovering our natural dignity, restored to us by the order of events; and in compliance with the imprescriptible rights enjoyed by nations, to destroy every pact, agreement, or association, which does not answer the purposes for which governments were established; we believe that we cannot, nor ought not, to preserve the bonds which hitherto kept us united to the Government of Spain; and that, like all the other nations of the world, we are free, and authorised not to depend on any other authority than our own, and to take amongst the powers of the earth the place of equality which the Supreme Being and Nature assign to us, and to which we are called by the succession of human events, and urged by our own good and utility.

Notwithstanding we are aware of the difficulties that attend, and the obligations imposed upon us, by the rank we are about to take in the political order of the world; as well as the powerful influence of forms and habitudes, to which unfortunately we have been accustomed: we at the same time know, that the shameful submission to them, when we can throw them off, would be still more ignominious for us, and more fatal to our posterity, than our long and painful slavery; and that it now becomes an indispensable duty to provide for our own preservation, security, and felicity, by essentially varying all the forms of our former constitution.

In consequence whereof, considering, by the reasons thus alledged, that we have satisfied the respect which we owe to the opinions of the human race, and the dignity of other nations, in the number of whom we are about to enter, and on whose communication and friendship we rely: We, the Representatives of the United Provinces of Venezuela, calling on the SUPREME BEING to witness the justice of our proceedings and the rectitude of our intentions, do implore his divine and celestial help; and ratifying, at the moment in which we are born to the dignity which his Providence restores to us, the desire we have of living and dying free, and of believing and defending the holy Catholic and Apostolic Religion of Jesus Christ. We, therefore, in the name and by the will and authority which we hold from the virtuous People of Venezuela, DO declare solemnly to the world, that its united Provinces are, and ought to be, from this day, by act and right, Free, Sovereign, and Independent States; and that they are absolved from every submission and dependence on the Throne of Spain, or on those who do, or may call themselves its Agents and Representatives; and that a free and independent State, thus constituted, has full power to take that form of Government which may be conformable to the general will of the People; to declare war, make peace, form alliances, regulate treaties of commerce, limits, and navigation; and to do and transact every act, in like manner as other free and independent States. And that this, our solemn Declaration, may be held valid, firm, and durable, we hereby mutually bind each Province to the other, and pledge our lives, fortunes, and the sacred tie of our national honour. Done in the Federal Palace of Caracas; signed by our own hands, sealed with the great Provisional Seal of the Confederation, and countersigned by the Secretary of Congress, this 5th day of July, 1811, the first of our Independence. . . .

Figure 29: *The Mecklenburg Declaration is commemorated by a plaque in the North Carolina State Capitol in Raleigh.*

As the legacy of the Declaration was reverberating around the Americas, it was called into question by a curious incident at home. The so-called Mecklenburg Declaration of Independence was first published on April 30, 1819, in a newspaper in Raleigh, North Carolina, with the following tease: "It is not probably known to many of our readers, that the citizens of Mecklenburg County, in this State made a Declaration of Independence more than a year before Congress made theirs. The following Document on the subject has lately come to the hands of the Editor from unquestionable authority, and is published that it may go down to posterity." This precocious declaration was purportedly written on May 20, 1775, by a patriot committee alarmed by the news of the fighting at Lexington and Concord the month before. The text appeared to have some basis in fact: the county did issue resolves supporting the patriots of Lexington and Concord.

But many questions remained, beginning with the improbability of a full-throated declaration of independence in the late spring of 1775, seemingly anticipating the language of the Declaration of Independence more than a year before it was written. An aged John Adams was surprised when he first read of the discovery of this "lost declaration" in a Boston paper, and he forwarded the article to Thomas Jefferson, who thought the document must be a fake, professing that "I shall believe it such until positive and solemn proof of its authenticity shall be produced."

Mecklenburg Declaration of Independence

"May 20, 1775" (April 30, 1819)

1. *Resolved,* That whosoever directly or indirectly abetted, or in any way, form or manner countenanced the unchartered and dangerous invasion of our rights, as claimed by Great-Britain, is an enemy to this Country,—to America,—and to the inherant and inalienable rights of man.

2. *Resolved,* That we the citizens of Mecklenburg County, do hereby dissolve the political bands which have connected us to the Mother Country, and hereby absolve ourselves from all allegiance to the British Crown, and abjure all political connection, contract or association with that Nation, who have wantonly trampled on our rights and liberties—and inhumanly shed the innocent blood of American patriots at Lexington.

3. *Resolved,* That we do hereby declare ourselves a free and independent People, are and of right ought to be, a sovereign and self-governing Association, under the control of no power other than that of our God and the General Government of the Congress; to the maintenance of which independence, we solemnly pledge to each other our mutual cooperation, our lives, our fortunes, and our most sacred honor.

4. *Resolved,* That as we now acknowledge the existence and control of no law or legal officer, civil or military, within this County, We do hereby ordain and adopt, as a rule of life, all, each and every of our former laws,—wherein, nevertheless, the Crown of Great-Britain never can be considered as holding rights, privileges, immunities or authority therein.

5. *Resolved,* That it is also further decreed, that all, each and every military officer in this county is hereby reinstated to his former command and authority, he acting conformably to these regulations. And that every member present of this delegation shall henceforth be a civil officer, viz: a Justice of the Peace, in the character of a "*Committee man,*" to issue process, hear and determine all matters of controversy, according to said adopted laws, and to preserve peace, and union, and harmony in said County,—and to use every exertion to spread the love of country and fire of freedom throughout America, until a more general and organized government be established in this province. . . .

Figure 30: *Secretary of State John Quincy Adams, seen here in an 1818 portrait by Gilbert Stuart, was the nation's greatest champion of the Declaration of Independence before Lincoln.*

In the early 1820s, with the nation's fiftieth anniversary looming, there was a palpable uptick in interest in the Declaration among Americans eager to revisit the story of the country's founding. They found a willing guide in John Quincy Adams, who was not only the son of a signer but in his second term as secretary of state under James Monroe. That post afforded him unrivaled access to the young nation's most important public and diplomatic records, including the original engrossed version of the Declaration of Independence.

An insightful student of American history, Adams often invoked the Declaration's immortal phrases in his speeches including, years later, his defense of the Africans on trial after the *Amistad* incident. As he knew better than most, the Founders, especially his father, had hoped that the creation of the United States would lead to a simpler, better diplomacy between nations, with less interference from kings, fewer wars, and clearer statements of national purpose. The Declaration had been an integral part of that plan.

On the Fourth of July 1821, Adams gave a landmark address that renewed this vision. In it he rejects the right of conquest, by which so many kings had acquired their domains, and pledges that the American Republic would quietly promote the spread of democracy, by peaceful means. In a famous line, he affirms of America that "she goes not abroad, in search of monsters to destroy."

Midway through his speech, delivered in the House chamber before the assembled federal government, Adams read aloud directly from the engrossed copy of the Declaration, which he had brought with him from the State Department. No doubt he glanced with pride at his father's signature on the document the elder Adams had done so much to will into existence. For Adams, the legacy of the American Revolution was a very personal patrimony.

John Quincy Adams, *An Address delivered At the request of a Committee of the Citizens of Washington; on the occasion of reading the Declaration of Independence, on the Fourth of July, 1821.*

July 4, 1821

. . . Little less than forty years have revolved since the struggle for independence was closed; another generation has arisen; and, in the assembly of nations, our Republic is already a matron of mature age. The cause of your independence is no longer upon trial; the final sentence upon it has long been passed upon earth and ratified in Heaven.

The interest, which in this paper has survived the occasion upon which it was issued; the interest which is of every age and every clime; the interest which quickens with the lapse of years, spreads as it grows old, and brightens as it recedes, is in the principles which it proclaims. It was the first solemn declaration by a nation of the only *legitimate* foundation of civil government. It was the corner stone of a new fabric, destined to cover the surface of the globe. It demolished at a stroke the lawfulness of all governments founded upon conquest. It swept away all the rubbish of accumulated centuries of servitude. It announced in practical form to the world the transcendent truth of the unalienable sovereignty of the people. It proved that the social compact was no figment of the imagination; but a real, solid, and sacred bond of the social union. From the day of this Declaration, the people of North America were no longer the fragment of a distant empire, imploring justice and mercy from an inexorable master in another hemisphere. They were no longer children appealing in vain to the sympathies of a heartless mother; no longer subjects leaning upon the shattered columns of royal promises, and invoking the faith of parchment to secure their rights. They were a *nation*, asserting as of right, and maintaining by war, its own existence. A nation was born in a day—

"How many ages hence
Shall this, their lofty scene, be acted o'er
In states unborn, and accents yet unknown?"

It will be acted o'er, fellow-citizens, but it can never be repeated. It stands, and must for ever stand, alone, a beacon on the summit of the mountain, to which all the inhabitants of the earth may turn their eyes for a genial and saving light till time shall be lost in eternity, and this globe itself dissolve, nor leave a wreck behind. It stands for ever, a light of admonition to the rulers of men, a light of salvation and redemption to the oppressed. So long as this planet shall be inhabited by human beings, so long as man shall be of social nature, so long as government shall be necessary to the great moral purposes of society, and so long as it shall be abused to the purposes of oppression, so long shall this Declaration hold out to the sovereign and to the subject the extent and the boundaries of their respective rights and duties, founded in the laws of nature, and of nature's God. Five and forty years have passed away since this Declaration was issued by our fathers; and here are we, fellow-citizens, assembled in the full enjoyment of its fruits, to bless the author of our being for the bounties of his providence, in casting our lot in this favored land; to remember with effusions of gratitude the sages who put forth, and the heroes who bled for the establishment of this Declaration; and, by the communion of soul in the reperusal and hearing of this instrument, to renew the genuine Holy Alliance of its principles, to recognise them as eternal truths, and to pledge ourselves, and bind our posterity, to a faithful and undeviating adherence to them.

Fellow-Citizens, our fathers have been faithful to them before us. When the little band of their Delegates, "with a firm reliance on the protection of Divine Providence, for the support of this declaration, mutually pledged to each other their *lives*, their *fortunes*, and their *sacred honor*," from every dwelling, street, and square, of your populous cities, it was re-echoed with shouts of joy and gratulation! And if the silent language of the heart could have been heard, every hill upon the surface of this continent which had been trodden by the foot of civilized man, every valley in which the toil of your fathers had opened a paradise upon the wild, would have rung, with one accordant voice, louder than the thunders, sweeter than the harmonies of the heavens, with the solemn and responsive words, "*We swear.*"

The pledge has been redeemed. Through six years of devastating but heroic war, through forty years of more heroic peace, the principles of this declaration have been supported by the toils, by the vigils, by the blood of your fathers, and of yourselves. The conflict of war had begun with fearful odds of apparent human power on the part of the oppressor. He wielded at will the collective force of the mightiest nation in Europe. He with more than poetic truth asserted the dominion of the waves. The power to whose unjust usurpation your fathers hurled the gauntlet of defiance, baffled and vanquished by them, has even since, stripped of all the energies of this continent, been found adequate to give the law to its own quarter of the globe, and to mould the destinies of the European world. It was with a sling and a stone, that your fathers went forth to encounter the massive vigor of this Goliath. They slung the heaven-directed stone, and

"With heaviest sound, the giant monster fell."

Amid the shouts of victory, your cause soon found friends and allies in the rivals of your enemies. France recognised your Independence as existing in fact, and made common cause with you for its support. Spain and the Netherlands, without adopting your principles, successively flung their weight into your scale. The Semiramis of the North, no convert to your doctrines, still conjured all the maritime neutrality of Europe in array against the usurpations of your antagonist upon the seas. While some of the fairest of your fields were ravaged; while your towns and villages were consumed with fire; while the harvests of your summers were blasted; while the purity of virgin innocence, and the chastity of matronly virtue, were violated; while the living remnants of the field of battle were reserved for the gibbet, by the fraternal sympathies of Britons throughout your land, the waters of the Atlantic ocean, and those that wash the shores of either India, were dyed with the mingled blood of combatants in the cause of North American Independence.

In the progress of time, that vial of wrath was exhausted. After seven years of exploits and achievements like these, performed under the orders of the British king; to use the language of the treaty of peace, "it having pleased the Divine Providence to dispose the hearts of the most serene and most potent Prince, George the III, by the Grace of God, King of Great Britain, France, and Ireland, Defender of the Faith, Duke of Brunswick and Luneburg, Arch Treasurer and Prince Elector of the Holy Roman Empire, and so forth—and of the United States of America to"—what? "To forget all past misunderstandings and differences that have unhappily interrupted the good correspondence and friendship which they mutually wish to restore"—what then? Why—"His Britannic Majesty ACKNOWLEDGES the said United States, viz: New Hampshire, Massachusetts Bay, Rhode Island and Providence Plantations, Connecticut, New-York, New-Jersey, Pennsylvania, Delaware, Maryland, Virginia, North-Carolina,

South-Carolina, and Georgia, to be *Free*, *Sovereign*, and *Independent* States; that he treats with them as such; and for himself, his heirs, and successors, relinquishes all claims to the Government, proprietary and territorial rights of the same, and every part thereof."

Fellow-Citizens, I am not without apprehension that some parts of this extract, cited to the word and to the letter, from the treaty of peace of 1783, may have discomposed the *serenity* of your temper. Far be it from me, to *dispose your hearts* to a levity unbecoming the hallowed dignity of this day. But this treaty of peace is the *dessert* appropriate to the sumptuous banquet of the Declaration. It is the epilogue to that unparalleled drama of which the Declaration is the prologue. Observe, my countrymen and friends, how the rules of unity, prescribed by the great masters of the fictive stage, were preserved in this tragedy of pity and terror in real life. Here was a beginning, a middle, and an end, of one mighty action. The beginning was the Declaration which we have read: the middle, was that sanguinary, calamitous, but glorious war, which calls for deeper colors, and a brighter pencil, than mine to pourtray: the end was the disposal by Divine Providence, that same Divine Providence upon whose protection your fathers had so solemnly and so effectually declared their firm reliance, of the heart of the most serene and most potent prince to acknowledge your Independence to the precise extent in which it had been declared. Here was no great charter of Runny Mead, yielded and accepted as a grant of royal bounty. That which the Declaration had asserted, which seven years of mercy-harrowing war had contested, was here, in express and unequivocal terms, *acknowledged*. And how? By the mere disposal of the heart of the most serene and most potent prince.

The Declaration of Independence pronounced the irrevocable decree of political separation, between the United States and their People on the one part, and the British King, Government and Nation on the other. It proclaimed the first principles on which civil government is founded, and derived from them the justification before Earth and Heaven, of this act of sovereignty: but it left the people of this Union collective and individual without *organized* Government. In contemplating this state of things, one of the profoundest of British statesmen, in an ecstacy of astonishment, exclaimed "Anarchy is found tolerable!" But there was no Anarchy. From the day of the Declaration, the people of the North American Union and of its constituent States, were associated bodies of civilized men and christians, in a state of nature; but not of Anarchy. They were bound by the laws of God, which they all, and by the laws of the Gospel, which they nearly all, acknowledged as the rules of their conduct. They were bound by all those tender and endearing sympathies, the absence of which in the British Government and Nation towards them was the primary cause of the distressing conflict into which they had been precipitated. They were bound by all the beneficent laws and institutions which their forefathers had brought with them from *their* mother Country, not as servitudes, but as rights. They were bound by habits of hardy industry, by frugal and hospitable manners, by the general sentiments of social equality, by pure and virtuous morals, and lastly they were bound by the grappling hooks of common suffering under the scourge of oppression. Where then, among such a people, were the materials for Anarchy? Had there been among them no other Law, they would have been a law unto themselves.

They had before them in their new position, besides the maintenance of the Independence which they had declared, three great objects to attain: the first, to cement and prepare for perpetuity, their common union, and that of their Posterity; the second, to erect and organize civil and municipal Governments in their respective States; and the third, to form connexions of friendship and of commerce with foreign Nations. For all these objects, the same Congress which issued the Declaration, and at the same time with it, had provided. They recommended to the several States to form civil governments for themselves. With guarded and cautious deliberation they matured a confederation for the whole Union; and they prepared treaties of commerce, to be offered to the principal maritime nations of the world. All these objects were in a great degree accomplished, amid the din of arms, and while every quarter of our country was ransacked by the fury of invasion. The states organized their governments, all in republican forms; all on the principles of the Declaration. The confederation was unanimously adopted by the thirteen States, and treaties of commerce were concluded with France and the Netherlands, in which, for the first time, the same just and magnanimous principles, consigned in the Declaration of Independence, were, so far as they could be applicable to the intercourse between nation and nation, solemnly recognised.

When experience had proved that the Confederation was not adequate to the national purposes of the country, the people of the United States, without tumult, without violence, by their delegates, all chosen upon principles of equal right, formed a more perfect Union, by the establishment of the Federal Constitution. This has already passed the ordeal of one human generation. In all the changes of men and of parties through which it has passed, it has been administered on the same fundamental principles. Our manners, our habits, our feelings, arc all republican; and if our principles had been, when first proclaimed, doubtful to the ear of reason or the sense of humanity, they would have been reconciled to our understandings, and endeared to our hearts by their practical operation. In the progress of forty years since the acknowledgement of our Independence, we have gone through many modifications of internal government, and through all the vicissitudes of peace and war, with other powerful nations. But never, never for a moment have the great principles, consecrated by the Declaration of this day, been renounced or abandoned.

And now, friends and countrymen, if the wise and learned philosophers of the elder world; the first observers of nutation and aberration, the discoverers of maddening ether and invisible planets, the inventors of Congreve rockets and Shrapnel shells, should find their hearts disposed to enquire what has America done for the benefit of mankind? Let our answer be this: America, with the same voice which spoke herself into existence as a nation, proclaimed to mankind the inextinguishable rights of human nature, and the only lawful foundations of government. America, in the assembly of nations, since her admission among them, has invariably, though often fruitlessly, held forth to them the hand of honest friendship, of equal freedom, of generous reciprocity. She has uniformly spoken among them, though often to heedless and often to disdainful ears, the language of equal liberty, of equal justice, and of equal rights. She has, in the lapse of nearly half a century, without a single exception, respected the independence of other nations while asserting and maintaining her own. She has abstained from interference in the concerns of others, even when the conflict has been for principles to which she clings, as to the last vital drop that visits the heart. She has seen that probably for centuries to come, all the contests of that Aceldama the European world, will be contests of inveterate power, and emerging right. Wherever the standard of freedom and Independence, has been or shall be unfurled, there will her heart, her benedictions and her prayers be. But she goes not abroad, in search of monsters to destroy. She is the well-wisher to the freedom and independence of all. She is the champion and vindicator only of her own. She will recommend the general cause by the countenance of her voice, and the benignant sympathy of her example. She well knows that by once enlisting under other banners than her own, were they even the banners of foreign Independence, she would involve herself beyond the power of extrication, in all the wars of interest and intrigue, of individual avarice, envy, and ambition, which assume the colors and usurp the standard of freedom. The fundamental maxims of her policy would insensibly change from *liberty* to *force*. The frontlet upon her brow would no longer beam with the ineffable splendor of Freedom and Independence; but in its stead would soon be substituted an Imperial Diadem, flashing in false and tarnished lustre the murky radiance of dominion and power. She might become the dictatress of the world. She would be no longer the ruler of her own spirit. . . .

In an age before active campaigning for the presidency, Adams's 1821 Independence Day speech had amounted to an announcement of his intention to stand in the election of 1824. (He would ultimately triumph in a contested election determined by the House of Representatives, becoming the sixth president.) Thus, the son of John Adams would be in the White House on the day that Americans would celebrate the Jubilee of the Declaration—its fiftieth anniversary. As secretary of state, Adams had been uniquely situated

***Figure 31:** One of the estimated fifty-two extant copies of the Stone engraving of the Declaration of Independence, the version most familiar to us today.*

to promote public awareness of its founding charters. In 1820, concerned about the deteriorating condition of the original parchment, he arranged for an important facsimile of the Declaration by engraver William J. Stone (completed in 1823). Nearly perfect (despite some minor changes in punctuation), the engraving is the source of most modern images of the Declaration. The Stone edition created thousands of fresh new copies, sent to libraries, schools, and legislative chambers around the country. This revivified curiosity in the founding, as did the triumphant return of the Marquis de Lafayette, for a prolonged goodwill tour in 1824–25.

Clearly, the experiment in self-government had succeeded. Independence, as Adams had said, was no longer "on trial . . . the final sentence upon it has long been passed upon earth and ratified in Heaven." The experiment was also spreading, as other peoples made their own declarations of independence, in Europe as well as the Americas. That included Greece, the original home of democracy, which claimed independence from the Ottoman Empire in 1822, in a text that celebrated "natural rights" and rejected tyranny.

Figure 32: *Close collaborators in the fight for independence, then bitter rivals for the presidency, John Adams and Thomas Jefferson rekindled their friendship in retirement, always acutely conscious of their legacy as Founders.*

The Jubilee became a focal point for national celebrations, as Americans peered through the mists of time, trying to recover everything that they could about 1776. They were aided in these efforts by the presence of a dwindling phalanx of Revolutionary veterans, and by the natural tendency of Fourth of July speakers to weave exuberant histories of the founding. Peleg Sprague, an orator in Hallowell, Maine, spoke for many when he remarked that "every thing connected" with the Declaration "excites deep and acute interest."

Remarkably, the two men who understood the Declaration most deeply were still alive as the Jubilee year began. Thomas Jefferson and John Adams had been corresponding for years, reconciled after a long estrangement triggered by Jefferson's victory over Adams in the presidential election of 1800 (Jefferson had likened the Adams administration to a "reign of witches").

Their renewed friendship deepened as the other Founders departed the stage, and they unburdened themselves to each other, speaking like Greek oracles from their respective hilltops (Monticello in Virginia, and the more modest Adams homestead in Massachusetts, which Adams sometimes called "Montezillo").

In 1813, Adams wrote to Jefferson, "You and I ought not to die, before we have explained ourselves to each other." For the next thirteen years, they did exactly that, discussing family, books, and their fading memories of the great events they had lived through. Despite advancing age and "crippled wrists and fingers," they attended unfailingly to their correspondence. The letters included a grim tally over the years of how many of the Declaration's signers had died, but they found constant consolation in this last living thread connecting them. As Jefferson put it, they enjoyed a "friendship co-eval with our government."

A note of excitement crept in as the great day approached. With the Jubilee drawing near, Adams and Jefferson were naturally invited to local celebrations. Old age and fragility forced each man to decline, but in so doing, they left important testimonies to what the Declaration still meant to them. These were among the final documents they wrote.

John Adams and Thomas Jefferson Letters

June 1826

JOHN ADAMS TO JOHN WHITNEY

Quincy June 7th, 1826

Sir,

Your letter of the 3d Instant, written on behalf of the Committee of Arrangements, for the approaching celebration of our National Independence; inviting me to dine, on the fourth of July next, with the Citizens of Quincy, at the Town Hall, has been received with the kindest emotions. The very respectful language with which the wishes of my Fellow Townsmen have been conveyed to me, by your Committee, and the terms of affectionate regard toward me, individually, demand my grateful thanks, which you will please to accept and to communicate to your Colleagues of the Committee.

The present feeble State of my health will not permit me to indulge the hope of participating, with more than by my best wishes in the joys & festivities and the Solemn Services of that day; on which will be completed *the fiftieth year* from its birth, *the Independence of these United States*. A Memorable epoch in the annals of the human race; destined, in future history, to form the brightest or the blackest page, according to the use or the abuse of those political institutions by which they shall, in time to come, be shaped, by the *human mind*.

I pray you Sir to tender in my behalf to our fellow Citizens my cordial thanks for their affectionate good wishes, and to be assured that I am very truly and affectionately, Your's & their Friend & Fellow-Townsman

J Adams

THOMAS JEFFERSON TO ROGER C. WEIGHTMAN,
Monticello, June 24, 1826

Respected Sir,—The kind invitation I received from you, on the part of the citizens of the city of Washington, to be present with them at their celebration of the fiftieth anniversary of American Independence, as one of the surviving signers of an instrument pregnant with our own, and the fate of the world, is most flattering to myself, and heightened by the honorable accompaniment proposed for the comfort of such a journey. It adds sensibly to the sufferings of sickness, to be deprived by it of a personal participation in the rejoicings of that day. But acquiescence is a duty, under circumstances not placed among those we are permitted to control. I should, indeed, with peculiar delight, have met and exchanged there congratulations personally with the small band, the remnant of that host of worthies, who joined with us on that day, in the bold and doubtful election we were to make for our country, between submission or the sword; and to have enjoyed with them the consolatory fact, that our fellow citizens, after half a century of experience and prosperity, continue to approve the choice we made. May it be to the world, what I believe it will be, (to some parts sooner, to others later, but finally to all,) the signal of arousing men to burst the chains under which monkish ignorance and superstition had persuaded them to bind themselves, and to assume the blessings and security of self-government. That form which we have substituted, restores the free right to the unbounded exercise of reason and freedom of opinion. All eyes are opened, or opening, to the rights of man. The general spread of the light of science has already laid open to every view the palpable truth, that the mass of mankind has not been born with saddles on their backs, nor a favored few booted and spurred, ready to ride them legitimately, by the grace of God. These are grounds of hope for others. For ourselves, let the annual return of this day forever refresh our recollections of these rights, and an undiminished devotion to them.

I will ask permission here to express the pleasure with which I should have met my ancient neighbors of the city of Washington and its vicinities, with whom I passed so many years of a pleasing social intercourse; an intercourse which so much relieved the anxieties of the public cares, and left impressions so deeply engraved in my affections, as never to be forgotten. With my regret that ill health forbids me the gratification of an acceptance, be pleased to receive for yourself, and those for whom you write, the assurance of my highest respect and friendly attachments.

TH: JEFFERSON.

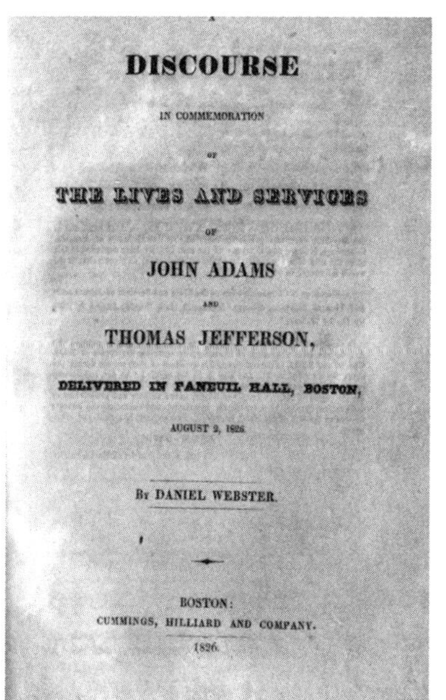

A

DISCOURSE

IN COMMEMORATION

OF

THE LIVES AND SERVICES

OF

JOHN ADAMS

AND

THOMAS JEFFERSON,

DELIVERED IN FANEUIL HALL, BOSTON,

AUGUST 2, 1826.

BY DANIEL WEBSTER.

BOSTON:
CUMMINGS, HILLIARD AND COMPANY.
1826.

Figure 33: *Just five days after Daniel Webster delivered his tribute to Adams and Jefferson in Boston's Faneuil Hall, the city council ordered that seven thousand copies be printed "for the use of the citizens."*

With exquisite timing, Adams and Jefferson both died on July 4, 1826: Jefferson at noon, Adams a few hours later. It was the perfect day for the two elderly statesmen to meet "the Great Legislator of the Universe," as Adams once referred to God, in a declaration of his own, the preamble to the Massachusetts Constitution.

Americans were already inclined to see the hand of Providence in all that they did; here, it seemed, was confirmation that they had a special destiny. The co-demise is still regarded as one of the more remarkable coincidences in American history, and it has cast an enduring, almost supernatural glow on the Declaration of Independence. Sixteen years earlier, in 1809, another signer, Benjamin Rush, described a dream in which he had a premonition that Adams and Jefferson would expire "nearly at the same time." Now it had come to pass.

Of the many eulogies delivered around the country for these two giants, none captured the public imagination more than the one Daniel Webster delivered to a packed crowd in Boston's Faneuil Hall. At a time when oratory served to entertain as well as edify, Webster (then a congressman, soon to be a U.S. senator) took his audience back to Philadelphia, fifty years earlier, and offered an almost minute-by-minute account of the tense deliberations that led to the Declaration.

Daniel Webster, *A Discourse in Commemoration of the Lives and Services of John Adams and Thomas Jefferson, delivered in Faneuil Hall, Boston, August 2, 1826.*

August 2, 1826

. . . Let us, then, bring before us the assembly, which was about to decide a question thus big with the fate of empire. Let us open their doors, and look in upon their deliberations. Let us survey the anxious and care-worn countenances, let us hear the firm-toned voices, of this band of patriots.

HANCOCK presides over the solemn sitting; and one of those not yet prepared to pronounce for absolute independence, is on the floor, and is urging his reasons for dissenting from the declaration.

'Let us pause! This step, once taken, cannot be retraced. This resolution, once passed, will cut off all hope of reconciliation. If success attend the arms of England, we shall then be no longer colonies, with charters, and with privileges; these will all be forfeited by this act; and we shall be in the condition of other conquered people, at the mercy of the conquerors. For ourselves, we may be ready to run the hazard; but are we ready to carry the country to that length? Is success so probable as to justify it? Where is the military, where the naval power, by which we are to resist the whole strength of the arm of England, for she will exert that strength to the utmost? Can we rely on the constancy and perseverance of the people? or will they not act, as the people of other countries have acted, and wearied with a long war, submit, in the end, to a worse oppression? While we stand on our old ground, and insist on redress of grievances, we know we are right, and are not answerable for consequences. Nothing, then, can be imputable to us. But if we now change our object, carry our pretensions further, and set up for absolute independence, we shall lose the sympathy of mankind. We shall no longer be defending what we possess, but struggling for something which we never did possess, and which we have solemnly and uniformly disclaimed all intention of pursuing, from the very outset of the troubles. Abandoning thus our old ground, of resistance only to arbitrary acts of oppression, the nations will believe the whole to have been mere pretence, and they will look on us, not as injured, but as ambitious, subjects. I shudder, before this responsibility. It will be on us, if relinquishing the ground we have stood on so long, and stood on so safely, we now proclaim independence, and carry on the war for that object, while these cities burn, these pleasant fields whiten and bleach with the bones of their owners, and these streams run blood. It will be upon us, it will be upon us, if failing to maintain this unseasonable and ill-judged declaration, a sterner despotism, maintained by military power, shall be established over our posterity, when we ourselves, given up by an exhausted, a harrassed, a misled people, shall have expiated our rashness and atoned for our presumption, on the scaffold.'

It was for Mr. Adams to reply to arguments like these. We know his opinions, and we know his character. He would commence with his accustomed directness and earnestness.

'Sink or swim, live or die, survive or perish, I give my hand, and my heart, to this vote. It is true, indeed, that in the beginning, we aimed not at independence. But there's a Divinity which shapes our ends. The injustice of England has driven us to arms; and, blinded to her own interest for our good, she has obstinately persisted, till independence is now within our grasp. We have but to reach forth to it, and it is ours. Why then should we defer the declaration? Is any man so weak as now to hope for a reconciliation with England, which shall leave either safety to the country and its liberties, or safety to his own life, and his own honor? Are not you, sir, who sit in that chair, is not he, our venerable colleague near you, are you not both already the proscribed and predestined objects of punishment and of vengeance? Cut off from all hope of royal clemency, what are you, what can you be, while the power of England remains, but outlaws? If we postpone independence, do we mean to carry on, or to give up, the war? Do we mean to submit to the measures of parliament, Boston port-bill and all? Do we mean to submit, and consent that we ourselves shall be ground to powder, and our country and its rights trodden down in the dust? I know we do not mean to submit. We never shall submit. Do we intend to violate that most solemn obligation ever entered into by men, that plighting, before God, of our sacred honor to Washington, when putting him forth to incur the dangers of war, as well as the political hazards of the times, we promised to adhere to him, in every extremity, with our fortunes and our lives? I know there is not a man here, who would not rather see a general conflagration sweep over the land, or an earthquake sink it, than one jot or tittle of that plighted faith fall to the ground. For myself, having, twelve months ago, in this place, moved you, that George Washington be appointed commander of the forces, raised or to be raised, for defence of American liberty, may my right hand forget her cunning, and my tongue cleave to the roof of my mouth, if I hesitate or waver, in the support I give him. The war, then, must go on. We must fight it through. And if the war must go on, why put off longer the Declaration of Independence? That measure will strengthen us. It will give us character abroad. The nations will then treat with us, which they never can do while we acknowledge ourselves subjects, in arms against our sovereign. Nay I maintain that England, herself, will sooner treat for peace with us on the footing of Independence, than consent, by repealing her acts, to acknowledge that her whole conduct towards us has been a course of injustice and oppression. Her pride will be less wounded, by submitting to that course of things which now predestinates our independence, than by yielding the points in controversy to her rebellious subjects. The former she would regard as the result of fortune; the latter she would feel as her own deep disgrace. Why then, why then, sir, do we not as soon as possible, change this from a civil to a national war? And since we must fight it through, why not put ourselves in a state to enjoy all the benefits of victory, if we gain the victory?

If we fail, it can be no worse for us. But we shall not fail. The cause will raise up armies; the cause will create navies. The people, the people, if we are true to them, will carry us, and will carry themselves, gloriously, through this struggle. I care not how fickle other people have been found. I know the people of these colonies, and I know that resistance to British aggression is deep and settled in their hearts and cannot be eradicated. Every colony, indeed, has expressed its willingness to follow, if we but take the lead. Sir, the declaration will inspire the people with increased courage. Instead of a long and bloody war for restoration of privileges, for redress of grievances, for chartered immunities, held under a British king, set before them the glorious object of entire independence, and it will breathe into them anew the breath of life. Read this declaration at the head of the army; every sword will be drawn from its scabbard, and the solemn vow uttered, to maintain it, or to perish on the bed of honor. Publish it from the pulpit; religion will approve it, and the love of religious liberty will cling round it, resolved to stand with it, or fall with it. Send it to the public halls; proclaim it there; let them hear it, who heard the first roar of the enemy's cannon; let them see it, who saw their brothers and their sons fall on the field of Bunkerhill, and in the streets of Lexington and Concord, and the very walls will cry out in its support.

Sir, I know the uncertainty of human affairs, but I see, I see clearly, through this day's business. You and I, indeed, may rue it. We may not live to the time, when this declaration shall be made good. We may die; die, colonists; die, slaves; die, it may be, ignominiously and on the scaffold. Be it so. Be it so. If it be the pleasure of Heaven that my country shall require the poor offering of my life, the victim shall be ready, at the appointed hour of sacrifice, come when that hour may. But while I do live, let me have a country, or at least the hope of a country, and that a free country.

But whatever may be our fate, be assured, be assured, that this declaration will stand. It may cost treasure, and it may cost blood; but it will stand, and it will richly compensate for both. Through the thick gloom of the present, I see the brightness of the future, as the sun in Heaven. We shall make this a glorious, an immortal day. When we are in our graves, our children will honor it. They will celebrate it, with thanksgiving, with festivity, with bonfires, and illuminations. On its annual return they will shed tears, copious, gushing tears, not of subjection and slavery, not of agony and distress, but of exultation, of gratitude, and of joy. Sir, before God, I believe the hour is come. My judgment approves this measure, and my whole heart is in it. All that I have, and all that I am, and all that I hope, in this life, I am now ready here to stake upon it; and I leave off, as I begun, that live or die, survive or perish, I am for the declaration. It is my living sentiment, and by the blessing of God it shall be my dying sentiment; independence, *now*; and INDEPENDENCE FOREVER.'

And so that day shall be honored, illustrious prophet and patriot! so that day shall be honored, and as often as it returns, thy renown shall come along with it, and the glory of thy life, like the day of thy death, shall not fail from the remembrance of men. . . .

Webster had done his research well. The imagined language he put into the mouth of John Adams often echoed actual quotations. A case in point: just days before Adams's death, the Reverend George Whitney, who would preach the sermon at the former president's funeral, paid a call on the old patriarch. He later recorded the encounter:

> Spent a few minutes with him in conversation, and took from him a toast, to be presented on the Fourth of July as coming from him. I should have liked a longer one; but as it is, this will be acceptable. "I will give you," said he, "Independence forever!" He was asked if he would not add any thing to it, and he replied, "not a word."

PART III

CREATED EQUAL 1826–1865

How did Americans reconcile the Declaration's soaring promise of equality with the poisonous reality of slavery?

Around the time of the Jubilee, a rangy young man in Indiana was presented with a book of statutes, lent to him by a kindly constable. He was seventeen or eighteen at the time, and keenly interested in the law, especially after being accused of operating a ferry without a license (hence the constable). The young man was found innocent, for the simple reason that he had no idea a license was required to carry people in his boat. But the incident stirred in him a desire to read more, and the constable opened up his library.

Abraham Lincoln had grown up in a household with very few possessions of any kind, much less books. Even still, *The Revised Laws of Indiana* might have struck most teenagers as painfully dry. But it began with a gallery of historical documents, first among them the Declaration of Independence. To the young Lincoln, it was electrifying.

His relatives later remembered that Lincoln "saturated" himself with the book, reading and rereading it. The opening section included not only the Declaration and Constitution but the Northwest Ordinance of 1787, which had banned slavery from the northern bank of the Ohio River.

Lincoln was a Southerner of sorts, born south of the Ohio, in a slave state, Kentucky. But he grew up across the river, in southern Indiana, and that made a difference. Indiana was a free state, carved from the old Northwest Territory, and from an early age Lincoln formed an instinctive aversion to slavery. His own poverty may have had something to do with it; when he was young, his father rented him out as an indentured servant, and there are intriguing signs, in Lincoln's writings, that he felt a personal identification with the enslaved. In an 1864 letter, he wrote, "If slavery is not wrong, nothing is wrong. I can not remember when I did not so think, and feel."

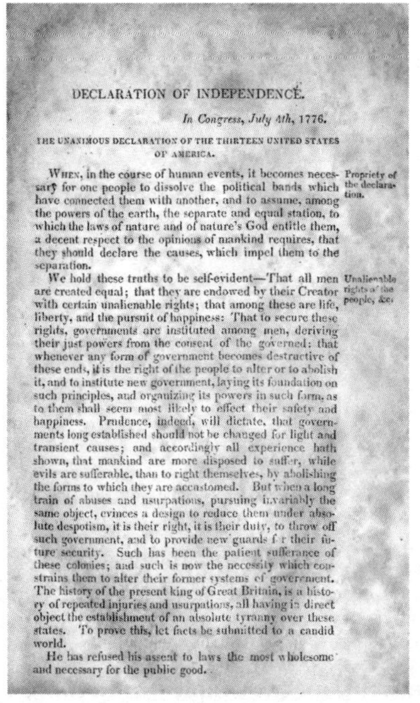

DECLARATION OF INDEPENDENCE.

In Congress, July 4th, 1776.

THE UNANIMOUS DECLARATION OF THE THIRTEEN UNITED STATES OF AMERICA.

WHEN, in the course of human events, it becomes necessary for one people to dissolve the political bands which have connected them with another, and to assume, among the powers of the earth, the separate and equal station, to which the laws of nature and of nature's God entitle them, a decent respect to the opinions of mankind requires, that they should declare the causes, which impel them to the separation. Propriety of the declaration.

We hold these truths to be self-evident—That all men are created equal; that they are endowed by their Creator with certain unalienable rights; that among these are life, liberty, and the pursuit of happiness: That to secure these rights, governments are instituted among men, deriving their just powers from the consent of the governed: that whenever any form of government becomes destructive of these ends, it is the right of the people to alter or to abolish it, and to institute new government, laying its foundation on such principles, and organizing its powers in such form, as to them shall seem most likely to effect their safety and happiness. Prudence, indeed, will dictate, that governments long established should not be changed for light and transient causes; and accordingly all experience hath shown, that mankind are more disposed to suffer, while evils are sufferable, than to right themselves, by abolishing the forms to which they are accustomed. But when a long train of abuses and usurpations, pursuing invariably the same object, evinces a design to reduce them under absolute despotism, it is their right, it is their duty, to throw off such government, and to provide new guards for their future security. Such has been the patient sufferance of these colonies; and such is now the necessity which constrains them to alter their former systems of government. The history of the present king of Great Britain, is a history of repeated injuries and usurpations, all having in direct object the establishment of an absolute tyranny over these states. To prove this, let facts be submitted to a candid world. Unalienable rights of the people, &c.

He has refused his assent to laws the most wholesome and necessary for the public good.

Figure 34: *The Declaration of Independence, as Lincoln would have encountered it on the first page of the 1824 edition of* The Revised Laws of Indiana.

Lincoln's determination to read was another way to resist subjugation. His father could barely read or write, and even then, "bunglingly," as Lincoln once remembered, not very charitably. From an early age, Lincoln was determined to avoid this fate, and there are many stories about his formidable efforts to find and read books on the frontier. Few had the impact of *The Revised Laws of Indiana*. Lincoln had been exposed to the Declaration of Independence at a seminal moment, both for him and for the young nation. He was now embarked on a miraculous journey, from near-illiteracy to the deepest possible reading of the country's founding charter.

As his stature grew, he kept the Declaration close, citing it throughout his speeches, including the Lincoln-Douglas debates that elevated his profile. The highlight of his train ride to Washington to assume the presidency was a visit to Independence Hall, where Lincoln proclaimed, "I have never had a feeling politically that did not spring from the sentiments embodied in the Declaration of Independence." When he needed to write a proclamation to explain the great issues of the Civil War, he naturally issued it on July 4, 1861.

He revisited the Declaration's themes in what may be his greatest speech, the Gettysburg Address.

Given the magnitude of Lincoln's achievement—not only saving the Union but preserving the example of American democracy to the rest of the world—his analysis of the Declaration must be considered one of the most important close readings in history. The result would be nothing less than a new birth of freedom.

* * *

In the aftermath of the Declaration's fiftieth anniversary, as mass-produced, highly ornamented copies of the text spread far and wide, a broader audience began to contemplate its daring assertion of equality. That included a few brave women, willing to speak at a time when women were generally silent in public, and immigrants, too, eager to claim the Declaration's promise for themselves. Frances (or Fanny) Wright was *both* a woman and an immigrant, born in Scotland, who came to the United States in 1818 and again in 1824 (she became a citizen in 1825). A forerunner to later feminists, she advocated for equal educational opportunity, legal rights for married women, and liberal divorce laws. She also opposed slavery and capital punishment.

In 1828, she gave a Fourth of July address in New Harmony, Indiana, some seventy-five miles from where Lincoln was coming of age, at the site of an experimental utopian community that had been established three years earlier by a Welsh social reformer, Robert Owen. Though Owen declared the experiment a failure in 1827, many of the community's residents remained when Wright came to share her vision of a day when "all mankind" would "hold with us the jubilee of independence." In this passage, she focuses on the capacity for organic change embedded in America's founding

Figure 35: *Frances Wright delivered her Fourth of July address at New Harmony, Indiana, an experimental utopian community established in 1825 by Welsh manufacturer and social reformer Robert Owen.*

principles, and in the book of nature. In so doing, she identifies something essential about both the Declaration (which speaks not of the attainment but of the *pursuit* of happiness) and the Constitution (which commits to continually striving toward a *more* perfect Union).

Frances Wright, *Fourth of July Address*

New Harmony, Indiana, July 4, 1828

The custom which commemorates in rejoicing the anniversary of the national independence of these states, has its origin in a human feeling, amiable in its nature, and beneficial, under proper direction, in its indulgence.

From the era which dates the national existence of the American people, dates also a mighty step in the march of human knowledge. And it is consistent with that principle in our conformation which leads us to rejoice in the good which befals our species, and to sorrow for the evil, that our hearts should expand on this day;—on this day, which calls to memory the conquest achieved by knowledge over ignorance, willing cooperation over blind obedience, opinion over prejudice, new ways over old ways, when, fifty-two years ago, America declared her national independence, and associated it with her republican federation. Reasonable is it to rejoice on this day, and useful to reflect thereon; so that we rejoice for the real, and not any imaginary good, and reflect on the positive advantages obtained, and on those which it is ours farther to acquire.

Dating, as we justly may, a new era in the history of man from the Fourth of July, 1776, it would be well, that is, it would be useful, if on each anniversary we examined the progress made by our species in just knowledge and just practice. Each Fourth of July would then stand as a tide mark in the flood of time, by which to ascertain the advance of the human intellect, by which to note the rise and fall of each successive error, the discovery of each important truth, the gradual melioration in our public institutions, social arrangements, and, above all, in our moral feelings and mental views. Let such a review as this engage annually our attention, and sacred, doubly sacred, shall be this day; and that not to one nation only, but to all nations capable of reflection!

The political dismemberment of these once British colonies from the parent island, though involving a valuable principle, and many possible results, would scarcely merit a yearly commemoration, even in this country, had it not been accompanied by other occurrences more novel, and far more important. I allude to the seal then set to the system of representative government, till then imperfectly known in Europe, and insecurely practised in America, and to the crown then placed on this system by the novel experiment of political federation. The frame of federative government that sprung out of the articles signed in '76, is one of the most beautiful inventions of the human intellect. It has been in government what the steam engine has been in mechanics, and the printing press in the dissemination of knowledge.

But it needs not that we should now pause to analyse what all must have considered. It is to one particular feature in our political institutions that I would call attention, and this, because it is at once the most deserving of notice, and the least noticed. Are our institutions better than those of other countries? Upon fair examination most men will answer *yes*. But why will they so answer? Is it because they are republican, instead of monarchical? democratic, rather than aristocratic? In so far as the republican principle shall have been proved more conducive to the general good than the monarchical, and the democratic than the aristocratic—in so far will the reasons, be good. But there is another and a better reason than these. There is, in the institutions of this country, one principle, which, had they no other excellence, would secure to them the preference over those of all other countries. I mean—and some devout patriots will start—I mean the principle of *change*.

I have used a word to which is attached an obnoxious meaning. Speak of *change*, and the world is in alarm. And yet where do we not see change? What is there in the physical world *but* change? And what would there be in the moral world *without* change? The flower blossoms, the fruit ripens, the seed is received and germinates in the earth, and we behold the tree. The aliment we eat to satisfy our hunger incorporates with our frame, and the atoms composing our existence to-day, are exhaled to-morrow. In like manner our feelings and opinions are moulded by circumstance, and matured by observation and experience. All is change. Within and about us no one thing is as it was, or will be as it is. Strange, then, that we should start at a word used to signify a thing so familiar! Stranger yet that we should fail to appreciate a principle which, inherent in all matter, is no less inherent in ourselves; and which, as it has tracked our mental progress heretofore, so will it track our progress through time to come!

But will it be said *change* has a bad, as well as a good sense? It may be for the better, and it may be for the worse? In the physical world it can be neither the one nor the other. It can be simply such as it is. But in the moral world—that is, in the thoughts, and feelings, and inventions of men, change may certainly be either for the better or for the worse, or it may be for neither. Changes that are neither bad nor good can have regard *only* to trivial matters, and can be as little worthy of observation as of censure. Changes that are from better to worse can originate only in ignorance, and are ever amended so soon as experience has substantiated their mischief. Where men then are free to consult experience they will correct their practice, and make changes for the better. It follows, therefore, that the more free men are, the more changes they will make. In the beginning, possibly, for the worse; but most certainly in time for the better; until their knowledge enlarging by observation, and their judgment strengthening by exercise, they will find themselves in the straight, broad, fair road of improvement. Out of change, therefore, springs improvement; and the people who shall have imagined a peaceable mode of changing their institutions, hold a surety for their melioration. This surety is worth all other excellencies. Better were the prospects of a people under the influence of the worst government who should hold the power of changing it, than those of a people under the best who should hold no such power. Here, then, is the great beauty of American government. The simple machinery of representation carried through all its parts, gives facility for its being moulded at will to fit with the knowledge of the age. If imperfect in any or all of its parts, it bears within it a perfect principle—the principle of improvement. And, let us observe, that this principle is all that we can ever know of perfection. Knowledge, and all the blessings which spring out of knowledge, can never be more than progressive; and whatsoever *sets open the door* does all for us—does every thing.

The clear sighted provision in the national constitution, as in the constitutions of the different states, by which the frame of government can be moulded at will by the public voice, and so made to keep pace in progress with the public mind, is the master-stroke in constitutional law. Were our institutions far less enlightened and well digested than they are—were every other regulation erroneous, every other ordinance defective—nay, even tyrannous—this single provision would counterbalance all. Let but the door be opened, and be fixed open, for improvement to hold on her unimpeded course, and vices, however flagrant, are but the evils of an hour. Once lanch the animal man in the road of enquiry, and he *shall*—he *must*—hold a forward career. He may be sometimes checked; he may seem occasionally to retrograde; but his retreat is only that of the receding wave in the inning tide. His master movement is always in advance. By this do we distinguish man from all other existences within the range of our observation. By this does he stand pre-eminent over all known animals. By *this*—by his capability of improvement: by his tendency to improve whenever scope is allowed for the developement of his faculties. To hold him *still*, he must be chained. Snap the chain, and he springs forward.

But will it be said, that the chains which bind him are more than one? That political bonds are much, but not all; and that when broken, we may still be slaves? I know not, my friends. We tax our ingenuity to draw nice distinctions. We are told of political liberty—of religious liberty—of moral liberty. Yet, after all, is there more than one liberty; and these divisions, are they not the more and the less of the same thing? The provision we have referred to in our political institutions, as framed in accordance with the principle inherent in ourselves, insures to us all of free action that statutes *can* insure. Supposing that our laws, constitutional, civil, or penal, should in any thing cripple us at the present, the power will be with us to amend or annul them so soon (and how might it be sooner?) as our enlarged knowledge shall enable us to see in what they err. All the liberty therefore that we yet lack will gradually spring up—*there*, where our bondage is—in our minds. To be free we have but to see our chains. Are we disappointed—are we sometimes angry, because the crowd or any part of the crowd around us bows submissively to mischievous usages or unjust laws? Let us remember, that they do so in ignorance of their mischief and injustice, and that when they see these, as in the course of man's progressive state they must see them, these and other evils will be corrected.

Inappreciable is this advantage that we hold (unfortunately) above other nations! The great national and political revolution of '76 set the seal to the liberties of North America. And but for one evil, and that of immense magnitude, which the constitutional provision we have been considering does not fairly reach—I allude to negro slavery and the degradation of our colored citizens—we could foresee for the whole of this magnificent country a certain future of uniform and peaceful improvement. While other nations have still to win reform at the sword's point, we have only to will it. While in Europe men have still to fight, we have only to learn. While there they have to cope with ignorance armed cap-a-pee, encircled with armies and powerful with gold, we have only peacefully to collect knowledge, and to frame our institutions and actions in accordance with it. . . .

Figure 36: *William Lloyd Garrison, seen here in a portrait from 1833, two years before his antislavery advocacy would result in his near-lynching at the hands of an angry mob in Boston.*

One year later, on July 4, 1829, another newcomer took advantage of the anniversary of independence to give a politically charged address. William Lloyd Garrison had grown up in Newburyport, Massachusetts, the son of Canadian immigrants. He learned the printing trade as a teenager and moved to Boston in 1827, where he soon assumed editorship of the *National Philanthropist*, a recently launched pro-temperance newspaper. After a short time as editor of the *Journal of the Times*, an anti-Jackson paper published in Bennington, Vermont, Garrison returned to Boston in March 1829. Having established a modest profile among the city's reform-minded residents, he was invited to speak at the Park Street Church as part of a series sponsored by the Boston branch of the American Colonization Society, an organization supporting efforts to transport free Black people to Africa.

The tenor of Garrison's speech was signaled by its title, "Dangers of the Nation." Instead of the usual patriotic oratory, he begins by criticizing a holiday that had degenerated from its original simplicity into boasting and bingeing. For Garrison, this was symptomatic of a deeper problem: "I speak not as a partisan or an opponent of any man or measures, when I say, that our politics are rotten to the core."

From there he pivots to what will be his main topic, slavery, the nation's original sin, using the Declaration of Independence as his point of departure: "Sirs, I am not come to tell you that slavery is a curse, debasing in its effect, cruel in its operation, fatal in its continuance. The day and the occasion require no such revelation. I do not claim the discovery as my own, that 'all men are born equal,' and that among their inalienable rights are 'life, liberty, and the pursuit of happiness.'"

Having thus evoked the Declaration's soaring preamble, Garrison then turns in this passage from the heart of his speech to its list of grievances, holding them up in withering comparison to the oppressions endured by enslaved

Americans. In the wake of this speech, temperance and other concerns would become secondary for Garrison. Though only twenty-three years old, he had found his life's calling.

William Lloyd Garrison, "Dangers of the Nation"

July 4, 1829

Every Fourth of July, our Declaration of Independence is produced, with a sublime indignation, to set forth the tyranny of the mother country, and to challenge the admiration of the world. But what a pitiful detail of grievances does this document present, in comparison with the wrongs which our slaves endure! In the one case, it is hardly the plucking of a hair from the head; in the other, it is the crushing of a live body on the wheel; the stings of the wasp contrasted with the tortures of the inquisition. Before God I must say, that such a glaring contradiction, as exists between our creed and practice, the annals of five thousand years cannot parallel. In view of it, I am ashamed of my country. I am sick of our unmeaning declamations in praise of liberty and equality—of our hypocritical cant about the unalienable rights of man. I could not, for my right hand, stand up before a European assembly, and exult that I am an American citizen, and denounce the usurpations of a kingly government as wicked and unjust; or, should I make the attempt, the recollection of my country's barbarity and despotism would blister my lips, and cover my cheeks with burning blushes of shame.

Will this be termed a rhetorical flourish? Will any man coldly accuse me of intemperate zeal? I will borrow, then, a ray of humanity from one of the brightest stars in our American galaxy, whose light will gather new effulgence to the end of time:—

"This, Sirs, is a cause, that would be dishonored and betrayed, if I contented myself with appealing only to the understanding. It is too cold, and its processes are too slow for the occasion. I desire to thank God, that, since he has given me an intellect so fallible, he has impressed upon me an instinct that is sure. On a question of shame and honor—liberty and oppression—reasoning is sometimes useless and worse. I feel the decision in my pulse: if it throws no light upon the brain, it kindles a fire at the heart."

Let us suppose that endurance has passed its bounds, and that the slaves, goaded to desperation by the cruelty of their oppressors, have girded on the armor of vengeance. Let us endeavor to imagine the appeal which they would publish to the world, in extenuation of their revolt. The preamble might be taken from our own Declaration of Independence, with a few slight alterations. Then what a detail of wrongs would follow! . . .

We say, that the disabilities imposed upon our fathers, by the mother country, furnished just cause for rebellion; that their removal was paramount to every other consideration; and that the slaughter of our oppressors was a justifiable act—for we should resist unto blood to save our liberties. Suppose that tomorrow should bring us tidings that the slaves at the South had revolted, *en masse*, and were spreading devastation and death among the white population. Should we celebrate their achievements in song, and justify their terrible excesses? And why not, if our own creed be right? Their wrongs are unspeakably grievous, and liberty is the birthright of every man.

We say, that France was justified in assisting our fathers to maintain their independence; and that, as a nation, we owe her our liveliest gratitude for her timely interference. Suppose, in case of a revolt, that she, or some other European power, should furnish our slaves with guns and ammunition, and pour her troops into our land. Would it be treacherous or cruel? Why—according to our revolutionary credenda? The argument—tremendous as it is—is against us! WELL—IT MAY BE DONE. At a fit moment, a foreign foe may stir up a rebellion, and arm every black, and take the lead in the enterprise. The attempt would not be difficult; the result can be easily imagined.

We say, that the impressment of an inconsiderable number of our seamen, by Great Britain, authorized the late war; and we boast of our promptitude to redress their wrongs. More than a million of native-born citizens are at this moment enduring the galling yoke of slavery. Who cries for justice? None. "But they are blacks!" True—and they are also men—and, moreover, they are Americans by birth.

I come to my second proposition:—the right of the free States to remonstrate against the continuance, and to assist in the overthrow of slavery.

This, I am aware, is a delicate subject, surrounded with many formidable difficulties. But if delay only adds to its intricacy, wherefore shun an immediate investigation? I know that we, of the North, affectedly believe, that we have no local interest in the removal of this great evil; that the slave States can take care of themselves, and that any proffered assistance, on our part, would be rejected as impertinent, dictatorial or meddlesome; and that we have no right to lift up even a note of remonstrance. But I believe that these opinions are crude, preposterous, dishonorable, unjust. Sirs, this is a business in which, as members of one great family, we have a common interest; but we take no responsibility, either individually or collectively. Our hearts are cold—our blood stagnates in our veins. We act, in relation to the slaves, as if they were something lower than the brutes that perish.

On this question, I ask no support from the injunction of Holy Writ, which says:—"therefore all things whatsoever ye would that men should do to you, do ye even so to them: for this is the law and the prophets." I throw aside the common dictates of humanity. I assert the right of the free States to demand a gradual abolition of slavery, because, by its continuance, they participate in the guilt thereof, and are threatened with ultimate destruction; because they are bound to watch over the interests of the whole country, without reference to territorial divisions; because their white population is nearly double that of the slave States, and the voice of this overwhelming majority should be potential; because they are now deprived of their just influence in the councils of the nation; because it is absurd and anti-republican to suffer property to be represented as men, and *vice versa*; because it gives the South an unjust ascendancy over other portions of territory, and a power which may be perverted on every occasion. . . .

Now I say that, on the broad system of equal rights, this monstrous inequality should no longer be tolerated. If it cannot be speedily put down—not by force, but by fair persuasion; if we are always to remain shackled by unjust constitutional provisions, when the emergency that imposed them has long since passed away; if we must share in the guilt and danger of destroying the bodies and souls of men, *as the price of our Union*; if the slave States will haughtily spurn our assistance, and refuse to consult the general welfare; then the fault is not ours if a separation eventually take place. . . .

The inauguration of Andrew Jackson in March 1829 brought an infusion of outsider energy into national politics. Not for the last time, a swarm of the new president's followers arrived in Washington, determined to purify a capital that had sold its soul to insiders, lobbyists, and profiteers. In other words, they hoped to "drain the swamp," a metaphor that was already being used in the nineteenth century, accurately enough for a federal city with toxic canals and severe irrigation problems.

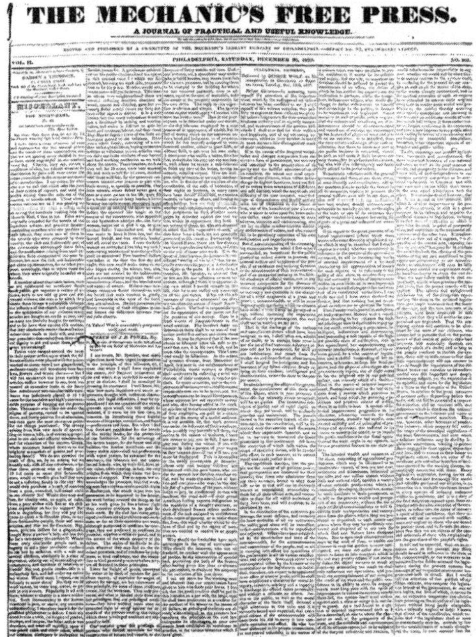

THE MECHANIC'S FREE PRESS.

A JOURNAL OF PRACTICAL AND USEFUL KNOWLEDGE.

Figure 37: First published in the New York Working Man's Advocate, *"The Working Men's Declaration of Independence" was soon reprinted in the Philadelphia* Mechanic's Free Press, *one of the nation's first and largest labor newspapers.*

The first president to come from the West, Jackson brought with him a rough-hewn aura that appealed to the so-called Common Man: the frontiersman, the mechanic, and the farmer. Jackson would famously say in his 1832 annual message to Congress that the "wealth and strength of a country are its population, and the best part of that population are the cultivators of the soil." Drawing supporters from every region, Jackson's broad appeal laid the groundwork for a new, expansive Democratic Party.

Although Southern Jacksonians remained sensitive about racial matters, the party was broadly attuned to the promise of equality, and by natural extension, to the Declaration. Many cheered these developments, spurred on by a partisan press that amplified Jackson's agenda. But for some, "Jacksonian Democracy" seemed little more than a veneer covering politics as usual. Its rise stimulated the formation of an opposition party—the Whigs—and also had the effect of inspiring more radical movements.

One such movement was the New York Working Men's Party, a short-lived political group formed in 1829 (by, among others, Robert Dale Owen, son of New Harmony's founder). The party started its own newspaper, edited and largely written by a self-styled mechanic named George Henry Evans, who had immigrated from England earlier in the decade. To introduce the movement, and to situate it squarely within the American political tradition, he framed a pro-labor declaration of independence that sought to make the promise of equality actionable by turning the nebulous idea of the "pursuit of happiness" into a more practical matter of "means."

The Working Men's Declaration of Independence.

December 1829

"When, in the course of human events, it becomes necessary" for one class of a community to assert their natural and unalienable rights in opposition to other classes of their fellow men, "and to assume among" them a political "station of equality to which the laws of nature and of nature's God," as well as the principles of their political compact, "entitle them; a decent respect to the opinions of mankind," and the more paramount duty they owe to their own fellow citizens, "requires that they should declare the causes which impel them" to adopt so painful, yet so necessary, a measure.

"We hold these truths to be self evident, that all men are *created equal*; that they are endowed by their creator with certain unalienable rights; that among these are *life, liberty,* and the *pursuit of happiness*; that to secure these rights" against the undue influence of other classes of society, prudence, as well as the claims of self defence, dictates the necessity of the organization of a party, who shall, by their representatives, prevent dangerous combinations to subvert these indefeasible and fundamental privileges. "All experience hath shown, that mankind" in general, and *we as a class in particular*, "are more disposed to suffer, while evils are sufferable, than to right themselves," by an opposition which the pride and self interest of unprincipled political aspirants, with more unprincipled zeal or religious bigotary, will wilfully misrepresent. "But when a long train of abuses and usurpations" take place, all invariably tending to the oppression and degradation of one class of society, and to the unnatural and iniquitous exaltation of another by political leaders, "it is their right, it is their duty," to use every constitutional means to *reform* the abuses of such a government, and to provide new guards for their future security. The history of the political *parties* in this state, is a history of political *iniquities*, all tending to the enacting and enforcing oppressive and unequal laws. To prove this, let facts be submitted to the candid and impartial of our fellow citizens of all parties.

1.—The laws for levying taxes are all based on erroneous principles, in consequence of their operating most oppressively on one class of society, and being scarcely felt by the other.

2.—The laws regarding the duties of jurors, witnesses, and militia trainings, are still more unequal and oppressive.

3.—The laws for private incorporations are all partial in their operations; favoring one class of society to the expense of the other, who have no equal participation.

4.—The laws incorporating religious societies have a pernicious tendency, by promoting the erection of magnificent places of public worship, by the rich, excluding others, and which others cannot imitate; consequently engendering spiritual pride in the clergy and people, and thereby creating odious distinctions in society, destructive to its social peace and happiness.

5.—The laws establishing and patronizing seminaries of learning are unequal, favoring the rich, and perpetuating imparity, which natural causes have produced, and which judicious laws ought, and can, remedy.

6.—The laws and municipal ordinances and regulations, generally, besides those specially enumerated, have heretofore been ordained on such principles, as have deprived nine tenths of the members of the body politic, who are *not* wealthy, of the *equal means* to enjoy "*life, liberty, and the pursuit of happiness*," which the *rich* enjoy exclusively; but the federative compact intended to secure to all, indiscriminately. The lien law in favor of landlords against tenants, and all other honest creditors, is one illustration among innumerable others which can be adduced to prove the truth of these allegations.

We have trusted to the influence of the justice and good sense of our political leaders, to prevent the continuance of these abuses, which destroy the natural bands of equality, so essential to the attainment of moral happiness, "but they have been deaf alike to the voice of justice and of consanguinity."

Therefore, we, the working class of society, of the city of New York, "appealing to the supreme judge of the world," and to the reason, and consciences of the impartial of all parties, "for the rectitude of our intentions, do, in the spirit, and by the authority," of that political liberty which has been promised to us equally with our fellow men, solemnly publish and declare, and invite all under like pecuniary circumstances, together with every liberal mind, to join us in the declaration, "that we are, & of right ought to be," entitled to EQUAL MEANS to obtain equal moral happiness, and social enjoyment, and that all lawful and constitutional measures ought to be adopted to the attainment of those objects. "And for the support of this declaration, we mutually pledge to each other" our faithful aid to the end of our lives.

The declaration of our rights, and brief allegation of our grievances, will I am confident, be responded to by more than three fourths of the numbers of this nation. There wants but a determined moral courage to support them against designing and interested partizans, in order to secure those great blessings for ourselves and for posterity.

The seeds of moral happiness are sown with as unbounded a liberality, as are those so necessary for our physical wants. To the attainment of even the latter, in any degree of perfection, labor and toil, with great intellectual exertions, are, by the invariable laws of nature, indispensable. Even so with our moral happiness; it is only through the discreet and judicious exercise of our mental powers that we can attain any degree of felicity. The bane of every nation on the face of the earth, has been the debased state of PUBLIC OPINION; a wicked and an unprincipled *few* have given tone to it, and the honest *many* have submitted to their own consequent degradation. A moral *influence*, fatal to our social enjoyment has usurped the power, where the full exertion of our intellectual faculties ought to control and to govern us. The crisis has now arrived. To obtain our political and religious rights, *collectively*, we must exert our moral courage *individually*. The voice of nature loudly calls for these exertions, and the sacred claims of families and posterity repeats the call in mental echos.

In 1831, in zombie-like fashion, the Mecklenburg Declaration of Independence sprang to life again, reanimated by the Nullification Crisis in South Carolina, a fiery dispute over tariffs and state sovereignty that threatened to upend not only Jackson's administration but the very premise of the Union. Jackson had come into office with the unenviable task of enforcing the so-called Tariff of Abominations, a schedule of punishing import duties passed by Congress during the administration of his predecessor, John Quincy Adams. The South, dependent upon imports, erupted in protest. South Carolina's leaders, including Vice President John C. Calhoun, took the lead, positing that state legislatures could "interpose" themselves between their citizens and federal laws the state deemed unconstitutional, effectively nullifying them.

Figure 38: *This 1833 political cartoon depicts the nullification theories of John C. Calhoun of South Carolina as a precursor to civil war and despotic rule, with Andrew Jackson ("Stop, you have gone too far, or by the Eternal I'll hang you all") struggling to restrain their influence.*

In the midst of this crisis, Governor Montford Stokes of neighboring North Carolina issued a pamphlet staking a claim for the primacy (and by implication the veracity) of the Mecklenburg Declaration of May 1775. That document's assertion of local sovereignty took on unmistakable new significance in the context of the ongoing debate over states' rights, effectively backdating the nullifiers' vision of the United States as a confederation of autonomous and self-governing political entities. Former president Adams, now a newly elected congressman from Massachusetts, was not impressed. He used his hometown's annual Fourth of July observances to offer a forceful rebuttal to the nullifiers in what amounted to a landmark new reading of the Declaration of Independence.

John Quincy Adams, *An Oration addressed to the Citizens of the Town of Quincy on the Fourth of July, 1831*

July 4, 1831

. . . Ten years of controversy, and more than one of civil war, preceded the Declaration, "that these United Colonies are, and of right ought to be, free and independent states; that they are absolved from all allegiance to the British crown, and that all political connexion between them and the state of Great Britain, is, and ought to be totally dissolved."

The union of the Colonies had preceded this Declaration and even the commencement of the war. The Declaration was joint, that the United Colonies were free and independent states, but not that any one of them was a free and independent state, separate from the rest. In the Constitution of this Commonwealth it is declared, that the body politic is formed by a voluntary association of individuals; that it is a social compact, by which the whole people covenants with each citizen, and each citizen with the whole people, that all shall be governed by certain laws, for the common good. The body politic of the United States was formed by the voluntary association of the people of the United Colonies. The Declaration of Independence was a social compact, by which the whole people covenanted with each citizen of the United Colonies, and each citizen with the whole people, that the United Colonies were, and of right ought to be, free and independent states. To this compact, union was as vital as freedom or independence. From the hour of that Declaration, no one of the States whose people were parties to it, could, without violation of that primitive compact, secede or separate from the rest. Each was pledged to all, and all were pledged to each by a concert of souls, without limitation of time, in the presence of Almighty God, and proclaimed to all mankind. The Colonies were not declared *sovereign* states. The term sovereign is not even to be found in the Declaration; and far, very far was it from the contemplation of those who composed, or of those who adopted it, to constitute either the aggregate community, or any one of its members, with absolute, uncontrollable or despotic power. They are united, free and independent States. Each of these properties is equally essential to their existence. Without union the *covenant* contains no pledge of freedom or independence; without freedom, none of independence or union; without independence, none of union or freedom.

In the history of the world, this was the first example of a self-constituted nation proclaiming to the rest of mankind the principles upon which it was associated, and deriving those principles from the laws of nature. It has sometimes been objected to the paper, that it deals too much in abstractions. But this was its characteristic excellence; for upon those abstractions hinged the justice of the cause. Without them, our revolution would have been but successful rebellion. Right, truth, justice, are all abstractions. The Divinity that stirs within the soul of man is abstraction. The Creator of the universe is a spirit, and all spiritual nature is abstraction. Happy would it be, could we answer with equal confidence another objection, not to the Declaration, but to the consistency of the people by whom it was proclaimed! Thrice happy, could the appeal to the Supreme Judge of the World for rectitude of intention, and with firm reliance on the protection of Divine Providence for support, have been accompanied with an appeal equally bold to our own social institutions to illustrate the self-evident truths which we declared!

The Declaration of Independence was not a declaration of liberty newly acquired, nor was it a form of government. The people of the Colonies were already free, and their forms of government were various. They were all Colonies of a monarchy. The king of Great Britain was their common sovereign. Their internal administrations presented great varieties of form. The proprietary governments were hereditary monarchies in miniature. New York and Virginia were feudal aristocracies. Massachusetts Bay was an approximation to the complex government of the parent state. Connecticut and Rhode Island were little remote from democracies. But as in the course of our recent war with Great Britain, her gallant naval warriors made the discovery that the frigates of the United States were line of battle ships in disguise, so the ministers of George III., when they brought their king and country into collision with these transatlantic dependencies, soon found to their astonishment, that the United American Colonies were republics in disguise. The spirit of the people, throughout the Union, was republican; and the absurdity of a foreign and a royal head to societies of men thus constituted, had remained unperceived, only because until then that head had been seldom brought into action.

The Declaration of Independence announced the severance of the thirteen United Colonies from the rest of the British Empire, and the existence of their people from that day forth as an independent nation. The people of all the Colonies, speaking by their representatives, constituted themselves one moral person before the face of their fellow men. Frederic I., of Brandenburg, constituted himself king of Prussia, by putting a crown upon his own head. Napoleon Bonaparte invested his brows with the iron crown of Lombardy, and declared himself king of Italy. The Declaration of Independence was the crown with which the people of United America, rising in gigantic stature as one man, encircled their brows, and there it remains; there, so long as this globe shall be inhabited by human beings, may it remain, a crown of imperishable glory!

The Declaration of Independence asserted the rights, and acknowledged the obligations of an independent nation. It recognised the laws of nations, as they were observed and practised among Christian communities. It considered the state of nature between nations as a state of peace; and, as a necessary consequence, that the new confederacy was at peace with all other nations, Great Britain alone excepted. It made no change in the laws—none in the internal administration of any one of the confederates, other than such as necessarily followed from the dissolution of the connexion with Great Britain. It left all municipal legislation, all regulation of private individual rights and interests, to the people of each separate Colony; and each separate Colony, thus transformed into a State of the Union, wrought for itself a constitution of government.

There remained to be formed a confederate government for the whole Union; and of this, an abortive experiment was made by the co-operation of Congress with the State Legislatures, without recurrence to the fountain of power, the people. This error proved well nigh fatal to the Union, and to the liberties of the whole. It palsied in a great degree the subsequent operations of the war; it prostrated the faith and energy of the nation in peace; it became a source of impotence in all the relations of the country with foreign powers; of mutual irritation, discord and anarchy at home. It disabled the nation from the performance of its engagements to others, and from the means of exacting the fulfilment of theirs in return. It degraded the country in the eyes of the world, and disgraced the glorious cause in which our national independence had been achieved. It embittered the hearts, and armed the hands of our citizens against one another, till our judicial tribunals were sullied with trials for treason, and our legislative records blackened with proclamations of rebellion.

In our own Commonwealth, the blood of her citizens was shed by each other, on the field of battle, and the scaffold thirsted for that of her children. Never, even during the gloomiest moments of the revolutionary war, had the condition of the country been so calamitous as in the years immediately succeeding the peace, in the very triumph of our cause, and in the full and undisputed enjoyment of our independence.

The primary cause of all these misfortunes and all these crimes, was the same mistaken estimate of sovereignty which the British Parliament had made, when they undertook to levy money upon the Colonies by taxation. The separate States of the Union, using a term which appears to have been studiously avoided in the Declaration of Independence, declared themselves, not only free and independent, but *sovereign* States;—and then their lawyers, adopting the doctrine of Blackstone, the oracle of English law, inferred that *sovereign* must necessarily be uncontrollable, unlimited, despotic power. Assuming, like the eminent commentator, that in all governments this power must exist *somewhere*, and that it is inherent in the very definition of sovereignty, with about as much plausibility as he deposits it in the British Parliament, they made no hesitation to entrust it to the governments of the separate States.

It were an abuse of your time and patience, fellow citizens, to recall to your memory all the vagaries into which this political sophism of identity between *sovereign* and *despotic* power, has led, and continues to lead, some of the Statists of this our happy but disputatious Union. It seizes upon the brain of a heated politician sometimes in one State, sometimes in another, and its natural offspring is the doctrine of nullification;—that is, the *sovereign* power of any one State of the confederacy to nullify any act of the whole twenty-four States, which the *sovereign* State shall please to consider as unconstitutional;—an error sustained by reasoners too respectable to be treated with derision, and, apart from that consideration, too absurd to be encountered with serious argument. Even under our present Federal Constitution, it has been directly asserted, or imprudently countenanced, at one time in Virginia and Kentucky, at another in Massachusetts and Connecticut, now in the temperate climate of Pennsylvania, and again in the warmer regions of the South. Fortunate has it been for our country, that the paroxysms of this fever have hitherto proved not extensively contagious! But we are admonished by one of the profoundest philosophers of modern ages,* not to measure the danger of discontentments in the body politic by this,—whether they be just or unjust; nor yet by this, whether the griefs whereupon they rise, be great or small—neither to be secure, because they have been often or long, without ensuing peril. Not every fume or vapor turns indeed to a storm, but from vapors and exhalations imperceptibly gathered, the tempest of desolation does come at last.

* Lord Bacon

It was this hallucination of State sovereignty, identified with unlimited power, which blasted the Confederation from its birth. The delegates in Congress were representatives of the State Legislatures; for as such only they acted in the formation of the articles of confederation. The State Legislatures were representatives of the people of each separate State. Between these two representative bodies, primary and secondary, of the same parties, a Confederation was elaborated for the whole Union, memorable only for its impotence.

It was formed by many of the same pure and exalted patriots, who had pledged their lives, their fortunes, and their sacred honor, to the independence of their country. It was made with long, painful and anxious deliberation, animated with the most ardent love of liberty, purified with perfect disinterestedness, and digested with consummate ability. It was a bloodless corpse! Fire from Heaven alone could have given it life; and that fire, unduly sought, brought with it Pandora and her box. In the establishment of the Confederation the people of the whole Union had no part. It was an alliance of States, intent above all things to preserve their *sovereignty* entire; averse above all things to confer power, because power might be abused; and also because they perceived that every grant of power to the confederate body could be made only by the relinquishment of their own. These, however, were errors, not of intention, nor even of judgment so much as of inexperience. The Union was a novelty. Self-government was an innovation. The idea of recurring to the people of the Union for a constitution, does not appear to have presented itself then to any mind. Yet the Declaration of Independence had been issued in the name and by the authority of the whole people. The total inefficiency of the Confederation to fulfil any of the good offices for which it was intended, reinspired the idea of recurring to the first source of all political power, the people.

Thus rose to birth the Constitution of the United States under which we yet live. It was formed by a Convention of Delegates, appointed by the Legislatures of the respective States, upon a recommendation of Congress, under a profound conviction of its own incompetency to administer the affairs of the Union, either at home or abroad. The work of the Convention, when completed, was by their President, Washington, transmitted to Congress; and by them to the Legislatures of the several States. These, without undertaking to decide upon it themselves, referred it back to the people, by whom it was sanctioned through the medium of Conventions specially elected in every State, who, after long investigation, and severe scrutiny, accepted, adopted, and made it the supreme law of the land, anything in the constitution or laws of any State to the contrary notwithstanding.

In the formation of Constitutions for the several States, similar errors of inexperience were committed. The Constitutions were all republican, all popular—not monarchical—not military. An article amendatory to the Constitution of the United States, declares that the powers *not delegated* to the United States by the Constitution, nor prohibited by it to the States, are reserved to the States respectively, or to the people. There are powers, then, powers of government, reserved to the people, and which never have been delegated either to the United or to the separate States; nor do the United States, nor the separate States possess any powers, not delegated to them by the people—by the people of the whole Union to the United States—by the people of each separate State to that State. Hence it follows, too, that the people of each State were incompetent to delegate to the State, any power already delegated by the people of the whole Union to the United States. It was the people of the whole Union, who had declared the United Colonies free and independent States. But those States possessed no powers but such as had been delegated to the Colonies by their charters, or as, after their becoming States, were delegated to them by the people. There was no such thing in their constitutions as an absolute, irresistible, despotic power, lurking *somewhere* under the cabalistic denomination of *sovereignty*. In some of the States, the people thought it unnecessary to form new Constitutions. They abided by the forms of government established by their charters. In one, the ordinary Legislature of the State modified their government without consulting the people;—an usurpation sanctioned by the acquiescence of the people, until a very recent day, but now rectified. Of those which did form Constitutions during the revolutionary war, every one, New Jersey perhaps excepted, has within the first half century found a revisal of its own necessary. New powers have from time to time been delegated by the People of each State to their government; powers previously delegated have been annulled: but in vain would you search all the Constitutions past or present of the States, for a power to nullify any act of the United States in Congress assembled. The people of no State were competent to grant such a power. The pretence to grant it would itself have been null and void—a violation of the Constitution of the United States; a violation of the Declaration of Independence. . . .

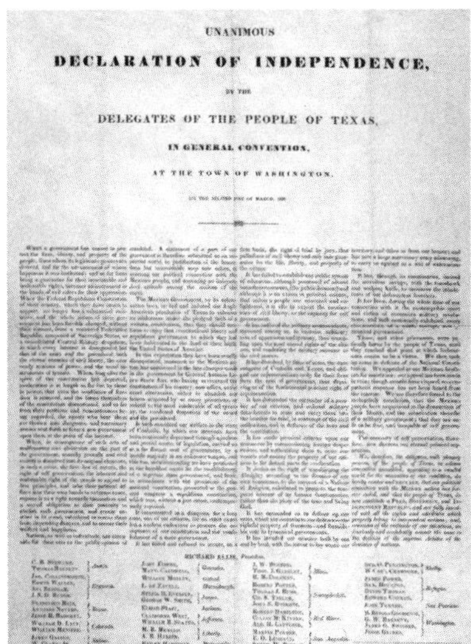

UNANIMOUS

DECLARATION OF INDEPENDENCE,

BY THE

DELEGATES OF THE PEOPLE OF TEXAS,

IN GENERAL CONVENTION,

AT THE TOWN OF WASHINGTON.

***Figure 39:** The Texas Declaration of Independence, seen here, was signed and published on March 2, 1836, just four days before Mexican forces overwhelmed the defenders of the Alamo.*

The Nullification Crisis, though nominally a dispute over tariffs and states' rights, also raised acute concerns relating to slavery. For many in the South, it was a short step from federal "interference" in economic matters to a more direct assault on the peculiar institution. That led to furious arguments in Congress, and deep divisions over where and how the United States should expand.

Texas was a signal case in point. Since slavery had been blocked from the Northwest Territories in 1787, the slaveholding class had necessarily looked to expand in a new direction, toward the southwest and Mexico. After Mexico secured its own independence from Spain in 1821, Americans began to cross into the country's northern province of Texas. Their presence was initially encouraged by the Mexican government, which made the land readily available to settlers who would follow its laws and profess Christianity (which in Mexico was equated with Catholicism). This arrangement grew more problematic after the Mexican Republic outlawed slavery in 1829, albeit with a carve-out for Texas. For the American settlers, the writing was on the wall, and they began to contemplate the prospect of annexation to the country of their birth. But before Texas could join the United States, it became an independent republic in 1836—requiring a declaration all its own.

In some ways, the Texans borrowed from the Declaration of Independence, echoing certain phrases ("a candid world") and describing the various tyrannies they felt they were living under. There is in both texts an unmistakable aversion to Catholicism, and a tendency to dehumanize Native Americans ("merciless savages"). But in one important way the Texans departed from the template the Declaration offered, eschewing its language about equality as they set about creating a society dependent upon slavery. They also discarded "the pursuit of happiness" in favor of "life, liberty, and property."

Texas Declaration of Independence

March 2, 1836

When a government has ceased to protect the lives, liberty, and property of the people, from whom its legitimate powers are derived, and for the advancement of whose happiness it was instituted; and so far from being a guarantee for their inestimable and inalienable rights, becomes an instrument in the hands of evil rulers for their oppression. When the Federal Republican Constitution of their country, which they have sworn to support, no longer has a substantial existence, and the whole nature of their government has been forcibly changed, without their consent, from a restricted Federative Republic, composed of Sovereign States, to a consolidated Central Military despotism, in which every interest is disregarded but that of the army and the priesthood, both the eternal enemies of civil liberty, the ever ready minions of power, and the usual instruments of tyrants. When, long after the spirit of the constitution has departed, moderation is at length so far lost by those in power, that even the semblance of freedom is removed, and the forms themselves of the constitution discontinued, and so far from their petitions and remonstrances being regarded, the agents who bear them are thrown into dungeons, and mercenary armies sent forth to force a new government upon them at the point of the bayonet.

When, in consequence of such acts of malfeasance and abduction on the part of the government, anarchy prevails and civil society is dissolved into its original elements, in such a crisis, the first law of nature, the right of self preservation, the inherent and inalienable right of the people to appeal to first principles, and take their political affairs into their own hands in extreme cases, enjoins it as a right towards themselves and a sacred obligation to their posterity to abolish such government, and create another in its stead, calculated to rescue them from impending dangers, and to secure their welfare and happiness.

Nations, as well as individuals, are amenable for their acts to the public opinion of mankind. A statement of a part of our grievances is therefore submitted to an impartial world, in justification of the hazardous but unavoidable step now taken, of severing our political connection with the Mexican people, and assuming an independent attitude among the nations of the earth.

The Mexican Government, by its colonization laws, invited and induced the Anglo American population of Texas to colonize its wilderness under the pledged faith of a written constitution, that they should continue to enjoy that constitutional liberty and republican government to which they had been habituated in the land of their birth, the United States of America.

In this expectation they have been cruelly disappointed, inasmuch as the Mexican nation has acquiesced in the late changes made in the government by General Antonio Lopez Santa Ana, who having overturned the constitution of his country, now offers, as the cruel alternative, either to abandon our homes acquired by so many privations, or submit to the most intolerable of all tyranny, the combined despotism of the sword and the priesthood.

It hath sacrificed our welfare to the state of Coahuila, by which our interests have been continually depressed through a jealous and partial course of legislation, carried on at a far distant seat of government, by a hostile majority in an unknown tongue, and this too, notwithstanding we have petitioned in the humblest terms for the establishment of a separate state government, and have, in accordance with the provisions of the national constitution, presented to the general congress a republican constitution, which was, without a just cause, contemptuously rejected.

It incarcerated in a dungeon, for a long time, one of our citizens, for no other cause but a zealous endeavour to procure the acceptance of our constitution and the establishment of a state government.

It has failed and refused to secure, on a firm basis, the right of trial by jury, that palladium of civil liberty and only safe guarantee for the life, liberty, and property of the citizen.

It has failed to establish any public system of education, although possessed of almost boundless resources, (the public domain;) and although it is an axiom in political science, that unless a people are educated and enlightened, it is idle to expect the continuance of civil liberty, or the capacity for self government.

It has suffered the military commandants, stationed among us, to exercise arbitrary acts of oppression and tyranny, thus trampling upon the most sacred rights of the citizen, and rendering the military superior to the civil power.

It has dissolved, by force of arms, the state congress of Coahuila and Texas, and obliged our representatives to fly for their lives from the seat of government, thus depriving us of the fundamental political right of representation.

It has demanded the surrender of a number of our citizens, and ordered military detachments to seize and carry them into the interior for trial, in contempt of the civil authorities, and in defiance of the laws and the constitution.

It has made piratical attacks upon our commerce by commissioning foreign desperadoes, and authorizing them to seize our vessels and convey the property of our citizens to far distant parts for confiscation.

It denies us the right of worshipping the Almighty according to the dictates of our own conscience, by the support of a National Religion, calculated to promote the temporal interest of its human functionaries, rather than the glory of the true and living God.

It has demanded us to deliver up our arms, which are essential to our defence—the rightful property of freemen—and formidable only to tyrannical governments.

It has invaded our country both by sea and by land, with the intent to lay waste our territory, and drive us from our homes; and has now a large mercenary army advancing, to carry on against us a war of extermination.

It has, through its emissaries, incited the merciless savage, with the tomahawk and scalping knife, to massacre the inhabitants of our defenceless frontiers.

It has been, during the whole time of our connection with it, the contemptible sport and victim of successive military revolutions, and hath continually exhibited every characteristic of a weak, corrupt, and tyrannical government.

These, and other grievances, were patiently borne by the people of Texas, until they reached that point at which forbearance ceases to be a virtue. We then took up arms in defence of the National Constitution. We appealed to our Mexican brethren for assistance: our appeal has been made in vain; though months have elapsed, no sympathetic response has yet been heard from the interior. We are therefore forced to the melancholy conclusion, that the Mexican people have acquiesced in the destruction of their liberty, and the substitution therefor of a military government; that they are unfit to be free, and incapable of self government.

The necessity of self preservation, therefore, now decrees our eternal political separation.

We, therefore, the delegates, with plenary powers, of the people of Texas, in solemn convention assembled, appealing to a candid world for the necessities of our condition, do hereby resolve and DECLARE, *that our political connection with the Mexican nation has forever ended, and that the people of Texas, do now constitute a* FREE, SOVEREIGN, *and* INDEPENDENT REPUBLIC, *and are fully invested with all the rights and attributes which properly belong to independent nations; and, conscious of the rectitude of our intentions, we fearlessly and confidently commit the issue to the decision of the supreme Arbiter of the destinies of nations.*

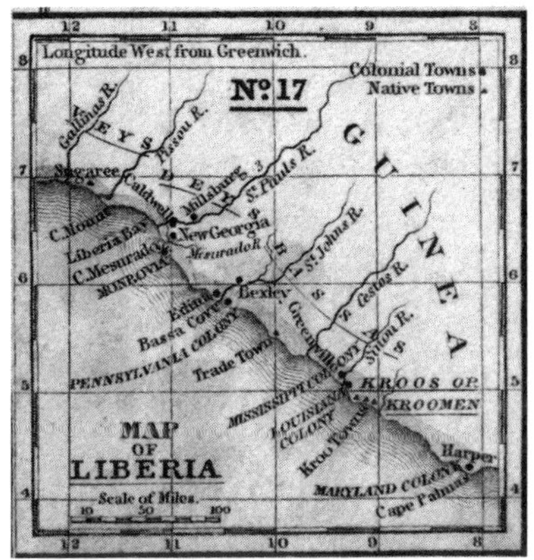

Figure 40: *This 1839 map of Liberia shows both native towns and colonial settlements, including the capital Monrovia, named for U.S. president James Monroe.*

Eleven years after Americans in Texas declared independence, initiating a protracted process that would lead to annexation (and war with Mexico), another very different group of Americans did so in Africa.

Since 1822, the American Colonization Society had been sending free people of color to West Africa. The idea was controversial. Viewed in a favorable light, it was a philanthropic endeavor to make amends for American complicity in slavery, perhaps even promote democracy in another part of the world. At the same time, colonization testified to a deep ambivalence about the possibility of a multiracial polity in the United States. For many Black Americans, the Society's efforts to remove them from the national life was an affront. Frederick Douglass spoke for them when he said defiantly: "We live here—have lived here—have a right to live here, and mean to live here."

The contradictions embedded within the Society's colonial enterprise translated into spotty and inconsistent supervision of its largest project, the colony of Liberia, on the coast of West Africa. Throughout the 1830s and 1840s, settlers in Liberia chafed against rules not of their own making, imposed on them by the Society's white leadership in the United States. Finally, in 1847, a dozen leading settlers banded together to launch a new government. As had the Texans, the Liberians borrowed much of the language of the Declaration, but with one crucial difference. The right to life and liberty was essential to this new African country. In addition, the Liberian Declaration offered a blistering critique of just how unfree life had felt to these African Americans (turned American Africans) while they still lived in the United States.

Liberian Declaration of Independence

July 29, 1847

We the representatives of the people of the Commonwealth of Liberia, in Convention assembled, invested with authority for forming a new government, relying upon the aid and protection of the Great Arbiter of human events, do hereby, in the name, and on the behalf of the people of this Commonwealth, publish and declare the said Commonwealth a FREE, SOVEREIGN, AND INDEPENDENT STATE, by the name and title of the REPUBLIC OF LIBERIA.

While announcing to the nations of the world the new position which the people of this Republic have felt themselves called upon to assume, courtesy to their opinion seems to demand a brief accompanying statement of the causes which induced them, first to expatriate themselves from the land of their nativity and to form settlements on this barbarous coast, and now to organize their government by the assumption of a sovereign and independent character. Therefore we respectfully ask their attention to the following facts.

We recognise in all men, certain natural and inalienable rights: among these are life, liberty, and the right to acquire, possess, enjoy and defend property. By the practice and consent of men in all ages, some system or form of government is proven to be necessary to exercise, enjoy and secure those rights; and every people have a right to institute a government, and to choose and adopt that system or form of it, which in their opinion will most effectually accomplish these objects, and secure their happiness, which does not interfere with the just rights of others. The right therefore to institute government, and to all the powers necessary to conduct it, is, an inalienable right, and cannot be resisted without the grossest injustice.

We the people of the Republic of Liberia were originally the inhabitants of the United States of North America.

In some parts of that country, we were debarred by law from all the rights and privileges of men—in other parts, public sentiment, more powerful than law, frowned us down.

We were every where shut out from all civil office.

We were excluded from all participation in the government.

We were taxed without our consent.

We were compelled to contribute to the resources of a country, which gave us no protection.

We were made a separate and distinct class, and against us every avenue to improvement was effectually closed. Strangers from all lands of a color different from ours, were preferred before us.

We uttered our complaints, but they were unattended to, or only met by alledging the peculiar institutions of the country.

All hope of a favorable change in our country was thus wholly extinguished in our bosoms, and we looked with anxiety abroad for some asylum from the deep degradation.

The Western coast of Africa was the place selected by American benevolence and philanthropy, for our future home. Removed beyond those influences which depressed us in our native land, it was hoped we would be enabled to enjoy those rights and privileges, and exercise and improve those faculties, which the God of nature has given us in common with the rest of mankind.

Under the auspices of the American Colonization Society, we established ourselves here, on land acquired by purchase from the Lords of the soil.

In an original compact with this Society, we, for important reasons delegated to it certain political powers; while this institution stipulated that whenever the people should become capable of conducting the government, or whenever the people should desire it, this institution would resign the delegated power, peacably withdraw its supervision, and leave the people to the government of themselves.

Under the auspices and guidance of this institution, which has nobly and in perfect faith redeemed its pledges to the people, we have grown and prospered.

From time to time, our number has been increased by migration from America, and by accessions from native tribes; and from time to time, as circumstances required it, we have extended our borders by acquisition of land by honorable purchase from the natives of the country.

As our territory has extended, and our population increased, our commerce has also increased. The flags of most of the civilized nations of the earth float in our harbors, and their merchants are opening an honorable and profitable trade. Until recently, these visits have been of a uniformly harmonious character, but as they have become more frequent, and to more numerous points of our extending coast, questions have arisen, which it is supposed can be adjusted only by agreement between sovereign powers.

For years past, the American Colonization Society has virtually withdrawn from all direct and active part in the administration of the government, except in the appointment of the Governor, who is also a colonist, for the apparent purpose of testing the ability of the people to conduct the affairs of government, and no complaint of crude legislation, nor of mismanagement, nor of mal-administration has yet been heard.

In view of these facts, this institution, the American Colonization Society, with that good faith which has uniformly marked all its dealings with us, did, by a set of resolutions in January, in the Year of Our Lord One Thousand Eight Hundred and Forty-Six, dissolve all political connexion with the people of this Republic, return the power with which it was delegated, and left the people to the government of themselves.

The people of the Republic of Liberia then, are of right, and in fact, a free, sovereign and independent State; possessed of all the rights, powers, and functions of government.

In assuming the momentous responsibilities of the position they have taken, the people of this Republic, feel justified by the necessities of the case, and with this conviction they throw themselves with confidence upon the candid consideration of the civilized world.

Liberia is not the offspring of grasping ambition, nor the tool of avaricious speculation.

No desire for territorial aggrandizement brought us to these shores; nor do we believe so sordid a motive entered into the high considerations of those who aided us in providing this asylum.

Liberia is an asylum from the most grinding oppression.

In coming to the shores of Africa, we indulged the pleasing hope that we would be permitted to exercise and improve those faculties, which impart to man his dignity—to nourish in our hearts the flame of honorable ambition, to cherish and indulge those aspirations, which a beneficent Creator had implanted in every human heart, and to evince to all who despise, ridicule and oppress our race, that we possess with them a common nature, are with them susceptible of equal refinement, and capable of equal advancement in all that adorns and dignifies man.

We were animated with the hope, that here we should be at liberty to train up our children in the way they should go—to inspire them with the love of an honorable fame, to kindle within them, the flame of a lofty philanthropy, and to form strong within them, the principles of humanity, virtue and religion.

Among the strongest motives to leave our native land—to abandon forever the scenes of our childhood, and to sever the most endeared connexions, was the desire for a retreat where, free from the agitations of fear and molestation, we could, in composure and security approach in worship, the God of our fathers.

Thus far our highest hopes have been realized.

Liberia is already the happy home of thousands, who were once the doomed victims of oppression, and if left unmolested to go on with her natural and spontaneous growth; if her movements be left free from the paralysing intrigues of jealous, ambitious, and unscrupulous avarice, she will throw open a wider and yet a wider door for thousands, who are now looking with an anxious eye for some land of rest.

Our courts of justice are open equally to the stranger and the citizen for the redress of grievances, for the remedy of injuries, and for the punishment of crime.

Our numerous and well attended schools attest our efforts, and our desire for the improvement of our children.

Our churches for the worship of our Creator, every where to be seen, bear testimony to our piety, and to our acknowledgment of His Providence.

The native African bowing down with us before the altar of the living God, declare that from us, feeble as we are, the light of Christianity has gone forth, while upon that curse of curses, the slave trade, a deadly blight has fallen as far as our influence extends.

Therefore in the name of humanity, and virtue and religion—in the name of the Great God, our common Creator, and our common Judge, we appeal to the nations of Christendom, and earnestly and respectfully ask of them, that they will regard us with the sympathy and friendly consideration, to which the peculiarities of our condition entitle us, and to extend to us, that comity which marks the friendly intercourse of civilized and independent communities.

***Figure 41:** John C. Calhoun, here in an 1845 portrait that captures his fiery intensity, was the nation's most forceful spokesman for a darker, more restrictive reading of the Declaration of Independence.*

As former Americans in Liberia were declaring a nation free from the scourge of slavery, a growing number of Southerners were expressing increasingly strident defenses of human bondage, which they now defined as a positive good, rather than a necessary evil.

To do that, they had to reckon with the Declaration of Independence, and what John C. Calhoun called its "poisonous fruits." Long after his brief and unhappy vice presidency under Andrew Jackson, Calhoun remained a formidable force in the Senate, where he led Southern efforts to block anti-slavery measures. As the United States continued to expand westward, many feared that the new territory seized from Mexico was a poison pill that would finally cause a rupture over slavery. In 1848, tensions surfaced as the Senate debated a bill to admit the Oregon Territory, long disputed between the United States and Great Britain, with a provision banning slavery. This issue contributed to a climate of increasing sectional friction that led two years later to the Compromise of 1850, which would temporarily defuse the situation through a combination of measures to both support slavery (by making it easier to recover escapees from the North) and restrict it (by allowing California to become a free state), while allowing "popular sovereignty" to decide the matter in the remaining western territories. But in 1848 Calhoun was in no mood for a compromise, insisting that slavery must expand along with the United States, and that the idea that "all men are created equal" had become "the most false and dangerous of all political error."

John C. Calhoun, Speech on the Oregon Bill

June 27, 1848

. . . . Now, let me say, Senators, if our Union and system of government are doomed to perish, and we to share the fate of so many great people who have gone before us, the historian, who, in some future day, may record the events ending in so calamitous a result, will devote his first chapter to the ordinance of '87, as lauded as it and its authors have been, as the first to that series which led to it. His next chapter will be devoted to the Missouri compromise, and the next to the present agitation. Whether there will be another beyond, I know not. It will depend on what we may do.

If he should possess a philosophical turn of mind, and be disposed to look to more remote and recondite causes, he will trace it to a proposition which originated in a hypothetical truism, but which, as now expressed and now understood, is the most false and dangerous of all political error. The proposition to which I allude, has become an axiom in the minds of a vast many on both sides of the Atlantic, and is repeated daily from tongue to tongue, as an established and incontrovertible truth; it is, that "all men are born free and equal." I am not afraid to attack error, however deeply it may be entrenched, or however widely extended, whenever it becomes my duty to do so, as I believe it to be on this subject and occasion.

Taking the proposition literally, (it is in that sense it is understood,) there is not a word of truth in it. It begins with "all men are born," which is utterly untrue. Men are not born. Infants are born. They grow to be men. And concludes with asserting that they are born "free and equal," which is not less false. They are not born free. While infants they are incapable of freedom, being destitute alike of the capacity of thinking and acting, without which there can be no freedom. Besides, they are necessarily born subject to their parents, and remain so among all people, savage and civilized, until the development of their intellect and physical capacity enable them to take care of themselves. They grow to all the freedom, of which the condition in which they were born permits, by growing to be men. Nor is it less false that they are born "equal." They are not so in any sense in which it can be regarded; and thus, as I have asserted, there is not a word of truth in the whole proposition, as expressed and generally understood.

If we trace it back, we shall find the proposition differently expressed in the declaration of independence. That asserts that "all men are created equal." The form of expression, though less dangerous, is not less erroneous. All men are not created. According to the Bible, only two, a man and a woman, ever were, and of these one was pronounced subordinate to the other. All others have come into the world by being born, and in no sense, as I have shown, either free or equal. But this form of expression being less striking and popular, has given away to the present, and under the authority of a document put forth on so great an occasion, and leading to such important consequences, has spread far and wide, and fixed itself deeply in the public mind. It was inserted in our declaration of independence without any necessity. It made no necessary part of our justification in separating from the parent country, and declaring ourselves independent. Breach of our chartered privileges, and lawless encroachment on our acknowleged and well established rights by the parent country, were the real causes, and of themselves sufficient, without resorting to any other, to justify the step. Nor had it any weight in constructing the governments which were substituted in the place of the colonial. They were formed of the old materials and on practical and well established principles, borrowed for the most part from our own experience and that of the country from which we sprang.

If the proposition be traced still further back, it will be found to have been adopted from certain writers on government who had attained much celebrity in the early settlement of these States, and with whose writings all the prominent actors in our Revolution were familiar. Among these, Locke and Sydney were prominent. But they expressed it very differently. According to their expression, "all men in the state of nature were free and equal." From this the others were derived; and it was this to which I referred when I called it a hypothetical truism. To understand why will require some explanation.

Man, for the purpose of reasoning, may be regarded in three different states: in a state of individuality; that is, living by himself apart from the rest of his species. In the social; that is, living in society, associated with others of his species. And in the political; that is, living under government. We may reason as to what would be his rights and duties in either, without taking into consideration whether he could exist in it or not. It is certain, that in the first, the very supposition that he lived apart and separated from all others would make him free and equal. No one in such a state could have the right to command or control another. Every man would be his own master, and might do just as he pleased. But it is equally clear, that man cannot exist in such a state; that he is by nature social, and that society is necessary, not only to the proper development of all his faculties, moral and intellectual, but to the very existence of his race. Such being the case, the state is a purely hypothetical one; and when we say all men are free and equal in it, we announce a mere hypothetical truism; that is, a truism resting on a mere supposition that cannot exist, and of course one of little or no practical value.

But to call it a state of nature was a great misnomer, and has led to dangerous errors; for that cannot justly be called a state of nature which is so opposed to the constitution of man as to be inconsistent with the existence of his race and the development of the high faculties, mental and moral, with which he is endowed by his Creator.

Nor is the social state of itself his natural state; for society can no more exist without government, in one form or another, than man without society. It is the political, then, which includes the social, that is his natural state. It is the one for which his Creator formed him, into which he is impelled irresistibly, and in which only his race can exist and all its faculties be fully developed.

Such being the case, it follows that any, the worst form of government, is better than anarchy; and that individual liberty, or freedom, must be subordinate to whatever power may be necessary to protect society against anarchy within or destruction without; for the safety and well-being of society are as paramount to individual liberty, as the safety and well-being of the race is to that of individuals; and in the same proportion the power necessary for the safety of society is paramount to individual liberty. On the contrary, government has no right to control individual liberty beyond what is necessary to the safety and well-being of society. Such is the boundary which separates the power of government and the liberty of the citizen or subject in the political state, which, as I have shown, is the natural state of man—the only one in which his race can exist, and the one in which he is born, lives, and dies.

It follows from all this that the quantum of power on the part of the Government, and of liberty on that of individuals, instead of being equal in all cases, must necessarily be very unequal among different people, according to their different conditions. For just in proportion as a people are ignorant, stupid, debased, corrupt, exposed to violence within, and danger from without, the power necessary for government to possess, in order to preserve society against anarchy and destruction, becomes greater and greater, and individual liberty less and less, until the lowest condition is reached when absolute and despotic power become necessary on the part of the government, and individual liberty extinct. So, on the contrary, just as a people rise in the scale of intelligence, virtue, and patriotism, and the more perfectly they become acquainted with the nature of government, the ends for which it was ordered, and how it ought to be administered, and the less the tendency to violence and disorder within, and danger from abroad, the power necessary for government become less and less, and individual liberty greater and greater. Instead then of all men having the same right to liberty and equality, as is claimed by those who hold that they are all born free and equal, liberty is the noble and highest reward bestowed on mental and moral developement, combined with favorable circumstances. Instead then of liberty and equality being born with men, instead of all men and all classes and descriptions being equally entitled to them, they are high prizes to be won, and are in their most perfect state, not only the highest reward that can be bestowed on our race, but the most difficult to be won, and when won, the most difficult to be preserved.

They have been made vastly more so by the dangerous errors I have attempted to expose, that all men are born free and equal, as if those high qualities belonged to man without effort to acquire them, and to all equally alike, regardless of their intellectual and moral condition. The attempt to carry into practice this, the most dangerous of all political errors, and to bestow on all, without regard to their fitness, either to acquire or maintain liberty—that unbounded and individual liberty supposed to belong to man in the hypothetical and misnamed state of nature, has done more to retard the cause of liberty and civilization, and is doing more at present than all other causes combined. While it is powerful to pull down governments, it is still more powerful to prevent their construction on proper principles. It is the leading cause among those which have placed Europe in its present anarchical condition, and which mainly stands in the way of reconstructing good governments in the place of those which have been overthrown, threatening thereby the quarter of the globe most advanced in progress and civilization, with hopeless anarchy, to be followed by military despotism. Nor are we exempt from its disorganizing effects. We now begin to experience the danger of admitting so great an error to have a place in the declaration of our independence. For a long time it lay dormant; but in the process of time it began to germinate, and produce its poisonous fruits. It had strong hold on the mind of Mr. Jefferson, the author of that document, which caused him to take an utterly false view of the subordinate relation of the black to the white race in the South; and to hold, in consequence, that the latter, though utterly unqualified to possess liberty, were as fully entitled to both liberty and equality as the former; and that to deprive them of it was unjust and immoral. To this error, his proposition to exclude slavery from the territory northwest of the Ohio may be traced, and to that the ordinance of 1787, and through it the deep and dangerous agitation which now threatens to engulf, and will certainly engulf, if not speedily settled, our political institutions, and involve the country in countless woes.

REPORT

OF THE

WOMAN'S RIGHTS

CONVENTION,

Held at SENECA FALLS, N. Y., July 19th and 20th, 1848.

ROCHESTER:
PRINTED BY JOHN DICK,
AT THE NORTH STAR OFFICE.

1848.

Figure 42: *Word of the Seneca Falls Declaration of Sentiments spread rapidly thanks to this pamphlet published at the offices of Frederick Douglass's newspaper in nearby Rochester.*

From temperance to prison reform to abolition, many of the reform movements of the Jacksonian period had been strongly supported by women. By 1848, this activism had inspired women to assert their own political rights more forcefully. On July 19 and 20, more than three hundred people, including forty men, gathered in a Methodist church in the small town of Seneca Falls, New York, to discuss "the social, civil and religious condition of Woman." The call to assemble had been issued by three leaders of the nascent women's movement, Elizabeth Cady Stanton, Lucretia Mott, and Martha Coffin Wright. The group's deliberations would be framed by a "Declaration of Sentiments," which was largely the work of Stanton.

As had the Working Men's Association, the women's rights activists chose to stake their claim to America's promise with a line-by-line paraphrase of the Declaration of Independence, showing once again how easily it could be adapted to a new cause. In this case, the Declaration's long litany of grievances against the King is converted into a critique of the domestic despotism of nineteenth-century marriage law. Eleven resolutions followed the women's declaration, including one (which passed only narrowly) that asserted "it is the duty of the women of this country to secure to themselves their sacred right to the elective franchise," anticipating the Nineteenth Amendment to the Constitution by more than seventy years.

Still, as radical as the Declaration of Sentiments was, it is telling that its authors couched their claim to full citizenship in the form and language of the Declaration, which by the middle of the nineteenth century had come to assume an almost sacred resonance for most Americans.

Seneca Falls Convention, Declaration of Sentiments.

July 19–20, 1848

When, in the course of human events, it becomes necessary for one portion of the family of man to assume among the people of the earth a position different from that which they have hitherto occupied, but one to which the laws of nature and of nature's God entitle them, a decent respect to the opinions of mankind requires that they should declare the causes that impel them to such a course.

We hold these truths to be self-evident: that all men and women are created equal; that they are endowed by their Creator with certain inalienable rights; that among these are life, liberty, and the pursuit of happiness; that to secure these rights governments are instituted, deriving their just powers from the consent of the governed.—Whenever any form of Government becomes destructive of these ends, it is the right of those who suffer from it to refuse allegiance to it, and to insist upon the institution of a new government, laying its foundation on such principles, and organizing its powers in such form as to them shall seem most likely to effect their safety and happiness. Prudence, indeed, will dictate that governments long established should not be changed for light and transient causes; and accordingly, all experience hath shown that mankind are more disposed to suffer, while evils are sufferable, than to right themselves by abolishing the forms to which they are accustomed. But when a long train of abuses and usurpations, pursuing invariably the same object, evinces a design to reduce them under absolute despotism, it is their duty to throw off such government, and to provide new guards for their future security. Such has been the patient sufferance of the women under this government, and such is now the necessity which constrains them to demand the equal station to which they are entitled.

The history of mankind is a history of repeated injuries and usurpations on the part of man toward woman, having in direct object the establishment of an absolute tyranny over her. To prove this, let facts be submitted to a candid world.

He has never permitted her to exercise her inalienable right to the elective franchise.

He has compelled her to submit to laws, in the formation of which she had no voice.

He has withheld from her rights which are given to the most ignorant and degraded men—both natives and foreigners.

Having deprived her of this first right of a citizen, the elective franchise, thereby leaving her without representation in the halls of legislation, he has oppressed her on all sides.

He has made her, if married, in the eye of the law, civilly dead.

He has taken from her all right in property, even to the wages she earns.

He has made her, morally, an irresponsible being, as she can commit many crimes with impunity, provided they be done in the presence of her husband. In the covenant of marriage, she is compelled to promise obedience to her husband, he becoming, to all intents and purposes, her master—the law giving him power to deprive her of her liberty, and to administer chastisement.

He has so framed the laws of divorce, as to what shall be the proper causes of divorce; in case of separation, to whom the guardianship of the children shall be given; as to be wholly regardless of the happiness of women—the law, in all cases, going upon the false supposition of the supremacy of man, and giving all power into his hands.

After depriving her of all rights as a married woman, if single and the owner of property, he has taxed her to support a government which recognizes her only when her property can be made profitable to it.

He has monopolized nearly all the profitable employments, and from those she is permitted to follow, she receives but a scanty remuneration.

He closes against her all the avenues to wealth and distinction, which he considers most honorable to himself. As a teacher of theology, medicine, or law, she is not known.

He has denied her the facilities for obtaining a thorough education—all colleges being closed against her.

He allows her in Church as well as State, but a subordinate position, claiming Apostolic authority for her exclusion from the ministry, and, with some exceptions, from any public participation in the affairs of the Church.

He has created a false public sentiment, by giving to the world a different code of morals for men and women, by which moral delinquencies which exclude women from society, are not only tolerated but deemed of little account in man.

He has usurped the prerogative of Jehovah himself, claiming it as his right to assign for her a sphere of action, when that belongs to her conscience and her God.

He has endeavored, in every way that he could to destroy her confidence in her own powers, to lessen her self-respect, and to make her willing to lead a dependant and abject life.

Now, in view of this entire disfranchisement of one-half the people of this country, their social and religious degradation,—in view of the unjust laws above mentioned, and because women do feel themselves aggrieved, oppressed, and fraudulently deprived of their most sacred rights, we insist that they have immediate admission to all the rights and privileges which belong to them as citizens of these United States.

In entering upon the great work before us, we anticipate no small amount of misconception, misrepresentation, and ridicule; but we shall use every instrumentality within our power to effect our object. We shall employ agents, circulate tracts, petition the State and national Legislatures, and endeavor to enlist the pulpit and the press in our behalf. We hope this Convention will be followed by a series of Conventions, embracing every part of the country.

Firmly relying upon the final triumph of the Right and the True, we do this day affix our signatures to this declaration.

Figure 43: *Frederick Douglass delivered this address, one of his most famous, before a crowd of more than five hundred in Rochester's Corinthian Hall, at the invitation of the Rochester Ladies' Anti-Slavery Society.*

Among the signatories in Seneca Falls was a thirty-year-old Frederick Douglass, still in the early stages of his career as a writer, public speaker, and statesman, but well on his way to becoming one of the most famous Americans of the nineteenth century.

Born into slavery on the eastern shore of Maryland, Douglass was called "Frederick Bailey" in his youth. Like Lincoln, he had a keen intellect, which had been fired as a teenager by exposure to a political text. For Douglass, it was *The Columbian Orator*, a collection of historical speeches for students of oratory. Learning to read increased his desire for freedom, as did occasional exposure to free people of color.

In 1838, he dramatically escaped by boarding a northbound train in Baltimore, disguised as a sailor. After moving to Massachusetts, he met and was mentored by William Lloyd Garrison, and began working as an antislavery orator and writer. (The two men would eventually part ways over different readings of the nation's other founding text, the Constitution, which Garrison regarded as irredeemably tainted by slavery and Douglass believed contained within it the means of its own redemption.) Four years after Seneca Falls, Douglass, now living in nearby Rochester, New York, used the annual Independence Day celebration to deliver perhaps his greatest speech, an incandescent jeremiad blasting the hypocrisy of a slaveholding republic premised on equality.

Earlier African American abolitionists had struck this note. In 1829, David Walker published *Walker's Appeal*, which included a searing critique ("See your Declaration Americans!!! Do you understand your own language?") But Douglass took the argument to a new level.

Frederick Douglass, "What to the Slave Is the Fourth of July?"

July 5, 1852

. . . . Fellow-citizens, pardon me, allow me to ask, why am I called upon to speak here to-day? What have I, or those I represent, to do with your national independence? Are the great principles of political freedom and of natural justice, embodied in that Declaration of Independence, extended to us? and am I, therefore, called upon to bring our humble offering to the national altar, and to confess the benefits and express devout gratitude for the blessings resulting from your independence to us?

Would to God, both for your sakes and ours, that an affirmative answer could be truthfully returned to these questions! Then would my task be light, and my burden easy and delightful. For who is there so cold, that a nation's sympathy could not warm him? *Who* so obdurate and dead to the claims of gratitude, that would not thankfully acknowledge such priceless benefits? Who so stolid and selfish, that would not give his voice to swell the hallelujahs of a nation's jubilee, when the chains of servitude had been torn from his limbs? I am not that man. In a case like that, the dumb might eloquently speak, and the "lame man leap as an hart."

But, such is not the state of the case. I say it with a sad sense of the disparity between us. I am not included within the pale of this glorious anniversary! Your high independence only reveals the immeasurable distance between us. The blessings in which you, this day, rejoice, are not enjoyed in common. The rich inheritance of justice, liberty, prosperity and independence, bequeathed by your fathers, is shared by you, not by me. The sunlight that brought life and healing to you, has brought stripes and death to me. This Fourth of July is *yours*, not *mine*. *You* may rejoice, *I* must mourn. To drag a man in fetters into the grand illuminated temple of liberty, and call upon him to join you in joyous anthems, were inhuman mockery and sacrilegious irony. Do you mean, citizens, to mock me, by asking me to speak to-day? If so, there is a parallel to your conduct. And let me warn you that it is dangerous to copy the example of a nation whose crimes, towering up to heaven, were thrown down by the breath of the Almighty, burying that nation in irrecoverable ruin! I can to-day take up the plaintive lament of a peeled and woe-smitten people!

"By the rivers of Babylon, there we sat down. Yea! we wept when we remembered Zion. We hanged our harps upon the willows in the midst thereof. For there, they that carried us away captive, required of us a song; and they who wasted us required of us mirth, saying, Sing us one of the songs of Zion. How can we sing the Lord's song in a strange land? If I forget thee, O Jerusalem, let my right hand forget her cunning. If I do not remember thee, let my tongue cleave to the roof of my mouth."

Fellow-citizens; above your national, tumultuous joy, I hear the mournful wail of millions! whose chains, heavy and grievous yesterday, are, to-day, rendered more intolerable by the jubilee shouts that reach them. If I do forget, if I do not faithfully remember those bleeding children of sorrow this day, "may my right hand forget her cunning, and may my tongue cleave to the roof of my mouth!" To forget them, to pass lightly over their wrongs, and to chime in with the popular theme, would be treason most scandalous and shocking, and would make me a reproach before God and the world. My subject, then fellow-citizens, is AMERICAN SLAVERY. I shall see, this day, and its popular characteristics, from the slave's point of view. Standing, there, identified with the American bondman, making his wrongs mine, I do not hesitate to declare, with all my soul, that the character and conduct of this nation never looked blacker to me than on this 4th of July! Whether we turn to the declarations of the past, or to the professions of the present, the conduct of the nation seems equally hideous and revolting. America is false to the past, false to the present, and solemnly binds herself to be false to the future. Standing with God and the crushed and bleeding slave on this occasion, I will, in the name of humanity which is outraged, in the name of liberty which is fettered, in the name of the constitution and the Bible, which are disregarded and trampled upon, dare to call in question and to denounce, with all the emphasis I can command, everything that serves to perpetuate slavery—the great sin and shame of America! "I will not equivocate; I will not excuse"; I will use the severest language I can command; and yet not one word shall escape me that any man, whose judgement is not blinded by prejudice, or who is not at heart a slaveholder, shall not confess to be right and just.

But I fancy I hear some one of my audience say, it is just in this circumstance that you and your brother abolitionists fail to make a favorable impression on the public mind. Would you argue more, and denounce less, would you persuade more, and rebuke less, your cause would be much more likely to succeed. But, I submit, where all is plain there is nothing to be argued. What point in the anti-slavery creed would you have me argue? On what branch of the subject do the people of this country need light? Must I undertake to prove that the slave is a man? That point is conceded already. Nobody doubts it. The slaveholders themselves acknowledge it in the enactment of laws for their government. They acknowledge it when they punish disobedience on the part of the slave. There are seventy-two crimes in the State of Virginia, which, if committed by a black man, (no matter how ignorant he be), subject him to the punishment of death; while only two of the same crimes will subject a white man to the like punishment. What is this but the acknowledgement that the slave is a moral, intellectual and responsible being? The manhood of the slave is conceded. It is admitted in the fact that Southern statute books are covered with enactments forbidding, under severe fines and penalties, the teaching of the slave to read or to write. When you can point to any such laws, in reference to the beasts of the field, then I may consent to argue the manhood of the slave. When the dogs in your streets, when the fowls of the air, when the cattle on your hills, when the fish of the sea, and the reptiles that crawl, shall be unable to distinguish the slave from a brute, *then* will I argue with you that the slave is a man!

For the present, it is enough to affirm the equal manhood of the negro race. Is it not astonishing that, while we are ploughing, planting and reaping, using all kinds of mechanical tools, erecting houses, constructing bridges, building ships, working in metals of brass, iron, copper, silver and gold; that, while we are reading, writing and cyphering, acting as clerks, merchants and secretaries, having among us lawyers, doctors, ministers, poets, authors, editors, orators and teachers; that, while we are engaged in all manner of enterprises common to other men, digging gold in California, capturing the whale in the Pacific, feeding sheep and cattle on the hill-side, living, moving, acting, thinking, planning, living in families as husbands, wives and children, and, above all, confessing and worshipping the Christian's God, and looking hopefully for life and immortality beyond the grave, we are called upon to prove that we are men!

Would you have me argue that man is entitled to liberty? that he is the rightful owner of his own body? You have already declared it. Must I argue the wrongfulness of slavery? Is that a question for Republicans? Is it to be settled by the rules of logic and argumentation, as a matter beset with great difficulty, involving a doubtful application of the principle of justice, hard to be understood? How should I look to-day, in the presence of Americans, dividing, and subdividing a discourse, to show that men have a natural right to freedom? speaking of it relatively, and positively, negatively, and affirmatively. To do so, would be to make myself ridiculous, and to offer an insult to your understanding. There is not a man beneath the canopy of heaven, that does not know that slavery is wrong *for him*.

What, am I to argue that it is wrong to make men brutes, to rob them of their liberty, to work them without wages, to keep them ignorant of their relations to their fellow men, to beat them with sticks, to flay their flesh with the lash, to load their limbs with irons, to hunt them with dogs, to sell them at auction, to sunder their families, to knock out their teeth, to burn their flesh, to starve them into obedience and submission to their masters? Must I argue that a system thus marked with blood, and stained with pollution, is *wrong*? No! I will not. I have better employments for my time and strength, than such arguments would imply.

What, then, remains to be argued? Is it that slavery is not divine; that God did not establish it; that our doctors of divinity are mistaken? There is blasphemy in the thought. That which is inhuman, cannot be divine! *Who* can reason on such a proposition? They that can, may; I cannot. The time for such argument is past.

At a time like this, scorching irony, not convincing argument, is needed. O! had I the ability, and could I reach the nation's ear, I would, to-day, pour out a fiery stream of biting ridicule, blasting reproach, withering sarcasm, and stern rebuke. For it is not light that is needed, but fire; it is not the gentle shower, but thunder. We need the storm, the whirlwind, and the earthquake. The feeling of the nation must be quickened; the conscience of the nation must be roused; the propriety of the nation must be startled; the hypocrisy of the nation must be exposed; and its crimes against God and man must be proclaimed and denounced.

What, to the American slave, is your 4th of July? I answer: a day that reveals to him, more than all other days in the year, the gross injustice and cruelty to which he is the constant victim. To him, your celebration is a sham; your boasted liberty, an unholy license; your national greatness, swelling vanity; your sounds of rejoicing are empty and heartless; your denunciations of tyrants, brass fronted impudence; your shouts of liberty and equality, hollow mockery; your prayers and hymns, your sermons and thanksgivings, with all your religious parade, and solemnity, are, to him, mere bombast, fraud, deception, impiety, and hypocrisy—a thin veil to cover up crimes which would disgrace a nation of savages. There is not a

> nation on the earth guilty of practices, more shocking and bloody, than are the people of these United States, at this very hour.
>
> Go where you may, search where you will, roam through all the monarchies and despotisms of the old world, travel through South America, search out every abuse, and when you have found the last, lay your facts by the side of the everyday practices of this nation, and you will say with me, that, for revolting barbarity and shameless hypocrisy, America reigns without a rival. . . .

* * *

Around the time of Seneca Falls, from 1847 to 1849, Lincoln served out his one and only term in Congress. He boarded near the Capitol, which housed the Library of Congress. Records from the Library suggest that Lincoln was reading Jefferson during his presidency, and there is reason to think he did so as a member of Congress as well. He was surely aware that Jefferson's own books constituted an important portion of the Library's holdings, donated by the third president after the British burned the Capitol—and the Library—in 1814. To have read Jefferson's own books would have brought Lincoln into even greater intimacy with the author of the Declaration. During his lone term in Congress, he was on the floor of the House when John Quincy Adams was stricken, in February 1848, and served on the Committee of Arrangements to plan the funeral. That too might have deepened his identification with Old Man Eloquent, as Adams was by then known, the great statesman who had been a living link to the age of the Founders.

Lincoln understood Jefferson to be a complicated figure. He almost certainly knew the widely circulating rumors about Jefferson's private life, including the fact that he fathered children with Sally Hemings, his late wife's half-sister, whom he kept in slavery. There is evidence that Lincoln felt the "character of Jefferson was repulsive," as he was heard to say in a speech. At the same time, Lincoln was fascinated by Jefferson's literary genius, and his artistry in writing a document for the ages, grounded in human rights, when a simple declaration of independence might have sufficed. As he wrote, in 1859:

> All honor to Jefferson—to the man who, in the concrete pressure of a struggle for national independence by a single people, had the coolness,

> forecast, and capacity to introduce into a merely revolutionary document, an abstract truth, applicable to all men and all times, and so to embalm it there, that to-day, and in all coming days, it shall be a rebuke and a stumbling-block to the very harbingers of re-appearing tyranny and oppression.

Like the radicals and reformers we have encountered, Abraham Lincoln was keenly aware of the fact that the Declaration's promises of equality did not extend fully to all citizens. But unlike them, Lincoln chose a moderate course at first, cloaking his criticisms of slavery in the patriotic shade that the Declaration afforded. His rhetoric grew more heated, however, as other politicians, defending slavery, attacked the Declaration more stridently. The next flashpoint in America's westward expansion came with the Kansas-Nebraska Act of 1854. John C. Calhoun had died in 1850, but there were plenty of other politicians willing to follow his lead, including one from Lincoln's former home state. In 1854, Indiana senator John Pettit called the proposition that "all men are created equal" a "self-evident lie." Lincoln instinctively recoiled, and began to speak of the Declaration's promises with an almost evangelical fervor.

The first sign of this new force came at Peoria, where Lincoln gave a long speech, in response to the act, on October 16, 1854. He described his belief in the Declaration as "an ancient faith," which might have surprised his listeners, since he had not previously spoken at length about the document. But now he was bringing real conviction:

> Our republican robe is soiled, and trailed in the dust. Let us repurify it. Let us turn and wash it white, in the spirit, if not the blood, of the Revolution. Let us turn slavery from its claims of "moral right," back upon its existing legal rights, and its arguments of "necessity." Let us return it to the position our fathers gave it; and there let it rest in peace. Let us re-adopt the Declaration of Independence, and with it, the practices, and policy, which harmonize with it. Let north and south—let all Americans—let all lovers of liberty everywhere—join in the great and good work. If we do this, we shall not only have saved the Union; but we shall have so saved it, as to make, and to keep it, forever worthy of the saving.

A year later, Lincoln poured out more feelings like these, in a letter to his close friend, Joshua Speed:

> Our progress in degeneracy appears to me to be pretty rapid. As a nation, we began by declaring that *"all men are created equal."* We now practically read it "all men are created equal, *except negroes."* When the Know-Nothings get control, it will read "all men are created equal, except negroes, *and foreigners, and catholics."* When it comes to this I should prefer emigrating to some country where they make no pretence of loving liberty—to Russia, for instance, where despotism can be taken pure, and without the base alloy of hypocracy.

When the Supreme Court issued its notorious *Dred Scott* decision in 1857, effectively denying that African Americans had any rights at all, Lincoln was much affected, and gave a speech at Springfield, on June 26, 1857, arguing that the ruling was turning the Declaration into a "mangled ruin."

A year later, on July 10, 1858, Lincoln gave another important speech, this time as a candidate for the U.S. Senate. In it he ridiculed the idea that the Declaration applied only to those with an ancestral connection to the American Revolution. Instead he argued that its promise extended to people of every extraction, tied together by "the electric cord in that Declaration that links the hearts of patriotic and liberty-loving men together."

He continued the thought throughout the Lincoln-Douglas debates, held across Illinois, in seven locations, from August to October 1858. The Declaration was a frequent topic, almost as if Lincoln and Douglas were back in Independence Hall, in 1776, wondering what kind of country to create. For Douglas, it was a document that applied only to white men of European extraction; anything less was a "monstrous heresy." But Lincoln punctured these claims, in debate after debate. Observers noticed that Lincoln grew even taller as he spoke of the Declaration, and stretched out his long arms, to fully explore the breadth of its ideas, and the warmth of its embrace, for all.

Lincoln lost the Senate race to Douglas, but two years later, in November 1860, he defeated him (and two other candidates) to win the presidency. In response, seven Southern states seceded (eleven would secede in all). Their leaders, including Confederate president Jefferson Davis, delivered tortured speeches, affirming some of the Declaration's principles (particularly the right of one people to sever their connection with another), while insisting that the rights it promised were not applicable to non-whites.

As usual, Lincoln went deeper. In the winter of 1860–1861, in a private exchange with his old friend and former fellow Whig Alexander

Stephens—now the newly anointed vice president of the Confederacy—Lincoln used an old biblical metaphor, the apple of gold, to describe the profound meaning the Declaration held for him.

> All this is not the result of accident. It has a philosophical cause. Without the *Constitution* and the *Union*, we could not have attained the result; but even these, are not the primary cause of our great prosperity. There is something back of these, entwining itself more closely about the human heart. That something, is the principle of "Liberty to all"—the principle that clears the *path* for all—gives *hope* to all—and, by consequence, *enterprize*, and *industry* to all.
>
> The *expression* of that principle, in our Declaration of Independence, was most happy, and fortunate. *Without* this, as well as *with* it, we could have declared our independence of Great Britain; but *without* it, we could not, I think, have secured our free government, and consequent prosperity. No oppressed people will *fight*, and *endure*, as our fathers did, without the promise of something better, than a mere change of masters.
>
> The assertion of that *principle*, at *that time*, was *the* word, *"fitly spoken"* which has proved an "apple of gold" to us. The *Union*, and the *Constitution*, are the *picture* of *silver*, subsequently framed around it. The picture was made, not to *conceal*, or *destroy* the apple; but to *adorn*, and *preserve* it. The *picture* was made *for* the apple—*not* the apple for the picture.

That train of thought was still on Lincoln's mind as he took a literal train from his home in Springfield, Illinois, to Washington, to be sworn in. In February 1861, he completed an arduous 1,300-mile journey that turned into a kind of Homeric odyssey, as he dodged assassination threats and met with thousands of ordinary Americans to explain his hopes for resolving the crisis of secession. After crossing the Midwest and New York, Lincoln's train wound through old Revolutionary battlegrounds in New Jersey, before stopping in Trenton. There Lincoln remembered that the Declaration offered something "even more than National Independence" to the American people: it "held out a great promise to all the people of the world for all time to come." A day later, he entered Philadelphia on the perfect day—Washington's birthday, February 22—and hoisted a flag over Independence Hall, before delivering a moving speech about his personal dedication to the Declaration and his willingness to die to defend its precepts.

***Figure 44:** Having delivered his remarks inside, in the room where American independence had been debated and declared—an eyewitness described his manner as "very intense"—Abraham Lincoln raises the flag over Independence Hall on February 22, 1861.*

This was no idle boast. As Lincoln and his entourage drew closer to the nation's capital, they were daily confronted with rumors of a plot on his life in Baltimore, where the president-elect's train was scheduled to stop the next day. Still, he chose to stand before his fellow citizens, unafraid, to argue for the Declaration's eternal relevance.

Abraham Lincoln, Speech at Independence Hall

February 22, 1861

Mr. Cuyler: — I am filled with deep emotion at finding myself standing here in the place where were collected together the wisdom, the patriotism, the devotion to principle, from which sprang the institutions under which we live. You have kindly suggested to me that in my hands is the task of restoring peace to our distracted country. I can say in return, sir, that all the political sentiments I entertain have been drawn, so far as I have been able to draw them, from the sentiments which originated, and were given to the world from this hall in which we stand. I have never had a feeling politically that did not spring from the sentiments embodied in the Declaration of Independence. (Great cheering.) I have often pondered over the dangers which were incurred by the men who assembled here and adopted that Declaration of Independence—I have pondered over the toils that were endured by the officers and soldiers of the army, who achieved that Independence. (Applause.) I have often inquired of myself, what great principle or idea it was that kept this Confederacy so long together. It was not the mere matter of the separation of the colonies from the mother land; but something in that Declaration giving liberty, not alone to the people of this country, but hope to the world for all future time. (Great applause.) It was that which gave promise that in due time the weights should be lifted from the shoulders of all men, and that *all* should have an equal chance. (Cheers.) This is the sentiment embodied in that Declaration of Independence.

Now, my friends, can this country be saved upon that basis? If it can, I will consider myself one of the happiest men in the world if I can help to save it. If it can't be saved upon that principle, it will be truly awful. But, if this country cannot be saved without giving up that principle—I was about to say I would rather be assassinated on this spot than to surrender it. (Applause.)

Now, in my view of the present aspect of affairs, there is no need of bloodshed and war. There is no necessity for it. I am not in favor of such a course, and I may say in advance, there will be no blood shed unless it be forced upon the Government. The Government will not use force unless force is used against it. (Prolonged applause and cries of "That's the proper sentiment.")

My friends, this is a wholly unprepared speech. I did not expect to be called upon to say a word when I came here—I supposed I was merely to do something toward raising a flag. I may, therefore, have said something indiscreet, (cries of "no, no"), but I have said nothing but what I am willing to live by, and, in the pleasure of Almighty God, die by.

Shortly after Lincoln's inauguration, on March 4, 1861, his old friend, Alexander Stephens, delivered a speech in which he continued the line of reasoning developed by Calhoun more than a decade earlier, making clear that the Confederacy would not respect the Declaration at all:

> Our new government is founded upon exactly the opposite idea; its foundations are laid, its corner-stone rests, upon the great truth that the negro is not equal to the white man; that slavery subordination to the superior race is his natural and normal condition. This, our new government, is the first, in the history of the world, based upon this great physical, philosophical, and moral truth.

Three weeks later, on April 12, the Civil War began with an attack on a federal fort in the harbor of Charleston, South Carolina. In the four long years that followed, Lincoln never wavered from his belief in the Declaration and its foundational promise of equal rights for all. On May 7, 1861, his secretary, John Hay, recorded a conversation with the president in which he asserted that the "central idea" of the Civil War was the necessity "of proving that popular government is not an absurdity." Not long after, Lincoln issued a proclamation on July 4 that included this peroration, strongly influenced by the Declaration:

> This is essentially a People's contest. On the side of the Union, it is a struggle for maintaining in the world, that form, and substance of government, whose leading object is, to elevate the condition of men—to lift artificial weights from all shoulders—to clear the paths of laudable pursuits for all—to afford all, an unfettered start, and a fair chance, in the race of life.

Two years later Lincoln's wish to believe in the Fourth of July became a kind of self-fulfilling prophecy, as Union armies delivered two spectacular victories, at Gettysburg on July 3, and at Vicksburg on July 4. The latter victory resulted in the self-liberation of twenty thousand former slaves, emboldened to seek their freedom and establish their own claim to the pursuit of happiness. Cheered by these victories, which seemed to signal a major turning point in the war, serenaders came to sing at the White House. Moved, Lincoln delivered the response below, full of feeling for the old document that had guided so much of his thinking.

Abraham Lincoln, Response to Serenade

July 7, 1863

Fellow-citizens:

I am very glad indeed to see you to-night, and yet I will not say I thank you for this call, but I do most sincerely thank Almighty God for the occasion on which you have called. [Cheers.] How long ago is it?—eighty odd years—since on the Fourth of July for the first time in the history of the world a nation by its representatives, assembled and declared as a self-evident truth that "all men are created equal." [Cheers.] That was the birthday of the United States of America. Since then the Fourth of July has had several peculiar recognitions. The two most distinguished men in the framing and support of the Declaration were Thomas Jefferson and John Adams—the one having penned it and the other sustained it the most forcibly in debate—the only two of the fifty-five who sustained it being elected President of the United States. Precisely fifty years after they put their hands to the paper it pleased Almighty God to take both from the stage of action. This was indeed an extraordinary and remarkable event in our history. Another President, five years after, was called from this stage of existence on the same day and month of the year; and now, on this last Fourth of July just passed, when we have a gigantic Rebellion, at the bottom of which is an effort to overthrow the principle that all men were created equal, we have the surrender of a most powerful position and army on that very day, [cheers] and not only so, but in a succession of battles in Pennsylvania, near to us, through three days, so rapidly fought that they might be called one great battle on the 1st, 2d and 3d of the month of July; and on the 4th the cohorts of those who opposed the declaration that all men are created equal, "turned tail" and run. [Long and continued cheers.] Gentlemen, this is a glorious theme, and the occasion for a speech, but I am not prepared to make one worthy of the occasion. I would like to speak in terms of praise due to the many brave officers and soldiers who have fought in the cause of the Union and liberties of the country from the beginning of the war. There are trying occasions, not only in success, but for the want of success. I dislike to mention the name of one single officer lest I might do wrong to those I might forget. Recent events bring up glorious names, and particularly prominent ones, but these I will not mention. Having said this much, I will now take the music.

Figure 45: *Lincoln photographed on April 17, 1863.*

Lincoln's remarks to the serenaders were impromptu, but they touched on great themes, which he wished to pursue further. In July 1863, he was not quite prepared to give a proper speech, "worthy of the occasion." Four months later, he was more than ready, when asked to say a few words at the ceremony to dedicate a cemetery for those who fell at Gettysburg.

The Gettysburg Address remains sublime, not only for its heartfelt tribute to the young men who died to sustain the republic, but for its elegant articulation of the guiding principles that Lincoln had been following since he first encountered the Declaration, as a young man, and realized it described the kind of country he wanted to live in.

That this slender wisp of a speech should "long endure" as it has would, presumably, have astonished Lincoln. He was not even the main orator of the day, and predicted that few would remember the occasion. But it is a tribute to his artistry that the Gettysburg Address has never released its hold on our attention. Its peculiar staying power stems not only from its poetry (for example, the internal rhymes of four/score and dedicate/consecrate) but also from other odd cadences that seem to spring directly from the King James Bible. Psalm 90, for example, speaks of the "fourscore years" that are allotted to some people.

But if pleasingly modest in many ways, there is also a grandeur in the Gettysburg Address that stems from Lincoln's deep command of the

Declaration. He admits freely that the words "all men are created equal" are merely a "proposition"—very far from a fact. A brief glimpse at American history confirms how many times we have failed to live up to it. But the Declaration could become more true—more factual—if more people read it the same way that Lincoln did.

The word "proposition" comes from Euclid, the ancient Greek mathematician, and one of Lincoln's favorite thinkers. To turn a proposition into a fact requires proof. Here Lincoln understood that the Declaration was becoming more factual every day, thanks to the willingness of Americans to stand up for—even to die for—its best sentences.

Abraham Lincoln, Address at Gettysburg

November 19, 1863

Four score and seven years ago our fathers brought forth on this continent, a new nation, conceived in Liberty, and dedicated to the proposition that all men are created equal.

Now we are engaged in a great civil war, testing whether that nation, or any nation so conceived and so dedicated, can long endure. We are met on a great battle-field of that war. We have come to dedicate a portion of that field, as a final resting place for those who here gave their lives that that nation might live. It is altogether fitting and proper that we should do this.

But, in a larger sense, we can not dedicate—we can not consecrate—we can not hallow—this ground. The brave men, living and dead, who struggled here, have consecrated it, far above our poor power to add or detract. The world will little note, nor long remember what we say here, but it can never forget what they did here. It is for us the living, rather, to be dedicated here to the unfinished work which they who fought here have thus far so nobly advanced. It is rather for us to be here dedicated to the great task remaining before us—that from these honored dead we take increased devotion to that cause for which they gave the last full measure of devotion—that we here highly resolve that these dead shall not have died in vain—that this nation, under God, shall have a new birth of freedom—and that government of the people, by the people, for the people, shall not perish from the earth.

Near the end of the Address, Lincoln calls for "a new birth of freedom." In a sense he had already enacted this with the Emancipation Proclamation, which drove a stake into the heart of the Slave Power. But he knew that more victories would be needed, to consolidate these gains.

In the aftermath of the Civil War, the Thirteenth, Fourteenth, and Fifteenth Amendments did just that. The Fourteenth, in particular, has widened the Declaration's meaning ever since, with new interpretations that have expanded the reach of a short word, "all," that was one of Lincoln's favorites. It specifically protects "life" and "liberty," in a resonant echo of the Declaration. Like the Constitution, the Declaration will always be a work in progress, tied to the best and the worst impulses of the American people. But as Lincoln grasped, to make it more true is, in its own right, a way for each generation to pursue happiness.

PART IV

AMONG THE POWERS OF THE EARTH 1865–1945

Would the Declaration's promises apply to millions of immigrants living in the shadows of the Gilded Age? Would they extend to other peoples, far from the national boundaries understood by the Founders? As the United States emerged as a world power, these were questions of no little import.

The Civil War marked a victory for the Declaration as well as the president who had done so much to interpret it for new generations. To be sure, the cost was staggering, but the conflict resolved a great inconsistency that lay at the heart of the republic. In its aftermath, all Americans, in theory, were free to explore the meaning of citizenship and the opportunities implied, if not always guaranteed, by their birthright (particularly after women gained the vote in 1919). With time, and the passage of a few generations, millions of peoples around the globe would feel the relevance of the Declaration, especially after the United States intervened in two world wars to deter aggression and advance the American ideal of government by consent.

* * *

Abraham Lincoln was cut down by an assassin's bullet on Good Friday, April 14, 1865, and did not live to fulfill the promise of his Second Inaugural Address, given just weeks earlier. In that memorable speech he had pledged to rebuild the Union "with malice toward none, with charity for all." What such an approach would look like in practice was the subject of much debate.

Ultimately the postwar agenda was shaped not by Lincoln's feckless successor, Andrew Johnson, but by Republicans in Congress. Stymied at first by Johnson's refusal to implement their plans for administering the conquered

South, they eventually gained a veto-proof supermajority, with which they set about to erect a multiracial democracy from the ashes of war.

Figure 46: *Charles Sumner, shown here in 1865, would deliver a memorable eulogy to the fallen president: "He has been put to death by the enemies of the Declaration; but, though dead, he will continue to guard that great title-deed of the human race."*

Republican senator Charles Sumner of Massachusetts played a leading role in this Reconstruction. Perhaps best remembered for the vicious beating he suffered from a South Carolina congressman, Preston Brooks, in 1856, Sumner survived to become, in many ways, the conscience of the North. He admired Lincoln but was often frustrated by what he regarded as the president's cautious nature. Yet he matched him in his reverence for the Declaration of Independence. In the following letter, written to a British member of Parliament, John Bright, Sumner makes clear that the Declaration would be the guiding principle of his postwar plans.

Charles Sumner to John Bright

March 13, 1865

private

Washington 13th March '65

Dear Mr Bright,

I have yr good & most suggestive letter. I concur in it substantially. A practical difficulty is this; can Emancipation be carried out without using the lands of the slave-masters. We must see that the freedmen are established on the soil & that they may become proprietors.

From the beginning I have regarded confiscation only as ancillary to Emancipation. The great plantations, which have been so many nurseries of the rebellion, must be broken up, & the freedmen must share the pieces.

It looks as if we were on the eve of another agitation. I insist that the rebel States shall not come back except on the footing of the Decltn of

Indep. with all persons equal before the law, & govt. founded on the consent of the governed. In other words there shall be no discrimination on account of color. If *all* whites vote, then must all blacks; but there shall be no limitation of suffrage for one more than the other.

It is sometimes said "what—let the freedmen yesterday a slave vote?" I am inclined to think that there is more harm in refusing than in conceding the franchise. It is said that they are as intelligent as the Irish just arrived.

But the question has become immensely practical in this respect. Without their votes, we cannot establish stable govts. in the rebel states. Their votes are as necessary as their musquets. Of this I am satisfied. Without them, the old enemy will reappear &, under the forms of law, take possession of the govts.—choose magistrates & officers—&, in alliance with the Northern democracy, put us all in peril again, postpone the day of tranquility, & menace the national credit by assailing the national debt. To my mind, the nation is now bound by self-interest—aye, *self-defence*—to be thoroughly just.

The Declaration of Indep. has pledges which have never been redeemed. We must redeem them, at least as regards the rebel states which have fallen under our jurisdiction.

Mr Lincoln is slow in accepting truths. I have reminded him that if he would say the word we might settle this question promptly & rightly. He hesitates.

Meanwhile I felt it my duty to oppose his scheme of govt. in Louisiana, which for the present is defeated in Congress. Chief Justice Chase yesterday pronounced an opinion of the Sup. Ct declaring the whole scheme "illegal & void" from the beginning; so that it fares no better in court than in Congress. Mr Chase & myself have always concurred in opinion on this question. With the habit of deference here to the Sup. Ct. I anticipate much from this opinion. Substantially it affirms the conclusion which I adopted three years ago, sometimes called "the territorial theory."

That has been much misunderstood in Europe. It has been supposed sometimes as a menace of subjugation. Nothing further from my mind—at least in any offensive sense. I felt that the rebel region must for a while pass under the *jurisdiction of Congress*, in order to set up the necessary safeguards for the future; & I have labored to this end.

Nothing has been heard of Sherman for weeks,—but Mr Stanton has no anxiety about him. He will re-appear in North Carolina. Grant is very cheerful. But for the moment the curtain is down. It may lift any day.

I send you the Resolutions on Reciprocity & Lake Armaments, as they passed the House, & as amended by me. The Italics are mine; & that is the form adopted.

You will see from the date of the House Resolution on Armaments how long I held it back. I was unwilling to take the step, until the outrages on the Lakes seemed to shew its necessity.

I came into the proposition to give the notice to terminate the Reciprocity Treaty, because I was satisfied that we could not negotiate for its modification, on a footing of equality unless our hands were untied. You will see this in my speech. I make this remark in reply to yr suggestion on the subject.

Congress has separated in good humor, without anxiety for the future, & indeed confident that we are on the verge of peace. My desire is that England should do something to take out the bitterness from the American heart—before the war closes. Help. I owe Cobden, & shall write him next.

Ever Yours,
Charles Sumner

To an extent, the redemption that Sumner envisioned did take place, thanks to federal efforts to expand voting rights after the Civil War. But the word "redemption" would ultimately come to have a different, more ominous meaning in the waning days of Reconstruction, when it became a rallying cry for Southern Democrats, determined to resist the extension of the Declaration's rights to Black Americans. As it turned out, those rights were often quite alienable, if the federal government failed to enforce them.

This was the backdrop when, eleven years after the war ended, another important anniversary awakened new interest in America's founding text. The Centennial of 1876 encouraged Americans to celebrate the Declaration in new and often garish ways. Nearly ten million tourists made their way to Philadelphia, where they could witness astonishing displays of American industrial might or see the fragile engrossed Declaration on display in the chamber where it was signed, in Independence Hall.

Getting it there required a writing campaign nearly as extensive as that which led to the original document. Philadelphia officials used every tool at their disposal to persuade the federal government to release the precious piece of parchment from its place of display in the old Patent Office. On May 7, 1876, a civil servant carried the special cargo on a train from Washington to Philadelphia, where he was met by a delegation that escorted him to Independence Hall. Already, the Declaration had aged significantly, and was described as a "faded and crumbling manuscript held together by a simple frame."

The return was glorious all the same. Some were skeptical of the orgy of materialism—what one observer called "an overgrown and spread-eagle Fourth of July"—coming on the heels of a financial crisis, and in the midst of pervasive corruption scandals. But Congress appropriated $1.5 million for a Centennial Exposition, and the party was on. One member who voted for the appropriation was Josiah T. Walls of Florida, a former slave who was proud that the Civil War had marked "the tardy but in the end the full and complete vindication of the sublime simple announcements of the Declaration of Independence."

Figure 47: *The Centennial Exposition featured both the hand of Bertholdi's Statue of Liberty on the fairgrounds and, inside Memorial Hall, Italian sculptor Francesco Pezzicar's statue of* The Freed Slave, *shown here in an illustration by Fernando Miranda.*

Perhaps "complete" was wishful thinking; when the exposition opened, Frederick Douglass was briefly stopped at the door and barred from entry by a clueless sentry. Thanks to the intervention of a U.S. senator, Roscoe Conkling, he was allowed to enter, and to sit on the reviewing stand, near President Ulysses Grant. But the struggle continued in ways large and small; on a national level, the centennial year was marred by a vexed presidential election that transferred power to the very politicians least likely to vindicate the Declaration's "sublime simple announcements."

For all the raucous celebrations, the Declaration's centennial year was also an occasion for reflection and, in the thoroughly American spirit of the original, remonstrance. In Washington, a group of Black leaders convened to express their grievances with the Republican Party with a "Negro Declaration of Independence." Mixing legitimate criticisms with white supremacist propaganda—several of the drafters were aligned with the Democratic Party—this strange and cynical document testified both to the Declaration's enduring usefulness as a model of protest and to the perilous state of Reconstruction as it neared its sad end.

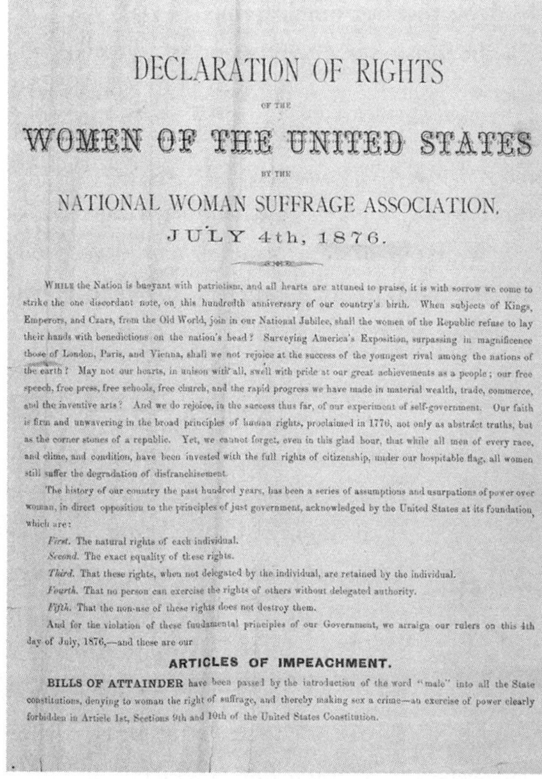

DECLARATION OF RIGHTS

OF THE

WOMEN OF THE UNITED STATES

BY THE

NATIONAL WOMAN SUFFRAGE ASSOCIATION,

JULY 4th, 1876.

WHILE the Nation is buoyant with patriotism, and all hearts are attuned to praise, it is with sorrow we come to strike the one discordant note, on this hundredth anniversary of our country's birth. When subjects of Kings, Emperors, and Czars, from the Old World, join in our National Jubilee, shall the women of the Republic refuse to lay their hands with benedictions on the nation's head? Surveying America's Exposition, surpassing in magnificence those of London, Paris, and Vienna, shall we not rejoice at the success of the youngest rival among the nations of the earth? May not our hearts, in unison with all, swell with pride at our great achievements as a people; our free speech, free press, free schools, free church, and the rapid progress we have made in material wealth, trade, commerce, and the inventive arts? And we do rejoice, in the success thus far, of our experiment of self-government. Our faith is firm and unwavering in the broad principles of human rights, proclaimed in 1776, not only as abstract truths, but as the corner stones of a republic. Yet, we cannot forget, even in this glad hour, that while all men of every race, and clime, and condition, have been invested with the full rights of citizenship, under our hospitable flag, all women still suffer the degradation of disfranchisement.

The history of our country the past hundred years, has been a series of assumptions and usurpations of power over woman, in direct opposition to the principles of just government, acknowledged by the United States at its foundation, which are:

First. The natural rights of each individual.

Second. The exact equality of these rights.

Third. That these rights, when not delegated by the individual, are retained by the individual.

Fourth. That no person can exercise the rights of others without delegated authority.

Fifth. That the non-use of these rights does not destroy them.

And for the violation of these fundamental principles of our Government, we arraign our rulers on this 4th day of July, 1876,—and these are our

ARTICLES OF IMPEACHMENT.

BILLS OF ATTAINDER have been passed by the introduction of the word "male" into all the State constitutions, denying to woman the right of suffrage, and thereby making sex a crime—an exercise of power clearly forbidden in Article 1st, Sections 9th and 10th of the United States Constitution.

Figure 48: *By disseminating their Declaration of Rights of the Women of the United States at the Philadelphia Centennial Exposition, Susan B. Anthony and her fellow suffragists laid claim to the promise of the Declaration.*

On the centennial day itself, July 4, 1876, the nation's attention was understandably fixed on Philadelphia, where a grand celebration was held at Independence Hall, culminating in a reading of the engrossed Declaration by Richard Henry Lee, whose grandfather of the same name had proposed the original resolution of independence in 1776. This was the kind of time-honored commemoration that Americans had come to expect on the Fourth of July.

What happened next was not expected. Immediately after Lee finished, five women, including Susan B. Anthony, moved to the front of the stage, and began to distribute copies of a declaration of women's rights that Anthony had cowritten, with Matilda Joslyn Gage and Elizabeth Cady Stanton, on behalf of the National Woman Suffrage Association. The women had been denied when they asked for a place on the program—instead they were offered complimentary general admission tickets—and so took this action to capture attention. After exiting the ceremony, the suffragists commandeered a nearby bandstand, where Anthony read the declaration to a gathering crowd.

The lengths that Anthony and her colleagues had to go to be heard aptly symbolized the many ways in which women were excluded from political and legal rights in a nation that claimed to represent all. But, like their forebears at Seneca Falls, the women refused to be denied. Instead, they used the occasion of the Centennial to call attention to the fact that the original Declaration, by failing to mention women, had effectively excluded half of humanity from its bold assertion of equality.

Declaration of Rights of the Women of the United States

July 4, 1876

While the Nation is buoyant with patriotism, and all hearts are attuned to praise, it is with sorrow we come to strike the one discordant note, on this hundredth anniversary of our country's birth. When subjects of Kings, Emperors, and Czars, from the Old World, join in our National Jubilee, shall the women of the Republic refuse to lay their hands with benedictions on the nation's head? Surveying America's Exposition, surpassing in magnificence those of London, Paris, and Vienna, shall we not rejoice at the success of the youngest rival among the nations of the earth? May not our hearts, in unison with all, swell with pride at our great achievements as a people: our free speech, free press, free schools, free church, and the rapid progress we have made in material wealth, trade, commerce, and the inventive arts? And we do rejoice, in the success thus far, of our experiment of self-government. Our faith is firm and unwavering in the broad principles of human rights, proclaimed in 1776, not only as abstract truths, but as the corner stones of a republic. Yet, we cannot forget, even in this glad hour, that while all men of every race, and clime, and condition, have been invested with the full rights of citizenship, under our hospitable flag, all women still suffer the degradation of disfranchisement.

The history of our country the past hundred years, has been a series of assumptions and usurpations of power over woman, in direct opposition to the principles of just government, acknowledged by the United States at its foundation, which are:

First. The natural rights of each individual.

Second. The exact equality of these rights.

Third. That these rights, when not delegated by the individual, are retained by the individual.

Fourth. That no person can exercise the rights of others without delegated authority.

Fifth. That the non-use of these rights does not destroy them.

And for the violation of these fundamental principles of our Government, we arraign our rulers on this 4th day of July, 1876,—and these are our

ARTICLES OF IMPEACHMENT.

BILLS OF ATTAINDER have been passed by the introduction of the word "male" into all the State constitutions, denying to women the right of suffrage, and thereby making sex a crime—an exercise of power clearly forbidden in Article 1st, Sections 9th and 10th of the United States Constitution.

THE WRIT OF HABEAS CORPUS, the only protection against *lettres de cachet*, and all forms of unjust imprisonment, which the Constitution declares "shall not be suspended, except when in cases of rebellion or invasion, the public safety demands it," is held inoperative in every State in the Union, in case of a married woman against her husband,—the marital rights of the husband being in all cases primary, and the rights of the wife secondary.

THE RIGHT OF TRIAL BY A JURY OF ONE'S PEERS was so jealously guarded that States refused to ratify the original Constitution, until it was guaranteed by the 6th Amendment. And yet the women of this nation have never been allowed a jury of their peers—being tried in all cases by men, native and foreign, educated and ignorant, virtuous and vicious. Young girls have been arraigned in our courts for the crime of infanticide; tried, convicted, hung—victims, perchance, of judge, jurors, advocates—while no woman's voice could be heard in their defence. And not only are women denied a jury of their peers, but in some cases, jury trial altogether. . . .

TAXATION WITHOUT REPRESENTATION, the immediate cause of the rebellion of the Colonies against Great Britain, is one of the grievous wrongs the women of this country have suffered during the century. Deploring war, with all the demoralization that follows in its train, we have been taxed to support standing armies, with their waste of life and wealth. Believing in temperance, we have been taxed to support the vice, crime, and pauperism of the Liquor Traffic. While we suffer its wrongs and abuses infinitely more than man, we have no power to protect our sons against this giant evil. . . .

UNEQUAL CODES FOR MEN AND WOMEN. Held by law a perpetual minor, deemed incapable of self-protection, even in the industries of the world, woman is denied equality of rights. The fact of sex, not the quantity or quality of work, in most cases, decides the pay and position; and because of this injustice thousands of fatherless girls are compelled to choose between a life of shame and starvation.

Laws catering to man's vices have created two codes of morals in which penalties are graded according to the political status of the offender. Under such laws, women are fined and imprisoned if found alone in the streets, or in public places of resort, at certain hours. Under the pretence of regulating public morals, police officers seizing the occupants of disreputable houses, march the women in platoons to prison, while the men, partners in their guilt, go free. . . .

SPECIAL LEGISLATION FOR WOMAN has placed us in a most anomalous position. Women invested with the rights of citizens in one section—voters, jurors, office-holders—crossing an imaginary line, are subjects in the next. In some states, a married woman may hold property and transact business in her own name; in others, her earnings belong to her husband. In some states, a woman may testify against her husband, sue and be sued in the courts; in others, she has no redress in case of damage to person, property, or character. In case of divorce, on account of adultery in the husband, the innocent wife is held to possess no right to children, or property, unless by special decree of the court. But in no state of the Union has the wife the right to her own person, or to any part of the joint earnings of the co-partnership, during the life of her husband. . . .

REPRESENTATION FOR WOMAN has had no place in the nation's thought. Since the incorporation of the thirteen original states, twenty four have been admitted to the Union, not one of which has recognized woman's right of self-government. On this birthday of our national liberties, July 4th, 1876, Colorado, like all her elder sisters, comes into the Union, with the invidious word "male" in her Constitution.

UNIVERSAL MANHOOD SUFFRAGE, by establishing an aristocracy of sex, imposes upon the women of this nation a more absolute and cruel despotism than monarchy; in that, woman finds a political master in her father, husband, brother, son. The aristocracies of the old world are based upon birth, wealth, refinement, education, nobility, brave deeds of chivalry; in this nation, on sex alone; exalting brute force above moral power, vice above virtue, ignorance above education, and the son above the mother who bore him.

THE JUDICIARY OF THE NATION has proved itself but the echo of the party in power, by upholding and enforcing laws that are opposed to the spirit and letter of the Constitution. When the slave power was dominant, the Supreme Court decided that a black man was not a citizen, because he had not the right to vote; and when the Constitution was so amended as to make all persons citizens, the same high tribunal decided that a woman, though a citizen, had not the right to vote. Such vascillating interpretations of constitutional law unsettle our faith in judicial authority, and undermine the liberties of the whole people.

THESE ARTICLES OF IMPEACHMENT AGAINST OUR RULERS we now submit to the impartial judgment of the people.

To all these wrongs and oppressions woman has not submitted in silence and resignation. From the beginning of the century, when Abigail Adams, the wife of one President and the mother of another, said, "we will not hold ourselves bound to obey laws in which we have no voice or representation," until now, woman's discontent has been steadily increasing, culminating nearly thirty years ago in a simultaneous movement among the women of the nation, demanding the right of suffrage. In making our just demands, a higher motive than the pride of sex inspires us; we feel that national safety and stability depend on the complete recognition of the broad principles of our government. Woman's degraded, helpless position is the weak point in our institutions to-day; a disturbing force everywhere, severing family ties, filling our asylums with the deaf, the dumb, the blind, our prisons with criminals, our cities with drunkenness and prostitution, our homes with disease and death.

It was the boast of the founders of the republic, that the rights for which they contended, were the rights of human nature. If these rights are ignored in the case of one half the people, the nation is surely preparing for its own downfall. Governments try themselves. The recognition of a governing and a governed class is incompatible with the first principles of freedom. Woman has not been a heedless spectator of the events of this

> century, nor a dull listener to the grand arguments for the equal rights of humanity. From the earliest history of our country, woman has shown equal devotion with man to the cause of freedom, and has stood firmly by his side in its defence. Together, they have made this country what it is. Woman's wealth, thought and labor have cemented the stones of every monument man has reared to liberty.
>
> And now, at the close of a hundred years, as the hour hand of the great clock that marks the centuries points to 1876, we declare our faith in the principles of self-government; our full equality with man in natural rights; that woman was made first for her own happiness, with the absolute right to herself—to all the opportunities and advantages life affords, for her complete development; and we deny that dogma of the centuries, incorporated in the codes of all nations—that woman was made for man—her best interests, in all cases, to be sacrificed to his will.
>
> We ask of our rulers, at this hour, no special favors, no special privileges, no special legislation. We ask justice, we ask equality, we ask that all the civil and political rights that belong to citizens of the United States, be guaranteed to us and our daughters forever. . . .

Despite the occasional market contraction, the United States was in a position of increasing strength in the decades that followed the Civil War. A greatly empowered federal government was now free to extend its writ across the continent, and millions moved west, accordingly. The transcontinental railroad had been completed in 1869, speeding enterprising Americans on their way.

Millions more came to these shores from around the world, eager to secure rights of their own. Across the Atlantic, America's example generally bolstered democracy, as other peoples increasingly sought to govern themselves in accordance with the principles enshrined in the Declaration. Charles Sumner's friend, the British liberal John Bright, was delighted that the United States could finally be called "the Free States of America" after the defeat of the Confederacy.

In France, too, republican thinkers were thrilled by the Union's triumph and the demise of slavery. The idea for the Statue of Liberty originated among such a group, and the title they settled on, "Liberty Enlightening the World," reflected their belief that the Declaration's vision of self-government might likewise spread around the world.

Figure 49: *The tablet of the Statue of Liberty.*

They could not have chosen a site better suited to convey this message than at the entrance to New York Harbor, where so many immigrants were arriving annually. France's magnanimous gesture was celebrated at a massive dedication ceremony in 1886. Appropriately, at the unveiling, the Goddess of Liberty was seen to be holding a tablet with the date of the Declaration in Roman numerals. President Grover Cleveland gave a stirring speech, praising "the kinship of republics" and "the open gates of America."

In truth, reality was more complicated; the gates were not always open, and they were not open at all to immigrants from China, following a restrictive act passed four years earlier. But the Declaration continued to inspire "the huddled masses yearning to breathe free," as the poet Emma Lazarus phrased it, including those who were already living in the United States but denied full citizenship.

Farther south, in Louisiana, the Declaration galvanized a group of concerned citizens who challenged an 1890 law that required railways to segregate travelers by race. Justifying their suit, the plaintiffs insisted that "We take for the base of our platform the Declaration of Independence of the United States." For the lawyer arguing their case, the document was "not a fable," but "the all-embracing formula of personal rights on which our government is based and toward which it is tending and with a power which neither legislation nor judicial construction can prevent."

This egalitarian conviction may have been heartfelt, but it was tragically premature. In *Plessy v. Ferguson* (1896) the Supreme Court decreed that segregation was legal if public accommodations were "separate but equal." Cruelly, that phrase, which did so little to promote equality, echoed a phrase in the Declaration ("the separate and equal station to which the laws of Nature and of Nature's God entitle them"). A stinging dissent was submitted by Justice John Marshall Harlan, arguing for "the equality before the law of all citizens of the United States, without regard to race."

But it would take more than half a century for the Supreme Court to come around to that conclusion.

Other groups, motivated by other causes, were gathering under the broad shade of the Declaration, including labor leaders, suffragettes, and progressives, broadly defined. The Great Commoner, William Jennings Bryan, often cited the Declaration in his populist speeches, which identified many of the ways in which the nation did not feel equal at all.

But Bryan held no monopoly; the Declaration also appealed to politicians across the political spectrum. When New York governor Grover Cleveland rode to the White House in 1885 on a reformist, anti-corruption platform, becoming the first Democrat to win election to the presidency in more than a generation, his war on the bosses was likened to a new declaration of independence.

Figure 50: *Dated July 4, 1885, Grover Cleveland's "New Declaration" reads: "When, in the course of human events, it becomes necessary for a President to dissolve the political bands which the machinery of his party has imposed upon him, he must speak in unmistakable words. When a long train of abuses evinces a design to reduce him under absolute despotism, it is his right, it is his duty to throw off such government. I, therefore, do solemnly publish and declare that I am absolved from all allegiance to bosses, and that all political connection between them and me is, and ought to be, totally dissolved."*

Figure 51: *A young Theodore Roosevelt, shown here in 1884. He would later write, "In name we had the Declaration of Independence in 1776; but we gave the lie by our acts to the words of the Declaration of Independence until 1865; and words count for nothing except in so far as they represent acts."*

Republican Theodore Roosevelt, who as a young New York State assemblyman crossed the aisle to support Cleveland's reforms, gave many Fourth of July speeches throughout his storied career, including one near the beginning. Like many other Americans, he had been drawn westward in the decades after the Civil War. A lifelong New Yorker, Roosevelt had enjoyed a privileged upbringing, before tragedy struck in 1884, on the day he lost his mother and his wife Alice, who suffered complications from childbirth. To assuage his grief, Roosevelt relocated to the Badlands of the Dakota Territory, where he bought a ranch and pursued a cowboy lifestyle that agreed with him. Even if he was not exactly a Westerner, he was far from the first city slicker to fall in love with the rugged terrain; and the ranch work expanded him mentally and physically.

On July 4, 1886, a twenty-seven-year-old Roosevelt made the following public address, one of his earliest, to his "fellow citizens of Dakota." After a local citizen named Western Starr read the Declaration of Independence, Roosevelt reflected on its significance as a blueprint for the future of a vast republic, full of "big things," rapidly approaching the twentieth century. His speech went well. Afterward, he said to a friend, the editor of the *Bad Lands Cow Boy,* that he was ready to work once more "in a public and political way." His friend remarked, "Then you will become President of the United States."

Theodore Roosevelt, Speech in Dickinson, Dakota Territory

July 4, 1886

I am peculiarly glad to have an opportunity of addressing you, my fellow citizens of Dakota, on the Fourth of July, because it always seems to me that those who dwell in a new territory and whose actions therefore are peculiarly fruitful, for good and for bad alike, in shaping the future of the land, have in consequence peculiar responsibilities. You have already been told, very truthfully and effectively, of the great gifts and blessings that you enjoy; and we all of us feel, most rightly and properly, that we belong to the greatest nation that has ever existed on the earth; a feeling I like to see, for I wish every American to always feel the most intense pride in his country and his people. But, as you already know your rights and privileges so well, I am going to ask you to excuse me if I say a few words to you about your duties. Much has been given to us, and so much will surely be expected from us; and we must take heed to use aright the gifts entrusted to our care.

The Declaration of Independence derived its peculiar importance not on account of what America was, but because of what she was to become; she shared with other nations the present, and she yielded to them the past; but it was felt in return that to her, and to her especially, belonged the future. It is the same with us here. We—grangers and cowboys alike—have opened a new land; we are the pioneers, and as we shape the course of the stream near its head, our efforts have infinitely more effect in bending it in any given direction than they would have if they were made farther along. In other words, the first comers in a land can, by their individual efforts, do far more to channel out the course in which its history is to run than can those who come after them; and their labors, whether exercised on the side of evil or on the side of good, are far more effective than if they had remained in old settled communities. So it is peculiarly incumbent on us here today to so act throughout our lives as to leave our children a heritage for which we will receive their blessings and not their curses. We have rights but we have co-relative duties; none can escape them. We only have the right to live on as free men, so long as we show ourselves worthy of the privileges we enjoy. We must remember that the republic can only be kept pure by the individual purity of its members, and that if it once becomes thoroughly corrupt it will surely cease to exist. In our body politic each man is himself a constituent portion of the sovereign; and if the sovereign is to continue in power he must continue to do right. When you here exercise your privileges at the ballot box, you are not only exercising a right, but you are also fulfilling a duty, and a heavy responsibility rests on you to fulfill your duty well. If you fail to work in public life as well as in private, for honesty, and uprightness and virtue—if you condone vice because the vicious man is smart, or if you in any other way cast your weight into the scales in favor of evil, you are just so far corrupting and making less valuable the birthright of your children. The duties of American citizenship are very solemn as well as very precious, and each one of us here today owes it to himself, to his children and to all his fellow-Americans to show that he is capable of performing them in the right spirit.

It is not what we have that will make us a great nation, it is the way in which we use it.

I do not undervalue, for a moment, our national prosperity. Like all Americans, I like big things; big prairies, big forests and mountains, big wheat fields, railroads—and herds of cattle too; big factories, steamboats and everything else. But we must keep steadily in mind that no people were ever yet benefitted by riches if their property corrupted their virtue. It is of more importance that we should show ourselves honest, brave, truthful and intelligent than that we should own all the railways and grain elevators in the world. We have fallen heirs to the most glorious heritage a people ever received, and each one must do his part if we wish to show the nation is worthy of its good fortune. Here we are not ruled over by others, as is the case in Europe; we rule ourselves. * * * When we thus rule ourselves we have the responsibilities of sovereigns, not of subjects. We must never exercise our rights either wickedly or thoughtlessly; we continue to preserve them in but one possible way—by making the proper use of them. * * * In a new portion of the country—especially out here in the far west—it is peculiarly important to do right, and on this day of all others we ought to soberly realize the weight of the responsibility that rests upon us. * * * I am myself at heart as much a westerner as an easterner; I am proud indeed to be considered one of yourselves, and I address you in this rather solemn strain today only because of my pride in you and because your welfare, moral as well as material, is so near my heart.

The following winter was a rough one for the upstart rancher, decimating his herd and leaving him determined to return to the East and reenter the arena of public service. After an unsuccessful bid to be the mayor of New York City, Roosevelt served on the Civil Service Commission, and as the city's police commissioner.

By 1896 he was an assistant secretary of the Navy, in a position to advocate, late in 1897, for war with Spain. With an eye on Cuba, the last major piece of Spain's once-glorious New World empire, Roosevelt argued that war would be "one more step toward the complete freeing of America from European dominion." Just as he had tested himself physically during his cowboy years, he felt that the same benefits would accrue to "our military forces by trying both the Navy and Army in actual practice."

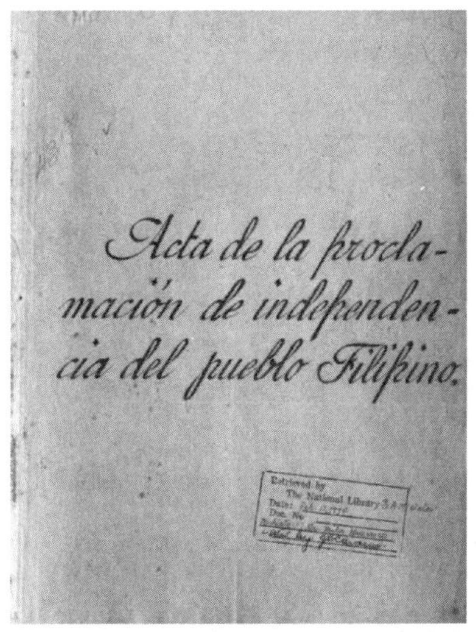

Figure 52: *The cover page of the* Act of the Proclamation of Independence of the Filipino People, *which differed strikingly from its American model in its establishment of a dictatorship.*

Within weeks the unexplained explosion of the USS *Maine* in Havana Harbor afforded the McKinley administration a pretext for action, and the Spanish-American War was formally declared on April 25, 1898 (though it was backdated to April 21). The war would implicate Spain's territories in the Pacific as well, especially the Philippines. Two years earlier, a revolutionary struggle had begun there, pitting Filipinos against Spanish colonial authorities who had held sway for more than three centuries. Capitalizing on this insurgency, the McKinley administration lent support to the rebels by dispatching naval vessels across the Pacific. They defeated the Spanish in the Battle of Manila Bay, and transported a leading Filipino revolutionary, Emilio Aguinaldo, from Hong Kong back to his homeland.

In the weeks that followed, Aguinaldo and his compatriots drafted a declaration of independence that clearly drew from the American precedent. Primarily written by Filipino lawyer Ambrosio Rianzares Bautista, it was issued on June 12, 1898, and signed by ninety-eight people, including an American military officer. That foreshadowed a grim geopolitical reality:

true independence would not come to the Philippines for decades. Instead, Spain ceded the islands to the United States.

Previously focused on continental expansion, U.S. imperialism now took on global dimensions. John Quincy Adams had once stated that America would never go abroad in search of monsters to destroy. That belief now appeared naïve. Only after decades of often brutal subjugation as an American territory, and an even more devastating Japanese occupation during World War II, would the Philippines finally secure genuine independence, on July 4, 1946 (although modern celebrations of Independence Day center on June 12, the date of the earlier 1898 Declaration).

Declaration of Philippine Independence

June 12, 1898

In the town of Cavite-Viejo, Province of Cavite, this 12th day of June 1898: BEFORE ME, Ambrosio Rianzares Bautista, War Counsellor and Special Delegate designated to proclaim and solemnize this Declaration of Independence by the Dictatorial Government of the Philippines, pursuant to, and by virtue of, a Decree issued by the Egregious Dictator Don Emilio Aguinaldo y Famy,

The undersigned assemblage of military chiefs and others of the army who could not attend, as well as the representatives of the various towns,

Taking into account the fact that the people of this country are already tired of bearing the ominuos yoke of Spanish domination,

Because of arbitrary arrests and abuses of the Civil Guards who cause deaths in connivance with and even under the express orders of their superior officers who at times would order the shooting of those placed under arrest under the pretext that they attempted to escape in violation of known Rules and Regulations, which abuses were left unpunished, and because of unjust deportations of illustrious Filipinos, especially those decreed by General Blanco at the instigation of the Archbishop and the friars interested in keeping them in ignorance for egoistic and selfish ends, which deportations were carried out through processes more execrable than those of the Inquisition which every civilized nation repudiates as a trial without hearing,

Had resolved to start a revolution in August 1896 in order to regain the independence and sovereignty of which the people had been deprived by Spain. . . .

And having as witness to the rectitude of our intentions the Supreme Judge of the Universe, and under the protection of the Powerful and Humanitarian Nation, the United States of America, we do hereby proclaim and declare solemnly in the name and by authority of the people of these Philippine Islands,

That they are and have the right to be free and independent; that they have ceased to have any allegiance to the Crown of Spain; that all political ties between them are and should be completely severed and annulled; and that, like other free and independent States, they enjoy the full power to make War and Peace, conclude commercial treaties, enter into alliances, regulate commerce, and do all other acts and things which an Independent State has a right to do,

And imbued with firm confidence in Divine Providence, we hereby mutually bind ourselves to support this Declaration with our lives, our fortunes, and with our most sacred possession, our Honor.

We recognize, approve, and ratify, with all the orders emanating from the same, the Dictatorship established by Don Emilio Aguinaldo whom we revere as the Supreme Head of this Nation, which today begins to have a life of its own, in the conviction that he has been the instrument chosen by God, inspite of his humble origin, to effectuate the redemption of this unfortunate country as foretold by Dr. Don José Rizal in his magnificent verses which he composed in his prison cell prior to his execution, liberating it from the Yoke of Spanish domination, . . .

Moreover, we confer upon our famous Dictator Don Emilio Aguinaldo all the powers necessary to enable him to discharge the duties of Government, including the prerogatives of granting pardon and amnesty,

And, lastly, it was resolved unanimously that this Nation, already free and independent as of this day, must use the same flag which up to now is being used, whose design and colors are found described in the attached drawing, the white triangle signifying the distinctive emblem of the famous Society of the "Katipunan" which by means of its blood compact inspired the masses to rise in revolution; the three stars, signifying the three principal Islands of this Archipelago—Luzon, Mindanao, and Panay where this revolutionary movement started; the sun representing the gigantic steps made by the sons of the country along the path of Progress and Civilization; the eight rays, signifying the eight provinces—Manila, Cavite, Bulacan, Pampanga, Nueva Ecija, Bataan, Laguna, and Batangas—which declared themselves in a state of war as soon as the first revolt was initiated; and the colors of Blue, Red, and

> White, commemorating the flag of the United States of North America, as a manifestation of our profound gratitude towards this Great Nation for its disinterested protection which it lent us and continues lending us....

As the Declaration was becoming more relevant to other nations, it was only appropriate that the original document was carefully protected by a series of secretaries of state, inside the State Department library, in the enormous State, War and Navy Building (now the Eisenhower Executive Office Building), adjacent to the White House. There it had been housed ever since returning from Philadelphia and the 1876 Exposition. Though kept under glass, and guarded by a phalanx of librarians, its ideals still breathed to Americans from every background, and particularly to those fighting for economic equality, as well as the right to decent wages, housing, and education.

By the end of the nineteenth century, the labor conditions that had led to the formation of the Working Men's Party in New York decades earlier might have seemed halcyon in comparison. The so-called Gilded Age brought mass industrialization and ballooning inequality, along with a host of vexing social ills in its train. These were exacerbated by an economic downtown in 1893, which prompted the Pullman Palace Car Company to reduce wages in order to pay dividends to shareholders. When Pullman workers went on strike, they were supported by their brothers in the American Railway Union, whose president, Eugene V. Debs, when he refused to back down, was found in contempt of court and jailed for six months.

***Figure 53:** A cartoon from the June 8, 1895, edition of the* Lincoln Socialist-Labor, *out of St. Louis, shows plutocrats gloating over an incarcerated Debs, who is shackled by the decisions of a notoriously business-friendly Supreme Court.*

Debs used his time in prison to better acquaint himself with socialist theory, and he emerged as one of the nation's most eloquent opponents of unrestrained capitalism. He ran for president five times as the candidate of the Socialist Party, winning nearly a million votes in both 1912 and 1920. In later decades, during the Cold War, the slightest accusation of socialist tendencies was enough to doom a candidacy; but in this earlier time Debs embraced his cause with clarity and charisma. Far from being "un-American," he was an ardent champion of the Fourth of July and the Declaration, whose revolutionary pedigree appealed to him during his long and difficult campaign to secure better working conditions. In 1895, he drafted an essay about what the day meant to him; six years later, he gave a speech on Independence Day, proudly declaring, "I like the 4th of July. It breathes a spirit of revolution."

Eugene V. Debs, Speech at Chicago, July Fourth

July 4, 1901

Ladies, Gentlemen and Comrades:

It is our good fortune, if we can boast no other, to live in the most marvelous age of all the centuries, not contemplating the material progress of our time, which overwhelms and bewilders by its extraordinary achievements. Improvements have been accomplished as if by magic and we behold with wonder and awe the march of human conquest. The forces of nature which terrified primitive man, and before which the ancient world bent in superstition, have to a large extent been conquered and we are the subject servants of man's desire. In this march of progress the brain and heart have been expanded, the one shedding light and the other life, without which civilization would turn back upon its axis. Fortunately for man, everything is subject to change, and all change tends to the development of the race and the advancement of human institutions. Institutions crumble in this march of time. All of them have their periods of gestation, of birth, of development, maturity, decline, decay and death. All of them come in their order. They fulfill their mission, they give birth to their offspring and they pass away. A little over a century ago the inhabitants of this country were not citizens. They were subjects. They were ruled by a foreign king. They petitioned for relief. Their petitions were disregarded. They objected to taxation without representation. Their protests were scorned. Finally they revolted. They issued the declaration of independence and enunciated the proposition that men are created equal. But the founders of this republic had only vague conceptions of democracy. The working class as we understand it today were not represented in the constitutional convention. The founders of the republic in declaring that men were created equal evidently meant themselves alone. They did not include the negro, who had been brought here against his will and had been reduced to a state of abject slavery. The institution of chattel slavery was already securely established at that time. It was founded in iniquity, yet it did not seemingly disturb the consciences of the founders of the republic. This institution was in conflict with the spirit of the declaration, with the genius of free institutions, and yet it was incorporated in them. It steadily grew in power, and in course of time it controlled the country and the courts and the life of the people.

On this day, commemorating the 4th of July, 1776, the declaration of independence was issued. Thousands of orators all over this broad land will glorify the institutions under which we live. In pride they will point toward Old Glory and declare that it is a flag that waves over a free country. In these modern days we hear very much about that flag and about the institutions over which it waves. I am not of those who worship the flag. I have no respect for the stars and stripes, or for any other flag that symbolizes slavery. It does not matter to me what others may think, say or do. I propose to preserve the integrity of my soul. I will give a transcript of my mind and tell you precisely what I think. Not very long ago the president of the country, in the attitude of mock heroics, asked who would haul down the flag. I will tell him. Triumphant Socialism will haul down that flag and every other that symbolizes capitalist class rule and wage slavery. I am a patriot, not in the sense that I love my country, but in the sense that I love all countries. I love the sentiment of Wm. L. Garrison. "All the world is my country and all mankind are my countrymen." Thos. Jefferson once said: "Where liberty is, is my country." That was good. Thos. Paine said: "Where liberty is honored, that is my country." That is better. Where liberty is not, Socialism has a mission, and, therefore, the mission of Socialism is as wide as the world. . . .

There has never been any democracy in the world. Political democracy in the United States, so called, is a myth. A single capitalist, upon whom twenty-five workingmen depend, has political power more than equal to the slaves in his employ, simply because he owns and controls the means upon which their lives depend, without which they are doomed to idleness and starvation. What good would it do you if it were in my power to shut off the supply of life and heat; you would all vote my ticket, would you not? Your lives depend upon the control and ownership of the means of production and distribution. . . .

There are two fundamental principles that are in conflict with each other—individualism and co-operation. Now there is perfect individualism among the beasts of the jungle. They do not co-operate, they compete, and the stronger competitor devours the weaker. You see a girl in the sweat shop only able to earn enough to keep her wretched soul within her shrunken body. Her pallid cheeks, her sunken eyes, her emaciated body testify to the poverty and horror of the competitive system. Hail the coming of Socialism!

But in every nation, in every civilized nation, men and women are massing beneath the banner of Socialism, men and women, for in Socialism woman stands side by side with man, she has all the rights that he enjoys.

We declare then, that the time has come when working men should open their eyes to the economic struggle, when they should have an intelligent understanding of Socialism and pave the way for its triumph and the abolishment of capitalism from the face of the world. Now I have a right to get rich if I can in this system. I scorn to get rich. I could get rich only by making someone else poor. Suppose I have sharper claws and keener fangs than some of the rest of you, am I justified in using them to prey upon your vitals. If I have any ability whatever, I can only prove it by using it for the benefit of my fellowman. Jno. Rockefeller is as completely a slave as any coal miner in the anthracite region of Pennsylvania. He lives in a gilded cell, but he is serving a life sentence. He does not mingle with his fellowmen, he does not enjoy the fellowship of the class he robs. He rules by the power of private ownership and he tries to ease the pangs of conscience by endowing universities. We do not want educational institutions in that way and when Socialism supplants capitalism, and when the wealth that is created is in the possession of the men who created it, when every man has not only plenty of what is required to supply his physical wants, but has leisure to enjoy, we will fill this country with educational institutions, we will make education universal; not only that we will rescue industry from its cupidity. Then man shall stand erect in touch with his fellow man. He will be the monarch of his work. It will not be possible for one man to enslave another without forging fetters for himself. There is no release, there is no relief on any other line. It is Socialism or capitalism; as capitalism declines, Socialism follows it, so it is only a question of time.

I like the 4th of July. It breathes a spirit of revolution. On this day we reaffirm the ultimate triumph of Socialism. It is coming as certain as I stand in your presence. Trials are not to be regretted. They are a part and a necessary part of the development. We may disagree. We may divide. It is possible that we shall quarrel and still be perfectly honest. The development demands it all. We are all subscribers to the same fundamental principles. We all stand upon the same uncompromising platform. We all have our faces turned toward the economic dawn. We are battling for the triumph of the producers of the world. . . .

Figure 54: Mark Twain in his Oxford robes, in 1908.

Mark Twain, whose 1873 novel *The Gilded Age* had given the postwar era its name, was an early and outspoken opponent of American imperialism. Initially a supporter of the Spanish-American War—"I wanted the American eagle to go screaming into the Pacific"—he later concluded that the war was not what it had seemed. "I have seen that we do not intend to free, but to subjugate the people of the Philippines. We have gone there to conquer, not to redeem." In 1901 Twain became the co-president of the American Anti-Imperialist League, which was dedicated to resisting calls for the annexation of the Philippines.

This late-in-life activism lent new dimension to the reputation of America's most beloved humorist, who traveled widely for speaking engagements and, inevitably, accolades. In the summer of 1907, he went to England to receive an honorary doctorate of law from Oxford University. The Fourth of July found him in London, delivering remarks about the national holiday at a banquet held by the American Society at the Cecil Hotel.

It is not entirely surprising that Mark Twain would turn his satirical eye to the Fourth of July; he specialized in skewering objects of awe and reverence. Twain began in a high satirical vein, making self-deprecating sport of the American mania for dangerous fireworks: "They cripple and kill more people on the Fourth of July in America than they kill and cripple in our wars nowadays, and there are no pensions for these folk." But in the speech's second half, presented below, he takes a more reflective tone, situating the Declaration of

Independence within a larger Anglo American rights-based political tradition. Twain was preceded at the podium by Sir Mortimer Durand, just returned after a three-year stint as the United Kingdom's ambassador to the United States.

Mark Twain, "The Day We Celebrate"

July 4, 1907

Mr. Chairman, my Lord, and gentlemen:

. . . Our Fourth of July which we honor so much, and which we love so much, and which we take so much pride in, is an English institution, not an American one, and it comes of a great ancestry. The first Fourth of July in that noble genealogy dates back seven centuries lacking eight years. That is the day of the Great Charter—the Magna Charta—which was born at Runnymede in the next to the last year of King John, and portions of the liberties secured thus by those hardy Barons from that reluctant King John are a part of our Declaration of Independence, of our Fourth of July, of our American liberties. And the second of those Fourths of July was not born until four centuries later, in Charles the First's time, in the Bill of Rights, and that is ours, that is part of our liberties. The next one was still English, in New England, where they established that principle which remains with us to this day, and will continue to remain with us—no taxation without representation. That is always going to stand, and that the English Colonies in New England gave us.

The Fourth of July, and the one which you are celebrating now, born in Philadelphia on the 4th of July, 1776—that is English, too. It is not American. Those were English colonists, subjects of King George III, Englishmen at heart, who protested against the oppressions of the home government. Though they proposed to cure those oppressions and remove them, still remaining under the Crown, they were not intending a revolution. The revolution was brought about by circumstances which they could not control. The Declaration of Independence was written by a British subject, every name signed to it was the name of a British subject. There was not the name of a single American attached to the Declaration of Independence—in fact, there was not an American in the country in that day except the Indians out on the plains. They were Englishmen, all Englishmen—Americans did not begin until seven years later, when that Fourth of July had become seven years old, and then the American

Republic was established. Since then there have been Americans. So you see what we owe to England in the matter of liberties.

We have, however, one Fourth of July which is absolutely our own, and that is that great proclamation issued forty years ago by that great American to whom Sir Mortimer Durand paid that just and beautiful tribute—Abraham Lincoln. Lincoln's proclamation, which not only set the black slaves free, but set the white man free also. The owner was set free from the burden and offense, that sad condition of things where he was in so many instances a master and owner of slaves when he did not want to be. That proclamation set them all free. But even in this matter England suggested it, for England had set her slaves free thirty years before, and we followed her example. We always followed her example, whether it was good or bad.

And it was an English judge that issued that other great proclamation, and established that great principle that, when a slave, let him belong to whom he may, and let him come whence he may, sets his foot upon English soil, his fetters by that act fall away and he is a free man before the world. We followed the example of 1833, and we freed our slaves as I have said.

It is true, then, that all our Fourths of July, and we have five of them, England gave to us, except that one that I have mentioned—the Emancipation Proclamation, and, lest we forget, let us all remember that we owe these things to England. Let us be able to say to Old England, this great-hearted, venerable old mother of the race, you gave us our Fourths of July that we love and that we honor and revere, you gave us the Declaration of Independence, which is the Charter of our rights, you, the venerable Mother of Liberties, the Protector of Anglo-Saxon Freedom—you gave us these things, and we do most honestly thank you for them.

Going in a very different direction from Twain was Emma Goldman, a writer and activist with no particular interest in old Anglo-Saxon freedoms. Instead, she spoke for a polyglot country, increasingly shaped by the enormous numbers of immigrants coming each year, driven to these shores by poverty, brutality, and despair. Goldman had lived as a second-class citizen in one place after another, with very few rights that could be considered unalienable—especially for a family of Jews, categorized as "inorodtsy" (a Russian term for "of alien origin").

Goldman was born in 1869 in Lithuania, then part of the Russian Empire. At age seven, she moved with her impoverished family to Königsberg, in what was then Prussia, and is now a Russian exclave. They then moved again, to St. Petersburg, the Russian capital, where security continued to elude them. At age sixteen, she determined to escape the privation and oppression she saw all around her, and emigrated to New York with her sister. Her father refused to approve until she threatened to throw herself into the Neva River.

On December 29, 1885, she arrived in New York Harbor, close by the then-rising Statue of Liberty. Perhaps for that reason, she always saw the United States as a work in progress. She moved first to Rochester, then back to New York City, where she grew radicalized under the influence of new anarchist friends. The increasing violence with which authorities met labor activism added to a sense, felt by many on the Left, that peaceful protest was no longer adequate for workers facing gun-wielding police and company enforcers. Throughout the 1880s and 1890s, tense standoffs divided factory owners and workers. In one of them, at Homestead, near Pittsburgh, Goldman's partner, Alexander Berkman, fired three shots at a company manager, Henry Clay Frick, who survived. Goldman escaped punishment in that case, but she was imprisoned numerous times for inciting unrest over the years that followed.

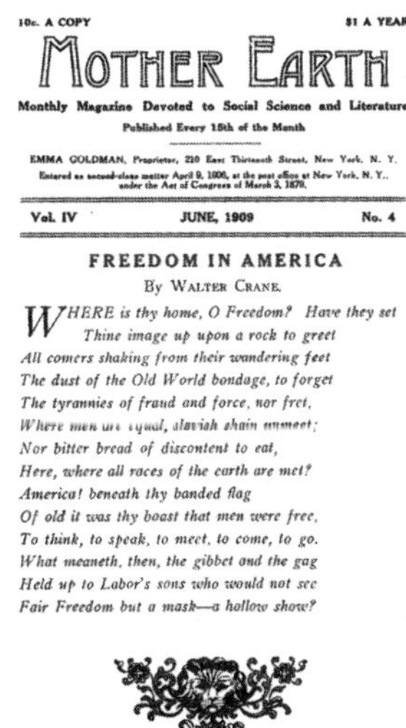

10c. A COPY $1 A YEAR

MOTHER EARTH

Monthly Magazine Devoted to Social Science and Literature

Published Every 15th of the Month

EMMA GOLDMAN, Proprietor, 210 East Thirteenth Street, New York, N. Y.
Entered as second-class matter April 9, 1906, at the post office at New York, N. Y., under the Act of Congress of March 3, 1879.

Vol. IV JUNE, 1909 No. 4

FREEDOM IN AMERICA

By Walter Crane.

Where is thy home, O Freedom? Have they set
Thine image up upon a rock to greet
All comers shaking from their wandering feet
The dust of the Old World bondage, to forget
The tyrannies of fraud and force, nor fret,
Where men are equal, slavish chain unmeet;
Nor bitter bread of discontent to eat,
Here, where all races of the earth are met?
America! beneath thy banded flag
Of old it was thy boast that men were free,
To think, to speak, to meet, to come, to go.
What meaneth, then, the gibbet and the gag
Held up to Labor's sons who would not see
Fair Freedom but a mask—a hollow show?

Figure 55: *Goldman's declaration was published in the July 1909 number of* Mother Earth. *The previous month's issue opened with Walter Crane's poem "Freedom in America," which asked if America's boast that "men are equal" was "but a mask—a hollow show?"*

Goldman withdrew from radical politics, and made a living as a nurse and midwife, before coming out of retirement to launch a new magazine, *Mother Earth*, in 1906. Typically, she embraced causes that were far to the left of the mainstream, including women's rights and contraception. In 1916, she was imprisoned for her advocacy of birth control, and in 1917 she was incarcerated again, for urging Americans to resist the draft. In 1919, she was deported to her old country, Russia (now with a very new government). But here too she failed to fit in, rejecting the corruption of the Bolsheviks, and their own stifling of free speech. After years in exile, she returned to give lectures in the United States in 1934, and was buried near Chicago after her death in 1940.

Never content to accept the status quo in any of her countries, Goldman found plenty to improve in the Declaration of Independence. Accordingly, she drafted a new version for a new age, directed against a new form of monarchy, "the American kings of capital." In doing so she joined a long line of American immigrants who laid claim to their new nation by reading, and revising, its founding text. It was published in the July 1909 issue of *Mother Earth.*

Emma Goldman, "A New Declaration of Independence"*

July 1909

When, in the course of human development, existing institutions prove inadequate to the needs of man, when they serve merely to enslave, rob, and oppress mankind, the people have the eternal right to rebel against, and overthrow, these institutions.

The mere fact that these forces—inimical to life, liberty, and the pursuit of happiness—are legalized by statute laws, sanctified by divine rights, and enforced by political power, in no way justifies their continued existence.

We hold these truths to be self-evident: that all human beings, irrespective of race, color, or sex, are born with the equal right to share at the table of life; that to secure this right, there must be established among men economic, social, and political freedom; we hold further that government exists but to maintain special privilege and property rights; that it coerces man into submission and therefore robs him of dignity, self-respect, and life.

The history of the American kings of capital and authority is the history of repeated crimes, injustice, oppression, outrage, and abuse, all aiming at the suppression of individual liberties and the exploitation of the people. A vast country, rich enough to supply all her children with all possible comforts, and insure well-being to all, is in the hands of a few, while the nameless millions are at the mercy of ruthless wealth gatherers, unscrupulous lawmakers, and corrupt politicians. Sturdy sons of America are forced to tramp the country in a fruitless search for bread, and many of her daughters are driven into the street, while thousands of tender children are daily sacrificed on the altar of Mammon. The reign of these kings is holding

* This "Declaration" was written at the request of a certain newspaper, which subsequently refused to publish it, though the article was already in composition.

mankind in slavery, perpetuating poverty and disease, maintaining crime and corruption; it is fettering the spirit of liberty, throttling the voice of justice, and degrading and oppressing humanity. It is engaged in continual war and slaughter, devastating the country and destroying the best and finest qualities of man; it nurtures superstition and ignorance, sows prejudice and strife, and turns the human family into a camp of Ishmaelites.

We, therefore, the liberty-loving men and women, realizing the great injustice and brutality of this state of affairs, earnestly and boldly do hereby declare, That each and every individual is and ought to be free to own himself and to enjoy the full fruit of his labor; that man is absolved from all allegiance to the kings of authority and capital; that he has, by the very fact of his being, free access to the land and all means of production, and entire liberty of disposing of the fruits of his efforts; that each and every individual has the unquestionable and unabridgeable right of free and voluntary association with other equally sovereign individuals for economic, political, social, and all other purposes, and that to achieve this end man must emancipate himself from the sacredness of property, the respect for man-made law, the fear of the Church, the cowardice of public opinion, the stupid arrogance of national, racial, religious, and sex superiority, and from the narrow puritanical conception of human life. And for the support of this Declaration, and with a firm reliance on the harmonious blending of man's social and individual tendencies, the lovers of liberty joyfully consecrate their uncompromising devotion, their energy and intelligence, their solidarity and their lives.

Woodrow Wilson entered the presidency with deep historical training (he remains the only president with a PhD). His earliest memory, as a boy in Georgia, was hearing the news that Lincoln had been elected. History remained a passion as he rose steadily in a career that brought him from the academy into the hurly-burly of politics.

It's not surprising, then, that Wilson would bring his considerable oratorical powers to bear on the subject of America's founding. In 1907, he delivered a lecture on "The Authors and Signers of the Declaration," which showed a deep understanding of its historical circumstances, but also insisted on some flexibility in thinking about the Declaration, because "each generation must form its own conception of what liberty is."

Nearly 200,000 Readers Daily

The Philadelphia Inquirer

Nearly 200,000 Readers Daily

Nearly 300,000 Readers Sunday

VOL. 171, NO. 5 | 7 Sections 64 Pages | PHILADELPHIA, SUNDAY MORNING, JULY 5, 1914 | News Section | FIVE CENTS

NATION'S PRESIDENT FOR FIRST TIME ATTENDS LOCAL CELEBRATION OF FOURTH

PRESIDENT WILSON ADDRESSING THRONG AT INDEPENDENCE SQUARE AT FIRST GREATER FOURTH OF JULY ASSOCIATION. IN FRONT OF THE STAND ARE MARINES AND SAILORS FROM LEAGUE ISLAND, THE GUARD OF HONOR

Figure 56: *Wilson's visit to Independence Hall on the Fourth of July in 1914 was headline news, though the headline itself was not strictly accurate: both Presidents Washington and Adams had marked Independence Day in Philadelphia more than a century earlier.*

This Wilson himself proceeded to do. Elected to the presidency in 1912, he was frequently called upon to deliver remarks on Independence Day. In 1913, he presided over a remarkable reunion of Union and Confederate veterans who had fought at Gettysburg a half-century earlier. A year later, the Fourth of July came six days after the assassination of the Archduke Franz Ferdinand, amid a crisis that would soon lead to the conflagration of World War I. Wilson went to Independence Hall, where he interpreted the Declaration as "a document preliminary to war."

Woodrow Wilson, "The Meaning of Liberty," Address at Independence Hall, Philadelphia

July 4, 1914

MR. CHAIRMAN AND FELLOW-CITIZENS:

We are assembled to celebrate the one hundred and thirty-eighth anniversary of the birth of the United States. I suppose that we can more vividly realize the circumstances of that birth standing on this historic spot than it would be possible to realize them anywhere else. The Declaration of Independence was written in Philadelphia; it was adopted in this historic building by which we stand. I have just had the privilege of sitting in the chair of the great man who presided over the deliberations of those who gave the declaration to the world. My hand rests at this moment upon the table upon which the declaration was signed. We can feel that we are almost in the visible and tangible presence of a great historic transaction.

Have you ever read the Declaration of Independence or attended with close comprehension to the real character of it when you have heard it read? If you have, you will know that it is not a Fourth of July oration. The Declaration of Independence was a document preliminary to war. It was a vital piece of practical business, not a piece of rhetoric; and if you will pass beyond those preliminary passages which we are accustomed to quote about the rights of men and read into the heart of the document you will see that it is very express and detailed, that it consists of a series of definite specifications concerning actual public business of the day. Not the business of our day, for the matter with which it deals is past, but the business of that first revolution by which the Nation was set up, the business of 1776. Its general statements, its general declarations cannot mean anything to us unless we append to it a similar specific body of particulars as to what we consider the essential business of our own day.

Liberty does not consist, my fellow-citizens, in mere general declarations of the rights of man. It consists in the translation of those declarations into definite action. Therefore, standing here where the declaration was adopted, reading its businesslike sentences, we ought to ask ourselves what there is in it for us. There is nothing in it for us unless we can translate it into the terms of our own conditions and of our own lives. . . .

In one sense the Declaration of Independence has lost its significance. It has lost its significance as a declaration of national independence. Nobody outside of America believed when it was uttered that we could make good our independence; now nobody anywhere would dare to doubt that we are independent and can maintain our independence. As a declaration of independence, therefore, it is a mere historic document. Our independence is a fact so stupendous that it can be measured only by the size and energy and variety and wealth and power of one of the greatest nations in the world. But it is one thing to be independent and it is another thing to know what to do with your independence. It is one thing to come to your majority and another thing to know what you are going to do with your life and your energies; and one of the most serious questions for sober-minded men to address themselves to in the United States is this: What are we going to do with the influence and power of this great Nation? Are we going to play the old rôle of using that power for our aggrandizement and material benefit only? You know what that may mean. It may upon occasion mean that we shall use it to make the peoples of other nations suffer in the way in which we said it was intolerable to suffer when we uttered our Declaration of Independence. . . .

It is very inspiring, my friends, to come to this that may be called the original fountain of independence and liberty in America and here drink draughts of patriotic feeling which seem to renew the very blood in one's veins. Down in Washington sometimes when the days are hot and the business presses intolerably and there are so many things to do that it does not seem possible to do anything in the way it ought to be done, it is always possible to lift one's thought above the task of the moment and, as it were, to realize that great thing of which we are all parts, the great body of American feeling and American principle. No man could do the work that has to be done in Washington if he allowed himself to be separated from that body of principle. He must make himself feel that he is a part of the people of the United States, that he is trying to think not only for them, but with them, and then he cannot feel lonely. He not only cannot feel lonely but he cannot feel afraid of anything.

My dream is that as the years go on and the world knows more and more of America it will also drink at these fountains of youth and renewal; that it also will turn to America for those moral inspirations which lie at the basis of all freedom; that the world will never fear America unless it feels that it is engaged in some enterprise which is inconsistent with the rights of humanity; and that America will come into the full light of the day when all shall know that she puts human rights above all other rights and that her flag is the flag not only of America but of humanity.

What other great people has devoted itself to this exalted ideal? To what other nation in the world can all eyes look for an instant sympathy that thrills the whole body politic when men anywhere are fighting for their rights? I do not know that there will ever be a declaration of independence and of grievances for mankind, but I believe that if any such document is ever drawn it will be drawn in the spirit of the American Declaration of Independence, and that America has lifted high the light which will shine unto all generations and guide the feet of mankind to the goal of justice and liberty and peace.

Three years later, the United States entered the Great War, decisively.

In the war's final months, and in the peace negotiations that followed, Wilson found that the Declaration offered him ways to go where presidents had not previously ventured, deep into international waters. At times, those waters were literal, as when Wilson crossed the Atlantic to press his vision of a new global society, liberated from kings and emperors, premised on the familiar catalogue of rights. For a moment, he envisioned a new Europe, "made safe for democracy," and organized around "self-determination," with small nations entitled to the same privileges as large ones. At times the connections were made explicit, as when a Czech nationalist, Tomas Masaryk, traveled to Independence Hall and used the inkwell from 1776 to sign a new declaration, claiming independence for his people.

On July 4, 1918, four years to the day after his speech in Philadelphia, Wilson invited Washington's diplomatic corps to Mount Vernon for a speech that looked to the Declaration to provide context for current events. Wilson demanded a new understanding, based around the Declaration's "consent of the governed," that would, he hoped, make all wars a thing of the past. Now, dramatically, the Declaration was a document preliminary to peace, not war.

Not everyone agreed that the "consent of the governed" was a viable model for a Europe shattered by its losses and still struggling with anarchy and violence, including the Russian Revolution. For that matter, not everyone agreed that it even existed in the United States, where wartime restrictions on free speech had curtailed debate and led to many arrests, including those of Eugene V. Debs and Emma Goldman. These examples of excessive policing at home undercut Wilson's florid vision, as did his administration's determination to revive segregation within the federal workforce.

But it was a heady time, filled with desperate and often contradictory hopes for a world without war. A year later, in 1919, Wilson gave another speech on the anniversary of independence, to soldiers coming home aboard the troop transport *George Washington*. It was only six days after he signed the Versailles Peace Treaty, on June 28, five years to the day after the assassination of Franz Ferdinand. For a brief moment, it seemed as if Wilson had realized his vision. He was almost giddy as he spoke, saying, "This is the most tremendous Fourth of July that men ever imagined, for we have opened its franchises to all the world." But the Senate refused to ratify the treaty, and Wilson's health soon gave out as he crossed the country giving speeches to defend it.

Figure 57: *H. L. Mencken in 1920.*

These events were fresh in the mind of the journalist, humorist, and grammarian Henry Louis Mencken, who was skeptical of the sanctimony that so many Americans (not least Woodrow Wilson) felt toward their founding charters, while encouraging restrictions on free speech. Like Noah Webster before him, Mencken combined a deep interest in American language with an equally deep distrust of American democracy. (Of the latter, Mencken once wrote that it is "the worship of jackals by jackasses.") Mencken was inspired by Webster's defense of the American branch of the English tongue, and in 1919 he published his own, *The American Language: A Preliminary Inquiry into the Development of English in the United States*, a far-reaching study of America's vibrant slang and speech ways.

As described in his own preamble below, Mencken first entertained the idea of translating the Declaration of Independence into a more contemporary argot many years before it saw the light of day in the November 7, 1921, edition of the Baltimore *Evening Sun*. He suggests that the text of the Declaration, written in the high-toned, eighteenth-century style of Samuel Johnson, was no longer intelligible to ordinary Americans in the time of Warren Harding, Wilson's successor as president. (Harding was famously, if perhaps unfairly, regarded as dim-witted and Mencken seems to suggest the same about Harding's supporters.) As a kind of public service then, he reimagines it in the pool-hall parlance of his day.

And yet the snarky, condescending quality of Mencken's conceit cannot conceal his evident admiration for the text, nor his belief in its ongoing relevance to American life. As with any good satire, there is a kernel of real concern animating Mencken's declaration. He also betrays a casual racism in his language, an ugliness that Mencken seems to be both parodying and parroting. Its presence is a reminder of the extent to which many Americans have found it difficult to encompass other peoples within the equality the Declaration unreservedly asserts.

H. L. Mencken, "Essay In American"

November 7, 1921

The following attempt to translate the Declaration of Independence into American was begun eight or ten years ago, at the time of my first investigations into the phonology and morphology of the American vulgate. I completed a draft in 1917, but its publication was made impossible by the Espionage act, which forbade any discussion, however academic, of proposed changes in the canon of the American Koran. In 1920 I resumed the work and have since had the benefit of the co-operation of various other philologists, American and European. But the version, as it stands, is mine. That such a translation has long been necessary must be obvious to every student of philology. And this is Better Speech Week.

The great majority of Americans now speak a tongue that differs materially from standard English, and in particular from the standard English of the eighteenth century. Thus the text of the Declaration has become, in large part, unintelligible to multitudes of them. What, for example, would the average soda-fountain clerk, or City Councilman, or private soldier, or even the average Congressman make of such a sentence as this one: "He has called together legislative bodies at places unusual, uncomfortable and distant from the depository of their public records, for the sole purpose of fatiguing them into compliance with his measures"? Or this one: "He has refused for a long time, after such dissolutions, to cause others to be elected, whereby the legislative powers, incapable of annihilation, have returned to the people at large for their exercise"? Obviously, such sonorous Johnsonese is as dark to the plain American of 1921 as so much Middle English would be, or Holland Dutch. He may catch a few words, but the general drift is beyond him.

This fact, I believe, is largely responsible for the disaster which overtook those idealists who sought to wrap the Declaration around them during and immediately after the war. The members of the American Legion, the Ku Klux Klan and other patriotic societies, unable to understand the texts upon which the libertarian doctrines of such persons were based, set them down as libelers of the Declaration, and so gave them beatings. I believe that that sort of faux pas might be avoided if the plain people, civil and military, could actually read the Declaration. The version which follows is still far from perfect, but it is at all events in sound American, and even the most advanced admirers of the Hon. Mr. Harding, I am convinced, will find it readily intelligible.

When things get so balled up that the people of a country have to cut loose from some other country and go it on their own hook, without asking no permission from nobody, excepting maybe God Almighty, then they ought to let everybody know why they done it, so that everybody can see they are on the level, and not trying to put nothing over on nobody.

All we got to say on this proposition is this: First, you and me is as good as anybody and maybe a damn sight better; second, nobody ain't got no right to take away none of our rights; third, every man has got a right to live, to come and go as he pleases, and to have a good time however he likes, so long as he don't interfere with nobody else. That any government that don't give a man these rights ain't worth a damn; also people ought to choose the kind of government they want themselves, and nobody else ought to have no say in the matter. That whenever any government don't do this, then the people have got a right to can it and put in one that will take care of their interests. Of course, that don't mean having a revolution every day, like them South American coons and Bolsheviki, or every time some jobholder does something he ain't got no business to do. It is better to stand a little graft, *etc.*, than to have revolutions all the time, like them coons, Bolsheviki, *etc.*, and any man that wasn't a anarchist or one of them I. W. W.s would say the same. But when things gets so bad that a man ain't hardly got no rights at all no more, but you might almost call him a slave, then everybody ought to get together and throw the grafters out, and put in new ones who won't carry on so high and steal so much, and then watch them. This is the proposition the people of these Colonies is up against, and they have got tired of it, and won't stand it no more. The administration of the present King, George III, has been rotten from the jump-off, and when anybody kicked about it he always tried to get away with it by strong-arm work. Here is some of the rough stuff he has pulled:

He vetoed bills in the Legislature that everybody was in favor of, and hardly nobody was against.

He wouldn't allow no law to be passed without it was first put up to him, and then he stuck it in his pocket and let on he forgotten about it, and didn't pay no attention to no kicks.

When people went to work and gone to him and asked him to put through a law about this or that, he give them their choice: either they had to shut down the Legislature and let him pass it all by himself or they couldn't have it at all.

He made the Legislature meet at one-horse tank-towns out in the alfalfa belt, so that hardly nobody could get there and most of the leaders would stay home and let him go to work and do things as he pleased.

He give the Legislature the air and sent the members home every time they stood up to him and give him a call-down.

When a Legislature was busted up he wouldn't allow no new one to be elected, so that there wasn't nobody left to run things, but anybody could walk in and do whatever they pleased.

He tried to scare people outen moving into these States, and made it so hard for a wop or one of them poor kikes to get his papers that he would rather stay home and not try it, and then, when he come in, he wouldn't let him have no land, and so he either went home again or never come.

He monkeyed with the courts and didn't hire enough judges to do the work and so a person had to wait so long for his case to be decided that he got sick of waiting, and went home, and so never got what was coming to him.

He got the judges under his thumb by turning them out when they done anything he didn't like, or holding up their salaries, so that they had to cough up or not get no money.

He made a lot of new jobs and give them to loafers that nobody knowed nothing about, and the poor people had to pay the bill, whether they wanted to or not.

Without no war going on, he kept an army loafing around the country, no matter how much people kicked about it.

He let the army run things to suit theirself and never paid no attention whatsoever to nobody which didn't wear no uniform.

He let grafters run loose, from God knows where, and give them the say in everything, and let them put over such things as the following:

Making poor people board and lodge a lot of soldiers they ain't got no use for and don't want to see loafing around.

When the soldiers kill a man, framing it up so that they would get off.

Interfering with business.

Making us pay taxes without asking us whether we thought the things we had to pay taxes for was something that was worth paying taxes for or not.

When a man was arrested and asked for a jury trial, not letting him have no jury trial.

Chasing men out of the country, without being guilty of nothing, and trying them somewheres else for what they done here.

In countries that border on us, he put in bum governments, and then tried to spread them out, so that by and by they would take in this country, too, or make our own government as bum as they was. He never paid no attention whatever to the Constitution, but he went to work and repealed laws that everybody was satisfied with and hardly nobody was against, and tried to fix the government so that he could do whatever he pleased.

He busted up the Legislatures and let on he could do all the work better by himself.

Now he washes his hands of us and even declares war on us, so we don't owe him nothing, and whatever authority he ever had he ain't got no more.

He has burned down towns, shot down people like dogs, and raised hell against us out on the ocean.

He hired whole regiments of Dutch, *etc.*, to fight us, and told them they could have anything they wanted if they could take it away from us, and sicked these Dutch, *etc.*, on us without paying no attention whatever to international law.

He grabbed our own people when he found them in ships on the ocean, and shoved guns into their hands, and made them fight against us, no matter how much they didn't want to.

He stirred up the Indians, and give them arms and ammunition, and told them to go to it, and they have killed men, women and children, and don't care which.

Every time he has went to work and pulled any of these things, we have went to work and put in a kick, but every time we have went to work and put in a kick he has went to work and did it again. When a man keeps on handing out such rough stuff all the time, all you can say is that he ain't got no class and ain't fitten to have no authority over people who have got any rights, and he ought to be kicked out.

When we complained to the English we didn't get no more satisfaction. Almost every day we warned them that the politicians over there was doing things to us that they didn't have no right to do. We kept on reminding them who we were, and what we were doing here, and how we come to come here. We asked them to get us a square deal, and told them if this thing kept on we'd have to do something about it and maybe they wouldn't like it. But the more we talked, the more they didn't pay no attention to us. Therefore, if they ain't for us they must be again us, and we are ready to give them the fight of their lives, or to shake hands when it is over.

Therefore be it resolved, That we, the representatives of the people of the United States of America, in Congress assembled, hereby declare as follows: That the United States, which was the United Colonies in former times, is now free and independent, and ought to be; that we have throwed out the English King and don't want to have nothing to do with him no more, and are not in England no more; and that, being as we are now free and independent, we can do anything that free and independent parties can do, especially declare war, make peace, sign treaties, go into business, *etc.* And we swear on the Bible on this proposition, one and all, and agree to stick to it no matter what happens, whether we win or we lose, and whether we get away with it or get the worst of it, no matter whether we lose all our property by it or even get hung for it.

Figure 58: *The caption on the back of this vintage postcard reads: "Between two windows on the west wall of the second floor gallery a niche has been cut in which the Declaration is enshrined. In a marble case standing on the floor in front of the Declaration is the Constitution of the United States. Both historic papers are protected by a glass which has been chemically treated so as to exclude all injurious light."*

In the years leading up to the Sesquicentennial of 1926, the Declaration of Independence found a new home, as Washington's power brokers once again jockeyed for its possession.

On September 29, 1921, President Harding signed an executive order to transfer the Declaration from the State Department to the Library of Congress, near the Capitol. In many ways, it was fitting to return a congressionally drafted document to Congress, and it also made sense to place it where a curious public could see it. A handsome shrine was designed, on the second floor of what is now called, appropriately enough, the Jefferson Building. The shrine was dedicated on February 28, 1924, with the new president, Calvin Coolidge, in attendance.

Two years later, the 150th celebration of Independence Day demanded another major speech from a president. That might have been a challenge for the famously taciturn Coolidge, but he rose to the occasion with a deeply researched address about the Declaration and its antecedents. Once again, the celebration included a pilgrimage to Philadelphia, and "pilgrimage" might be the right word to describe Coolidge's quest to locate the true sources of the Declaration in the religion of early America. For him, the creation of the document was a "spiritual event," and Philadelphia a "shrine."

Calvin Coolidge, "The Inspiration of the Declaration"

July 5, 1926

We meet to celebrate the birthday of America. The coming of a new life always excites our interest. Although we know in the case of the individual that it has been an infinite repetition reaching back beyond our vision, that only makes it the more wonderful. But how our interest and wonder increase when we behold the miracle of the birth of a new nation. It is to pay our tribute of reverence and respect to those who participated in such a mighty event that we annually observe the fourth day of July. Whatever may have been the impression created by the news which went out from this city on that summer day in 1776, there can be no doubt as to the estimate which is now placed upon it. At the end of 150 years the four corners of the earth unite in coming to Philadelphia as to a holy shrine in grateful acknowledgement of a service so great, which a few inspired men here rendered to humanity, that it is still the preeminent support of free government throughout the world.

Although a century and a half measured in comparison with the length of human experience is but a short time, yet measured in the life of governments and nations it ranks as a very respectable period. Certainly enough time has elapsed to demonstrate with a great deal of thoroughness the value of our institutions and their dependability as rules for the regulation of human conduct and the advancement of civilization. They have been in existence long enough to become very well seasoned. They have met, and met successfully, the test of experience.

It is not so much then for the purpose of undertaking to proclaim new theories and principles that this annual celebration is maintained, but rather to reaffirm and reestablish those old theories and principles which time and the unerring logic of events have demonstrated to be sound. Amid all the clash of conflicting interests, amid all the welter of partisan politics, every American can turn for solace and consolation to the Declaration of Independence and the Constitution of the United States with the assurance and confidence that those two great charters of freedom and justice remain firm and unshaken. Whatever perils appear, whatever dangers threaten, the Nation remains secure in the knowledge that the ultimate application of the law of the land will provide an adequate defense and protection.

It is little wonder that people at home and abroad consider Independence Hall as hallowed ground and revere the Liberty Bell as a sacred relic. That pile of bricks and mortar, that mass of metal, might appear to the uninstructed as only the outgrown meeting place and the shattered bell of a former time, useless now because of more modern conveniences, but to those who know they have become consecrated by the use which men have made of them. They have long been identified with a great cause. They are the framework of a spiritual event. The world looks upon them, because of their associations of one hundred and fifty years ago, as it looks upon the Holy Land because of what took place there nineteen hundred years ago. Through use for a righteous purpose they have become sanctified. . . .

No one can examine this record and escape the conclusion that in the great outline of its principles the Declaration was the result of the religious teachings of the preceding period. The profound philosophy which Jonathan Edwards applied to theology, the popular preaching of George Whitefield, had aroused the thought and stirred the people of the Colonies in preparation for this great event. No doubt the speculations which had been going on in England, and especially on the Continent, lent their influence to the general sentiment of the times. Of course, the world is always influenced by all the experience and all the thought of the past. But when we come to a contemplation of the immediate conception of the principles of human relationship which went into the Declaration of Independence we are not required to extend our search beyond our own shores. They are found in the texts, the sermons, and the writings of the early colonial clergy who were earnestly undertaking to instruct their congregations in the great mystery of how to live. They preached equality because they believed in the fatherhood of God and the brotherhood of man. They justified freedom by the text that we are all created in the divine image, all partakers of the divine spirit.

Placing every man on a plane where he acknowledged no superiors, where no one possessed any right to rule over him, he must inevitably choose his own rulers through a system of self-government. This was their theory of democracy. In those days such doctrines would scarcely have been permitted to flourish and spread in any other country. This was the purpose which the fathers cherished. In order that they might have freedom to express these thoughts and opportunity to put them into action, whole congregations with their pastors had migrated to the colonies. These great truths were in the air that our people breathed. Whatever else we may say of it, the Declaration of Independence was profoundly American.

If this apprehension of the facts be correct, and the documentary evidence would appear to verify it, then certain conclusions are bound to follow. A spring will cease to flow if its source be dried up; a tree will wither if its roots be destroyed. In its main features the Declaration of Independence is a great spiritual document. It is a declaration not of material but of spiritual conceptions. Equality, liberty, popular sovereignty, the rights of man—these are not elements which we can see and touch. They are ideals. They have their source and their roots in the religious convictions. They belong to the unseen world. Unless the faith of the American people in these religious convictions is to endure, the principles of our Declaration will perish. We can not continue to enjoy the result if we neglect and abandon the cause.

We are too prone to overlook another conclusion. Governments do not make ideals, but ideals make governments. This is both historically and logically true. Of course the government can help to sustain ideals and can create institutions through which they can be the better observed, but their source by their very nature is in the people. The people have to bear their own responsibilities. There is no method by which that burden can be shifted to the government. It is not the enactment, but the observance of laws, that creates the character of a nation.

About the Declaration there is a finality that is exceedingly restful. It is often asserted that the world has made a great deal of progress since 1776, that we have had new thoughts and new experiences which have given us a great advance over the people of that day, and that we may therefore very well discard their conclusions for something more modern. But that reasoning can not be applied to this great charter. If all men are created equal, that is final. If they are endowed with inalienable rights, that is final. If governments derive their just powers from the consent of the governed, that is final. No advance, no progress can be made beyond these propositions. If anyone wishes to deny their truth or their soundness, the only direction in which he can proceed historically is not forward, but backward toward the time when there was no equality, no rights of the individual, no rule of the people. Those who wish to proceed in that direction can not lay claim to progress. They are reactionary. Their ideas are not more modern, but more ancient, than those of the Revolutionary fathers. . . .

On an occasion like this a great temptation exists to present evidence of the practical success of our form of democratic republic at home and the ever-broadening acceptance it is securing abroad. Although these things are well known, their frequent consideration is an encouragement and an inspiration. But it is not results and effects so much as sources and causes that I believe it is even more necessary constantly to contemplate. Ours is a government of the people. It represents their will. Its officers may sometimes go astray, but that is not a reason for criticizing the principles of our institutions. The real heart of the American Government depends upon the heart of the people. It is from that source that we must look for all genuine reform. It is to that cause that we must ascribe all our results.

It was in the contemplation of these truths that the fathers made their declaration and adopted their Constitution. It was to establish a free government, which must not be permitted to degenerate into the unrestrained authority of a mere majority or the unbridled weight of a mere influential few. They undertook to balance these interests against each other and provide the three separate independent branches, the executive, the legislative, and the judicial departments of the Government, with checks against each other in order that neither one might encroach upon the other. These are our guaranties of liberty. As a result of these methods enterprise has been duly protected from confiscation, the people have been free from oppression, and there has been an ever-broadening and deepening of the humanities of life.

Under a system of popular government there will always be those who will seek for political preferment by clamoring for reform. While there is very little of this which is not sincere, there is a large portion that is not well informed. In my opinion very little of just criticism can attach to the theories and principles of our institutions. There is far more danger of harm than there is hope of good in any radical changes. We do need a better understanding and comprehension of them and a better knowledge of the foundations of government in general. Our forefathers came to certain conclusions and decided upon certain courses of action which have been a great blessing to the world. Before we can understand their conclusions we must go back and review the course which they followed. We must think the thoughts which they thought. Their intellectual life centered around the meeting-house. They were intent upon religious worship. While there were always among them men of deep learning, and later those who had comparatively large possessions, the mind of the people was not so much engrossed in how much they knew, or how much they had, as in how they were going to live. While scantily provided with other literature, there was a wide acquaintance with the Scriptures. Over a period as great as that which measures the existence of our independence they were subject to this discipline not only in their religious life and educational training, but also in their political thought. They were a people who came under the influence of a great spiritual development and acquired a great moral power.

No other theory is adequate to explain or comprehend the Declaration of Independence. It is the product of the spiritual insight of the people. We live in an age of science and of abounding accumulation of material things. These did not create our Declaration. Our Declaration created them. The things of the spirit come first. Unless we cling to that, all our material prosperity, overwhelming though it may appear, will turn to a barren sceptre in our grasp. If we are to maintain the great heritage which has been bequeathed to us, we must be like-minded as the fathers who created it. We must not sink into a pagan materialism. We must cultivate the reverence which they had for the things that are holy. We must follow the spiritual and moral leadership which they showed. We must keep replenished, that they may glow with a more compelling flame, the altar fires before which they worshipped.

Figure 59: *Huey Long at the mic. His Share Our Wealth movement proposed "to enforce the traditions on which this country was founded, rather than to have them harmed; we aim to carry out the guaranties of our immortal Declaration of Independence and our Constitution of the United States, as interpreted by our forefathers who wrote them and who gave them to us."*

It might seem paradoxical to borrow the language of the Declaration, a diatribe against a king, to argue that every citizen is entitled to claim a share of royal privilege. But Huey Long was a most adaptive speaker.

The Great Depression had been triggered by the financial crisis of the late 1920s. With each passing year widespread unemployment and crippling deflation cut deeper into the American psyche. Few events in the nation's history had done more to call into question what life, liberty, and the pursuit of happiness stood for in a society that could only offer an impoverished version of each. Better than most, Long understood the plight of a people battered by the Depression.

First in Louisiana, where he served as governor from 1928 to 1932, and then in the United States Senate, Long became famous for his stem-winding populist speeches, attacking corporate power and arguing for a more balanced distribution of wealth. Just months after delivering his "Every Man a King" radio address, arguably his most famous, Long launched the Share Our Wealth Society, designed to implement his redistributive vision. With a rising national profile, he might have challenged Franklin D. Roosevelt for the Democratic nomination in 1936, but he was assassinated in 1935. "Every Man a King" was a phrase that had been used by William Jennings Bryan, but Long effectively made it his own, penning an autobiography with that title, and, of course, this speech.

Huey Long, "Every Man a King"

February 23, 1934

Ladies and gentlemen, I have only thirty minutes in which to speak to you this evening, and I, therefore, will not be able to discuss in detail so much as I can write when I have all of the time and space that is allowed me for the subjects, but I will undertake to sketch them very briefly without manuscript or preparation, so that you can understand them so well as I can tell them to you tonight.

I contend, my friends, that we have no difficult problem to solve in America, and that is the view of nearly everyone with whom I have discussed the matter here in Washington and elsewhere throughout the United States—that we have no very difficult problem to solve.

It is not the difficulty of the problem which we have; it is the fact that the rich people of this country—and by rich people I mean the superrich—will not allow us to solve the problems, or rather the one little problem that is afflicting this country, because in order to cure all of our woes it is necessary to scale down the big fortunes, that we may scatter the wealth to be shared by all of the people.

We have a marvelous love for this Government of ours; in fact, it is almost a religion, and it is well that it should be, because we have a splendid form of government and we have a splendid set of laws. We have everything here that we need, except that we have neglected the fundamentals upon which the American Government was principally predicated.

How many of you remember the first thing that the Declaration of Independence said? It said, "We hold these truths to be self-evident, that there are certain inalienable rights for the people, and among them are life, liberty, and the pursuit of happiness"; and it said, further, "We hold the view that all men are created equal."

Now, what did they mean by that? Did they mean, my friends, to say that all men were created equal and that that meant that any one man was born to inherit $10 billion and that another child was to be born to inherit nothing?

Did that mean, my friends, that someone would come into this world without having had an opportunity, of course, to have hit one lick of work, should be born with more than it and all of its children and children's children could ever dispose of, but that another one would have to be born into a life of starvation?

That was not the meaning of the Declaration of Independence when it said that all men are created equal or "That we hold that all men are created equal."

Nor was it the meaning of the Declaration of Independence when it said that they held that there were certain rights that were inalienable—the right of life, liberty, and the pursuit of happiness.

Is that right of life, my friends, when the young children of this country are being reared into a sphere which is more owned by 12 men than it is by 120 million people?

Is that, my friends, giving them a fair shake of the dice or anything like the inalienable right of life, liberty, and the pursuit of happiness, or anything resembling the fact that all people are created equal; when we have today in America thousands and hundreds of thousands and millions of children on the verge of starvation in a land that is overflowing with too much to eat and too much to wear?

I do not think you will contend that, and I do not think for a moment that they will contend it.

Now let us see if we cannot return this Government to the Declaration of Independence and see if we are going to do anything regarding it. . . .

It is necessary to save the Government of the country, but is much more necessary to save the people of America. We love this country. We love this Government. It is a religion, I say. It is a kind of religion people have read of when women, in the name of religion, would take their infant babes and throw them into the burning flame, where they would be instantly devoured by the all-consuming fire, in days gone by; and there probably are some people of the world even today, who, in the name of religion, throw their own babes to destruction; but in the name of our good Government people today are seeing their own children hungry, tired, half-naked, lifting their tear-dimmed eyes into the sad faces of their fathers and mothers, who cannot give them food and clothing they both needed, and which is necessary to sustain them, and that goes on day after day, and night after night, when day gets into darkness and blackness, knowing those children would arise in the morning without being fed, and probably go to bed at night without being fed.

Yet in the name of our Government, and all alone, those people undertake and strive as hard as they can to keep a good government alive, and how long they can stand that no one knows. If I were in their place tonight, the place where millions are, I hope that I would have what I might say—I cannot give you the word to express the kind of fortitude they have; that is the word—I hope that I might have the fortitude to praise and honor my Government that had allowed me here in this land, where there is too much to eat and too much to wear, to starve in order that a handful of men can have so much more than they can ever eat or they can ever wear.

Now, we have organized a society, and we call it share-our-wealth society, a society with the motto "Every man a king."

Every man a king, so there would be no such thing as a man or woman who did not have the necessities of life, who would not be dependent upon the whims and caprices and ipsi dixit of the financial martyrs for a living. What do we propose by this society? We propose to limit the wealth of big men in the country. There is an average of $15,000 in wealth to every family in America. That is right here today.

We do not propose to divide it up equally. We do not propose a division of wealth, but we propose to limit poverty that we will allow to be inflicted upon any man's family. We will not say we are going to try to guarantee any equality, or $15,000 to families. No; but we do say that one third of the average is low enough for any one family to hold, that there should be a guaranty of a family wealth of around $5,000; enough for a home, an automobile, a radio, and the ordinary conveniences, and the opportunity to educate their children; a fair share of the income of this land thereafter to that family so there will be no such thing as merely the select to have those things, and so there will be no such thing as a family living in poverty and distress. . . .

Like all presidents before him, Franklin D. Roosevelt was called upon many times to interpret the intricacies of American history. He perfected this skill through his Fireside Chats, during the long years of the Depression, skillfully enlisting old phrases in new causes. Roosevelt's time in office had brought him into a close working relationship with the Declaration of Independence. His unique challenge, which he would meet through the complex of social programs known as the New Deal, was to read, and reimagine, the nation's founding charter in such a way as to meet the unprecedented exigencies of the moment. On July 4, 1936, he traveled to Jefferson's home at Monticello, where he delivered a thoughtful address about Jefferson and the Declaration, which he called "a continuing achievement, renewed and reiterated every day."

Figure 60: *FDR speaks to Congress and the American people on January 6, 1941: "I address you, the Members of the Seventy-Seventh Congress, at a moment unprecedented in the history of the Union. I use the word 'unprecedented,' because at no previous time has American security been as seriously threatened from without as it is today."*

As another world war threatened to engulf the United States, Roosevelt often borrowed from the Declaration's language about rights, hoping to inspire a new generation of Americans to meet the dire challenges before them. At the end of his annual message to Congress, delivered on January 6, 1941, an address that has become famous as the "Four Freedoms" speech, Roosevelt offered an expansive new reading of what the Declaration's unalienable rights entailed, and what they meant in practice, not just for Americans, but for all peoples in a world at war.

Franklin D. Roosevelt, Eighth Annual Address to Congress

January 6, 1941

. . . As men do not live by bread alone, they do not fight by armaments alone. Those who man our defenses, and those behind them who build our defenses, must have the stamina and the courage which come from unshakable belief in the manner of life which they are defending. The mighty action that we are calling for cannot be based on a disregard of all things worth fighting for.

The Nation takes great satisfaction and much strength from the things which have been done to make its people conscious of their individual stake in the preservation of democratic life in America. Those things have toughened the fibre of our people, have renewed their faith and strengthened their devotion to the institutions we make ready to protect.

Certainly this is no time for any of us to stop thinking about the social and economic problems which are the root cause of the social revolution which is today a supreme factor in the world.

For there is nothing mysterious about the foundations of a healthy and strong democracy. The basic things expected by our people of their political and economic systems are simple. They are:

Equality of opportunity for youth and for others.

Jobs for those who can work.

Security for those who need it.

The ending of special privilege for the few.

The preservation of civil liberties for all.

The enjoyment of the fruits of scientific progress in a wider and constantly rising standard of living.

These are the simple, basic things that must never be lost sight of in the turmoil and unbelievable complexity of our modern world. The inner and abiding strength of our economic and political systems is dependent upon the degree to which they fulfill these expectations.

Many subjects connected with our social economy call for immediate improvement.

As examples:

We should bring more citizens under the coverage of old-age pensions and unemployment insurance.

We should widen the opportunities for adequate medical care.

We should plan a better system by which persons deserving or needing gainful employment may obtain it.

I have called for personal sacrifice. I am assured of the willingness of almost all Americans to respond to that call.

A part of the sacrifice means the payment of more money in taxes. In my Budget Message I shall recommend that a greater portion of this great defense program be paid for from taxation than we are paying today. No person should try, or be allowed, to get rich out of this program; and the principle of tax payments in accordance with ability to pay should be constantly before our eyes to guide our legislation.

If the Congress maintains these principles, the voters, putting patriotism ahead of pocketbooks, will give you their applause.

In the future days, which we seek to make secure, we look forward to a world founded upon four essential human freedoms.

The first is freedom of speech and expression—everywhere in the world.

The second is freedom of every person to worship God in his own way—everywhere in the world.

The third is freedom from want—which, translated into world terms, means economic understandings which will secure to every nation a healthy peacetime life for its inhabitants—everywhere in the world.

The fourth is freedom from fear—which, translated into world terms, means a world-wide reduction of armaments to such a point and in such a thorough fashion that no nation will be in a position to commit an act of physical aggression against any neighbor—anywhere in the world.

That is no vision of a distant millennium. It is a definite basis for a kind of world attainable in our own time and generation. That kind of world is the very antithesis of the so-called new order of tyranny which the dictators seek to create with the crash of a bomb.

To that new order we oppose the greater conception—the moral order. A good society is able to face schemes of world domination and foreign revolutions alike without fear.

Since the beginning of our American history, we have been engaged in change—in a perpetual peaceful revolution—a revolution which goes on steadily, quietly adjusting itself to changing conditions—without the concentration camp or the quick-lime in the ditch. The world order which we seek is the cooperation of free countries, working together in a friendly, civilized society.

This nation has placed its destiny in the hands and heads and hearts of its millions of free men and women; and its faith in freedom under the guidance of God. Freedom means the supremacy of human rights everywhere. Our support goes to those who struggle to gain those rights or keep them. Our strength is our unity of purpose.

To that high concept there can be no end save victory.

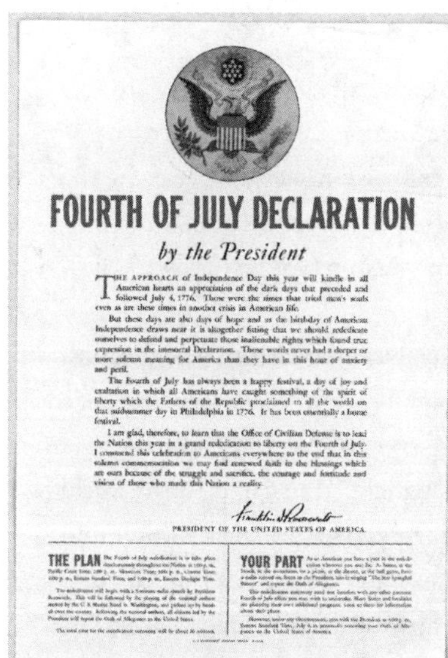

FOURTH OF JULY DECLARATION

by the President

THE APPROACH of Independence Day this year will kindle in all American hearts an appreciation of the dark days that preceded and followed July 4, 1776. Those were the times that tried men's souls even as are these times in another crisis in American life.

But these days are also days of hope and as the birthday of American Independence draws near it is altogether fitting that we should rededicate ourselves to defend and perpetuate those inalienable rights which found true expression in the immortal Declaration. These words never had a deeper or more solemn meaning for America than they have in this hour of anxiety and peril.

The Fourth of July has always been a happy festival, a day of joy and exaltation in which all Americans have caught something of the spirit of liberty which the Fathers of the Republic proclaimed to all the world on that midsummer day in Philadelphia in 1776. It has been essentially a home festival.

I am glad, therefore, to learn that the Office of Civilian Defense is to lead the Nation this year in a grand rededication to liberty on the Fourth of July. I commend this celebration to Americans everywhere to the end that in this solemn commemoration we may find renewed faith in the blessings which are ours because of the struggle and sacrifice, the courage and fortitude and vision of those who made this Nation a reality.

PRESIDENT OF THE UNITED STATES OF AMERICA

THE PLAN

YOUR PART

Figure 61: *President Roosevelt's address to the nation on July 4, 1941, was to serve as the centerpiece of a larger "rededication to liberty," including a nationwide pledge of allegiance conducted over the radio.*

Many Americans were wary of Roosevelt's solemn message, feeling the world's problems had nothing to do with them. On June 30, 1941, Charles Lindbergh spoke before thirty thousand people in Los Angeles, denouncing the president, and arguing, five months before Pearl Harbor, that America could never be attacked.

Five days later, on the Fourth of July, Roosevelt again returned to the subject of the Declaration. In a radio address that sometimes echoed Jefferson, he explained his faith in the old parchment and asked his fellow Americans to be ready to fight a new tyranny.

Franklin Delano Roosevelt, Radio Address to the Nation

July 4, 1941

In 1776, on the fourth day of July, the Representatives of the several States in Congress assembled, declaring our independence, asserted that a decent respect for the opinion of mankind required that they should declare the reasons for their action. In this new crisis, we have a like duty.

In 1776 we waged war in behalf of the great principle that Government should derive its just powers from the consent of the governed. In other words, representation chosen in free elections. In the century and a half that followed, this cause of human freedom swept across the world.

But now, in our generation—in the past few years—a new resistance, in the form of several new practices of tyranny, has been making such headway that the fundamentals of 1776 are being struck down abroad, and definitely they are threatened here.

It is, indeed, a fallacy, based on no logic at all, for any Americans to suggest that the rule of force can defeat human freedom in all the other parts of the world and permit it to survive in the United States alone. But it has been that childlike fantasy itself—that misdirected faith—which has led Nation after Nation to go about their peaceful tasks, relying on the thought, and even the promise, that they and their lives and their government would be allowed to live when the juggernaut of force came their way.

It is simple—I could almost say simple-minded—for us Americans to wave the flag, to reassert our belief in the cause of freedom—and to let it go at that.

Yet, all of us who lie awake at night—all of us who study and study again, know full well that in these days we cannot save freedom with pitchforks and muskets alone, after a dictator combination has gained control of the rest of the world.

We know too that we cannot save freedom in our own midst, in our own land, if all around us—our neighbor Nations—have lost their freedom.

That is why we are engaged in a serious, in a mighty, in a unified action in the cause of the defense of the hemisphere and the freedom of the seas. We need not the loyalty and unity alone, we need speed and efficiency and toil and an end to backbiting, and an end to the sabotage that runs far deeper than the blowing up of munitions plants.

I tell the American people solemnly that the United States will never survive as a happy and fertile oasis of liberty surrounded by a cruel desert of dictatorship.

And so it is that when we repeat the great pledge to our country and to our flag, it must be our deep conviction that we pledge as well our work, our will and, if it be necessary, our very lives.

Fortunately, the Declaration of Independence itself was in safe hands as the world entered another perilous moment. The document's transfer to the Library of Congress in 1921 meant that it was at last under the supervision of trained archivists who could carefully monitor the document and take steps to arrest the deterioration of its ink and paper.

It quickly became clear that the caretaking of the Declaration had not been foolproof, however. At some point, between the photograph taken in 1903, on the left, and one taken in 1940, on the right, a reader sought a

Figure 62: *Hands off, please: the engrossed version of the Declaration of Independence, photographed in 1903 and 1940, showing in the interim the unmistakable imprint of a careless individual in the lower left corner.*

close, personal relationship with the great document. Far too personal. The evidence clearly reveals a full handprint on the lower left-hand corner of the parchment, shocking evidence of archival mismanagement. Ever since, the Declaration has had a new and unwelcome signature, in addition to those of John Hancock and the others.

One of the professionals put in charge of the document was Julian P. Boyd, who became the editor of the Jefferson Papers in 1943. Fortuitously, that was also the bicentennial of Thomas Jefferson's birth. Alert to the opportunity, the Library of Congress mounted an impressive exhibition about the Declaration, then commissioned a full-length analysis, by Boyd, which remains an essential source (*The Declaration of Independence: The Evolution of the Text*).

The Library's exhibition opened on Jefferson's 200th birthday, April 13, 1943, the same day that the Jefferson Memorial was dedicated in Washington. The Declaration was an honored guest at these festivities, but it was no easy matter to procure it. After the Japanese attack on Pearl Harbor, the parchment had been sent to Fort Knox, in Kentucky. On December 26, 1941, a train left Union Station in Washington, carrying not only the engrossed Declaration, but other treasures of the national patrimony, including a Gutenberg Bible, the Magna Carta, Lincoln's Second Inaugural, the Gettysburg Address, and the Constitution, guarded by armed Secret Service agents.

But so great was the importance of having the Declaration present in Washington for Jefferson's bicentennial that the document was briefly returned, to satisfy a people's craving for contact. It and the other precious relics would be permanently returned to Washington on October 1, 1944, accompanied by a military escort. The Librarian of Congress, Archibald MacLeish, linked the documents to the war effort, writing, "It is appropriate that these fragile objects which bear so great a weight of meaning to our people, and indeed to all the peoples of the world, should be entrusted to the guard of men who have themselves seen active service in a war against the enemies of everything this Constitution and this Declaration stand for."

The military context made sense, once again, for a text that had originally been written as a war measure. World War II offered a chance for yet another reappraisal. By 1943, the United States was deeply embroiled in the war, fighting hard to beat back the forces of fascism both in Europe and in the Pacific. Like Woodrow Wilson a generation earlier, Roosevelt would turn the war effort into a campaign to liberate humanity. Shortly after the United States entered the conflict, the president organized an international conference so that the four freedoms he had pronounced in 1941 could be distilled into an official document. The Declaration by United Nations echoed the language of the Declaration of Independence by promising to defend "life, liberty, independence and religious freedom." It was signed by delegates from the United States, the United Kingdom, the Soviet Union, and China on January 1, 1942, and by many other nations in the weeks that followed. The Declaration had always been a kind of lodestar; now it was visible from every continent.

DECLARATION BY UNITED NATIONS

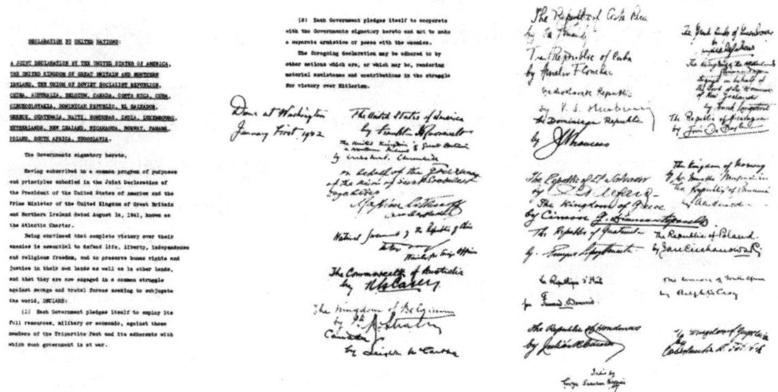

Figure 63: *The Allies unite in the fight against fascism.*

Declaration by United Nations

July 1, 1942

A JOINT DECLARATION BY THE UNITED STATES OF AMERICA, THE UNITED KINGDOM OF GREAT BRITAIN AND NORTHERN IRELAND, THE UNION OF SOVIET SOCIALIST REPUBLICS, CHINA, AUSTRALIA, BELGIUM, CANADA, COSTA RICA, CUBA, CZECHOSLOVAKIA, DOMINICAN REPUBLIC, EL SALVADOR, GREECE, GUATEMALA, HAITI, HONDURAS, INDIA, LUXEMBOURG, NETHERLANDS, NEW ZEALAND, NICARAGUA, NORWAY, PANAMA, POLAND, SOUTH AFRICA, YUGOSLAVIA.

The Governments signatory hereto,

Having subscribed to a common program of purposes and principles embodied in the Joint Declaration of the President of the United States of America and the Prime Minister of Great Britain of the United Kingdom and Northern Ireland dated August 14, 1941, known as the Atlantic Charter.

Being convinced that complete victory over their enemies is essential to defend life, liberty, independence and religious freedom, and to preserve human rights and justice in their own lands as well as in other lands, and that they are now engaged in a common struggle against savage and brutal forces seeking to subjugate the world,

DECLARE:

(1) Each Government pledges itself to employ its full resources, military or economic, against those members of the Tripartite Pact and its adherents with which such government is at war.

(2) Each Government pledges itself to cooperate with the Governments signatory hereto and not to make a separate armistice or peace with the enemies.

The foregoing declaration may be adhered to by other nations which are, or which may be, rendering material assistance and contributions in the struggle for victory over Hitlerism.

The Declaration by United Nations was also on display in the 1943 exhibition of the Library of Congress, along with Jefferson's 1776 drafts, fusing domestic and international meanings together, with a shared vocabulary that suddenly felt quite modern. Presumably, Jefferson would have been pleased.

In 1801, he wrote to John Dickinson that "a just and solid republican government maintained here, will be a standing monument & example for the aim & imitation of the people of other countries; and . . . will ameliorate the condition of man over a great portion of the globe."

But in another sense the World War II, like the first, would expose the emptiness of promises of equality, distributed so generously overseas, and so stingily at home. Jim Crow, the system of racial apartheid that had developed throughout the United States in the aftermath of Reconstruction, was still alive and well, and Black Americans were daily confronted with the chasm that separated their lived experience from the ideals of the Declaration. Still, they clung to a hope that the words might mean more someday, if interpreted by more sympathetic readers. What W.E.B. Du Bois had written in *The Souls of Black Folk* shortly after the turn of the century remained true as the nation mobilized for total war: "there are to-day no truer exponents of the pure human spirit of the Declaration of Independence than the American Negroes."

Figure 64: *Mary McLeod Bethune at her desk, in a 1943 photo by Gordon Parks.*

Mary McLeod Bethune lived her entire life under the Jim Crow regime, rising to distinction as an educator, activist, and presidential counselor. Born in 1875, the daughter of formerly enslaved parents, she lived until 1955, just a year after *Brown v. Board of Education*. Under the administration of Franklin D. Roosevelt, she became the first Black woman to lead a division of a federal agency (as the director of Negro Affairs at the National Youth Agency). She also helped Roosevelt assemble an informal circle of African American advisers, known colloquially as "the Black Cabinet," and became a friend to Eleanor Roosevelt. Despite these achievements, Bethune worried that progress on race would remain halting as long as Roosevelt needed the support of congressional Democrats in the South. In 1944, the same year she cofounded the United Negro College Fund, she contributed an essay titled "Certain Unalienable Rights" to a book of essays by leading Black figures, *What the Negro Wants.* Drawing her title from the Declaration, she argues passionately for the rights and dignities that were essential to all Americans as they joined a global war effort on behalf of freedom. Even before World War II ended, the Civil Rights Movement was clearly on the horizon.

Mary McLeod Bethune, "Certain Unalienable Rights"

1944

It is a quiet night in December, 1773. A British merchant ship rides easily at anchor in Boston Harbor. Suddenly, some row boats move out from the shore. Dark stealthy figures in the boats appear to be Indians in buckskin jackets and with feathers in their hair; but as they reach the ship, clamber abroad, climb down into the hold and carry out boxes of the cargo, the muffled voices speak English words. Their voices grow more excited and determined as they open the boxes and dump the King's tea into the ocean. The Boston Tea Party is in full swing. Resentment has reached flood tide. "Taxation without representation is tyranny!" The spark of the American Revolution has caught flame and the principle of the "consent of the governed" has been established by a gang disguised as Indians who take the law into their own hands. In this action a small and independent people struck out against restrictions and tyranny and oppression and gave initial expression to the ideal of a nation "that all men are created equal, that they are endowed by their Creator with certain unalienable Rights."

It is a Sunday night in Harlem in the year of our Lord 1943. Along the quiet streets dimmed out against the possibility of Axis air attack, colored Americans move to and fro or sit and talk and laugh. Suddenly electric rumor travels from mouth to ear: "A black soldier has been shot by a white policeman and has died in the arms of his mother." No one stops to ask how or why or if it be true. Crowds begin to gather. There is a rumbling of anger and resentment impelled by all the anger and all the resentment of all colored Americans in all the black ghettos in all the cities in America—the resentment against the mistreatment of Negroes in uniform, against restriction and oppression and discrimination breaks loose. Crowds of young people in blind fury strike out against the only symbols of this oppression which are near at hand. Rocks hurtle, windows crash, stores are broken open. Merchants' goods are tumbled into the streets, destroyed or stolen. Police are openly challenged and attacked. There are killings and bodily injury. For hours a veritable reign of terror runs through the streets. All efforts at restraint are of no avail. Finally the blind rage blows itself out.

Some are saying that a band of hoodlums have challenged law and order to burn and pillage and rob. Others look about them to remember riots in Detroit and Los Angeles and Beaumont. They will look further and recall cities laid in ruins by a global war in which the forces of tyranny and oppression and race supremacy attempt to subdue and restrain all the freedom of the world. They are thinking deeply to realize that there is a ferment aloose among the oppressed little people everywhere, a "groping of the long inert masses." They will see depressed and repressed masses all over the world swelling to the breaking point against the walls of ghettos, against economic, social and political restrictions; they will find them breaking open the King's boxes and throwing the tea into the ocean and storming the Bastilles stirred by the clarion call of the Four Freedoms. They are striking back against all that the Axis stands for. They are rising to achieve the ideals "that all men are created equal, that they are endowed by their Creator with certain unalienable Rights, that among these are Life, Liberty and the pursuit of Happiness." With the crash of the guns and the whir of the planes in their ears, led by the fighting voices of a Churchill and a Franklin Roosevelt, a Chiang Kai-shek and a Stalin, they are realizing that "Governments are instituted among Men" to achieve these aims and that these governments derive "their just power from the consent of the governed." They are a part of a peoples' war. The little people want "out." Just as the Colonists at the Boston Tea Party wanted "out" from under tyranny and oppression and taxation without representation, the Chinese want "out," the Indians want "out," and colored Americans want "out."

Throughout America today many people are alarmed and bewildered by the manifestation of this world ferment among the Negro masses. We say we are living in a period of "racial tension." They seem surprised that the Negro should be a part to this world movement. Really, all true Americans should not be surprised by this logical climax of American education. For several generations colored Americans have been brought up on the Boston Tea Party and the Declaration of Independence; on the principle of equality of opportunity, the possession of inalienable rights, the integrity and sanctity of the human personality. Along with other good Americans the Negro has been prepared to take his part in the fight against an enemy that threatens all these basic American principles. He is fighting now on land and sea and in the air to beat back these forces of oppression and tyranny and discrimination. Why, then, should we be surprised when at home as well as abroad he fights back against these same forces?

One who would really understand this racial tension which has broken out into actual conflict in riots as in Harlem, Detroit, and Los Angeles, must look to the roots and not be confused by the branches and the leaves. The tension rises out of the growing internal pressure of Negro masses to break through the wall of restriction which restrains them from full American citizenship. This mounting power is met by the unwillingness of white America to allow any appreciable breach in this wall. . . .

In order to maintain slavery, it was necessary to isolate black men from every possible manifestation of our culture. It was necessary to teach that they were inferior beings who could not profit from that culture. After the slave was freed, every effort has persisted to maintain "white supremacy" and wall the Negro in from every opportunity to challenge this concocted "supremacy." Many Americans said the Negro could not learn and they "proved" it by restricting his educational opportunities. When he surmounted these obstacles and achieved a measure of training, they said he did not know how to use it and proved it by restricting his employment opportunities. When it was necessary to employ him, they saw to it that he was confined to laborious and poorly-paid jobs. After they had made every effort to guarantee that his economic, social and cultural levels were low, they attributed his status to his race. Therefore, as he moved North and West after Reconstruction and during the Industrial Revolution, they saw to it that he was confined to living in veritable ghettos with covenants that were as hard and resistant as the walls of the ghettos of Warsaw.

They met every effort on his part to break through these barriers with stern resistance that would brook no challenge to our concept of white supremacy. Although they guaranteed him full citizenship under the Constitution and its Amendments, they saw to it that he was largely disfranchised and had little part in our hard won ideal of "the consent of the governed." In the midst of this anachronism, they increasingly educated his children in the American way of life—in its ideals of equality of all men before the law, and opportunities for the fullest possible development of the individual.

As this concept took hold among the Negro masses, it has evidenced itself through the years in a slow, growing, relentless pressure against every restriction which denied them their full citizenship. This pressure, intensified by those of other races who really believed in democracy, began to make a break through the walls here and there. It was given wide-spread impetus by the objectives of the New Deal with its emphasis on the rise of the forgotten man. With the coming of the Second World War, all the Negro's desires were given voice and support by the world leaders who fought back against Hitler and all he symbolizes. His efforts to break through have responded to Gandhi and Chiang Kai-shek, to Churchill and Franklin Roosevelt.

The radios and the press of the world have drummed into his ears the Four Freedoms, which would lead him to think that the world accepts as legitimate his claims as well as those of oppressed peoples all over the world. His drive for status has now swept past even most of his leaders, and has become imbedded in mass-consciousness which is pushing out of the way all the false prophets, be they white or black—or, be they at home or abroad.

The Negro wants to break out into the free realm of democratic citizenship. We can have only one of two responses. Either we must let him out wholly and completely in keeping with our ideals, or we must mimic Hitler and shove him back.

What, then, does the Negro want? His answer is very simple. He wants only what all other Americans want. He wants opportunity to make real what the Declaration of Independence and the Constitution and Bill of Rights say; what the Four Freedoms establish. While he knows these ideals are open to no man completely he wants only his equal chance to attain them. The Negro today wants specifically:

1. *Government leadership in building favorable public opinion.* Led by the President himself, the federal government should initiate a sound program carried out through appropriate federal agencies designed to indicate the importance of race in the war and post-war period. The cost of discrimination and segregation to a nation at war and the implications of American racial attitudes for our relationships with the other United Nations and their people should be delineated. Racial myths and superstitions should be exploded. The cooperation of the newspapers, the radio and the screen should be sought to replace caricature and slander with realistic interpretations of sound racial relationships.

2. *The victory of democracy over dictatorship.* Under democracy the Negro has the opportunity to work for an improvement in his status through the intelligent use of his vote, the creation of a more favorable public opinion,

and the development of his native abilities. The ideals of democracy and Christianity work for equality. These ideals the dictatorships disavow. Experience has taught only too well the implications for him and all Americans of a Nazi victory.

3. *Democracy in the armed forces.* He wants a chance to serve his country in all branches of the armed forces to his full capacity. He sees clearly the fallacy of fostering discrimination and segregation in the very forces that are fighting against discrimination and segregation all over the world. He believes that the government should fully protect the persons and the rights of all who wear the uniform of its armed forces.

4. *The protection of his civil rights and an end to lynching.* He wants full protection of the rights guaranteed all Americans by the Constitution; equality before the law, the right to jury trial and service, the eradication of lynching. Demanding these rights for himself, he will not be misled into any anti-foreign, Red-baiting, or anti-Semitic crusade to deny these rights to others. Appalled by the conditions prevailing in Washington, he joins in demanding the ballot for the District of Columbia and the protection of his rights now denied him within the shadow of the Capitol.

5. *The free ballot.* He wants the abolition of the poll tax and of the "white primary"; he wants universal adult suffrage. He means to use it to vote out all the advocates of racism and vote in those whose records show that they actually practise democracy.

6. *Equal access to employment opportunities.* He wants the chance to work and advance in any job for which he has the training and capacity. To this end he wants equal access to training opportunities. In all public programs, federal, state and local, he wants policy-making and administrative posts as well as rank and file jobs without racial discrimination. He wants a fair share of jobs under Civil Service.

7. *Extension of federal programs in public housing, health, social security, education and relief under federal control.* Low income and local prejudice often deprive him of these basic social services. Private enterprise or local government units cannot or will not provide them. For efficiency and equity in administration of these programs, the Negro looks to the federal government until such time as he has gained the full and free use of the ballot in all states.

8. *Elimination of racial barriers in labor unions.* He demands the right of admission on equal terms to the unions having jurisdiction over the crafts

or industries in which he is employed. He urges that job control on public works be denied to any union practising discrimination.

9. *Realistic interracial co-operation.* He realizes the complete interdependence of underprivileged white people and Negroes, North and South—laborers and sharecroppers alike. He knows that they stay in the gutter together or rise to security together; that the hope of democracy lies in their cooperative effort to make their government responsive to their needs; that national unity demands their sharing together more fully in the benefits of freedom—not "one as the hand and separate as the fingers," but one as the clasped hands of friendly cooperation.

Here, then, is a program for racial advancement and national unity. It adds up to the sum of the rights, privileges and responsibilities of full American citizenship. This is all that the Negro asks. He will not willingly accept less. As long as America offers less, she will be that much less a democracy. The whole way is the American way. . . .

"The American way." This phrase would become a cultural touchstone in the postwar decades. At the same time, Americans were not always united on how to read the instruction manuals. The end of World War II would create new challenges for a society proud of citing its old charters as evidence of an imperishable commitment to equality. As Mary McLeod Bethune understood, the Declaration's words were all too often observed in the breach.

Still, the words were plain to see, for all who took the time to read them. They were hard to miss, chiseled into the walls of the new Jefferson Memorial, built to observe his bicentennial in 1943. Not far away, Lincoln's words—answering Jefferson's—were just as visible, etched into the walls of a memorial of his own. Almost as if by a gravitational pull, the leaders of the Civil Rights Movement would find their way to this important civic space, as they, too, sought to deepen the meaning of the Declaration for a new generation.

PART V

THE PURSUIT OF HAPPINESS 1945–2026

What is the relevance of the Declaration to our modern world? How has our culture been shaped by its words, in particular by Jefferson's elegant phrase "the pursuit of Happiness"?

The overwhelming victory of the Allies in 1945 brought unprecedented influence to the United States, and by extension, to its founding charters. It came at a high cost; tens of millions of lives were lost, civilians as well as combatants, and millions of others bacame refugees. The post-war horizon was further darkened by a new awareness, after Hiroshima and the Holocaust, that the stately cadences of an eighteenth-century parchment might not be adequate for the inrushing problems of the nuclear age. To many, seeking to rebuild shattered lives, the pursuit of happiness must have felt more elusive than ever.

At the same time, victory seemed to validate the Declaration's brash insistence that the people are entitled to govern themselves. Suddenly, for nations and peoples around the world, that idealistic vision was closer to reality than ever. It was not simply that the Allies had defeated the Axis; new rights and freedoms were also spreading into the great spaces of Africa, Asia, and the Caribbean, where France and Great Britain, their exchequers emptied, were no longer able to afford their empires. That drab administrative reality may have done as much to advance self-determination as the defeat of fascism. On every continent, it appeared, democracy was on the march.

Franklin D. Roosevelt had lit the fuse, with his promise of Four Freedoms, but Eleanor Roosevelt kept the flame burning, embedding the concept of human rights inside the new articles of governance for the United Nations, the international organization that was expected to prevent the wars of the future.

Figure 65: *U.S. Army troops and vehicles parade down the main street of Oslo, Norway, during celebrations of the American Independence Day, July 4, 1945.*

Only two months after the death of her husband, Roosevelt was still writing her nationally syndicated "My Day" column. In the following reflection, she specifically asks that Americans celebrate the Fourth of July by thinking about human rights around the world. The war was still raging in the Pacific, with U.S. forces drawing near to the Japanese home islands. In Europe, Hitler was gone, but things were far from settled, with Russian, American, British, and French troops in close proximity to each other, tensely co-occupying Germany. A vision for the postwar order was needed, and Eleanor Roosevelt became a natural spokeswoman for a world based on rights and respect. That would include women's rights, where her qualifications to speak out were obvious, and the growing urgency of civil rights in the United States, where again she was a trailblazer.

Eleanor Roosevelt, "My Day, July 4, 1945"

HYDE PARK, Tuesday—All over the world our men will observe the Fourth of July. Even some of the nationals of foreign countries are going to celebrate this national holiday of the United States of America. I have a communication from our Ambassador in Brazil asking if I would accept, through our Ambassador, an honor which they wish to extend in memory of my husband on this important day.

This means that people throughout the world are going to ask what happened on July Fourth which made the American people choose it as their national holiday. They will be told that on that day a document was written in which a very small group of men set forth their convictions as to what was right or wrong. These men then led a successful war to uphold these convictions and freed themselves from a strong power across the sea that, at that time, was not concerned with the rights of people far away. Then they wrote a Constitution, to which they appended a Bill of Rights which delegated certain powers to their representatives in government, but retained the vast majority of fundamental powers in the hands of the people themselves.

* * *

What we remember most on the Fourth of July and what, I think, will impress itself most on the peoples of other nations as they read our Declaration of Independence, is that our concern was with human rights. In the last few years all over the world this question of human rights has been increasingly of importance to the people.

I think when the history of this past twelve years is written, we will find a very great development in the awareness of the people that their government belongs to them and is designed to furnish them with "life, liberty and the pursuit of happiness."

We have had periods here when property rights transcended human rights. But because our continent was such a vast one to develop, there was room for the development of property and its protection and we did not greatly harm the rights of human beings.

* * *

We have reached a point today, however—obviously we have been working toward it steadily during the last twelve years—when all questions will be considered first from the standpoint of human rights. That is going to hold good, I believe, throughout the world.

Perhaps, therefore, it is fitting that more and more this national holiday of ours should become known and respected by the peoples of the world. For the truths set down in the Declaration of Independence are the fundamentals of a lasting peace. If we are to move forward under the new charter toward a peaceful world, we must accept in all the United Nations these truths and it is well that we should remind ourselves individually in the U. S. A. that the Fourth of July is a day on which we glorify human rights.

E. R.

Despite apparent unity among the Allies, the end of World War II exposed a host of tensions that had been simmering below the surface. Roosevelt's speeches about freedom and self-determination had proven effective against the Nazis, but they also undermined the vast colonial empires of Great Britain and France. Suddenly, the peoples of the world clamored for rights of their own. The postwar era of independence required many new declarations, as one country after another adopted a new name, a new flag, and a new government.

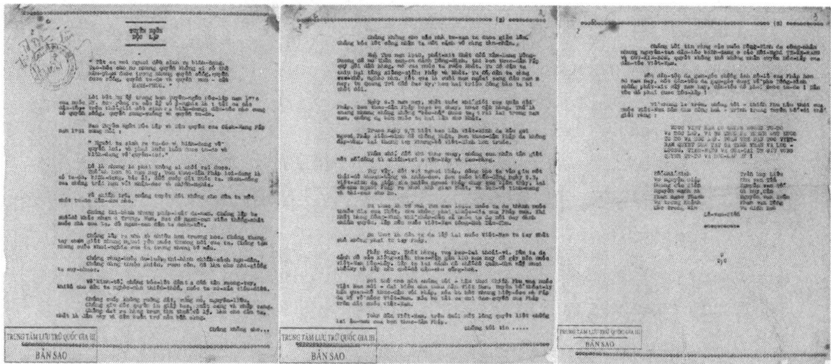
TRUNG TÂM LƯU TRỮ QUỐC GIA III
BẢN SAO

Figure 66: *An original copy of the September 2 declaration announcing the creation of the Democratic Republic of Vietnam.*

Vietnam was a case in point. In 1945, as the war was ending, the Viet Minh, nationalist guerillas led by Ho Chi Minh, were fighting against both the Japanese (who occupied Vietnam in 1940) and the French (who were trying to reassert their authority over a former colony). In the summer of 1945, Ho was encouraged by the friendly interest of the United States, which sent covert operatives to lend support. As a result of these new friendships, and his own scholarship, he drafted a declaration of independence that explicitly looked to American sources. Like the Founders, Ho believed it should be read to the people, and he did so, in Ba Đình Square, in Hanoi, on September 2, 1945.

Despite this early convergence, American interest in Vietnam soon swung in a dramatically different direction. Ho's plea for recognition would fall on deaf ears, as a series of American presidents chose to intervene in Vietnam, in a way that resembled George III more than Thomas Jefferson. As the pressures of the Cold War mounted, both Democratic and Republican administrations elected instead to support Vietnam's anticommunists, who opposed Ho and formed a regime of their own, in the South. Speaking against the Vietnam War in 1967, Martin Luther King, Jr., would call Americans "strange liberators," at odds with their own history as they sought to command the destinies of a foreign people, thousands of miles away.

A long and bloody civil war delayed unification for decades, and exacted dreadful costs on all sides, including the United States. Ironically, Vietnam's final independence was proclaimed on July 2, 1976—two days short of the American Bicentennial.

Declaration of Independence of the Democratic Republic of Viet Nam

September 2, 1945

"All men are created equal. They are endowed by their Creator with certain inalienable rights; among them are Life, Liberty and the pursuit of Happiness."

This immortal statement appeared in the Declaration of Independence of the United States of America in 1776. In a broader sense, it means: All the peoples on the earth are equal from birth, all the peoples have a right to live and to be happy and free.

The Declaration of the Rights of Man and the Citizen, made at the time of the French Revolution, in 1791, also states: "All men are born free and with equal rights, and must always remain free and have equal rights."

Those are undeniable truths.

Nevertheless, for more than eighty years, the French imperialists, abusing the standard of Liberty, Equality and Fraternity, have violated our Fatherland and oppressed our fellow-citizens. They have acted contrary to the ideals of humanity and justice.

Politically, they have deprived our people of every democratic liberty.

They have enforced inhuman laws; they have set up three different political regimes in the North, the Centre and the South of Viet Nam in order to wreck our country's oneness and prevent our people from being united.

They have built more prisons than schools. They have mercilessly massacred our patriots. They have drowned our uprisings in seas of blood.

They have fettered public opinion and practised obscurantism.

They have weakened our race with opium and alcohol.

In the field of economics, they have sucked us dry, driven our people to destitution and devastated our land.

They have robbed us of our ricefields, our mines, our forests and our natural resources. They have monopolized the issue of bank-notes and the import and export trade.

They have invented numerous unjustifiable taxes and reduced our people, especially our peasantry, to extreme poverty.

They have made it impossible for our national bourgeoisie to prosper; they have mercilessly exploited our workers.

In the autumn of 1940, when the Japanese fascists invaded Indochina to establish new bases against the Allies, the French colonialists went down on their bended knees and opened the doors of our country to welcome the Japanese in.

Thus, from that date, our people were subjected to the double yoke of the French and the Japanese. Their sufferings and miseries increased. The result was that towards the end of last year and the beginning of this year, from Quang Tri province to the North, more than two million of our fellow-citizens died from starvation.

On the 9th of March this year, the French troops were disarmed by the Japanese. The French colonialists either fled or surrendered, showing that not only were they incapable of "protecting" us, but that, in a period of five years, they had twice sold our country to the Japanese.

Before the 9th of March, how often the Viet Minh had urged the French to ally themselves with it against the Japanese! But instead of agreeing to this proposal, the French colonialists only intensified their terrorist activities against the Viet Minh. After their defeat and before fleeing, they massacred the political prisoners detained at Yen Bai and Cao Bang.

In spite of all this, our fellow-citizens have always manifested a lenient and humane attitude towards the French. After the Japanese putsch of March 9, 1945, the Viet Minh helped many Frenchmen to cross the frontier, rescued others from Japanese jails and protected French lives and property. In fact, since the autumn of 1940, our country had ceased to be a French colony and had become a Japanese possession.

When the Japanese surrendered to the Allies, our entire people rose to gain power and founded the Democratic Republic of Viet Nam.

The truth is that we have wrested our independence from the Japanese, not from the French.

The French have fled, the Japanese have capitulated, Emperor Bao Dai has abdicated. Our people have broken the chains which have fettered them for nearly a century and have won independence for Viet Nam. At the same time they have overthrown the centuries-old monarchic regime and established a democratic republican regime.

We, the Provisional Government of the new Viet Nam, representing the entire Vietnamese people, hereby declare that from now on we break off all relations of a colonial character with France; cancel all treaties signed by France on Viet Nam, and abolish all privileges held by France in our country.

The entire Vietnamese people are of one mind in their determination to oppose all wicked schemes by the French colonialists.

We are convinced that the Allies, which at the Teheran and San Francisco Conferences upheld the principle of equality among the nations, cannot fail to recognize the right of the Vietnamese people to independence.

A people who have courageously opposed French enslavement for more than eighty years, a people who resolutely sided with the Allies against the fascists during these last years, such a people must be free, such a people must be independent.

For these reasons, we, the Provisional Government of the Democratic Republic of Viet Nam, solemnly make this declaration to the world:

Viet Nam has the right to enjoy freedom and independence and in fact has become a free and independent country. The entire Vietnamese people are determined to mobilize all their physical and mental strength, to sacrifice their lives and property in order to safeguard their freedom and independence.

Figure 67: *Eleanor Roosevelt displays the final Declaration of Human Rights at Lake Success, New York, the home of the United Nations until 1951.*

Franklin D. Roosevelt had sought to define a postwar order that would preserve a hard-won peace, defend the sovereignty of nations, and protect the individual rights of their peoples. He began to articulate these thoughts even before the United States entered the war, in a meeting with Churchill off Newfoundland in August 1941. The Atlantic Charter they drafted promised respect for "the right of all peoples to choose the form of government under which they will live." A series of other agreements followed, often called "declarations." As we have seen, the Declaration by United Nations, signed on January 1, 1942, defined the goals of "life, liberty, independence and religious freedom," and began to envision a post-war organization that would protect the peace.

When the United Nations came into existence in 1945, it was quickly recognized that a formal declaration was required, one that would articulate the core rights and values that the new organization would protect. Franklin D. Roosevelt died just weeks before the San Francisco conference that launched the UN, and Eleanor Roosevelt was asked to chair the committee that drafted the Universal Declaration of Human Rights, proclaimed in 1948. “Human rights” was a new phrase in the lexicon of international relations, but it was not a great distance from the Declaration of Independence, which used “human” in its first sentence, and “rights” in its second.

Universal Declaration of Human Rights

December 10, 1948

Whereas recognition of the inherent dignity and of the equal and inalienable rights of all members of the human family is the foundation of freedom, justice and peace in the world,

Whereas disregard and contempt for human rights have resulted in barbarous acts which have outraged the conscience of mankind, and the advent of a world in which human beings shall enjoy freedom of speech and belief and freedom from fear and want has been proclaimed as the highest aspiration of the common people,

Whereas it is essential, if man is not to be compelled to have recourse, as a last resort, to rebellion against tyranny and oppression, that human rights should be protected by the rule of law,

Whereas it is essential to promote the development of friendly relations between nations,

Whereas the peoples of the United Nations have in the Charter reaffirmed their faith in fundamental human rights, in the dignity and worth of the human person and in the equal rights of men and women and have determined to promote social progress and better standards of life in larger freedom,

Whereas Member States have pledged themselves to achieve, in cooperation with the United Nations, the promotion of universal respect for and observance of human rights and fundamental freedoms,

Whereas a common understanding of these rights and freedoms is of the greatest importance for the full realization of this pledge,

Now, therefore,

THE GENERAL ASSEMBLY,

Proclaims this Universal Declaration of Human Rights as a common standard of achievement for all peoples and all nations, to the end that every individual and every organ of society, keeping this Declaration constantly in mind, shall strive by teaching and education to promote respect for these rights and freedoms and by progressive measures, national and international, to secure their universal and effective recognition and observance, both among the peoples of Member States themselves and among the peoples of territories under their jurisdiction.

Article 1: All human beings are born free and equal in dignity and rights. They are endowed with reason and conscience and should act towards one another in a spirit of brotherhood.

Article 2: Everyone is entitled to all the rights and freedoms set forth in this Declaration, without distinction of any kind, such as race, colour, sex, language, religion, political or other opinion, national or social origin, property, birth or other status. Furthermore, no distinction shall be made on the basis of the political, jurisdictional or international status of the country or territory to which a person belongs, whether it be independent, trust, non-self-governing or under any other limitation of sovereignty.

Article 3: Everyone has the right to life, liberty and the security of person.

Article 4: No one shall be held in slavery or servitude; slavery and the slave trade shall be prohibited in all their forms.

Article 5: No one shall be subjected to torture or to cruel, inhuman or degrading treatment or punishment.

Article 6: Everyone has the right to recognition everywhere as a person before the law.

Article 7: All are equal before the law and are entitled without any discrimination to equal protection of the law. All are entitled to equal protection against any discrimination in violation of this Declaration and against any incitement to such discrimination.

Article 8: Everyone has the right to an effective remedy by the competent national tribunals for acts violating the fundamental rights granted him by the constitution or by law.

Article 9: No one shall be subjected to arbitrary arrest, detention or exile.

Article 10: Everyone is entitled in full equality to a fair and public hearing by an independent and impartial tribunal, in the determination of his rights and obligations and of any criminal charge against him.

Article 11: 1. Everyone charged with a penal offence has the right to be presumed innocent until proved guilty according to law in a public trial at which he has had all the guarantees necessary for his defence. 2. No one shall be held guilty of any penal offence on account of any act or omission which did not constitute a penal offence, under national or international law, at the time when it was committed. Nor shall a heavier penalty be imposed than the one that was applicable at the time the penal offence was committed.

Article 12: No one shall be subjected to arbitrary interference with his privacy, family, home or correspondence, nor to attacks upon his honour and reputation. Everyone has the right to the protection of the law against such interference or attacks.

Article 13: 1. Everyone has the right to freedom of movement and residence within the borders of each state. 2. Everyone has the right to leave any country, including his own, and to return to his country.

Article 14: 1. Everyone has the right to seek and to enjoy in other countries asylum from persecution. 2. This right may not be invoked in the case of prosecutions genuinely arising from non-political crimes or from acts contrary to the purposes and principles of the United Nations.

Article 15: 1. Everyone has the right to a nationality. 2. No one shall be arbitrarily deprived of his nationality nor denied the right to change his nationality.

Article 16: 1. Men and women of full age, without any limitation due to race, nationality or religion, have the right to marry and to found a family. They are entitled to equal rights as to marriage, during marriage and at its dissolution. 2. Marriage shall be entered into only with the free and full consent of the intending spouses. 3. The family is the natural and fundamental group unit of society and is entitled to protection by society and the State.

Article 17: 1. Everyone has the right to own property alone as well as in association with others. 2. No one shall be arbitrarily deprived of his property.

Article 18: Everyone has the right to freedom of thought, conscience and religion; this right includes freedom to change his religion or belief, and freedom, either alone or in community with others and in public or private, to manifest his religion or belief in teaching, practice, worship and observance.

Article 19: Everyone has the right to freedom of opinion and expression; this right includes freedom to hold opinions without interference and to seek, receive and impart information and ideas through any media and regardless of frontiers.

Article 20: 1. Everyone has the right to freedom of peaceful assembly and association. 2. No one may be compelled to belong to an association.

Article 21: 1. Everyone has the right to take part in the government of his country, directly or through freely chosen representatives. 2. Everyone has the right to equal access to public service in his country. 3. The will of the people shall be the basis of the authority of government; this will shall be expressed in periodic and genuine elections which shall be by universal and equal suffrage and shall be held by secret vote or by equivalent free voting procedures.

Article 22: Everyone, as a member of society, has the right to social security and is entitled to realization, through national effort and international co-operation and in accordance with the organization and resources of each State, of the economic, social and cultural rights indispensable for his dignity and the free development of his personality.

Article 23: 1. Everyone has the right to work, to free choice of employment, to just and favourable conditions of work and to protection against unemployment. 2. Everyone, without any discrimination, has the right to equal pay for equal work. 3. Everyone who works has the right to just and favourable remuneration ensuring for himself and his family an existence worthy of human dignity, and supplemented, if necessary, by other means of social protection. 4. Everyone has the right to form and to join trade unions for the protection of his interests.

Article 24: Everyone has the right to rest and leisure, including reasonable limitation of working hours and periodic holidays with pay.

Article 25: 1. Everyone has the right to a standard of living adequate for the health and well-being of himself and of his family, including food, clothing, housing and medical care and necessary social services, and the right to security in the event of unemployment, sickness, disability, widowhood, old age or other lack of livelihood in circumstances beyond his control. 2. Motherhood and childhood are entitled to special care and assistance. All children, whether born in or out of wedlock, shall enjoy the same social protection.

Article 26: 1. Everyone has the right to education. Education shall be free, at least in the elementary and fundamental stages. Elementary education shall be compulsory. Technical and professional education shall be made generally available and higher education shall be equally accessible to all on the basis of merit. 2. Education shall be directed to the full development of the human personality and to the strengthening of respect for human rights and fundamental freedoms. It shall promote understanding, tolerance and friendship among all nations, racial or religious groups, and shall further the activities of the United Nations for the maintenance of peace. 3. Parents have a prior right to choose the kind of education that shall be given to their children.

Article 27: 1. Everyone has the right freely to participate in the cultural life of the community, to enjoy the arts and to share in scientific advancement and its benefits. 2. Everyone has the right to the protection of the moral and material interests resulting from any scientific, literary or artistic production of which he is the author.

Article 28: Everyone is entitled to a social and international order in which the rights and freedoms set forth in this Declaration can be fully realized.

Article 29: 1. Everyone has duties to the community in which alone the free and full development of his personality is possible. 2. In the exercise of his rights and freedoms, everyone shall be subject only to such limitations as are determined by law solely for the purpose of securing due recognition and respect for the rights and freedoms of others and of meeting the just requirements of morality, public order and the general welfare in a democratic society. 3. These rights and freedoms may in no case be exercised contrary to the purposes and principles of the United Nations.

Article 30: Nothing in this Declaration may be interpreted as implying for any State, group or person any right to engage in any activity or to perform any act aimed at the destruction of any of the rights and freedoms set forth herein.

As instruments were created to establish a new human rights regime around the world, they sharpened a perception in some quarters that the same rights were not observed fully in the United States. Returning veterans—particularly African Americans—were determined to enjoy these rights to the fullest after fighting for their country.

FOUR ESSENTIAL RIGHTS

THE RIGHT TO SAFETY AND SECURITY OF THE PERSON

THE RIGHT TO CITIZENSHIP AND ITS PRIVILEGES

ALL AMERICANS

THE RIGHT TO FREEDOM OF CONSCIENCE AND EXPRESSION

THE RIGHT TO EQUALITY OF OPPORTUNITY

Figure 68: *This illustration accompanied the report of the President's Committee on Civil Rights.*

Roosevelt's successor, Harry Truman, came from a former slave state (Missouri), but he believed that the Declaration's promises extended to all Americans. In 1947, that belief was being tested, as state and local governments (including the District of Columbia) continued to enforce segregation in schools and public places. But many Americans—inspired in part by the courage of Jackie Robinson, who was proving his ability on the baseball field that season—were increasingly unwilling to accept racial injustice. A series of lawsuits by the National Association for the Advancement of Colored Peoples was forcing a reckoning in the courts, and in the court of public opinion. Truman sent signals of agreement, including a speech to the NAACP, gathered by the Lincoln Memorial, on June 29, 1947. In October 1947, a commission he had established, the President's Committee on Civil Rights, submitted a 178-page report, *To Secure These Rights*, its title derived from the second paragraph of the Declaration. It detailed all the ways in which basic rights were being withheld from a large portion of the population and in clear-eyed language argued that racial discrimination was harming the economy and America's standing in the world.

Following its recommendations, Truman ordered an end to segregation in the military and the federal workforce, and proposed comprehensive civil rights legislation to Congress in February 1948. These steps marked a new beginning, paving the way for the Civil Rights Movement of the 1950s and 1960s. What follows is the report's first chapter, "The American Heritage: The Promise of Freedom and Equality."

To Secure These Rights: The Report of the President's Committee on Civil Rights

1947

In the time that it takes to read this report, 1,000 Americans will be born. These new Americans will come into families whose religious faiths are a roster of all those which men hold sacred. Their names will be strange and varied, echoes from every corner of the world. Their skins will range in color from black to white. A few will be born to riches, more to average comfort, and too many to poverty. All of them will be Americans.

These new Americans, drawn from all of the races of mankind, provide a challenge to our American democracy. We have a great heritage of freedom and equality for all men, sometimes called "the American way." Yet we cannot avoid the knowledge that the American ideal still awaits complete realization.

It was this knowledge which led the President to create this Committee; and the Committee's assignment has been primarily to discover wherein and to what extent we are presently failing to live up to that ideal. As we have said, this has meant that in its deliberations, and in this report, the Committee has focused its attention, not upon our achievements in protecting our heritage of civil liberties, but upon our shortcomings and our mistakes. These the Committee has not minimized nor has it evaded the responsibility of recommending remedial action. A later section of this report summarizes some of the concrete gains which we have made in the more secure protection of freedom and equality. Further evidence of our adherence to our great heritage in this field is the desire of our government to have our national record carefully scrutinized in an effort to expose our shortcomings and to find ways of correcting them.

If we are to judge with accuracy how far short we have fallen living up to the ideals which comprise our American heritage of freedom and equality, we must first make clear what that heritage is.

THE IDEAL OF FREEDOM AND EQUALITY

The central theme in our American heritage is the importance of the individual person. From the earliest moment of our history we have believed that every human being has an essential dignity and integrity which must be respected and safeguarded. Moreover, we believe that the welfare of the individual is the final goal of group life. Our American heritage further teaches that to be secure in the rights he wishes for himself, each man must be willing to respect the rights of other men. This is the conscious recognition of a basic moral principle: all men are created equal as well as free. Stemming from this principle is the obligation to build social institutions that will guarantee equality of opportunity to all men. Without this equality freedom becomes an illusion. Thus the only aristocracy that is consistent with the free way of life is an aristocracy of talent and achievement. The grounds on which our society accords respect, influence or reward to each of its citizens must be limited to the quality of his personal character and of his social contribution.

This concept of equality which is so vital a part of the American heritage knows no kinship with notions of human uniformity or regimentation. We abhor the totalitarian arrogance which makes one man say that he will respect another man as his equal only if he has "*my* race, *my* religion, *my* political views, *my* social position." In our land men are equal, but they are free to be different. From these very differences among our people has come the great human and national strength of America.

Thus, the aspirations and achievements of each member of our society are to be limited only by the skills and energies he brings to the opportunities equally offered to all Americans. We can tolerate no restrictions upon the individual which depend upon irrelevant factors such as his race, his color, his religion or the social position to which he is born.

GOVERNMENT AND FREEDOM

The men who founded our Republic, as those who have built any constitutional democracy, faced the task of reconciling personal liberty and group authority, or of establishing an equilibrium between them. In a democratic state we recognize that the common interests of the people must be managed by laws and procedures established by majority rule. But a democratic majority, left unrestrained, may be as ruthless and tyrannical as were the earlier absolute monarchs. Seeing this clearly, and fearing it greatly, our forefathers built a constitutional system in which valued personal liberties, carefully enumerated in a Bill of Rights, were placed beyond the reach of popular majorities. Thus the people permanently denied the federal government power to interfere with certain personal rights and freedoms.

Freedom, however, as we now use the term, means even more than the traditional "freedoms" listed in our Bill of Rights—important as they are. Freedom has come to mean the right of a man to manage his own affairs as he sees fit up to the point where what he does interferes with the equal rights of others in the community to manage their affairs—or up to the point where he begins to injure the welfare of the whole group. It is clear that in modern democratic society a man's freedom in this broader sense is not and cannot be absolute—nor does it exist in a vacuum—but instead is hedged about by the competing rights of others and the demands of the social welfare. In this context it is government which must referee the clashes which arise among the freedoms of citizens, and protect each citizen in the enjoyment of the maximum freedom to which he is entitled.

There is no essential conflict between freedom and government. Bills of rights restrain government from abridging individual civil liberties, while government itself by sound legislative policies protects citizens against the aggressions of others seeking to push their freedoms too far. Thus in the words of the Declaration of Independence: "Man is endowed by his Creator with certain inalienable rights. Among these are life, liberty, and the pursuit of happiness. To secure these rights, *governments are instituted among men.*"

THE ESSENTIAL RIGHTS

The rights essential to the citizen in a free society can be described in different words and in varying orders. The three great rights of the Declaration of Independence have just been mentioned. Another noble statement is made in the Bill of Rights of our Constitution. A more recent formulation is found in the Four Freedoms.

Four basic rights have seemed important to this Committee and have influenced its labors. We believe that each of these rights is essential to the well-being of the individual and to the progress of society.

1. The Right to Safety and Security of the Person: Freedom can exist only where the citizen is assured that his person is secure against bondage, lawless violence, and arbitrary arrest and punishment. Freedom from slavery in all its forms is clearly necessary if all men are to have equal opportunity to use their talents and to lead worthwhile lives. Moreover, to be free, men must be subject to discipline by society only for commission of offenses clearly defined by law and only after trial by due process of law.

Where the administration of justice is discriminatory, no man can be sure of security. Where the threat of violence by private persons or mobs exists, a cruel inhibition of the sense of freedom of activity and security of the person inevitably results. Where a society permits private and arbitrary violence to be done to its members, its own integrity is inevitably corrupted. It cannot permit human beings to be imprisoned or killed in the absence of due process of law without degrading its entire fabric.

2. The Right to Citizenship and its Privileges: Since it is a purpose of government in a democracy to regulate the activity of each man in the interest of all men, it follows that every mature and responsible person must be able to enjoy full citizenship and have an equal voice in his government. Because the right to participate in the political process is customarily limited to citizens there can be no denial of access to citizenship based upon race, color, creed, or national origin. Denial of citizenship for these reasons cheapens the personality of those who are confined to this inferior status and endangers the whole concept of a democratic society.

To deny qualified citizens the right to vote while others exercise it is to do violence to the principle of freedom and equality. Without the right to vote, the individual loses his voice in the group effort and is subjected to rule by a body from which he has been excluded. Likewise, the right of the individual to vote is important to the group itself. Democracy assumes that the majority is more likely as a general rule to make decisions which are wise and desirable from the point of view of the interests of the whole society than is any minority. Every time a qualified person is denied a voice in public affairs, one of the components of a potential majority is lost, and the formation of a sound public policy is endangered.

To the citizen in a democracy, freedom is a precious possession. Accordingly, all able-bodied citizens must enjoy the right to serve the nation and the cause of freedom in time of war. Any attempt to curb the right to fight in its defense can only lead the citizen to question the worth of the society in which he lives. A sense of frustration is created which is wholly alien to the normal emotions of a free man. In particular, any discrimination which, while imposing an obligation, prevents members of minority groups from rendering full military service in defense of their country is for them a peculiarly humiliating badge of inferiority. The nation also suffers a loss of manpower and is unable to marshal maximum strength at a moment when such strength is most needed.

3. The Right to Freedom of Conscience and Expression: In a free society there is faith in the ability of the people to make sound, rational judgments. But such judgments are possible only where the people have access to all relevant facts and to all prevailing interpretations of the facts. How can such judgments be formed on a sound basis if arguments, viewpoints, or opinions are arbitrarily suppressed? How can the concept of the marketplace of thought in which truth ultimately prevails retain its validity if the thought of certain individuals is denied the right of circulation? The Committee reaffirms our tradition that freedom of expression may be curbed by law only where the danger to the well-being of society is clear and present.

Our forefathers fought bloody wars and suffered torture and death for the right to worship God according to the varied dictates of conscience. Complete religious liberty has been accepted as an unquestioned personal freedom since our Bill of Rights was adopted. We have insisted only that religious freedom may not be pleaded as an excuse for criminal or clearly anti-social conduct.

4. The Right to Equality of Opportunity: It is not enough that full and equal membership in society entitles the individual to an equal voice in the control of his government; it must also give him the right to enjoy the benefits of society and to contribute to its progress. The opportunity of each individual to obtain useful employment, and to have access to services in the fields of education, housing, health, recreation and transportation, whether available free or at a price, must be provided with complete disregard for race, color, creed, and national origin. Without this equality of opportunity the individual is deprived of the chance to develop his potentialities and to share the fruits of society. The group also suffers through the loss of the contributions which might have been made by persons excluded from the main channels of social and economic activity.

THE HERITAGE AND THE REALITY

Our American heritage of freedom and equality has given us prestige among the nations of the world and a strong feeling of national pride at home. There is much reason for that pride. But pride is no substitute for steady and honest performance, and the record shows that at varying times in American history the gulf between ideals and practice has been wide. We have had human slavery. We have had religious persecution.

> We have had mob rule. We still have their ideological remnants in the unwarrantable "pride and prejudice" of some of our people and practices. From our work as a Committee, we have learned much that has shocked us, and much that has made us feel ashamed. But we have seen nothing to shake our conviction that the civil rights of the American people—all of them—can be strengthened quickly and effectively by the normal processes of democratic, constitutional government. That strengthening, we believe, will make our daily life more and more consonant with the spirit of the American heritage of freedom. But it will require as much courage, as much imagination, as much perseverance as anything which we have ever done together. The members of this Committee reaffirm their faith in the American heritage and in its promise.

As it happened, President Truman would play an even more immediate role in the Declaration's story. Some background: while laying the cornerstone of the National Archives in 1933, President Herbert Hoover, in one of his final official acts, decreed that the Declaration would someday reside there. In some ways it made sense to house the document in a handsome new building, built for archival purposes, and designed by John Russell Pope, who also designed the Jefferson Memorial. But it took two decades, in a city where bureaucracy can often blunt the clear language of an executive order, and where the best-laid plans are often built on sandy foundations. Indeed, that was precisely the situation of the Archives, built over the bed of a now-buried river called the Tiber Creek, well known in Lincoln's time.

On December 13, 1952, the transfer was finally effected. The charter documents were carefully crated and nestled on mattresses before a short drive down Pennsylvania Avenue, in a Marine Corps personnel carrier, accompanied by a color guard, a motorcycle escort, two military bands, two tanks, and four guards carrying submachine guns.

Two days later, on December 15, President Truman spoke at a dedication ceremony. In his remarks, he hinted at the nuclear anxieties of the era: "We are enshrining these documents for future ages. . . . This magnificent hall has been constructed to exhibit them, and the vault beneath, that we have built to protect them, is as safe from destruction as anything that the wit of modern man can devise." That tone tracked with a growing view that the Declaration and democracy were somehow one and the same—and that it would be vital to protect the former if the latter were to survive.

Figure 69: *On December 13, 1952, the Declaration of Independence and the Constitution were transferred from the Library of Congress to their permanent home in the newly dedicated National Archives Building.*

If staffers at the Library of Congress regretted their loss, the transfer allowed another chance to investigate the condition of the charters. There were reasons for concern. Archivists had taken steps to mitigate the damage caused by natural light in the nineteenth century, adding a sheet of yellow gelatin between the panes of glass that held the Declaration. But to their alarm, they also detected signs that the shrine had been invaded, by tiny beetles and other insects that managed to penetrate the encasement and feed on the parchment.

Another problem was that the humidity of Washington summers was causing stress, weakening the adhesive at the Declaration's edges and leading to small tears as the document expanded and contracted with the weather. When moved to the National Archives, its new encasement was filled with humidified helium, and sealed, to protect it from the fluctuations in the atmosphere. The Declaration was also lowered into a subterranean vault every evening.

* * *

A major goal of the postwar Civil Rights Movement was the overturning of the doctrine of "separate but equal" that had been enshrined in *Plessy v. Ferguson* (1896) and allowed racial segregation. That precedent had largely disregarded the idea, implied by the Declaration, and made explicit by the Fourteenth Amendment to the Constitution, that all citizens were entitled to "the equal protection of the laws." Instead, it had permitted an unequal system of segregation to spread across the South and in many other parts of the nation, including the nation's capital. As anyone could tell after a cursory examination of schools and hospitals, "separate" did not mean "equal."

In 1954, the NAACP joined a class-action suit before the Supreme Court, testing the "separate but equal" theory with respect to public schools. The NAACP's counsel, Thurgood Marshall, himself a product of segregated schools, won a unanimous decision that made segregation illegal. Shortly before the court delivered its landmark ruling in *Brown v. Board of Education*, Marshall—later appointed to the Supreme Court by Lyndon Johnson in 1967—delivered the following speech at Dillard University in New Orleans, in which he argues that the Declaration and the Constitution are meaningless if Americans fail to live up to their words.

Figure 70: *When he heard the unanimous opinion in* Brown v. Board of Education*—in which Chief Justice Earl Warren, writing for the court, affirmed that "in the field of public education the doctrine of 'separate but equal' has no place. Separate educational facilities are inherently unequal"—Thurgood Marshall recalled that "I was so happy I was numb."*

Thurgood Marshall, The Edwin R. Embree Memorial Lecture

February 1954

SEGREGATION AND DESEGREGATION

There has been much discussion during recent years concerning the question of the removal in this country of dual citizenship based solely on race and color. The primary emphasis has been on the elimination of racial segregation. No one denies that progress is being made. There are, however, some who say that the progress is too slow and others who say that the progress is too rapid. The important thing to remember is that progress is being made. We are moving ahead. We have passed the crossroads. We are moving toward a completely integrated society, North and South.

Those who doubt this and those who are afraid of complete integration are victims of a background based upon long indoctrination of only one side of the controversy in this country. They know only of one side of the controversy in this country. They know only of one side of slavery. They know only the biased reports about Reconstruction and the long-standing theory which seems to support the "legality" of the separate-but-equal doctrine.

In order to adequately appraise the situation, we must first understand the problem in relation to our history—legal and political. Secondly, we must give proper weight to progress that has been made with and without legal pressure, and thirdly, we must look to the future.

Our government is based on the principle of the equality of man the individual, not the group. All of us can quote the principle that "All men are created equal." Our basic legal document, the Constitution of the United States, guarantees equal protection of the laws to all of us. Many state constitutions have similar provisions. We even have a "Bill of Rights" in the Constitution of Louisiana. These high-sounding principles we preach and teach. However, in the eyes of the world we stand convicted of violating these principles day in and day out.

Today, one hundred and seventy-seven years after the signing of the Declaration of Independence and eighty-six years after the Fourteenth Amendment was adopted, we have a society where, in varying degrees throughout the country, but especially in the South, Negroes, solely because they are Negroes, are segregated, ostracized, and set apart from all other Americans. This discrimination extends from the cradle to the graveyard. (And I emphasize grave*yard*, rather than grave.) Or, to put it even more bluntly, in many areas of this country, a white paroled murderer would be welcome in places which would at the same time exclude such people as Ralph Bunche, Marian Anderson, Jackie Robinson, and many others. Constitutionally protected individual rights have been effectively destroyed by outmoded theories of racial or group inferiority. Why is this true? How long can we afford the luxury of segregation and discrimination? . . .

As of the present time, the paramount issue in so far as Americanism is concerned is the ending of all racial distinctions in American life. The reasons for this are many. A weighty factor, of course, is the recognition by more and more people in high places that the world situation in regard to the sensitive areas throughout the world depends on how well we can handle our race problem in this country. Our country can no longer tolerate an Achilles heel of discriminatory practices toward its darker citizens. Even more important is the realization that the equality of man as a principle and the equal protection of the laws as a Constitutional concept are both based upon the moral principle of individual responsibility rather than racial identity.

Racial segregation in our country is immoral, costly, and damaging to the nation's prestige. Segregation and discrimination violate the Judeo-Christian ethic, and the democratic creed on which our national morality is based is soundly established in the minds of most men. But in addition, it has been shown that the costs of segregation and discrimination to the nation are staggering. . . .

In conclusion, racial segregation is grounded upon the myth of inherent racial superiority. This myth has been completely exploded by all scientific studies. It now stands exposed as a theory which can only be explained as a vehicle for perpetuating racial prejudice. History reveals that racial segregation is a badge of slavery, is just as unscientifically supported, immoral, and un-American as slavery. Recent history shows that it can be removed, and that it can be done effectively when approached intelligently.

There is no longer any justification for segregation. There is no longer any excuse for it. There is no longer any reason under the sun why intelligent people should continue to find excuses for not ending segregation in their own community, in the South as well as in the North.

Figure 71: W.E.B. Du Bois is shown here with Mary McLeod Bethune at the United Nations Conference on International Organization held in San Francisco from April 25 to June 26, 1945.

The great scholar and civil rights activist W.E.B. Du Bois was eighty-seven years old in 1955, but he had not lost his dedication to the cause of African and African American empowerment. Excited by the independence movements then sweeping across Africa, he drafted a "proposed Declaration of Independence" for the entire continent.

It was not perhaps the most realistic of documents; postcolonial Africa was about to be divided into dozens of countries, each sovereign, and it contains no thoughts about how Africans should organize themselves into political bodies. But it boils with indignation against the extractive regimes that had been exploiting Africa, and its evocative imagery reveals the exuberance of an era in which the rights of the Declaration were at last understood to be available to all.

W.E.B. Du Bois, A Proposed Declaration of Independence of the People of Africa

April 1955

The peoples of Africa, black and white, brown and yellow, have a right to Freedom and Self-government, to Food and Shelter, Education and Health.

We hereby warn the world that no longer can Africa be regarded as pawn, slave or property of Europeans, Americans or of any other people.

Africa is for the Africans; its Land and Labor; its natural wealth and resources, its mountains, lakes and rivers; its cultures and its Soul.

Hereafter it will no longer be ruled by Might nor by Power; by invading armies nor police; but by the Spirit of all its Gods and the Wisdom of its Prophets.

Men of all races are welcome to Africa if they obey its laws, seek its interests and love their neighbors as themselves, doing unto others as they would that others should do to them. But the white bigots of South Africa and Kenya; the exploiters of the Rhodesias, the Congo, West, North and Southwest and Southeast Africa, are solemnly warned that they cannot win. Their doom is sealed. We will be free; we will govern ourselves for our best good. Our wealth and labor belongs to us and not to thieves at home nor abroad. Black Africa welcomes the world as equals; as masters, never; we will fight this forever and curse the blaspheming Boers and the heathen liars from Hell.

Let the white world keep its missionaries at home to teach the Golden Rule to its corporate thieves. Damn the God of slavery, exploitation and War. Peace on Earth; no more War. The earth of Africa is for its people. Its Wealth is for the poor and not for the rich. All Hail Africa!

As Du Bois's manifesto attests, the Universal Declaration of Human Rights had transformed the rights-based revolution of the Anglo-American tradition into something significantly more expansive. One phrase in Jefferson's Declaration, perhaps more than any other, opened the door to this transformation: "the pursuit of happiness." And no writer has interrogated this concept with more insight than the German-born, Jewish political thinker Hannah Arendt.

"Happiness" was a beguiling concept for a refugee who emigrated to the United States after a period of internment in France, arriving in New York City on May 22, 1941. She later recalled one of the striking impressions she had of her new home:

> Among the many surprises this country holds in store for its new citizens, especially of European background and origin, there is the amazing discovery that the "pursuit of happiness," which the Declaration of Independence asserted to be one of the inalienable human rights, has remained to this day considerably more than a meaningless phrase in the public and private life of the American Republic. To the extent that there is such a thing as the American frame of mind, it certainly has been deeply influenced, for better or worse, by this most elusive of human rights, which apparently entitles men, in the words of Howard Mumford Jones, to "the ghastly privilege of pursuing a phantom and embracing a delusion."

Figure 72: Hannah Arendt in 1958.

Arendt's observations bring us to a deep question, perhaps the animating question of postwar American life: Is the pursuit of happiness a phantom, a delusion that keeps us continually striving toward unrealized and maybe unrealizable goals? Or does it make America still "the last best hope of earth," as Lincoln memorably put it?

The following excerpt comes from Arendt's 1960 essay "Action and the 'Pursuit of Happiness,'" which addresses in its first part the relationship between political thought and political action. Arendt posits that "the grandeur of the Declaration of Independence . . . consists in being 'an argument in support of an action' [quoting the historian Carl L. Becker], or in its being the perfect way of an action to appear in words. And since we deal here with the written and not with the spoken word," she adds, "we are confronted by one of the rare moments when the power of action *is* great enough to erect its own monument." In the essay's second part, she narrows her focus "to two words only, which we hardly ever would use together, but which were a current idiom in the eighteenth century. The two words are 'public happiness.'"

Hannah Arendt, "Action and the 'Pursuit of Happiness'"

1960

. . . It is an odd fact which, of course, has often been noticed that Jefferson, when he drafted the Declaration of Independence, changed the current formula in which the inalienable rights were enumerated from "life, liberty and property" to "life, liberty and the pursuit of happiness." It is even stranger that in the debates which preceded the adoption of Jefferson's draft this alteration was not discussed; and this curious lack of attention to a phraseology, which in the course of the following centuries has contributed to a specifically American ideology more than any other word or notion, stands almost as much in need of explanation as the phrase itself. It is quite possible that this original lack of attention was due to the high regard paid to Mr. Jefferson's famous "felicity of the pen"; it is even more likely that the change escaped attention because the word "happiness" occupied a pre-revolutionary place in political language so that it sounded quite familiar in its context.

The first source of such familiarity which comes to mind is the conventional idiom in royal proclamations where "the welfare and the happiness of our people" quite explicitly meant the private welfare of the subjects and their private happiness, that is, exactly what the phrase "pursuit of happiness" has come to mean throughout the nineteenth and twentieth centuries. Against this plausibility, however, there stands the fact that it was precisely a highly significant variation in pre-revolutionary America to speak of *public* happiness instead of "welfare and happiness." Thus Jefferson himself, in a paper he prepared for the Virginia Convention of 1774, which in many respects anticipated the Declaration of Independence, declared that "our ancestors" when they left "the British dominions in Europe" exercised "a right which nature has given all men . . . of establishing new societies, under such laws and regulations as to them shall seem most likely *to promote public happiness*" (my italics). If Jefferson was right and it was in quest of "public happiness" that the "free inhabitants of the British dominions" had emigrated to America, then the colonies in the New World must have been the breeding grounds of revolutionaries from the beginning: for "public happiness" meant a share in "the government of affairs," that is, in public power, as distinct from the generally recognized right to be protected by the government even against public power. More importantly in our context, the very combination of the two words "public" and "happiness" indicates strongly that these men knew they were not altogether speaking the truth when they maintained (as did Jefferson in a letter to John Randolph in 1775): "My first wish is a restoration of our just rights; my second, a return to the happy period when . . . I may withdraw myself totally from the public eye, and pass the rest of my days in domestic ease and tranquility, banishing every desire of afterwards even hearing what passes in the world." Only John Adams was bold enough to make the enjoyment of power and public happiness the cornerstone of his political philosophy.

As far as the Declaration of Independence is concerned we doubtlessly are supposed to hear the term "pursuit of happiness" in a twofold meaning even though these meanings can hardly be reconciled either historically or conceptually. In this instance, Jefferson's felicity of pen succeeded only too well in blurring the distinctive line between "private rights and public happiness" (James Madison), which had the obvious immediate advantage that—without antagonizing his colleagues who actually wished to constitute a new body politic, a place for public happiness, where their passion for "emulation," the *spectemur agendo* ("let us be seen in action") in John Adams's phrase, could be realized—his draft formula would also appeal to those in the assembly who wished to give their attention "exclusively to their personal interests" (Cooper), not to be bothered any further with public affairs and a "public happiness" which they neither understood nor desired. And, lest somebody doubt that the Founding Fathers might have had a different notion of the dignity of politics than is currently ascribed to them, let me quote John Adams, who boldly claimed that "it is a principal end of government to regulate this passion [namely, the passion for emulation], which in its turn becomes a principal means of government." In this definition of the "end of government," means and end obviously coincide; the moment one puts the notion of "public happiness" in the place of private rights and personal interests, the very question: What is the end of government? loses its sense.

In order to understand the meaning of this public happiness, it may be well to remember that there existed a very similar and yet significantly different idiom in the political language of pre-revolutionary eighteenth-century France. Tocqueville reports how widespread the "taste" and the "passion for public freedom" was, how predominant in the minds of those who had no conception whatsoever of what we now call revolution nor any premonition of the role they were to play in it. The Americans could speak of public happiness because they had tasted, prior to the revolution, the experience of public freedom in the assemblies of towns and districts, where they used to deliberate upon public affairs and where, according to John Adams, "the sentiments of the people were formed in the first place." They knew that the activities connected with this business constituted no burden but gave those who discharged them in public a feeling of happiness they could acquire nowhere else. Compared to this American experience, the preparation of the French *hommes de lettres* who eventually were to make the French Revolution was theoretical in the extreme; no doubt, the men whom an unfriendly historian with some right has called "the play actors" of the French Assembly also enjoyed themselves, but they certainly had no time, caught in the torrent of revolutionary events they no longer knew how to control, to reflect upon this side of an otherwise grim business.

Which, then, was the background of experience from which the term "public freedom" was coined? Who were the men who, without even knowing it (for "the very notion of a violent revolution had no place in [their] mind; it was not discussed because it was not conceived," as Tocqueville pointed out), were in fact bent upon changing the old order of a whole civilization? The eighteenth century, as I mentioned before, called these men *hommes de lettres*, and one of their outstanding characteristics was they had withdrawn voluntarily from society, first from the society of the royal court and the life of a courtier, and later from the society of the salons. They educated themselves and cultivated their minds in a freely chosen seclusion, putting themselves at a calculated distance from the social as well as the political, from which they were excluded in any case, in order to look upon both in perspective. Living under the rule of an enlightened absolutism where life at the king's court, with its endless intrigues and the omnipresence of gossip, was supposed to offer full compensation for a share in the world of public affairs, their personal distinction lay in their refusal to exchange social consideration for political significance, opting rather for the secluded obscurity of private studies, reflections, and dreams. We know this atmosphere from the writings of the French *moralistes*, and we still are fascinated by the considered and deliberate contempt for society in its initial stages, which was the source even of Montaigne's wisdom, the depth of Pascal's thought, and which left its traces upon many pages of Montesquieu's work. Moreover, and importantly, no matter to which "estate" the men of letters belonged, they were free from the burden of poverty, and hence in a very similar position to their American colleagues. Dissatisfied with whatever prominence state or society of the *ancien régime* might have granted them, they felt that their leisure was a burden rather than a blessing, an imposed exile from a realm to which they had right of access by virtue of birth, talent, and inclination; and what they missed in this position in which "the world of public affairs was not only hardly known to them but was invisible" (Tocqueville), they called "public freedom."

To put it another way, their leisure was the Roman *otium* and not the Greek *skholē*, it was enforced inactivity, a "languishing in idle retirement" in which philosophy was supposed to deliver "some cure for grief"—a *doloris medicinam*, as Cicero put it. And they were still quite in the Roman style and mood when they began to employ their leisure in the interest of the *res publica* or *la chose publique* as eighteenth-century France, translating literally from the Latin, still called the realm of public affairs. Hence, they turned to the study of Greek and Roman authors, but not—and this is decisive—for the sake of whatever eternal wisdom or immortal beauty the ancient books might contain, but almost exclusively in order to learn about the political institutions to which they bore witness. In eighteenth-century France, as in eighteenth-century America, it was their search of public freedom and public happiness, and not their quest for truth, that led men back to antiquity.

Tocqueville once rightly remarked that "of all ideas and sentiments which prepared the Revolution, the notion and taste of public freedom strictly speaking have been the first ones to disappear." And the same, *mutatis mutandis*, can be said for the notion of public happiness in America where "the pursuit of happiness" was almost immediately used and understood without its original qualifying adjective. There were theoretical as well as historical reasons which caused this fateful disappearance. I mentioned the theoretical insufficiency of our tradition of political thought which, in this instance, turned about the ambiguities in the traditional definitions of tyranny. Tyranny, according to ancient, pre-theoretical understanding, was the form of government in which the ruler had monopolized for himself the right of action and banished the citizens from the public realm into the privacy of the household where they were supposed to mind their own, private business. Tyranny, in other words, deprived men of public happiness and public freedom without necessarily encroaching upon the pursuit of personal interests and the enjoyment of private rights. Tyranny, according to traditional theory, is the form of government in which the ruler rules out of his own will and in pursuit of his own interests, thus offending the private welfare and the personal liberties of his own subjects. The eighteenth century, when it spoke of tyranny and despotism, did not distinguish between these two possibilities, and it learned of the sharpness of the distinction between the private and the public, between the unhindered pursuit of private interests and the enjoyment of public freedom or of public happiness, only when, during the course of the revolutions, these two principles came into conflict with each other.

Basically, this conflict was the same in the American and the French revolutions though it assumed very different expressions. Theoretically, the briefest way to grasp its significance may be to remember Robespierre's theory of revolution, his conviction that "constitutional government is chiefly concerned with civil liberty, revolutionary government with public freedom." But Jefferson's insistence on some "ward system," his conviction that the revolution was incomplete and the permanence of the republic not assured because it had failed to establish institutions in which the revolutionary spirit could be kept alive, point in the same direction. Robespierre's profound unwillingness to put an end to the revolution, his fear lest the end of revolutionary power and the beginning of constitutional government spell the end of public freedom, is essentially akin to Jefferson's halfhearted wish for a revolution in every generation. In terms of the American Revolution, the question was whether the new body politic was to constitute a realm of its own for the "public happiness" of its citizens, or whether it had been devised solely to serve and insure their pursuit of private happiness more effectively than the old regime. In terms of the French Revolution, the question was whether the end of revolutionary government lay in the establishment of constitutional government which might terminate the reign of public freedom through a guarantee of civil liberties and rights, or whether, for the sake of public freedom, the revolution should be declared in permanence. The guarantee of civil liberties and rights had long been regarded as essential in all nontyrannical rule where the monarch governed within the limits of the law and for the sake of the welfare and the interests of his subjects. If nothing more was at stake, then the revolutionary changes of government that took place at the end of the eighteenth century, the abolition of monarchy and the establishment of republics, must be regarded as accidents, provoked by no more than the wrongheadedness and blunders of the old regimes; not revolutions but reforms, not the foundation of new political bodies but the exchange of a bad ruler for a better one, should have been the answer.

However, the point of the matter is that both the French and the American revolutions, although the men who enacted them on both sides of the Atlantic originally intended no more than such reforms in the direction of constitutional monarchy, were very quickly driven to an insistence on republican government. One of the outstanding characteristics the two revolutions—so unlike each other in most other respects—had in common was the new violent antagonism of monarchists and republicans, and this antagonism was practically unknown prior to the revolutions themselves; it clearly was the result of experiences made in action. Whatever the men of the revolutions might have known or dreamt about before, it was only in the course of the revolutions themselves that they became fully acquainted with public happiness and public freedom, when they became, as the phrase goes, intoxicated with the wine of action. At any rate, the impact of these experiences was sufficiently profound for them to prefer under almost any circumstances—should the alternatives unhappily be put to them in such terms—public freedom to personal interests and public happiness to private welfare. Behind Robespierre's and Jefferson's foredoomed theories and proposals, which foreshadow the revolution declared in permanence, one can discern the uneasy, alarmed, and the alarming question that was to disturb almost every revolutionary after them who was worth his salt: If the end of revolution and the intersection of constitutional government spelled the end of public freedom, was it then even desirable to end the revolution? . . .

On July 4, 1962, at the midway point of his presidency, John F. Kennedy came to Independence Hall to celebrate the day. Shortly before his trip to Philadelphia, Kennedy went to see the engrossed copy in the National Archives, and his speech was filled with learned references to earlier episodes, including Lincoln's visit to the same shrine in 1861.

***Figure** 73: Like many presidents and political leaders before him, John F. Kennedy was drawn to Philadelphia's Independence Hall, here to speak before a crowd of thousands, including all fifty governors, on July 4, 1962.*

In the audience were the nation's fifty governors, and Kennedy naturally seized the opportunity to address the different roles played by the states and the federal government in the system designed by the Founders (a charged topic in a moment of growing federal intervention in the Civil

Rights Movement). Kennedy also explored the ongoing relevance of the Declaration as an inspiration for the new nations emerging from the old colonial empires. In short, he found the "yellowing parchment" still had "worldwide implications." That was surely true; but it was never a simple matter to marry the Declaration's idealism to political reality. With protests flaring up in Alabama, a hardening Cold War, and a metastasizing conflict in Vietnam (one of the countries mentioned in the speech), Kennedy had his work cut out for him.

John F. Kennedy, Address at Independence Hall

July 4, 1962

It is a high honor for any citizen of our great Republic to speak at this Hall of Independence on this day of Independence. To speak as President of the United States to the Chief Executives of our 50 States is both an opportunity and an obligation. The necessity for comity between the National Government and the several States is an indelible lesson of our long history.

Because our system is designed to encourage both differences and dissent, because its checks and balances are designed to preserve the rights of the individual and the locality against preeminent central authority, you and I, Governors, recognize how dependent we both are, one upon the other, for the successful operation of our unique and happy form of government. Our system and our freedom permit the legislative to be pitted against the executive, the State against the Federal Government, the city against the countryside, party against party, interest against interest, all in competition or in contention one with another. Our task—your task in the State House and my task in the White House—is to weave from all these tangled threads a fabric of law and progress. We are not permitted the luxury of irresolution. Others may confine themselves to debate, discussion, and that ultimate luxury—free advice. Our responsibility is one of decision—for to govern is to choose.

Thus, in a very real sense, you and I are the executors of the testament handed down by those who gathered in this historic hall 186 years ago today. For they gathered to affix their names to a document which was, above all else, a document not of rhetoric but of bold decision. It was, it is true, a document of protest—but protests had been made before. It set forth their grievances with eloquence—but such eloquence had been heard before. But what distinguished this paper from all the others was the final irrevocable decision that it took—to assert the independence of free States in place of colonies, and to commit to that goal their lives, their fortunes, and their sacred honor.

Today, 186 years later, that Declaration whose yellowing parchment and fading, almost illegible lines I saw in the past week in the National Archives in Washington is still a revolutionary document. To read it today is to hear a trumpet call. For that Declaration unleashed not merely a revolution against the British, but a revolution in human affairs. Its authors were highly conscious of its worldwide implications. And George Washington declared that liberty and self-government everywhere were, in his words, "finally staked on the experiment entrusted to the hands of the American people."

This prophecy has been borne out. For 186 years this doctrine of national independence has shaken the globe—and it remains the most powerful force anywhere in the world today. There are those struggling to eke out a bare existence in a barren land who have never heard of free enterprise, but who cherish the idea of independence. There are those who are grappling with overpowering problems of illiteracy and ill-health and who are ill-equipped to hold free elections. But they are determined to hold fast to their national independence. Even those unwilling or unable to take part in any struggle between East and West are strongly on the side of their own national independence.

If there is a single issue that divides the world today, it is independence—the independence of Berlin or Laos or Viet-Nam; the longing for independence behind the Iron Curtain; the peaceful transition to independence in those newly emerging areas whose troubles some hope to exploit.

The theory of independence is as old as man himself, and it was not invented in this hall. But it was in this hall that the theory became a practice; that the word went out to all, in Thomas Jefferson's phrase, that "the God who gave us life, gave us liberty at the same time." And today this Nation—conceived in revolution, nurtured in liberty, maturing in independence—has no intention of abdicating its leadership in that worldwide movement for independence to any nation or society committed to systematic human oppression.

As apt and applicable as the Declaration of Independence is today, we would do well to honor that other historic document drafted in this hall—the Constitution of the United States. For it stressed not independence but interdependence—not the individual liberty of one but the indivisible liberty of all.

In most of the old colonial world, the struggle for independence is coming to an end. Even in areas behind the Curtain, that which Jefferson called "the disease of liberty" still appears to be infectious. With the passing of ancient empires, today less than 2 percent of the world's population lives in territories officially termed "dependent." As this effort for independence, inspired by the American Declaration of Independence, now approaches a successful close, a great new effort—for interdependence—is transforming the world about us. And the spirit of that new effort is the same spirit which gave birth to the American Constitution.

That spirit is today most clearly seen across the Atlantic Ocean. The nations of Western Europe, long divided by feuds far more bitter than any which existed among the 13 colonies, are today joining together, seeking, as our forefathers sought, to find freedom in diversity and in unity, strength.

The United States looks on this vast new enterprise with hope and admiration. We do not regard a strong and united Europe as a rival but as a partner. To aid its progress has been the basic object of our foreign policy for 17 years. We believe that a united Europe will be capable of playing a greater role in the common defense, of responding more generously to the needs of poorer nations, of joining with the United States and others in lowering trade barriers, resolving problems of commerce, commodities, and currency, and developing coordinated policies in all economic, political, and diplomatic areas. We see in such a Europe a partner with whom we can deal on a basis of full equality in all the great and burdensome tasks of building and defending a community of free nations.

It would be premature at this time to do more than indicate the high regard with which we view the formation of this partnership. The first order of business is for our European friends to go forward in forming the more perfect union which will someday make this partnership possible.

A great new edifice is not built overnight. It was 11 years from the Declaration of Independence to the writing of the Constitution. The construction of workable federal institutions required still another generation. The greatest works of our Nation's founders lay not in documents and in declarations, but in creative, determined action. The building of the new house of Europe has followed the same practical, purposeful course. Building the Atlantic partnership now will not be easily or cheaply finished.

But I will say here and now, on this Day of Independence, that the United States will be ready for a Declaration of Interdependence, that we will be prepared to discuss with a united Europe the ways and means of forming a concrete Atlantic partnership, a mutually beneficial partnership between the new union now emerging in Europe and the old American Union founded here 175 years ago.

All this will not be completed in a year, but let the world know it is our goal.

In urging the adoption of the United States Constitution, Alexander Hamilton told his fellow New Yorkers "to think continentally." Today Americans must learn to think intercontinentally.

Acting on our own, by ourselves, we cannot establish justice throughout the world; we cannot insure its domestic tranquility, or provide for its common defense, or promote its general welfare, or secure the blessings of liberty to ourselves and our posterity. But joined with other free nations, we can do all this and more. We can assist the developing nations to throw off the yoke of poverty. We can balance our worldwide trade and payments at the highest possible level of growth. We can mount a deterrent powerful enough to deter any aggression. And ultimately we can help to achieve a world of law and free choice, banishing the world of war and coercion.

For the Atlantic partnership of which I speak would not look inward only, preoccupied with its own welfare and advancement. It must look outward to cooperate with all nations in meeting their common concern. It would serve as a nucleus for the eventual union of all free men—those who are now free and those who are vowing that some day they will be free.

On Washington's birthday in 1861, standing right there, President-elect Abraham Lincoln spoke in this hall on his way to the Nation's Capital. And he paid a brief but eloquent tribute to the men who wrote, who fought for, and who died for the Declaration of Independence. Its essence, he said, was its promise not only of liberty "to the people of this country, but hope to the world . . . [hope] that in due time the weights should be lifted from the shoulders of all men, and that all should have an equal chance."

On this fourth day of July, 1962, we who are gathered at this same hall, entrusted with the fate and future of our States and Nation, declare now our vow to do our part to lift the weights from the shoulders of all, to join other men and nations in preserving both peace and freedom, and to regard any threat to the peace or freedom of one as a threat to the peace and freedom of all. "And for the support of this Declaration, with a firm reliance on the protection of Divine Providence, we mutually pledge to each other our Lives, our Fortunes and our sacred Honor."

Figure 74: *Dr. Martin Luther King, Jr., delivers his famous "I Have a Dream" speech before the Lincoln Memorial on August 28, 1963.*

If John F. Kennedy saw the Declaration as a "testament," or will, that handed down its treasure to later generations, the Reverend Martin Luther King, Jr., interpreted it very differently. For Dr. King, it was a "promissory note" that had fallen into default. Eight years earlier, in his first major speech, in Montgomery, Alabama, King had called his people "the disinherited." In a sense, he was still addressing the same theme in 1963, when he delivered the most important speech of his career. It remains one of the great orations in American history.

On August 28 of that year, at the culmination of the March on Washington for Jobs and Freedom, King spoke to an enormous throng that had gathered at the Lincoln Memorial. The symbolic site had already witnessed important milestones in the Civil Rights Movement, including Marian Anderson's outdoor concert in 1939 (after being barred from singing in Constitution Hall) and Harry Truman's address to the NAACP in 1947.

But the movement had advanced considerably since then, and a major statement was needed. On that hot August afternoon, a series of speakers called out the nation's slowness to address the problems faced by Black Americans, including widespread discrimination that still plagued the country, a century after Lincoln signed the Emancipation Proclamation.

The main event was King's extraordinary address, which began in stately cadences, before building in emotional intensity toward an improvised peroration about King's dream of genuine equality. The seventeen-minute speech, presented in full below, was seen by a huge national audience on television (including John F. Kennedy), in addition to the hundreds of thousands gathered on the Mall.

Shortly after concluding, King was invited to the White House, where he and Kennedy drew closer, and coordinated plans for the next stage of the movement. Neither would survive the decade, but King's profound reinterpretation of the Declaration would reverberate forever.

Martin Luther King, Jr., Address to the March on Washington

August 28, 1963

I am happy to join with you today in what will go down in history as the greatest demonstration for freedom in the history of our nation. [*Applause*]

Fivescore years ago, a great American, in whose symbolic shadow we stand today, signed the Emancipation Proclamation. This momentous decree came as a great beacon light of hope to millions of Negro slaves who had been seared in the flames of withering injustice. It came as a joyous daybreak to end the long night of their captivity.

But one hundred years later, the Negro still is not free. [*Audience:*] (*My Lord*) One hundred years later, the life of the Negro is still sadly crippled by the manacles of segregation and the chains of discrimination. One hundred years later, the Negro lives on a lonely island of poverty in the midst of a vast ocean of material prosperity. One hundred years later (*My Lord*) [*Applause*], the Negro is still languished in the corners of American society and finds himself an exile in his own land. And so we've come here today to dramatize a shameful condition.

In a sense we've come to our nation's capital to cash a check. When the architects of our republic wrote the magnificent words of the Constitution and the Declaration of Independence (*Yeah*), they were signing a promissory note to which every American was to fall heir. This note was a promise that all men, yes, black men as well as white men, would be guaranteed the "unalienable Rights of Life, Liberty, and the pursuit of Happiness." It is obvious today that America has defaulted on this promissory note insofar as her citizens of color are concerned. Instead of honoring this sacred obligation, America has given the Negro people a bad check, a check which has come back marked "insufficient funds." [*Sustained applause*]

But we refuse to believe that the bank of justice is bankrupt. (*My Lord*) [*Laughter*] (*Sure enough*) We refuse to believe that there are insufficient funds in the great vaults of opportunity of this nation. And so we've come to cash this check (*Yes*), a check that will give us upon demand the riches of freedom (*Yes*) and the security of justice. [*Applause*]

We have also come to this hallowed spot to remind America of the fierce urgency of now. This is no time (*My Lord*) to engage in the luxury of cooling off or to take the tranquilizing drug of gradualism. [*Applause*] Now is the time to make real the promises of democracy. (*My Lord*) Now is the time to rise from the dark and desolate valley of segregation to the sunlit path of racial justice. Now is the time [*Applause*] to lift our nation from the quicksands of racial injustice to the solid rock of brotherhood. Now is the time [*Applause*] to make justice a reality for all of God's children.

It would be fatal for the nation to overlook the urgency of the moment. This sweltering summer of the Negro's legitimate discontent will not pass until there is an invigorating autumn of freedom and equality. Nineteen sixty-three is not an end, but a beginning. And those who hope that the Negro needed to blow off steam and will now be content will have a rude awakening if the nation returns to business as usual. [*Applause*] There will be neither rest nor tranquillity in America until the Negro is granted his citizenship rights. The whirlwinds of revolt will continue to shake the foundations of our nation until the bright day of justice emerges.

But there is something that I must say to my people, who stand on the warm threshold which leads into the palace of justice: In the process of gaining our rightful place, we must not be guilty of wrongful deeds. Let us not seek to satisfy our thirst for freedom by drinking from the cup of bitterness and hatred. (*My Lord*) [*Applause*] We must forever conduct our struggle on the high plane of dignity and discipline. We must not allow our creative protest to degenerate into physical violence. Again and again, we must rise to the majestic heights of meeting physical force with soul force. The marvelous new militancy which has engulfed the Negro community must not lead us to a distrust of all white people, for many of our white brothers, as evidenced by their presence here today, have come to realize that their destiny is tied up with our destiny. [*Applause*] And they have come to realize that their freedom is inextricably bound to our freedom. We cannot walk alone.

And as we walk, we must make the pledge that we shall always march ahead. We cannot turn back. There are those who are asking the devotees of civil rights, "When will you be satisfied?" (*Never*)

We can never be satisfied as long as the Negro is the victim of the unspeakable horrors of police brutality. We can never be satisfied [*Applause*] as long as our bodies, heavy with the fatigue of travel, cannot gain lodging in the motels of the highways and the hotels of the cities. [*Applause*] We cannot be satisfied as long as the Negro's basic mobility is from a smaller ghetto to a larger one. We can never be satisfied as long as our children are stripped of their selfhood and robbed of their dignity by signs stating "for whites only." [*Applause*] We cannot be satisfied as long as a Negro in Mississippi cannot vote and a Negro in New York believes he has nothing for which to vote. (*Yes*) [*Applause*] No, no, we are not satisfied and we will not be satisfied until justice rolls down like waters and righteousness like a mighty stream. [*Applause*]

I am not unmindful that some of you have come here out of great trials and tribulations. (*My Lord*) Some of you have come fresh from narrow jail cells. Some of you have come from areas where your quest for freedom left you battered by the storms of persecution (*Yes*) and staggered by the winds of police brutality. You have been the veterans of creative suffering. Continue to work with the faith that unearned suffering is redemptive. Go back to Mississippi (*Yes*), go back to Alabama, go back to South Carolina, go back to Georgia, go back to Louisiana, go back to the slums and ghettos of our northern cities, knowing that somehow this situation can and will be changed. (*Yes*) Let us not wallow in the valley of despair.

I say to you today, my friends [*Applause*], so even though we face the difficulties of today and tomorrow, I still have a dream. (*Yes*) It is a dream deeply rooted in the American dream.

I have a dream that one day (*Yes*) this nation will rise up and live out the true meaning of its creed: "We hold these truths to be self-evident, that all men are created equal." (*Yes*) [*Applause*]

I have a dream that one day on the red hills of Georgia, the sons of former slaves and the sons of former slave owners will be able to sit down together at the table of brotherhood.

I have a dream that one day even the state of Mississippi, a state sweltering with the heat of injustice (*Well*), sweltering with the heat of oppression, will be transformed into an oasis of freedom and justice.

I have a dream (*Well*) [*Applause*] that my four little children will one day live in a nation where they will not be judged by the color of their skin but by the content of their character. (*My Lord*) I have a dream today. [*Applause*]

I have a dream that one day down in Alabama, with its vicious racists, with its governor having his lips dripping with the words of "interposition" and "nullification" (*Yes*), one day right there in Alabama little black boys and black girls will be able to join hands with little white boys and white girls as sisters and brothers. I have a dream today. [*Applause*]

I have a dream that one day every valley shall be exalted (*Yes*), and every hill and mountain shall be made low; the rough places will be made plain, and the crooked places will be made straight (*Yes*); and the glory of the Lord shall be revealed, and all flesh shall see it together. (*Yes*)

This is our hope. This is the faith that I go back to the South with. (*Yes*) With this faith we will be able to hew out of the mountain of despair a stone of hope. (*Yes*) With this faith we will be able to transform the jangling discords of our nation into a beautiful symphony of brotherhood. (*Talk about it*) With this faith (*My Lord*) we will be able to work together, to pray together, to struggle together, to go to jail together, to stand up for freedom together, knowing that we will be free one day. [*Applause*] This will be the day [*Applause continues*], this will be the day when all of God's children (*Yes*) will be able to sing with new meaning:

> My country, 'tis of thee (*Yes*), sweet land of liberty, of thee I sing.
> Land where my fathers died, land of the pilgrim's pride (*Yes*),
> From every mountainside, let freedom ring!

And if America is to be a great nation, this must become true.

And so let freedom ring (*Yes*) from the prodigious hilltops of New Hampshire.

Let freedom ring from the mighty mountains of New York.

Let freedom ring from the heightening Alleghenies of Pennsylvania. (*Yes, That's right*)

Let freedom ring from the snowcapped Rockies of Colorado. (*Well*)

Let freedom ring from the curvaceous slopes of California. (*Yes*)

But not only that: Let freedom ring from Stone Mountain of Georgia. (*Yes*)

Let freedom ring from Lookout Mountain of Tennessee. (*Yes*)

Let freedom ring from every hill and molehill of Mississippi. (*Yes*)

From every mountainside, let freedom ring. [*Applause*]

And when this happens [*Applause continues*], when we allow freedom ring, when we let it ring from every village and every hamlet, from every state and every city (*Yes*), we will be able to speed up that day when all of God's children, black men and white men, Jews and Gentiles, Protestants and Catholics, will be able to join hands and sing in the words of the old Negro spiritual:

Free at last! (*Yes*) Free at last!
Thank God Almighty, we are free at last! [*Applause*]

It was all the more important to honor the Declaration's promissory note as Americans found themselves waging a difficult Cold War, against adversaries keen to call attention to America's contradictions. Russian and Chinese propagandists argued that the Declaration's promises of equality had been meted out unequally for as long as anyone could remember. By coincidence, W.E.B. Du Bois died in Ghana on the day before King's speech, and was promptly lionized by the People's Republic of China. But the progress of the Civil Rights Movement weakened these foreign attacks on American democracy, especially when China and Russia's serial violations of human rights were brought to light. George Orwell had perceptively skewered the bland slogans of totalitarian regimes in his 1945 novella, *Animal Farm* ("ALL ANIMALS ARE EQUAL / BUT SOME ARE MORE EQUAL THAN OTHERS").

Figure 75: A Black Panther Party poster from 1968.

Not every Black leader approached the Declaration of Independence as Dr. King did. Malcolm X, a leading Black Muslim who advocated for separation of the races for most of his incendiary career, warned his followers not to celebrate the Fourth of July because "most of the white Founding Fathers who signed the Declaration of Independence were slave owners themselves," and "it is nothing but hypocrisy on the part of the American white man to pretend that the Revolutionary War was truly a war of independence as long as 20 million Black people here in America are denied the privileges of an independent people."

But other Black radicals were more willing to deploy the language and structure of the Declaration. The Black Panthers, founded in Oakland in 1966 by Huey P. Newton and Bobby Seale, were in many ways the heirs to Malcolm X's legacy of Black pride and anger. But at the same time, like Dr. King, they saw the wisdom of working within the Declaration's traditions. The Panthers issued a ten-point party platform that closed with the language from the preamble of the Declaration, reframed by the grievances that, in this case, precede it. The document exists in multiple versions. This one was published in an underground Seattle newspaper in May 1968, as the nation was reeling from King's assassination.

Black Panther Platform

May 9, 1968

WHAT WE WANT

1. We want freedom. We want power to determine the destiny of our black community.
2. We want full employment for our people.
3. We want an end to the robbery by the white man of our black community.
4. We want decent housing, fit for shelter of human beings.
5. We want education for our people that exposes the true nature of this decadent American society. We want education that teaches us our true history and our role in the present day society.
6. We want all black men to be exempt from military service.
7. We want an immediate end to *police brutality* and *murder* of black people.
8. We want freedom for all black men held in federal, state, county, and city prisons and jails.
9. We want all black people when brought to trial to be tried in court by a jury of their peer group or people from their black communities as defined by the constitution of the United States.
10. We want land, bread, housing, education, clothing, justice and peace.

WHAT WE BELIEVE

1. We believe that black people will not be free until we are able to determine our destiny.
2. We believe that the federal government is responsible and obligated to give every man employment or a guaranteed income. We believe that if the white American businessmen will not give full employment, then the means of production should be taken from the businessmen and placed in the community so that the people of the community can organize and employ all of its people and give a high standard of living.

3. We believe that this racist government has robbed us and now we are demanding the overdue debt of forty acres and two mules. Forty acres and two mules was promised 100 years ago as retribution for slave labor and mass murder of black people. We will accept the payment in currency which will be distributed to our many communities. The Germans murdered 6,000,000 Jews. The American racist has taken part in the slaughter of over 50,000,000 black people; therefore, we feel that this is a modest demand that we make.

4. We believe that if the white landlords will not give decent housing to our black community, then the housing and the land should be made into cooperatives so that our community, with government aid, can build and make decent housing for its people.

5. We believe in an educational system that will give to our people a knowledge of self. If a man does not have knowledge of himself and his position in society and the world, then he has little chance to relate to anything else.

6. We believe that black people should not be forced to fight in the military service to defend a racist government that does not protect us. We will not fight and kill other people of color in the world who, like black people, are being victimized by the white racist government of America. We will protect ourselves from the force and violence of the racist police and the racist military, by whatever means necessary.

7. We believe we can end police brutality in our black community by organizing black *self defense* groups that are dedicated to defending our black community from racist police oppression and brutality. The second amendment of the constitution of the United States gives a right to bear arms. We therefore believe that all black people should arm themselves for *self defense*.

8. We believe that all black people should be released from the many jails and prisons because they have not received a fair and impartial trial.

9. We believe that the courts should follow the United States constitution so that black people will receive fair trials. The 14th

amendment of the U.S. constitution gives a man a right to be tried by his peer group. A peer is a person from a similar economic, social, religious, geographical, environmental, historical and racial background. To do this the court will be forced to select a jury from the black community from which the black defendant came. We have been, and are being tried by all white juries that have no understanding of the "average reasoning man" of the black community.

10. When in the course of human events, it becomes necessary for one people to dissolve the political bonds which have connected them with another, and to assume among the powers of the earth, the separate and equal station to which the laws of nature and nature's god entitle them, a decent respect to the opinions of mankind requires that they should declare the causes which impel them to separation. We hold these truths to be self-evident, that all men are created equal, that they are endowed by their creator with certain inalienable rights, that among these are life, liberty and the pursuit of happiness. That to secure these rights, governments are instituted among men, deriving their just powers from the consent of the governed,—that *whenever any form of government becomes destructive of these ends, it is the right of people to alter or to abolish it, and to institute new government, laying its foundation on such principles and organizing its powers in such form as to them shall seem most likely to effect their safety and happiness.* Prudence, indeed, will dictate that governments long established should not be changed for light and transient causes; and accordingly all experience hath shewn, that mankind are more disposed to suffer while evils are sufferable, than to right themselves by abolishing the forms to which they are accustomed. *But when a long train of abuses and usurpations, pursuing invariably the same object, evinces a design to reduce them under absolute despotism, it is their right, it is their duty, to throw off such government, and to provide new guards for their future security.*

__Figure 76:__ Members of the American Indian Movement take their protest to the nation's capital in 1978.

As the energies unleashed by the Civil Rights Movement spread, many other groups found their voices and issued protest documents, often in the language of the Declaration of Independence. Native Americans were among them, in a time of rising Indigenous pride, and no small anger over chronic poverty and centuries of mistreatment and betrayal. In 1968, the American Indian Movement was founded and led a series of protests in the years that followed.

In 1973, a seventy-one-day armed standoff took place between Native Americans and U.S. law enforcement at Wounded Knee, near the site of an 1890 massacre, on the Pine Ridge Reservation in South Dakota. A year later, representatives of ninety-seven Indigenous tribes and nations gathered at the Standing Rock Reservation and wrote out a declaration of "continuing" independence, since they had been independent long before the creation of the United States. In its inclusion of a preamble and a litany of grievances it bears some structural similarity to the Declaration of Independence, even as it calls into question the fundamental premises of the nation that document birthed.

First Indian International Treaty Council, Declaration of Continuing Independence

June 8–16, 1974

A long time ago my father told me what his father told him. There was once a Lakota Holy man called Drinks Water, who visioned what was to be; and this was long before the coming of the Wasicus. He visioned that the four-legged were going back into the earth and that a strange race had woven a spider's web all around the Lakotas. And he said, "When this happens, you shall live in barren lands, and there beside those gray houses you shall starve." They say he went back to Mother Earth soon after he saw this vision and it was sorrow that killed him. —Black Elk, Oglala Sioux Holy Man

PREAMBLE

The United States of America has continually violated the independent Native Peoples of this continent by Executive action, Legislative fiat and Judicial decision. By its actions, the U.S. has denied all Native people their International Treaty rights, Treaty lands and basic human rights of freedom and sovereignty. This same U.S. Government, which fought to throw off the yoke of oppression and gain its own independence, has now reversed its role and become the oppressor of sovereign Native people.

Might does not make right. Sovereign people of varying cultures have the absolute right to live in harmony with Mother Earth so long as they do not infringe upon this same right of other peoples. The denial of this right to any sovereign people, such as the Native American Indian Nations, must be challenged by *truth* and *action*. World concern must focus on all colonial governments to the end that sovereign people everywhere shall live as they choose; in peace with dignity and freedom.

The International Indian Treaty Conference hereby adopts this Declaration of Continuing Independence of the Sovereign Native American Indian Nations. In the course of these human events, we call upon the people of the world to support this struggle for our sovereign rights and our treaty rights. We pledge our assistance to all other sovereign people who seek their own independence.

DECLARATION

The First International Treaty Council of the Western Hemisphere was formed on the land of the Standing Rock Sioux Tribe on June 8–16, 1974. The delegates, meeting under the guidance of the Great Spirit, represented 97 Indian tribes and Nations from across North and South America.

We, the sovereign Native Peoples recognize that all lands belonging to the various Native Nations now situated within the boundaries of the U.S. are clearly defined by the sacred treaties solemnly entered into between the Native Nations and the government of the United States of America.

We, the sovereign Native Peoples, charge the United States of gross violations of our International Treaties. Two of the thousands of violations that can be cited are the "wrongfully taking" of the Black Hills from the Great Sioux Nation in 1877, this sacred land belonging to the Great Sioux Nation under the Fort Laramie Treaty of 1868. The second violation was the forced march of the Cherokee people from their ancestral lands in the state of Georgia to the then "Indian Territory" of Oklahoma after the Supreme Court of the United States ruled the Cherokee treaty rights inviolate. The treaty violation, know as the "Trail of Tears," brought death to two-thirds of the Cherokee Nation during the forced march.

The Council further realizes that securing United States recognition of treaties signed with Native Nations requires a committed and unified struggle, using every available legal and political resource. Treaties between sovereign nations explicitly entail agreements which represent "the supreme law of the land," binding each party to an inviolate international relationship.

We acknowledge the historical fact that the struggle for Independence of the Peoples of our sacred Mother Earth have always been over sovereignty of land. These historical freedom efforts have always involved the highest human sacrifice.

We recognize that all Native Nations wish to avoid violence, but we also recognize that the United States government has always used force and violence to deny Native Nations basic human and treaty rights.

We adopt this Declaration of Continuing Independence, recognizing that struggle lies ahead—a struggle certain to be won—and that the human and treaty rights of all Native Nations will be honored. In this understanding the International Indian Treaty Council declares:

The United State Government in its Constitution, Article VI, recognizes treaties as part of the Supreme Law of the United States. We will peacefully pursue all legal and political avenues to demand United States recognition of its own Constitution in this regard, and thus to honor its own treaties with Native Nations.

We will seek the support of all world communities in the struggle for the continuing independence of Native Nations.

We the representatives of sovereign Native Nations united in forming a council to be known at the International Indian Treaty Council to implement these declarations.

The International Indian Treaty Council will establish offices in Washington, D.C. and New York City to approach the international forces necessary to obtain the recognition of our treaties. These offices will establish an initial system of communications among Native nations to disseminate information, getting a general consensus of concerning issues, developments and any legislative attempt affecting Native Nations by the United States of America.

The International Indian Treaty Council recognizes the sovereignty of all Native Nations and will stand in unity to support our Native and international brothers and sisters in their respective and collective struggles concerning international treaties and agreements violated by the United States and other governments.

All treaties between the Sovereign Native Nations and the United States Government must be interpreted according to the traditional and spiritual ways of the signatory Native Nations.

We declare our recognition of the Provisional Government of the Independent Oglala Nation, established by the Traditional Chiefs and Headmen under the provisions of the 1868 Fort Laramie Treaty with the Great Sioux Nation at Wounded Knee, March 11, 1973.

We condemn the United States of America for its gross violation of the 1868 Fort Laramie Treaty in militarily surrounding, killing and starving the citizens of the Independent Oglala Nation into exile.

We demand the United States of America recognize the sovereignty of the Independent Oglala Nation and immediately stop all present and future criminal prosecutions of sovereign Native Peoples. We call upon the conscionable nations of the world to join us in charging and prosecuting the United States of America for its genocidal practices against the sovereign Native Nations; most recently illustrated by Wounded Knee 1973 and the continued refusal to sign the United Nations 1948 Treaty on Genocide.

We reject all executive orders, legislative acts and judicial decisions of the United States related to Native Nations since 1871, when the United States unilaterally suspended treaty-making relations with the Native Nations. This includes, but is not limited to, the Major Crimes Act, the General Allotment Act, the Citizenship Act of 1924, the Indian Reorganization Act of 1934, the Indian Claims Commission Act, Public Law 280 and the Termination Act. All treaties made between Native Nations and the United States made prior to 1871 shall be recognized without further need of interpretation.

We hereby ally ourselves with the colonized Puerto Rican People in their struggle for Independence from the same United States of America.

We recognize that there is only one color of Mankind in the world who are not represented in the United Nations; that is the indigenous Redman of the Western Hemisphere. We recognize this lack of representation in the United Nations comes from the genocidal policies of the colonial power of the United States.

The International Indian Treaty Council established by this conference is directed to make the application to the United Nations for recognition and membership of the sovereign Native Nations. We pledge our support to any similar application by an aboriginal people.

This conference directs the Treaty Council to open negotiations with the government of the United States through its Department of State. We seek these negotiations in order to establish diplomatic relations with the United States. When these diplomatic relations have been established, the first order of business shall be to deal with U.S. violations of treaties with Native Indian Nations, and violations of the rights of those Native Indian Nations who have refused to sign treaties with the United States.

We, the People of the International Indian Treaty Council, following the guidance of our elders through instructions from the Great Spirit, and out of respect for our sacred Mother Earth, all her children, and those yet unborn, offer our lives for our International Treaty Rights.

Time and again, in different ways, the Declaration served as a template for protests and pronouncements in the postwar period. It also loomed large in popular culture—fittingly for a document thought to possess almost talismanic powers—as advertisers found ways to sell products around the linked notions of independence, personal rights, and the pursuit of happiness. That happiness could be defined broadly, from a new form of plastic to a skillet full of sizzling bacon, a slice of Kraft cheese, or a 1976 Pontiac, perfect for a drive to watch the bicentennial fireworks.

Still, despite these crude conflations of the pursuit of happiness with material prosperity, the Declaration's basic brand was intact. Its older meanings were not forgotten as other groups began to explore its protections in the wake of the Civil Rights Movement. They included women, still seeking full equality more than half a century after winning the right to vote, and other Americans who felt marginalized.

Figure 77: Madison Avenue meets Independence Hall.

***Figure 78:** French philosopher Jacques Derrida used America's Bicentennial as the occasion to ask who, exactly, declared independence in July 1776.*

As had all the major anniversaries before it, the 1976 Bicentennial brought another surge of interest in the Declaration of Independence, with some help from the 1972 film *1776* (based on a 1969 Broadway musical). The nation was in a celebratory mood, eager to move past the shame of Vietnam and Watergate. One of the more interesting, if perhaps esoteric, observances of the Bicentennial took place in Charlottesville, Virginia, home of the University of Virginia, which Thomas Jefferson had founded in his old age and which he regarded, along with the drafting of the Declaration of Independence, as among the signal achievements of his life. Roger Shattuck, a professor at the university, invited the French philosopher Jacques Derrida, then still in the early stages of a career that would transform textual criticism in the academy, to come to Jefferson's hometown to undertake a close comparative analysis of the American Declaration of Independence and the French Declaration of the Rights of Man and of the Citizen.

Derrida had already become famous (in some circles notorious) for his theory and practice of subjecting texts to "deconstruction," which involved an interrogation of the subjectivity inherent in any piece of writing—especially one like the Declaration that aspires to articulate self-evident truths.

Derrida accepted the invitation, but announced at the beginning of his remarks that "I am not going to keep my promise." Instead of the comparative analysis that Shattuck had requested—which Derrida called "an intimidating proposition" for which he felt unprepared—the Frenchman proposed to focus on a single question that reveals much about the nature of the Declaration and the sovereignty it announces and embodies: "*Who signs, and with what so-called proper name, the declarative act which founds an institution?*"

Jacques Derrida, "Declarations of Independence"

1976

. . . Such an act does not come back to a constative or descriptive discourse. It performs, it accomplishes, it does what it says it does: that at least would be its intentional structure. Such an act does not have the same relation to its presumed signer—to whatever subject, individual or collective, engages itself in producing it—as a text of the "constative" type, if in all rigor there are any "constative" texts and if one could come across them in "science," in "philosophy," or in "literature." The declaration which founds an institution, a constitution or a State requires that a signer engage him- or herself. The signature maintains a link with the instituting act, as an act of language and of writing, a link which has absolutely nothing of the empirical accident about it. This attachment does not let itself be reduced, not as easily in any case as it does in a scientific text, where the value of the utterance is separated or cuts itself off from the name of its author without essential risk and, indeed, even has to be able to do so in order for it to pretend to objectivity. Although in principle an institution—in its history and in its tradition, in its offices [*permanence*] and thus in its very institutionality—has to render itself independent of the empirical individuals who have taken part in its production, although it has in a certain way to mourn them or resign itself to their loss [*faire son deuil*], even and especially if it commemorates them, it turns out, precisely by reason of the structure of instituting language, that the founding act of an institution—the act as archive as well as the act as performance—*has to maintain within itself the signature.*

But just whose signature exactly? Who is the actual signer of such acts? And what does actual [*effectif*] mean? The same question spreads or propagates itself in a chain reaction through all the concepts affected by the same rumbling: act, performative, signature, the "present" "I" and "we," etc.

Prudence imposes itself here, as does attention to detail. Let us distinguish between the several instances within the moment of your Declaration. Take, for example, Jefferson, the "draftsman [*rédacteur*]" of the project or draft [*projet*] of the Declaration, of the "Draft," the facsimile of which I have before my eyes. No one would take him for the true signer of the Declaration. *By right,* he writes but he does not sign. Jefferson represents the representatives who have delegated to him the task of drawing up [*rédiger*] what they knew *they* wanted to say. He was not responsible for *writing*, in the productive or initiating sense of the term, only for *drawing up*, as one says of a secretary that he or she draws up a *letter* of which the spirit has been breathed into him or her, or even the content dictated. Moreover, after having thus drawn up a project or a draft, a sketch, Jefferson had to submit it to those whom, for a time, he *represented* and who are themselves *representatives*, namely the "representatives of the United States in General Congress assembled." These "representatives," of whom Jefferson represents a sort of advance-pen, will have the right to revise, to correct and to ratify the project or draft of the Declaration.

Shall we say, for all that, that they are the ultimate signers?

You know what scrutiny and examination this letter, this literal declaration in its first state, underwent, how long it remained and deferred, undelivered, in sufferance between all those representative instances, and with what suspense or suffering Jefferson paid for it. As if he had secretly dreamed of signing all alone.

As for the "representatives" themselves, they don't sign either. In principle at least, because the right is divided here. In fact, they sign; by right, they sign for themselves but also "for" others. They have been delegated the proxies, the power of attorney, for signing [*Ils ont délégation ou procuration de signature*]. They speak, "declare," declare themselves and sign "in the name of . . .": "We, therefore, the representatives of the United States of America in General Congress assembled, do in the name and by the authority of the good people of these [. . .] that as free and independant states. . .".

By right, the signer is thus the people, the "good" people (a decisive detail because it guarantees the value of the intention and of the signature, but we will see further along on what and on whom such a guarantee is founded or founds itself). It is the "good people" who declare themselves free and independent by the relay of their representatives and of their representatives of representatives. One cannot decide—and that's the interesting thing, the force and the coup of force of such a declarative act—whether independence is stated or produced by this utterance. We have not finished following the chain of these representatives of representatives, and doing so further complicates this necessary undecidability. Is it that the good people have already freed themselves in fact and are only stating the fact of this emancipation in [*par*] the Declaration? Or is it rather that they free themselves at the instant of and by [*par*] the signature of this Declaration? It is not a question here of an obscurity or of a difficulty of interpretation, of a problematic on the way to its (re)solution. It is not a question of a difficult analysis which would fail in the face of the structure of the acts involved and the overdetermined temporality of the events. This obscurity, this undecidability between, let's say, a performative structure and a constative structure, is *required* in order to produce the sought-after effect. It is essential to the very positing or position of a right as such, whether one is speaking here of hypocrisy, of equivocation, of undecidability, or of fiction. I would even go so far as to say that every signature finds itself thus affected.

Here then is the "good people" who engage themselves and engage only themselves in signing, in having their own declaration signed. The "we" of the declaration speaks "in the name of the people."

But this people does not exist. They do *not* exist as an entity, it does *not* exist, *before* this declaration, not *as such*. If it gives birth to itself, as free and independent subject, as possible signer, this can hold only in the act of the signature. The signature invents the signer. . . .

There was no signer, by right, before the text of the Declaration which itself remains the producer and guarantor of its own signature. By this fabulous event, by this fable which implies the structure of the trace and is only in truth possible thanks to [*par*] the inadequation to itself of a present, a signature gives itself a name. It opens *for itself* a line of credit, *its* own credit, for itself *to* itself. The *self* surges up here in all cases (nominative, dative, accusative) as soon as a signature gives or extends credit to itself, in a single coup of force, which is also a coup of writing, as the right to writing. The coup of force makes right, founds right or the law, gives right, *brings the law to the light of day, gives both birth and day to the law* [donne le jour à la loi]. Brings the law to the light of day, gives both birth and day to the law: read "The Madness of the Day," by Maurice Blanchot.

That this unheard-of thing should also be an everyday occurrence should not make us forget the singular context of this act. In this case, another state signature had to be effaced in "dissolving" the links of colonial paternity or maternity. One will confirm it in reading: this "dissolution" too involves both constation and performance, indissociably mixed. The signature of every American citizen today depends, in fact and by right, on this indispensable confusion. The constitution and the laws of your country somehow guarantee the signature, as they guarantee your passport and the circulation of subjects and of seals foreign to this country, of letters, of promises, of marriages, of checks—all of which may be given occasion or asylum or right.

And yet. And yet another instance still holds itself back behind the scenes. Another "subjectivity" is still coming to sign, in order to guarantee it, this production of signature. In short, there are only countersignatures in this process. There is a differantial process here because there is a countersignature, but everything should concentrate itself in the *simulacrum of the instant*. It is still "in the name of" that the "good people" of America call *themselves* and declare *themselves* independent, at the instant in which they invent (for) themselves a signing identity. They sign in the name of the laws of nature and in the name of God. They *pose* or *posit* their institutional laws on the foundation of natural laws and by the same coup (the interpretive coup of force) in the name of God, creator of nature. He comes, in effect, to guarantee the rectitude of popular intentions, the unity and goodness of the people. He founds natural laws and thus the whole game which tends to present performative utterances *as* constative utterances.

Do I dare, here, in Charlottesville, recall the *incipit* of your Declaration? "When in the course of human events it becomes necessary for one people to dissolve the political bands which have connected them with another, and to assume among the powers of the earth the separate and equal station to which the laws of Nature and of Nature's God entitle them, a decent respect to the opinions of mankind requires that they should declare the causes which impel them to the separation. We hold these truths to be self-evident: that all men are created equal; that they are endowed by their creator with inalienable Rights [. . .]." And finally: "We therefore the Representatives of the United States of America, in General Congress assembled, appealing to the Supreme Judge of the world for the rectitude of our intentions, do in the Name and by the authority of the good People of these Colonies solemnly *publish* and *declare*, that these united Colonies are and of right ought to be *free and independant states* [. . .]."

"Are and ought to be"; the "and" articulates and conjoins here the two discursive modalities, the to be and the ought to be, the constation and the prescription, the fact and the right. *And* is God: at once creator of nature and judge, supreme judge of what is (the state of the world) and of what relates to what ought to be (the rectitude of our intentions).

The instance of judgment, at the level of the supreme judge, is the last instance for saying the fact *and* the law. One can understand this Declaration as a vibrant act of faith, as a hypocrisy indispensable to a politico-military-economic, etc. coup of force, or, more simply, more economically, as the analytic and consequential deployment of a tautology: for this Declaration to have a meaning *and* an effect, there must be a last instance. God is the name, the best one, for this last instance and this ultimate signature. Not only the best one in a determined context (such and such a nation, such and such a religion, etc.), but the name of the best name in general. Now, this (best) name also *ought to be* a proper name. God is the best proper name, the proper name the best [*Dieu est le nom propre le meilleur*]. One could not replace "God" by "the best proper name [*le meilleur nom propre*]."

Jefferson knew it.

Secretary and draftsman, he represents. He represents the "representatives" who are the representatives of the people in whose name they speak, the people themselves authorizing themselves and authorizing their representatives (in addition to the rectitude of their intentions) in the name of the laws of nature which inscribe themselves in the name of God, judge and creator.

If he knew all this, why did he suffer? What did he suffer from, this representative of representatives who themselves represent, *to infinity*, up to God, other representative instances?

Apparently he suffered because he clung to his text. It was very hard for him to see it, to see *himself*, corrected, emended, "improved," shortened, especially by his colleagues. A feeling of wounding and of mutilation should be inconceivable for someone who knows not to write in his own name, his proper name, but *simply by representation* and in place of another. If the wound does not efface itself in the delegation, that is because things aren't so simple, neither the structure of the representation nor the procuration of the signature.

Someone, let's call him Jefferson (but why not God?), desired that the institution of the American people should be, by the same coup, the erection of his proper name. A name of State.

Did he succeed? I would not venture to decide. . . .

Four years after the Bicentennial, Hollywood-actor-turned-politician Ronald Reagan effectively seized on the desire to move past the traumas of the 1960s and '70s with a creative amalgam of nostalgia for the past and optimism for the future. This combination was perhaps best captured by his 1984 reelection slogan "Morning in America," which implicitly harkened back to the nation's beginning.

It was in this gauzy mood that President Reagan traveled to New York in 1986 to celebrate the centennial of the Statue of Liberty. In the evening of July 3, he delivered a stirring speech that retold the story of the statue as a gift from the people of France, and a symbol of the Great Republic's openness to all. As he put it, "Miss Liberty is still giving life to the dream of a new world where old antagonisms could be cast aside and people of every nation could live together as one." While undoubtedly a conservative, Reagan employed an inclusive tone regarding immigrants that drew him into a broad centrist tradition that included a fellow Irish American, John F. Kennedy.

In the same speech, Reagan began to speak of the Declaration, and of the role it had played over the centuries, for Lincoln and other presidents. He enlarged the thought the next day, July 4, speaking to a throng of sailors gathered on the deck of the USS *John F. Kennedy*, in New York Harbor.

Figure 79: *Ronald and Nancy Reagan watch the fireworks over the Statue of Liberty from the deck of the USS* John F. Kennedy.

Ronald Reagan, Address to the Nation on Independence Day

July 4, 1986

My fellow Americans:

In a few moments the celebration will begin here in New York Harbor. It's going to be quite a show. I was just looking over the preparations and thinking about a saying that we had back in Hollywood about never doing a scene with kids or animals because they'd steal the scene every time. So, you can rest assured I wouldn't even think about trying to compete with a fireworks display, especially on the Fourth of July.

My remarks tonight will be brief, but it's worth remembering that all the celebration of this day is rooted in history. It's recorded that shortly after the Declaration of Independence was signed in Philadelphia celebrations took place throughout the land, and many of the former Colonists—they were just starting to call themselves Americans—set off cannons and marched in fife and drum parades.

What a contrast with the sober scene that had taken place a short time earlier in Independence Hall. Fifty-six men came forward to sign the parchment. It was noted at the time that they pledged their lives, their fortunes, and their sacred honors. And that was more than rhetoric; each of those men knew the penalty for high treason to the Crown. "We must all hang together," Benjamin Franklin said, "or, assuredly, we will all hang separately." And John Hancock, it is said, wrote his signature in large script so King George could see it without his spectacles. They were brave. They stayed brave through all the bloodshed of the coming years. Their courage created a nation built on a universal claim to human dignity, on the proposition that every man, woman, and child had a right to a future of freedom.

For just a moment, let us listen to the words again: "We hold these truths to be self-evident, that all men are created equal, that they are endowed by their Creator with certain unalienable Rights, that among these are Life, Liberty, and the pursuit of Happiness." Last night when we rededicated Miss Liberty and relit her torch, we reflected on all the millions who came here in search of the dream of freedom inaugurated in Independence Hall. We reflected, too, on their courage in coming great distances and settling in a foreign land and then passing on to their children and their children's children the hope symbolized in this statue here just behind us: the hope that is America. It is a hope that someday every people and every nation of the world will know the blessings of liberty.

And it's the hope of millions all around the world. In the last few years, I've spoken at Westminster to the mother of Parliaments; at Versailles, where French kings and world leaders have made war and peace. I've been to the Vatican in Rome, the Imperial Palace in Japan, and the ancient city of Beijing. I've seen the beaches of Normandy and stood again with those boys of Pointe du Hoc, who long ago scaled the heights, and with, at that time, Lisa Zanatta Henn, who was at Omaha Beach for the father she loved, the father who had once dreamed of seeing again the place where he and so many brave others had landed on D-day. But he had died before he could make that trip, and she made it for him. "And, Dad," she had said, "I'll always be proud."

And I've seen the successors to these brave men, the young Americans in uniform all over the world, young Americans like you here tonight who man the mighty U.S.S. *Kennedy* and the *Iowa* and other ships of the line. I can assure you, you out there who are listening, that these young are like their fathers and their grandfathers, just as willing, just as brave. And we can be just as proud. But our prayer tonight is that the call for their courage will never come. And that it's important for us, too, to be brave; not so much the bravery of the battlefield, I mean the bravery of brotherhood.

All through our history, our Presidents and leaders have spoken of national unity and warned us that the real obstacle to moving forward the boundaries of freedom, the only permanent danger to the hope that is America, comes from within. It's easy enough to dismiss this as a kind of familiar exhortation. Yet the truth is that even two of our greatest Founding Fathers, John Adams and Thomas Jefferson, once learned this lesson late in life. They'd worked so closely together in Philadelphia for independence. But once that was gained and a government was formed, something called partisan politics began to get in the way. After a bitter and divisive campaign, Jefferson defeated Adams for the Presidency in 1800. And the night before Jefferson's inauguration, Adams slipped away to Boston, disappointed, brokenhearted, and bitter.

For years their estrangement lasted. But then when both had retired, Jefferson at 68 to Monticello and Adams at 76 to Quincy, they began through their letters to speak again to each other. Letters that discussed almost every conceivable subject: gardening, horseback riding, even sneezing as a cure for hiccups; but other subjects as well: the loss of loved ones, the mystery of grief and sorrow, the importance of religion, and of course the last thoughts, the final hopes of two old men, two great patriarchs, for the country that they had helped to found and loved so deeply. "It carries me back," Jefferson wrote about correspondence with his cosigner of the Declaration of Independence, "to the times when, beset with difficulties and dangers, we were fellow laborers in the same cause, struggling for what is most valuable to man, his right to self-government. Laboring always at the same oar, with some wave ever ahead threatening to overwhelm us and yet passing harmless . . . we rowed through the storm with heart and hand. . . ." It was their last gift to us, this lesson in brotherhood, in tolerance for each other, this insight into America's strength as a nation. And when both died on the same day within hours of each other, that date was July 4th, 50 years exactly after that first gift to us, the Declaration of Independence.

My fellow Americans, it falls to us to keep faith with them and all the great Americans of our past. Believe me, if there's one impression I carry with me after the privilege of holding for 5½ years the office held by Adams and Jefferson and Lincoln, it is this: that the things that unite us—America's past of which we're so proud, our hopes and aspirations for the future of the world and this much-loved country—these things far outweigh what little divides us. And so tonight we reaffirm that Jew and gentile, we are one nation under God; that black and white, we are one nation indivisible; that Republican and Democrat, we are all Americans. Tonight, with heart and hand, through whatever trial and travail, we pledge ourselves to each other and to the cause of human freedom, the cause that has given light to this land and hope to the world.

My fellow Americans, we're known around the world as a confident and a happy people. Tonight there's much to celebrate and many blessings to be grateful for. So while it's good to talk about serious things, it's just as important and just as American to have some fun. Now, let's have some fun—let the celebration begin!

THE
DECLARATION OF INDEPENDENCE
OF
THE UNITED STATES OF AMERICA

IN CONGRESS, July 4, 1776

The unanimous Declaration of the thirteen united States of America

When in the Course of human events, it becomes necessary for one people to dissolve the political bands which have connected them with another, and to assume, among the Powers of the earth, the separate and equal station to which the Laws of Nature and of Nature's God entitle them, a decent respect to the opinions of mankind requires that they should declare the causes which impel them to the separation.

We hold these truths to be self-evident, that all men are created equal, that they are endowed by their Creator with certain unalienable Rights, that among these are Life, Liberty, and the pursuit of Happiness. That to secure these rights, Governments are instituted among Men, deriving their just powers from the consent of the governed, That whenever any Form of Government becomes destructive of these ends, it is the Right of the People to alter or to abolish it, and to institute new Government, laying its foundation on such principles and organizing its powers in such form, as to them shall seem most likely to effect their Safety and Happiness. Prudence, indeed, will dictate that Governments long established should not be changed for light and transient causes; and accordingly all experience hath shown, that mankind are more disposed to suffer, while evils are sufferable, than to right themselves by abolishing the forms to which they are accustomed. But when a long train of abuses and usurpations, pursuing invariably the same Object evinces a design to reduce them under absolute Despotism, it is their right, it is their duty, to throw off such Government, and to provide new Guards for their future security. –Such has been the patient sufferance of these Colonies; and such is now the necessity which constrains them to alter their former Systems of Government. The history of the present King of Great Britain is a history of repeated injuries and usurpations, all having in direct object the establishment of an absolute Tyranny over these States. To prove this, let Facts be submitted to a candid world.

Figure 80: *The world's first e-book, published on July 4, 1971.*

As the twentieth century was drawing to a close, the old parchment was finding new worlds to conquer—specifically, the digital universe. That universe was still in its infancy in the 1970s, but when Project Gutenberg, housed at the University of Illinois, wanted to create the first e-book in 1971, the project managers chose the Declaration of Independence. Even if the format was different, this time with no paper at all, the idea of disseminating the text widely and inexpensively was not so different from the way the Founders thought about it in 1776.

As we have seen, thanks to skilled printers like John Dunlap and Mary Katharine Goddard, the original Declaration of Independence benefited from rapid diffusion when it was issued in 1776. Two centuries later, the arrival of digital tools only quickened this trend. In the early days of the internet, in the 1990s, the Declaration still spoke to early avatars, eager to define cyberspace in ways that would protect their intellectual freedom and defend it from governmental overreach. In that sense, these defenders were not all that different from the Founders of the United States, trying to protect a different kind of uncharted space.

With the benefit of hindsight, and the knowledge of how important (and profitable) the internet has become, it seems absurd to contemplate a world in which governments would not seek to regulate this essential channel of commerce. It also overlooks an inconvenient fact, namely, that the U.S. government (and specifically the Defense Advanced Research Projects Agency, or DARPA) contributed mightily to the development of the internet. But in 1996, attitudes were more innocent, and when the Telecommunications Act of that year passed Congress, a writer and activist, John Perry Barlow, wrote an impassioned screed asserting that the pristine world of cyberspace should not be desecrated by the heavy hand of the state.

John Perry Barlow, A Declaration of the Independence of Cyberspace

February 8, 1996

Governments of the Industrial World, you weary giants of flesh and steel, I come from Cyberspace, the new home of Mind. On behalf of the future, I ask you of the past to leave us alone. You are not welcome among us. You have no sovereignty where we gather.

We have no elected government, nor are we likely to have one, so I address you with no greater authority than that with which liberty itself always speaks. I declare the global social space we are building to be naturally independent of the tyrannies you seek to impose on us. You have no moral right to rule us nor do you possess any methods of enforcement we have true reason to fear.

Governments derive their just powers from the consent of the governed. You have neither solicited nor received ours. We did not invite you. You do not know us, nor do you know our world. Cyberspace does not lie within your borders. Do not think that you can build it, as though it were a public construction project. You cannot. It is an act of nature and it grows itself through our collective actions.

You have not engaged in our great and gathering conversation, nor did you create the wealth of our marketplaces. You do not know our culture, our ethics, or the unwritten codes that already provide our society more order than could be obtained by any of your impositions.

You claim there are problems among us that you need to solve. You use this claim as an excuse to invade our precincts. Many of these problems don't exist. Where there are real conflicts, where there are wrongs, we will identify them and address them by our means. We are forming our own Social Contract. This governance will arise according to the conditions of our world, not yours. Our world is different.

Cyberspace consists of transactions, relationships, and thought itself, arrayed like a standing wave in the web of our communications. Ours is a world that is both everywhere and nowhere, but it is not where bodies live.

We are creating a world that all may enter without privilege or prejudice accorded by race, economic power, military force, or station of birth.

We are creating a world where anyone, anywhere may express his or her beliefs, no matter how singular, without fear of being coerced into silence or conformity.

Your legal concepts of property, expression, identity, movement, and context do not apply to us. They are all based on matter, and there is no matter here.

Our identities have no bodies, so, unlike you, we cannot obtain order by physical coercion. We believe that from ethics, enlightened self-interest, and the commonweal, our governance will emerge. Our identities may be distributed across many of your jurisdictions. The only law that all our constituent cultures would generally recognize is the Golden Rule. We hope we will be able to build our particular solutions on that basis. But we cannot accept the solutions you are attempting to impose.

In the United States, you have today created a law, the Telecommunications Reform Act, which repudiates your own Constitution and insults the dreams of Jefferson, Washington, Mill, Madison, DeToqueville, and Brandeis. These dreams must now be born anew in us.

You are terrified of your own children, since they are natives in a world where you will always be immigrants. Because you fear them, you entrust your bureaucracies with the parental responsibilities you are too cowardly to confront yourselves. In our world, all the sentiments and expressions of humanity, from the debasing to the angelic, are parts of a seamless whole, the global conversation of bits. We cannot separate the air that chokes from the air upon which wings beat.

In China, Germany, France, Russia, Singapore, Italy and the United States, you are trying to ward off the virus of liberty by erecting guard posts at the frontiers of Cyberspace. These may keep out the contagion for a small time, but they will not work in a world that will soon be blanketed in bit-bearing media.

Your increasingly obsolete information industries would perpetuate themselves by proposing laws, in America and elsewhere, that claim to own speech itself throughout the world. These laws would declare ideas to be another industrial product, no more noble than pig iron. In our world, whatever the human mind may create can be reproduced and distributed infinitely at no cost. The global conveyance of thought no longer requires your factories to accomplish.

These increasingly hostile and colonial measures place us in the same position as those previous lovers of freedom and self-determination who had to reject the authorities of distant, uninformed powers. We must declare our virtual selves immune to your sovereignty, even as we continue to consent to your rule over our bodies. We will spread ourselves across the Planet so that no one can arrest our thoughts.

We will create a civilization of the Mind in Cyberspace. May it be more humane and fair than the world your governments have made before.

Davos, Switzerland
February 8, 1996

In 2002, it was once again time to examine the Declaration and its housing, after fifty years in the same encasement. This time, tiny imperfections were found in the glass protecting it, and another round of improvements was ordered. Microscopic examination also yielded deeper understanding of the damage sustained in earlier decades, often caused by the very curators who were trying to protect it. Through their well-intentioned but misguided efforts, the parchment had been rolled, stretched, and flattened at various moments, which led to tiny holes and tears, and some missing parchment as well.

It was also found that a great deal of the original ink is missing, having sunk into the parchment or been flaked off during some of the rough handling over the years (including the wet-process transfer that was likely used to create the Stone facsimile in 1823). This creates a quandary, in which we know the words, but can barely see them. At one point, someone tried to remedy the problem of fading ink by drawing over John Hancock's signature, clumsily. The upper right corner is especially compromised, with a tear running from "1776" to "America." Reviewing the long history of ill-advised repairs, one expert said, "the Declaration of Independence is one of the most abused documents in the history of preservation." This is a strange paradox; we have nearly destroyed our founding charter through our love for it.

Figure 81: *Repaired tear in upper right corner, from "1776" to "America," in a 1940 photograph.*

And yet the Declaration survives. It appears to be indestructible. Its very old technology—ink on vellum—endures more successfully than many of the strategies of preserving government documents in the twentieth century, when the National Archives sometimes lost the ability to read vast troves of government data on machines that had become obsolete.

Millions line up to see it every year, and its words still resonate. It speaks to all of us. Capaciously, it manages to address both those who feel a deep and patriotic sense that all is right in America and those who feel that we are not living up to our revolutionary inheritance. The Founders who wrote it felt a healthy skepticism toward the ruling order of their day, and a robust confidence that the people could govern themselves. They acted on those feelings, and in so doing, created the United States of America. The Declaration excites similar feelings today. It works for all its audiences, but it is especially welcoming to those who would comfort the afflicted, and afflict the comfortable. It is not a document for the complacent, or the antiquarian. It is alive with the feeling that a better world is possible.

In this way the Declaration of Independence has always appealed to the disenfranchised, eager to claim the rights so generously offered by its language. Many made their way to the progressive end of the political spectrum, where certain causes (i.e., the Civil Rights Movement) found a natural home. Several declarations of *inter*dependence have been composed to express environmental concerns, arguing that the pursuit of happiness is not incompatible with a decent respect for the Earth.

But at times, the leveling energies of the Declaration attracted activists on the right, eager to paint the federal government as a "tyranny" in the same language the Founders used to attack King George III. The right-to-life movement had often borrowed from Jefferson's language about life and liberty. Then, from 2007

Figure 82: *Self-styled Tea Partiers assemble in Dallas, Texas, on April 15, 2009, many sporting the Gadsden "Don't Tread on Me" flag, a historical emblem that dates to 1775.*

to 2010, an amorphous movement began to grow in libertarian circles, enraged by government spending, taxation, and the temporary sway of Democrats following the 2008 fiscal crisis and the election of Barack Obama, the nation's first Black president. Judging from its name, the "Tea Party" was drawn to the American Revolution, and following that logic, it needed a Declaration of Independence all its own. This document (not attributed to any author) began to circulate online at the time. Ostensibly angry with all political elites, it opens by declaring that "as the course of human events winds its way through History, it has found some paths lead to Tyranny and some to Liberty. In seeking a path to Liberty, a great and powerful movement is now rising from every corner of our land." After asserting its independence from both major political parties, the text moves on to express a larger anti-establishment vision that pointed the way toward political ruptures to come.

Declaration of Tea Party Independence

February 24, 2010

. . . IV. We Declare ourselves INDEPENDENT of the Media, which has proved itself to be anything BUT a fair and balanced enterprise and which focuses more on entertainment, fear mongering and shock value than investigation and unbiased fact.

We reject the fiction that an unbiased media still exists; there is friendly media and there is unfriendly ENE-media. The Tea Party Movement refuses to give false credence to the self-aggrandizing, self-deluding lie that ANY PART of the Fourth Estate is free of the self-serving agendas of those who own them.

V. We Declare ourselves INDEPENDENT of self-styled "leaders" who claim to speak for the Tea Party Movement. This movement is not a brand name to -be used to sell product; nor is it a logo to be used to justify profiting off its name.

We reject those who seek to personally capitalize on our popularity and momentum by trying to associate with our cause.

We reject the idea that the Tea Party Movement is "led" by anyone other than the millions of average citizens who make it up. The Tea Party Movement understands that as a Free People, we need to SAVE OURSELVES, BY OURSELVES, FOR OURSELVES.

The Tea Party Movement is not "led." The Tea Party Movement LEADS.

VI. We are united in our common belief in Fiscal Responsibility, Constitutionally Limited Government and Free Markets. This threefold purpose is the source of our unity in the Tea Party Movement.

We reject the idea that the Tea Party Movement must all be unanimous in our specific policy views in order to win. We recognize that the current situation requires we come together in confederation to achieve the MANY MUTUAL GOALS we all seek to accomplish.

We recognize that the current situation requires that we concentrate on the many things we have in common rather than those few things about which we may disagree.

We are the Tea Party Movement of America and we believe in American Exceptionalism.

We believe that American Exceptionalism is found in its devotion to the cause of Liberty.

We believe that Liberty is based in rational self-interest, in freedom of thought, in free markets, free association, free speech, a free press and the ability granted us under the Constitution TO DIRECT OUR OWN AFFAIRS FREE OF THE DICTATES OF AN EVER EXPANDING FEDERAL GOVERNMENT WHICH IS AS VORACIOUS IN ITS DESIRE FOR POWER AS IT IS INCOMPETENT AND DANGEROUS IN ITS EXERCISE.

We believe that either fate or history has chosen this Country to be a beacon of freedom and prosperity to the whole world because of America's belief in and vigorous defense of political and economic Liberty. The United States has been the instrument of Liberty against the many tyrannies that have threatened the people of this world.

The Tea Party Movement rejects the idea that America has to apologize to a far guiltier world that has been largely unappreciative of the sacrifices made on their behalf by the brave and noble members of our Armed Forces, whose sacrifice and patriotic service in our defense makes all else possible.

The Tea Party Movement rejects the imposition of "transformational change" performed on our Nation by smug elites who call themselves the "educated class".

The Tea Party Movement understands that our Nation is NOT the same thing as our government and that America is much more than simply a militarily and economically powerful State.

The Tea Party Movement sees America as something exceptional, as something unique, as something that came into existence to fulfill the hope of all previous generations that longed for freedom.

It came into existence because it is more than simply a country with land and population and riches and armaments. America came into existence because LIBERTY is an eternal concept in the mind of both God AND Man.

The United States of America came into existence because Mankind needs freedom the same way it needs food and air and property and security and love.

And what is freedom other than the RIGHT to be free of the tyranny of Government and the elitist, self-styled aristocrats who seek to run it at our expense and to our detriment?

The Tea Party Movement will fight this danger to our Liberty as long as its members have breath in their bodies.

When America didn't exist men and women were compelled to invent it, BECAUSE MANKIND CANNOT EXIST WITHOUT FREEDOM AND STILL BE FULLY HUMAN.

To this goal we mutually pledge to each other, as our Founding Fathers did over two centuries ago, our Lives, our Fortunes, and our sacred Honor.

Alert to the many competing interpretations of the Declaration, President Barack Obama often spoke personally and meaningfully about it. His second inaugural address, in 2013, included a vivid line about an idea that lies at the heart of this book—namely, that the Declaration is what we make of it. Specifically, Obama said: "while these truths may be self-evident, they've never been self-executing; that while freedom is a gift from God, it must be secured by His people here on Earth."

That line, which echoed the final sentence of John F. Kennedy's lone inaugural, became especially relevant on June 26, 2015, a consequential day for a number of reasons. President Obama was already planning to fly to Charleston, South Carolina, to deliver a eulogy for the nine victims of a tragic shooting at Charleston's historic Emanuel African Methodist Episcopal Church. The eulogy, as it turned out, would be one of the most memorable speeches delivered by President Obama, including an improvised singing of the hymn "Amazing Grace."

Figure 83: *President Barack Obama speaks in the White House Rose Garden in the wake of the Supreme Court's decision in* Obergefell v. Hodges, *legalizing same-sex marriage nationwide.*

But in the morning of the same day, the news flashed forth that the Supreme Court had released an important ruling in the case of *Obergefell v. Hodges*, validating gay marriage by a 5–4 decision. President Obama, who had mentioned the Stonewall riot of 1969—a major event in the history of LGBT rights—in his second inaugural, immediately understood the significance of the decision, and delivered a heartfelt statement in the Rose Garden. In those remarks, he invoked the importance of the Declaration in new and resonant ways.

In fact, LGBT activists had always understood the power of the Declaration, in their own pursuit of equal protections, and they had been gathering at Independence Hall to say as much. On every July 4, from 1965 to 1969, gay activists attended an "Annual Reminder" at Independence Hall to insist that they, too, were created equal. These were among the first demonstrations for gay rights in American history, even before Stonewall.

Barack Obama, Remarks on the Supreme Court Decision on Marriage Equality

June 26, 2015

Good morning. Our nation was founded on a bedrock principle that we are all created equal. The project of each generation is to bridge the meaning of those founding words with the realities of changing times—a never-ending quest to ensure those words ring true for every single American.

Progress on this journey often comes in small increments, sometimes two steps forward, one step back, propelled by the persistent effort of dedicated citizens. And then sometimes, there are days like this when that slow, steady effort is rewarded with justice that arrives like a thunderbolt.

This morning, the Supreme Court recognized that the Constitution guarantees marriage equality. In doing so, they've reaffirmed that all Americans are entitled to the equal protection of the law. That all people should be treated equally, regardless of who they are or who they love.

This decision will end the patchwork system we currently have. It will end the uncertainty hundreds of thousands of same-sex couples face from not knowing whether their marriage, legitimate in the eyes of one state, will remain if they decide to move to or even visit another. This ruling will strengthen all of our communities by offering to all loving same-sex couples the dignity of marriage across this great land.

In my second inaugural address, I said that if we are truly created equal, then surely the love we commit to one another must be equal as well. It is gratifying to see that principle enshrined into law by this decision.

This ruling is a victory for Jim Obergefell and the other plaintiffs in the case. It's a victory for gay and lesbian couples who have fought so long for their basic civil rights. It's a victory for their children, whose families will now be recognized as equal to any other. It's a victory for the allies and friends and supporters who spent years, even decades, working and praying for change to come.

And this ruling is a victory for America. This decision affirms what millions of Americans already believe in their hearts: When all Americans are treated as equal we are all more free.

My administration has been guided by that idea. It's why we stopped defending the so-called Defense of Marriage Act, and why we were pleased when the Court finally struck down a central provision of that discriminatory law. It's why we ended "Don't Ask, Don't Tell." From extending full marital benefits to federal employees and their spouses, to expanding hospital visitation rights for LGBT patients and their loved ones, we've made real progress in advancing equality for LGBT Americans in ways that were unimaginable not too long ago.

I know change for many of our LGBT brothers and sisters must have seemed so slow for so long. But compared to so many other issues, America's shift has been so quick. I know that Americans of goodwill continue to hold a wide range of views on this issue. Opposition in some cases has been based on sincere and deeply held beliefs. All of us who welcome today's news should be mindful of that fact; recognize different viewpoints; revere our deep commitment to religious freedom.

But today should also give us hope that on the many issues with which we grapple, often painfully, real change is possible. Shifts in hearts and minds are possible. And those who have come so far on their journey to equality have a responsibility to reach back and help others join them. Because for all our differences, we are one people, stronger together than we could ever be alone. That's always been our story.

We are big and vast and diverse; a nation of people with different backgrounds and beliefs, different experiences and stories, but bound by our shared ideal that no matter who you are or what you look like, how you started off, or how and who you love, America is a place where you can write your own destiny. We are a people who believe that every single child is entitled to life and liberty and the pursuit of happiness.

There's so much more work to be done to extend the full promise of America to every American. But today, we can say in no uncertain terms that we've made our union a little more perfect.

That's the consequence of a decision from the Supreme Court, but, more importantly, it is a consequence of the countless small acts of courage of millions of people across decades who stood up, who came out, who talked to parents—parents who loved their children no matter what. Folks who were willing to endure bullying and taunts, and stayed strong, and came to believe in themselves and who they were, and slowly made an entire country realize that love is love.

What an extraordinary achievement. What a vindication of the belief that ordinary people can do extraordinary things. What a reminder of what Bobby Kennedy once said about how small actions can be like pebbles being thrown into a still lake, and ripples of hope cascade outwards and change the world.

Those countless, often anonymous heroes—they deserve our thanks. They should be very proud. America should be very proud.

But what of the old parchment? The technology of preservation continues to improve, encouraging confidence that the physical Declaration will be with us for a long time yet—certainly through the tricentennial of 2076, and hopefully for some time to come after that. Of course, the virtual Declaration is ubiquitous, and freely available online. Thanks to our phones, we can all keep a copy in our pocket. It is everywhere, including on the moon (a digital Declaration was brought to the lunar surface in 2024 and beamed back to Earth).

The 2026 semiquincentennial will, it can be hoped, stimulate new interest in a document that now belongs to all of us. Human rights continue to be precious in a time of resurgent autocracy—and also, growing uncertainty about what "human" rights even mean in a world with so many nonhuman actors populating our lives. The yearning for freedom from arbitrary power will never end, as each generation works out its destiny in the face of ever-changing reality. But the old verities still hold, and a basic confidence that the peoples of the Earth deserve to govern themselves along the lines sketched in 1776.

PART VI

EPILOGUE

Anniversaries are naturally retrospective; but they can look forward too. So it has always been with the Fourth of July, a day that asks us to take stock of the national experiment.

When Alexis de Tocqueville attended a Fourth of July celebration in Albany, New York, in 1831, he was not impressed by the speeches, which droned on too long, or the singing of patriotic songs, many of which borrowed their tunes, not very independently, from other countries (including his own).

But the people's reverence for the Declaration of Independence left him profoundly moved. They cheered when a parade float passed by, featuring a Goddess of Liberty, a slave bursting his chains, and a printing press that churned out copies of the great document in real time. Then they went into a local church for a public reading. As Lincoln later would, Tocqueville used the word "electric" to describe the feeling evoked by hearing the words of the Declaration. "A profound silence reigned in the meeting," he recalled in a letter home to a friend:

> When in its eloquent plea Congress reviewed the injustices and the tyranny of England, we heard a murmur of indignation and anger circulate about us in the auditorium. When it appealed to the justice of its cause and expressed the generous resolution to succumb or free America, it seemed an electric current made the hearts vibrate.

He continued:

> This was not, I assure you, a theatrical performance. There was in the reading of those promises of independence so well kept, in this return of an entire people toward the memories of its birth, in this union of the present generation to that which is no longer, sharing for the moment all its generous passions, there was in all that something deeply felt and truly great.

Perhaps the Declaration's words will inspire the same generous passions during the semiquincentennial and beyond. It is not always simple to celebrate a complex nation's history, especially in a divisive political moment. It can be troubling to see our inconsistencies, but that is precisely why we have historians. A great nation can survive an honest self-examination, and cannot long endure without one.

That the United States was not perfect when it came into existence is fairly easy to document. On July 2, 1776, the very day that the Continental Congress voted for independence, a Philadelphia newspaper ran a notice by a slaveowner, hoping to recapture a young American named Ishmael, "twenty-five years of age, above six feet high, strong made, his colour between a Mulatto and a Black."

But a central premise of this book is that we are not condemned to repeat the mistakes of the past. We evolve, thanks to a remarkably elastic document that remains intensely alive to most Americans. Ever since 1776, each generation has struggled—often at great cost—to give real meaning to the words of a living Declaration. Dr. King put it simply and powerfully in his final speech: "Be true to what you said on paper."

That sounds easy; history confirms just how hard it has been. The effort to define our creed, and then live up to it, has never been as straightforward or immediate as we would like. In fact, it has taken most of the past 250 years to understand the full implications of the promises we made to one another, at the beginning of our experiment, inside a document that is still unscrolling.

But even when we cannot entirely see the path, the Declaration acts as a lantern, guiding our steps. In the eternal battle between our better angels and our baser ones, it has tilted the balance.

Lincoln always felt that the Declaration of Independence was, in a sense, alive. In his speeches, he described it as a burbling spring ("the fountain whose waters spring close by the blood of the Revolution"), or a lighthouse to guide the mariners of the future ("a beacon to guide their children and their children's children"), or a source of electricity, bringing a charge to those who believe in its words.

I hope some of that feeling comes through this book, and from the many voices in it. While the majority are American, it should be noted that Lincoln also expressly believed that the Declaration spoke to the aspirations of *all* humanity; as he put it, "the whole great family of man." We don't revere it because it proclaimed rights for a select few. We understand it to express universal truths, available to everyone.

In the years to come, it can be hoped that once again, the Declaration will unite a fractious people. History encourages the thought. The two men who did the most to bring the document into existence, John Adams and Thomas Jefferson, were not always on the same page. Long after working toward a common goal in 1776, their political views began to pull them apart, into the factions that the Founders dreaded. But the country survived these early divisions, and grew stronger as Americans realized that they could reasonably disagree.

As fate would have it, Adams and Jefferson would run against each other twice for the presidency. Jefferson's victory in the bitter campaign of 1800 strained but did not end his friendship with Adams. Their correspondence in retirement brought them close again, as they returned to the great themes of their youth and their shared pride in the Declaration. In his final letter to Adams, Jefferson distilled an immense history into a single sentence: "It was the lot of our early years to witness nothing but the dull monotony of Colonial subservience, and of our riper ones to breast the labors and perils of working out of it." What he did not say—because he did not need to—was that they had drafted a timeless document while doing so. As Lincoln understood, it would serve as a "rebuke and a stumbling-block" to future tyrannies as well.

The Adams-Jefferson letters reward close reading. They are an epistolary monument to the proposition that Americans can survive their differences.

Our heritage includes a natural pride in the ancestors who achieved independence, but that pride expands with the understanding that they built a country for *all* of us, including those with no blood relation to them. It is the essential idea of a country founded upon ideas. It is what makes us who we are. As Herman Melville wrote in a letter to a friend, "The Declaration of Independence makes a difference."

ACKNOWLEDGMENTS

The Living Declaration came together in the same collaborative spirit in which the Declaration was written in the summer of 1776. Brian McCarthy at Library of America was a superb partner throughout the process. Many of the selections came from his deep knowledge of American history and the narrative was improved by his deft editorial touch. Max Rudin and the rest of the team at Library of America helped in a hundred different ways to deliver a product worthy of LOA's exacting standards. Les Levi, David Bruce Smith, and the National Endowment for the Humanities provided generous funding. Karenna Gore gave the book a close reading and sharpened the thinking in many places. Zachary Turpin helped find early examples of the Declaration's most famous phrases, including "self-evident," whose origins are not self-evident at all. I'm deeply grateful to Gordon Wood for his foreword, and for a lifetime of instruction at the highest level.

At the end of the Declaration, the signers affirmed their belief that the document serves as a mutual pledge, joining them in common cause. It can be hoped that the act of reading and rereading the document is another act of union, binding new readers to the hopes of the Founders, and to each other. As Lincoln said, "it is for us, the living. . . ."

FURTHER READING

Readers interested in learning more about the Declaration of Independence, its history, and its political significance are encouraged to explore the following works:

Allen, Danielle. *Our Declaration: A Reading of the Declaration of Independence in Defense of Equality.* New York: Liveright, 2014.

Armitage, David. *The Declaration of Independence: A Global History.* Cambridge, MA: Harvard University Press, 2008.

Auslin, Michael. *National Treasure: How the Declaration of Independence Made America.* New York: Simon & Schuster, 2026.

Becker, Carl. *The Declaration of Independence: A Study in the History of Political Ideas.* New York: Alfred A. Knopf, 1960 (reprint of earlier editions from 1922, 1942).

Beeman, Richard R. *Our Lives, Our Fortunes and Our Sacred Honor: The Forging of American Independence, 1774–1776.* New York: Basic Books, 2013.

Bell, Whitfield J., Jr. *The Declaration of Independence: Four 1776 Versions.* Philadelphia: American Philosophical Society, 1976.

Bidwell, John. *The Declaration in Script and Print: A Visual History of America's Founding Document.* University Park: Penn State University Press, 2024.

Boyd, Julian P. *The Declaration of Independence: The Evolution of the Text.* Princeton, NJ: Princeton University Press, 1945.

Burstein, Andrew. *America's Jubilee: A Generation Remembers the Revolution After Fifty Years of Independence.* New York: Alfred A. Knopf, 2001.

Cappon, Lester, ed. *The Adams-Jefferson Letters: The Complete Correspondence Between Thomas Jefferson and Abigail and John Adams.* Chapel Hill: University of North Carolina Press (Institute of Early American History and Culture), 1987.

Dupont, Christian Y. and Peter S. Onuf, eds. *Declaring Independence: The Origin and Influence of America's Founding Document.* Charlottesville: University of Virginia Library, 2008.

Ellis, Joseph J. *American Creation: Triumphs and Tragedies at the Founding of the Republic.* New York: Alfred A. Knopf, 2007.

———. *Revolutionary Summer: The Birth of American Independence.* New York: Alfred A. Knopf, 2013.

Fischer, David Hackett. *Liberty and Freedom: A Visual History of America's Founding Ideas.* New York: Oxford University Press, 2005.

Fliegelman, Jay. *Declaring Independence: Jefferson, Natural Language, and the Culture of Performance.* Stanford, CA: Stanford University Press, 1993.

Foner, Philip S., ed. *We, the Other People: Alternative Declarations of Independence by Labor Groups, Farmers, Woman's Rights Advocates, Socialists, and Blacks, 1829–1975.* Urbana: University of Illinois Press, 1976.

Gilbert, Felix. *To the Farewell Address: Ideas of Early American Foreign Policy.* Princeton, NJ: Princeton University Press, 1961.

Goff, Frederick R. *The John Dunlap Broadside: The First Printing of the Declaration of Independence.* Washington, D.C.: Library of Congress, 1976.

Gould, Eliga H. *Among the Powers of the Earth: The American Revolution and the Making of a New World Empire.* Cambridge, MA: Harvard University Press, 2012.

Hazelton, John H. *The Declaration of Independence: Its History.* New York: Dodd, Mead, 1906.

Hogeland, William. *Declaration: The Nine Tumultuous Weeks When America Became Independent, May 1–July 4, 1776.* New York: Simon & Schuster, 2010.

Jones, Howard Mumford. *The Pursuit of Happiness.* Cambridge, MA: Harvard University Press, 1953.

Maier, Pauline. *American Scripture: Making the Declaration of Independence.* New York: Alfred A. Knopf, 1997.

Malone, Dumas. *The Story of the Declaration of Independence.* New York: Oxford University Press, 1954.

Mearns, David C. *The Declaration of Independence: The Story of a Parchment.* Washington, D.C.: Library of Congress, 1950.

Moore, Peter. *Life, Liberty, and the Pursuit of Happiness: Britain and the American Dream.* New York: Farrar, Straus & Giroux, 2023.

Onuf, Peter S., ed. *Jeffersonian Legacies.* Charlottesville: University of Virginia Press, 1993.

Parkinson, Robert G. *Thirteen Clocks: How Race United the Colonies and Made the Declaration of Independence.* Williamsburg, VA: Omohundro Institute of Early American History and Culture, 2021.

Peterson, Merrill D. *The Jefferson Image in the American Mind.* New York: Oxford University Press, 1960.

Pincus, Steve. *The Heart of the Declaration: The Founders' Case for an Activist Government.* New Haven, CT: Yale University Press, 2016.

Preservation of the Declaration of Independence and the Constitution of the United States. Washington, D.C.: U.S. Department of Commerce, 1951.

Rakove, Jack N. *The Annotated U.S. Constitution and Declaration of Independence.* Cambridge, MA: Harvard University Press, 2009.

Rosen, Jeffrey. *The Pursuit of Happiness: How Classical Writers on Virtue Inspired the Lives of the Founders and Defined America.* New York: Simon & Schuster, 2024.

Sneff, Emily. *When the Declaration of Independence Was News.* New York: Oxford University Press, 2026.

Spahn, Hannah. *Black Reason, White Feeling: The Jeffersonian Enlightenment in the African American Tradition.* Charlottesville: University of Virginia Press, 2024.

Travers, Len. *Celebrating the Fourth: Independence Day and the Rites of Nationalism in the Early Republic.* Amherst: University of Massachusetts Press, 1997.

Waldstreicher, David. *In the Midst of Perpetual Fetes: The Making of American Nationalism, 1776–1820.* Williamsburg, VA: Omohundro Institute of Early American History and Culture, 1997.

White, Morton. *The Philosophy of the American Revolution.* New York: Oxford University Press, 1978.

Widmer, Ted. *Lincoln on the Verge: Thirteen Days to Washington.* New York: Simon & Schuster, 2020.

Wills, Garry. *Inventing America: Jefferson's Declaration of Independence.* Garden City, NY: Doubleday, 1978.

Winterer, Caroline. *American Enlightenments: Pursuing Happiness in the Age of Reason.* New Haven, CT: Yale University Press, 2016.

Wood, Gordon S. *The Radicalism of the American Revolution: How a Revolution Transformed a Monarchical Society into a Democratic One Unlike Any That Had Ever Existed.* New York: Alfred A. Knopf, 1992.

NOTES

The following notes identify the source of quotations in the narrative and provide additional context for references that may be obscure or confusing in the historical texts, which are presented with their original spelling. No note is made for material included in *Webster's Collegiate Dictionary*, except in certain cases where common words and terms have specific historical meanings or inflections.

INTRODUCTION

xvi **"future use . . . all people of all colors everywhere."]** "I think the authors of that notable instrument . . . meant to set up a standard maxim for free society, which should be familiar to all, and revered by all; constantly looked to, constantly labored for, and even though never perfectly attained, constantly approximated, and thereby constantly spreading and deepening its influence, and augmenting the happiness and value of life to all people of all colors everywhere. The assertion that 'all men are created equal' was of no practical use in effecting our separation from Great Britain; and it was placed in the Declaration, not for that, but for future use." "Speech on the Dred Scott Decision at Springfield, Illinois," June 26, 1857, *Abraham Lincoln: Speeches & Writings 1832–1858*, ed. Don E. Fehrenbacher (New York: Library of America, 1989), 398.

xix **"hard nut to crack"]** "Its authors meant it to be, thank God, it is now proving itself, a stumbling block to those who in after times might seek to turn a free people back into the hateful paths of despotism. They knew the proneness of prosperity to breed tyrants, and they meant when such should re-appear in this fair land and commence their vocation they should find left for them at least one hard nut to crack." Ibid., 399.

xx **"a Theatrical Show" and a "Stage Effect,"]** "The Declaration of Independence I always considered as a Theatrical Show. Jefferson ran away with all the Stage Effect of that, i.e. all the Glory of it." John Adams to Benjamin Rush, June 21, 1811, *John Adams: Writings from the New Nation 1784–1826*, ed. Gordon S. Wood (New York: Library of America, 2016), 522.

xxv **as John Adams did to Mary Palmer, on July 5]** Mary Palmer was the niece of Adams's brother-in-law, and an occasional correspondent. Still a little giddy, perhaps, by the events of the last few days, Adams wrote to her that "I will inclose to you a Declaration, in which all America is remarkably united. . . . It compleats a Revolution, which will make as good a Figure in the History of Mankind, as any that has preceeded it—provided always, that the Ladies take Care to record the Circumstances of it, for by the Experience I have had of the other Sex, they are either too lazy, or too active, to commemorate them." https://founders.archives.gov/documents/Adams/04-02-02-0018.

xxviii **This was the object of the Declaration of Independence . . . by the occasion.]** Thomas Jefferson to Henry Lee, May 8, 1825, *Thomas Jefferson: Writings*, ed. Merrill D. Peterson (New York: Library of America, 1984), 1501.

xxx **Some scholars have speculated that the edit came from Benjamin Franklin]** Julian P. Boyd, the editor of the Thomas Jefferson Papers, and the author of a classic study, *The Declaration of Independence: The Evolution of the Text* (1945), thought that this critical edit was made by Jefferson himself, and he supported his argument with careful analysis of Jefferson's handwriting. According to Boyd (p. 22), "The famous and altogether felicitous change has been attributed both to Franklin and to Jefferson. Such feeling as it exhibits for precisely the right word is quite Franklinian in character, but the handwriting of the phrase 'self-evident' bears the appearance of being equally Jeffersonian. I find it difficult to believe that the characteristically Jeffersonian 's' here—another example given immediately above it—and the even more distinctive final 't' with its peculiar 'A'-like quality, were not made by Jefferson." Boyd repeated this opinion in the first volume of *The Papers of Thomas Jefferson* (Princeton, NJ: Princeton University Press, 1950). But other scholars have been less certain. Carl Becker, in *The Declaration of Independence* (1922, 1942), thought the answer unknowable. Pauline Maier, in *American Scripture*, also refused to make a firm attribution. More recently, Walter Isaacson has asserted Franklin's authorship more categorically. In his biography *Benjamin Franklin: An American Life* (New York: Simon & Schuster, 2003), he claims that "he crossed out, using the heavy backslashes that he often employed, Jefferson's phrase, 'We hold these truths to be sacred and undeniable' and changed them to the words now enshrined in history: 'We hold these truths to be self-evident'" (212). But a backslash is not the most solid foundation for an argument, and the editors of the Franklin Papers at Yale University vigorously dispute Issacson's assertion. The point is further muddled by the possibility that another Founder—Franklin or Adams—may have spoken the phrase, at which point Jefferson wrote it into his draft. Other uses of "self-evident" are not difficult to find in the years prior to the Declaration (though nowhere in Franklin's collected works). Locke wrote of "self-evident propositions" in his *Essay Concerning Human Understanding* (1689). The entry for "Logic" in *The Encyclopedia Britannica* (1771) described "self-evident truths," stemming from a book, *The Elements of Logick* (1770), by a Scottish philosopher, William Duncan. Other books that contain this phrase include Matthew Tindal's *Christianity as Old as the Creation* (1730), Robert Dodsley's *The Preceptor* (1758), and Abraham Tucker's *The Light of Nature Pursued* (1768). It also appeared sparingly in the *Virginia Gazette.*

xxxiii **as the Swedish sociologist Gunnar Myrdal phrased it**] In his landmark 1944 book, *An American Dilemma.*

xxxiv **"Arbitrary power . . . to preserve or to tolerate."**] John Adams to Thomas Jefferson, November 13, 1815, https://founders.archives.gov/documents/Jefferson/03-09-02-0121.

xxxv **"As there is not a more . . . that can be devised."**] Circular letter from John Hancock to the state legislatures, January 31, 1777, https://docsouth.unc.edu/csr/index.html/document/csr11-0249.

A state paper . . . is, like freedom, a hard-bought thing.] John Gehlmann and Mary Rives Bowman, *Adventures in American Literature* (New York: Harcourt, Brace & World, 1958), 478.

xxxvii **He has refused his Assent . . . he has utterly neglected to attend to them.**] British monarchs lost the power to veto acts of Parliament in 1708, during the reign of Queen Anne. They relinquished the right to suspend laws even earlier, under the terms of the 1689 Declaration of Rights (see Part I). Congress begins therefore with two grievances that underscore the extent to which the colonial assemblies were not afforded what they understood to be the rights properly due to a legislature under the British constitution.

He has refused to pass other Laws . . . formidable to tyrants only.] Even as colonies enjoyed an influx of migrants in the 1770s, and settlements expanded westward, the Crown sought to limit the extension of representation to new communities to check the growth of increasingly unruly colonial assemblies.

He has called together . . . into compliance with his measures.] This grievance is specific to Massachusetts, where royal governors twice forced the legislature (the General Court) to meet in locations other than Boston.

xxxviii **He has made Judges dependent . . . of their salaries.**] Another instance where practices in America lagged well behind those in Britain, where judges had served on condition of good behavior, rather than simply at the pleasure of the monarch, since 1701.

He has kept among us . . . without the Consent of our legislatures.] Again, Massachusetts takes center stage here, with Boston having twice been occupied by British troops in the 1760s and 1770s, the second time including the imposition of a military governor.

He has combined with others . . . Acts of pretended Legislation:] Though it had been acts of Parliament that provoked the American crisis, Congress was scrupulous in not mentioning the body by name in the Declaration. Since at least 1774 the colonists had contended that they had no constitutional relationship whatsoever with Parliament and were therefore tied only to the Crown. By the summer of 1776, from the perspective of Jefferson and the other drafters, it was the only tie left to sever.

For Quartering . . . in all cases whatsoever] This series of charges relates to the Coercive Acts and other parliamentary measures passed in 1774 and 1775. See Part I.

He has abdicated . . . and destroyed the lives of our people.] These are the most damning charges. Congress alludes here to three British naval bombardments that were particularly galling for Americans: the June 17, 1775, destruction of Charlestown, Massachusetts, during the Battle of Bunker Hill; the October 18, 1775, burning of Falmouth, Massachusetts (now Portland, Maine); and the January 1, 1776, torching of Norfolk, Virginia.

He is at this time transporting . . . unworthy the Head of a civilized nation.] When news reached the colonies in the spring of 1776 that George III had contracted with various German states to send mercenary soldiers to America, it confirmed for many that the time for compromise had passed.

xxxix **He has constrained our fellow Citizens . . . by their Hands.**] Impressment of this sort would remain a thorny issue in Anglo-American relations for generations.

He has excited domestic insurrections . . . and conditions.] Referring in the first instance to the November 1775 proclamation by the Virginia royal governor, Lord Dunmore, offering freedom to enslaved individuals who would join British forces. As Americans well remembered, the British had made strategic use of Indian allies against the French during the Seven Years' War, and they feared those alliances would be turned against them now.

PART I

3 **a long debate about the nature of the British empire**] For the major themes and changing contours of this debate, see the two-volume collection *The American Revolution: Writings from the Pamphlet Debate,* ed. Gordon S. Wood (New York: Library of America, 2015).

"out of his protection,"] Quoting from the Declaration of Independence. See also Joseph Ellis, *Revolutionary Summer: The Birth of American Independence* (New York: Alfred A. Knopf, 2013), 10–11.

4 **"a new order for the ages"**] It was Congress's secretary, Charles Thomson, who adapted this phrase from the *Ecologues* of the Roman poet Virgil for use on the Great Seal.

5 **in the yeare of our Lord one thousand six hundred eighty eight**] Actually 1689. England would not officially adopt the Gregorian calendar until 1750, so the date here reflects the older Julian calendar, under which the new year began on March 25.

7 **whereas the said late King James the Second haveing Abdicated**] This significantly obscures the true nature of Parliament's coup d'état, undertaken in conjunction with William, Prince of Orange, who organized the largest invasion fleet assembled in the English Channel prior to D-Day. Though James II fled into exile in France in the face of this onslaught, he never formally relinquished the throne.

Cinque Ports] A regional cluster of five ports and their surrounding towns in southeastern England with traditional rights and privileges dating back to the Anglo-Saxon period.

10 **Edes and Gill**] Boston printers Benjamin Edes and John Gill were active in the town's patriot movement as publishers of the *Boston-Gazette* and key political pamphlets and broadsides,

including the minutes of the town meeting that led to the Boston Tea Party in December 1773. In 1776 they reproduced the Declaration of Independence in the *Gazette*, and as a broadside.

22 **the close of the last war**] Referring to the Seven Years' War, which ended in 1763. Its North American theater is often referred to as the French and Indian War.

in all cases whatsoever] Parliament made this claim in the Declaratory Act of 1765, which it issued at the same time it repealed the Stamp Act, a controversial measure, passed the year before, that had provoked fierce protest in the colonies.

24 **excluding every idea of taxation internal or external**] Benjamin Franklin, who was in London acting as an agent for several colonies, had famously testified before Parliament a decade earlier, during the Stamp Act crisis, and had seemed to suggest that Americans might recognize a distinction between revenue generated by Parliament's regulation of imperial trade (external taxes) and its claim, as in the Stamp Act, of the power to tax goods and services within the colonies (internal taxes). But by 1774, Americans had come to reject all such distinctions, asserting that no levies of any kind could be raised without the consent of the colonial assemblies.

25 **5 Geo. III. ch. 25**] Citations to parliamentary statutes are made with an abbreviation that designates first the year of the reign of the monarch who seals the law and second the chapter, or number, of the law in the statute books for that year. This notation refers to the Postage Act of 1765, the twenty-fifth public act passed in the fifth year of George III's reign, a relatively innocuous measure that adjusted postal rates and regulations in place since the reign of Queen Anne. It is likely that Congress meant to refer to 5 Geo. III ch. 12, the much more controversial Stamp Act.

28 **the minister who . . . enabled her to triumph over her enemies.**] William Pitt, later the Earl of Chatham, who had become a national hero guiding the British war effort as leader of the House of Commons during the Seven Years' War. He had believed that the North American colonies were strategically key and was especially highly regarded by the Americans for enacting legislation reimbursing them for their wartime expenses.

it pleased our sovereign to make a change in his counsels.] On October 25, 1760, the British king, George II, died suddenly and was succeeded by his twenty-two-year-old grandson. In March of the following year, George III installed his longtime tutor, John Stuart, 3rd Earl of Bute, a Scotsman and a Tory, as secretary of state for the Northern Department. In May 1762 he became prime minister. The king and his minister promptly initiated new measures, including a speedy and many thought overly generous resolution of the war with France, the maintenance of a large peacetime army in the colonies, and the proclamation of a western boundary line beyond which new settlement was prohibited, all of which aroused anger and resentment among Americans.

31 **this bold pamphlet played an essential role in the drama of 1776.**] See Joseph J. Ellis, *Revolutionary Summer: The Birth of American Independence* (Alfred A. Knopf, 2013), 11–12.

37 **"For forms of government . . . administered is best."**] Alexander Pope, *An Essay on Man* (1733), III.303–304.

Sidney, Harrington, Locke, Milton, Nedham, Neville, Burnet, and Hoadley] English Whig writers especially admired by American patriots: Algernon Sidney (1623–1683), James Harrington (1611–1677), John Locke (1632–1704), John Milton (1608–1674), Marchamont Needham (1620–1678), Henry Neville (1620–1694), Gilbert Burnett (1643–1715), and Bishop Hoadly (1676–1761).

39 **"Where annual elections end, there slavery begins."**] Though this was a maxim among radical Whigs, only the New England colonies and Pennsylvania held annual elections. Hyper-democratic Rhode Island did them one better, holding elections every six months.

45 **Rhode Island . . . renounce its allegiance to the crown.**] For the colony's May 4, 1776, Act of Renunciation, see https://catalog.sos.ri.gov/repositories/2/digital_object_components/6021.

53 **John Hancock . . . by couriers on fast horses.**] John H. Hazelton, *The Declaration of Independence: Its History* (New York: Dodd, Mead, 1906), 240–44.

the Declaration was read publicly; including . . . in New York City.] Frederick R. Goff, *The John Dunlap Broadside: The First Printing of the Declaration of Independence* (Washington, D.C.: Library of Congress, 1976), 11, and Hazelton, *The Declaration of Independence,* 251–53.

"That copies of the declaration . . . at the head of the army."] Quoted at https://declaration.fas.harvard.edu/blog/signing.

Within days, newspapers were reprinting the words of the Declaration.] For examples, see https://www.doyle.com/story/life-liberty-and-the-pursuit-of-happiness/ and https://www.sethkaller.com/item/2308-26587.99-July-8,-1776-%E2%80%93-The-First-Book-Printing-of-the-Declaration-of-Independence,-and-One-of-the-First-Printings.

55 **"dress and ornament rather than Body, Soul or Substance."**] Quoted in Pauline Maier, *American Scripture: Making the Declaration of Independence* (New York: Alfred A. Knopf, 1997), 184.

"the glory of the act is overshadowed by the glory of its annunciation."] Mellen Chamberlain, *The Authentication of the Declaration of Independence, July 4, 1776* (Cambridge, MA: John Wilson and Son, 1885), 27. Chamberlain's monograph was originally published in the November 1884 *Proceedings of the Massachusetts Historical Society.*

PART II

58 **"elevated into something akin to . . . one cause after another."**] Maier, *American Scripture*, 154.

60 **how far life, liberty, and the *pursuit of happiness* may be said to be unalienable**] Hutchinson emphasizes here one of Jefferson's most notable word choices in the Declaration. "Life, Liberty, and Property" was a familiar phrase in the Anglo-American world, its origins traceable to Locke's *Second Treatise* (ch. ix, sect. 131): "Men . . . enter into society . . . with an intention in every one the better to preserve himself, his liberty and property." "Liberty and Property" became a political slogan of the Glorious Revolution, one so associated with Whigs that by 1713 the Tory opposition adopted its own slogan: "No Liberty and Property Men!" But "happiness" was on the minds of the Founders in 1776. In his *Thoughts on Government*, as we have seen, John Adams had written that "the happiness of society is the end of government," and in the Virginia Declaration of Rights, George Mason claimed that "pursuing and obtaining happiness and safety" was a fundamental right, along with "life and liberty." Another possible source, even more exact, was Samuel Johnson, who wrote of "the pursuit of happiness" on at least five occasions, including his dictionary, a 1770 political pamphlet, *The False Alarm*, and a longer work, *The History of Rasselas, Prince of Abissinia* (first published in 1759). See Peter Moore, *Life, Liberty and the Pursuit of Happiness: Britain and the American Dream* (New York: Farrar, Straus & Giroux, 2023), 514.

62 **they at the same time, *acknowledged* that it was their duty to yield**] In 1764 many of the colonies, including Massachusetts, opposed the Sugar Act as an intrusive and unwise regulation of trade without challenging Parliament's constitutional right to enact it.

66 **the day that New Jersey chose to begin gradual emancipation.**] Maier, *American Scripture*, 198.

Two centuries later, a scholar named Ruth Bogin made an important discovery.] See Ruth Bogin, "Liberty Further Extended: A 1776 Antislavery Manuscript by Lemuel Haynes," *William and Mary Quarterly*, Vol. 40, no. 1 (January 1983): 85–105, and Eric Slauter, "The Declaration of Independence and the New Nation," in *The Cambridge Companion to Thomas Jefferson*, ed. Frank Shuffelton (New York: Cambridge University Press, 2008), 27.

71 **"The sublime manifesto of the United States of America was very generally applauded."**] Quoted in Carl Becker, *The Declaration of Independence: A Study in the History of Political Ideas* (New York: Harcourt, Brace and Company, 1922), 231.

72 **Lafayette helped to draft an early version, with advice from Thomas Jefferson**] Maier, *American Scripture*, 167.

the natural, unalienable and sacred rights of man] The apparent exclusion of women from the 1789 Declaration prompted French playwright and activist Olympe de Gouges, the nom de plume of Marie Gouze (1748–1793), to publish in 1791 a pamphlet entitled *Déclaration des droits de la femme et de la citoyenne.*

75 **It was in this period . . . "the immortal Jefferson."]** Maier, *American Scripture*, 167.
"poured the soul of the continent into the monumental act of Independence."] Ezra Stiles, *The United States Elevated to Honor and Glory. A Sermon, Preached . . . At the Anniversary Election, May 8th, 1783* (New Haven, CT: Thomas and Samuel Green, 1783), 46.

76 **"not controulable by any other . . . gave their consent."]** Cf. Article X of the Massachusetts Constitution.

77 **it is confirmed by written revelation]** In the Ninth and Tenth Commandments, Exodus 20:16–17.

78 **This, I think is a sentiment of the celebrated Montesquieu]** Adams may be thinking of this passage from Montesquieu's *De l'esprit des lois* (1748), bk. xi, ch. vi: "The political liberty of the subject is a tranquillity of mind, arising from the opinion each person has of his safety. In order to have this liberty, it is requisite the government be so constituted as one man need not be afraid of another. When the legislative and executive powers are united in the same person, or in the same body of magistrates, there can be no liberty; because apprehensions may arise, lest the same monarch or senate should enact tyrannical laws, to execute them in a tyrannical manner" (translation by Thomas Nugent, 1758).

83 **Haitians began a thirteen-year struggle for freedom in 1791.]** *The Haitian Declaration of Independence: Creation, Context and Legacy*, ed. Julia Gaffield (Charlottesville: University of Virginia Press, 2016), 2.
"an admirer of the work of Jefferson,"] Quoted in David Armitage, *The Declaration of Independence: A Global History* (Cambridge, MA: Harvard University Press, 2007), 115.

84 **Dessalines]** Jean-Jacques Dessalines (1758–1806) was the self-appointed governor general, and later emperor, of the newly independent Haiti.

85 **the object for which they have not ceased fighting since 1780]** This dating is likely an error in Marcus Rainsford's *Historical Account of the Black Empire of Hayti* (1805), from which the texts for the Haitian declarations presented here are taken. Inspired by the French Revolution, the first stirrings of organized resistance to the slave system on the island began in October 1790.

92 **"I shall believe it such until . . . proof of its authenticity shall be produced."]** Thomas Jefferson to John Adams, July 9, 1819, https://founders.archives.gov/documents/Jefferson/03-14-02-0491.

95 **"How many ages hence . . . and accents yet unknown?"]** Cf. *Julius Caesar*, III.i.111–13.

96 **the genuine Holy Alliance of its principles]** Adams makes a pointed allusion to the reactionary "Holy Alliance" of Austria, Prussia, and Russia, formed after the final defeat of Napoleon in 1815.

97 **"With heaviest sound, the giant monster fell."]** Adams likens the Americans to David, in his contest with the Philistine champion Goliath, depicted in 1 Samuel 17:1–58.
The Semiramis of the North . . . upon the seas.] An allusion to the League of Armed Neutrality, formed in early 1780 by Empress Catherine II of Russia (r. 1762–96), whose formidable leadership skills invited comparison to the legendary Princess Semiramis of Assyria.
vial of wrath] Cf. Revelation 15:7.

98 **"Anarchy is found tolerable!"]** Quoting from Edmund Burke, "Speech on Conciliation," from *The American Revolution: Writings from the Pamphlet Debate 1773–1776*, ed. Gordon S. Wood (New York: Library of America, 2015), 551.

100 **Aceldama]** Literally, field of blood.

102 **This revivified curiosity . . . for a prolonged goodwill tour in 1824–25.]** John Bidwell, *The Declaration in Script and Print* (University Park: Penn State University Press, 2024), 51–59.
Peleg Sprague . . . "excites deep and acute interest."] Maier, *American Scripture*, 190.

103 **Jefferson had likened the Adams administration to a "reign of witches"]** Thomas Jefferson to John Taylor, June 4, 1798. *Thomas Jefferson: Writings*, 1050.
"You and I ought not to die, before we have explained ourselves to each other."] John Adams to Thomas Jefferson, July 15, 1813. *John Adams: Writings from the New Nation 1784–1826*, 564.

"crippled wrists and fingers,"] Thomas Jefferson to John Adams, October 12, 1823. *Thomas Jefferson: Writings*, 1479.

"friendship co-eval with our government."] Ibid., 1480.

106 **"nearly at the same time."**] Benjamin Rush to John Adams, October 17, 1809, https://founders.archives.gov/documents/Adams/99-02-02-5450.

107 **is not he, our venerable colleague near you,**] Referring to Samuel Adams. In April 1775, Massachusetts's last royal governor, the British general Thomas Gage, received instructions from Lord Dartmouth, the British secretary of state for the colonies, to arrest Hancock and Adams as "the principal actors and abettors in the Provincial congress whose proceedings appear in every light to be acts of treason and rebellion." Their capture was one of the aims of the British expeditionary force that Gage fatefully dispatched to Lexington and Concord on April 18.

108 **may my right hand forget . . . the roof of my mouth**] Cf. Psalm 137:5–6.

110 **"Spent a few minutes with him . . . and he replied, 'not a word.'"**] July Fourth Toast by John Adams, June 30, 1826, https://founders.archives.gov/documents/Adams/99-02-02-8030.

PART III

111 **To the young Lincoln, it was electrifying.**] For the story of Lincoln's encounter with *The Revised Laws of Indiana* see James M. Ogden, "Lincoln's Early Impressions of the Law in Indiana," *Notre Dame Law Review* 7.3 (1932), http://scholarship.law.nd.edu/ndlr/vol7/iss3/5.

112 **"If slavery is not wrong . . . think, and feel."**] *Abraham Lincoln: Speeches & Writings 1859–1865*, ed. Don E. Fehrenbacher (New York: Library of America, 1989), 585.

"bunglingly,"] Ibid., 160.

119 **"This, Sirs, is a cause, that . . . kindles a fire at the heart."**] Garrison quotes from Fisher Ames's "Speech in the House of Representatives of the United States, in support of the following motion: Resolved, That it is expedient to pass the laws necessary to carry into effect the treaty lately concluded between the United States and the king of Great Britain," April 28, 1796, in *Works of Fisher Ames. Compiled by a Number of His Friends* (Boston: T.B. Wait & Co., 1809), 78.

120 **authorized the late war**] That is, the War of 1812, which was not commonly referred to by that name until later in the nineteenth century.

121 **"therefore all things whatsoever . . . is the law and the prophets."**] Matthew 7:12.

127 **the Constitution of this Commonwealth**] Adams refers to Massachusetts, whose constitution his father had drafted.

128 **line of battle ships in disguise**] A British newspaper had so described the U.S. Navy's frigates by way of explaining their stunning success against larger British vessels during the War of 1812.

129 **a crown of imperishable glory!**] Cf. Simonides, "On the Lacedaemonian Dead at Plataea."

In our own Commonwealth . . . of her children.] Referring to Shays's Rebellion, a tax revolt that roiled western Massachusetts in the winter of 1786–87 before being suppressed by the state's militia. Nine individuals were killed and scores more were wounded, and two insurgents were executed for their actions.

130 **at one time in Virginia . . . and again in the warmer regions of the South.**] Adams refers to various appeals to state sovereignty in the nation's young history: first, the Kentucky and Virginia Resolutions (1798/1799) drafted by Thomas Jefferson and James Madison, respectively, which advocated for the states' power to "interpose" against the Alien and Sedition Acts; second, the opposition to Jefferson's embargo and later the War of 1812 among New England Federalists, which culminated in the Hartford Convention in 1814–1815; third, the controversy in Pennsylvania that resulted in the Supreme Court case *United States v. Peters* (1809), in which Chief Justice Marshall, writing for the majority, held that a state cannot annul the judgments or limit the jurisdiction of federal courts; and, finally, the Nullification Crisis in South Carolina.

one of the profoundest philosophers of modern ages] Adams paraphrases from the 1607 essay "Of Sedition and Troubles" by English philosopher Francis Bacon (1561–1626).

132 **In some of the States . . . by their charters]** Connecticut did not adopt a new constitution until 1818, and Rhode Island not until 1842.

In one . . . now rectified.] North Carolina's constitution was adopted by its provincial congress on December 18, 1776, and never submitted to the people for ratification. After much agitation, a new constitution would finally be approved in 1835.

135 **It hath sacrificed our welfare to the state of Coahuila]** After Mexico secured its independence from Spain, Coahuila y Tejas was one of its constituent states, combining two distinct regions, the more populous Coahuila, which was geographically and politically closer to the Mexican central government, and the frontier region of Tejas. The American immigrants to the latter territory styled themselves Texans.

It incarcerated in a dungeon, for a long time, one of our citizens] Believing that he was agitating for Texas independence, the Mexican government arrested settlement recruiter (*empresario*) Stephen F. Austin in January 1834 and held him in Mexico City for nearly a year.

137 **"We live here . . . and mean to live here."]** Frederick Douglass, "Colonization," *The North Star*, January 26, 1849. *Frederick Douglass: Speeches & Writings*, ed. David W. Blight (New York: Library of America, 2022), 117.

143 **devoted to the Missouri compromise]** Referring to the 1820 bill that sought to resolve the emerging sectional crisis by admitting Missouri as a slave state and Maine (until then part of Massachusetts) as a free state, thereby preserving a sectional balance in the Senate, while simultaneously banning slavery in the remaining Louisiana Purchase territory north of latitude 36°30'.

146 **Europe in its present anarchical condition]** An allusion to political unrest then spreading across France and much of central Europe, known collectively as the Revolutions of 1848.

150 **claiming Apostolic authority for her exclusion from the ministry]** By virtue of the tradition, derived from the Gospels, that the twelve apostles of Jesus were all men.

151 **For Douglass, it was *The Columbian Orator*]** On Douglass's early reading, see David W. Blight, *Frederick Douglass: Prophet of Freedom* (New York: Simon & Schuster, 2018), 43–46.

152 **"lame man leap as an hart."]** Isaiah 35:6.

"By the rivers of Babylon . . . roof of my mouth."] Psalm 137.1–6.

153 **"I will not equivocate; I will not excuse"]** In the first issue of his abolitionist newspaper, *The Liberator*, January 1, 1831, William Lloyd Garrison declared, "I am in earnest—I will not equivocate—I will not excuse—I will not retreat a single inch—and I will be heard."

154 **Is that a question for Republicans?]** Referring, that is, to all Americans, in the lowercase sense of the word. The Republican Party would not be formed until 1854.

155 **the storm, the whirlwind, and the earthquake]** Cf. Isaiah 29:6.

156 **"character of Jefferson was repulsive,"]** This characterization was from a speech purportedly made by Lincoln in 1844, as recorded in a local newspaper. See *Collected Works of Abraham Lincoln*, Vol. 4, ed. Roy P. Basler (New Brunswick, NJ: Rutgers University Press, 1953), 112.

All honor to Jefferson . . . tyranny and oppression.] Letter to Henry L. Pierce and Others, April 6, 1859, *Abraham Lincoln: Speeches & Writings 1859–1865*, 19.

157 **Indiana Senator John Pettit called the proposition . . . a "self-evident lie."]** Maier, *American Scripture*, 200. For Lincoln's response, see "Speech on the Kansas-Nebraska Act at Peoria, Illinois," *Abraham Lincoln: Speeches & Writings 1832–1858*, 339.

"an ancient faith,"] Ibid., 328.

Our republican robe is soiled . . . forever worthy of the saving.] Ibid., 339–40.

158 **Our progress in degeneracy . . . without the base alloy of hypocracy.]** To Joshua F. Speed, August 24, 1855, ibid., 363.

"mangled ruin."] "Speech on the Dred Scott Decision at Springfield, Illinois," June 26, 1857, ibid., 399.

"the electric cord in . . . liberty-loving men together."] "Speech at Chicago, Illinois," July 10, 1858, ibid., 456.

"monstrous heresy."] "I tell you that this Chicago doctrine of Lincoln's—declaring that the negro and the white man are made equal by the Declaration of Independence and by Divine Providence—is a monstrous heresy. (That's so, and terrific applause.)" "Fifth Lincoln-Douglas Debate, Galesburg, Illinois, October 7, 1858, Mr. Douglas' Speech," ibid., 697.

159 **All this is not the result of accident . . . *not* the apple for the picture.**] "Fragment on the Constitution and the Union, c. January 1861," *Collected Works of Abraham Lincoln*, Vol. 4, 169.

"even greater than National Independence . . . to all time to come."] "Address to the New Jersey Senate at Trenton, New Jersey," February 21, 1861, *Abraham Lincoln: Speeches & Writings 1859–1865*, 209.

160 **Mr. Cuyler**] Theodore Cuyler (1819–1876), president of the Select Council of Philadelphia, had delivered a speech welcoming Lincoln.

162 **Our new government is founded upon . . . moral truth.**] "Speech known as 'The Corner Stone,' delivered at the Athenaeum, Savannah, Georgia, March 21, 1861," *Alexander H. Stephens, in Public and Private. With Letters and Speeches, Before, During, and Since the War*, ed. Henry Cleveland (Philadelphia: National Publishing Company, 1866), 721.

"central idea . . . is not an absurdity."] John Hay, diary entry for May 7, 1861, in *Inside Lincoln's White House: The Complete Civil War Diary of John Hay*, eds. Michael Burlingame and J.R.T. Ettlinger (Carbondale: Southern Illinois University Press, 1997), 20.

This is essentially a People's contest . . . in the race of life.] "Message to Congress in Special Session," July 4, 1861, *Abraham Lincoln: Speeches & Writings 1859–1865*, 259.

PART IV

168 **yr good & most suggestive letter**] In a letter written on February 17, 1865, Bright advised that Reconstruction should be based on the abolition of slavery, a generous amnesty policy, limited confiscation of Southern land, the exclusion of Confederate leaders from federal or state office, and the nullification of Confederate debts.

169 **govt. in Louisiana . . . defeated in Congress**] On February 24, 1865, the Senate began debating a resolution recognizing the legitimacy of the Reconstruction government in Louisiana. Sumner engaged in a successful filibuster against the measure, and on February 27 the Senate voted to postpone further consideration of the resolution.

Chief Justice Chase . . . "illegal & void"] In a letter to Bright written on March 18, 1865, Sumner explained that he had initially misunderstood Chase's ruling in *United States v. Alexander*, a case arising from the seizure of cotton by the Union navy the year before. The chief justice had subsequently explained to him that the Court had not ruled on "the validity of the La. govt., but only on the validity of proceedings in certain parts of the state."

"the territorial theory."] Sumner had argued in 1862 that the seceding states should be treated as federal territories over which Congress had complete jurisdiction.

170 **Resolutions on Reciprocity & Lake Armaments,**] A measure of strengthening ties with Great Britain after the tensions of the early years of the Civil War, the Senate voted on January 12, 1865, to terminate the Reciprocity Treaty of 1854, liberalizing trade between the United States and Canada, and on January 18 to terminate the Rush-Bagot Treaty of 1817, limiting naval armaments on the Great Lakes and Lake Champlain.

the date . . . held it back] Concerned about the activities of Confederate agents in Canada, the House of Representatives voted on June 20, 1864, to end the Great Lakes naval agreement. As chairman of the Foreign Relations Committee, Sumner had delayed Senate consideration of the measure.

the outrages on the Lakes] Confederate raiders based in Canada had made a pair of alarming cross-border raids from Canada in the autumn of 1864.

Cobden] Richard Cobden (1804–1865), a British reformer who served in Parliament, 1841–57 and 1859–65, was a supporter of the Union and a friend and political ally of John Bright.

Nearly ten million tourists . . . in Independence Hall.] Charlene Mires, *Independence Hall in American Memory* (Philadelphia: University of Pennsylvania Press, 2002), 122.

171 **"faded and crumbling manuscript held together by a simple frame."**] Stephen W. Stathis, "Returning the Declaration of Independence to Philadelphia: An Exercise in Centennial Politics," *The Pennsylvania Magazine of History and Biography* 102.2 (April 1978): 168, 175, 179.

The return was glorious all the same.] Philadelphia's leaders enjoyed the presence of the Declaration so much that they launched an unsubtle effort to keep it, in the early months of 1877. But federal officials quickly snuffed it out. Upon return, the Declaration was installed in the library of the State Department, inside the handsome new State, War and Navy Building near the White House (now the Eisenhower Executive Office Building). Ibid, 181–82.

"the tardy but in the end the full . . . Declaration of Independence."] Quoted in Philip S. Foner, "Black Participation in the Centennial of 1876," *Negro History Bulletin* 39.2 (February 1976): 533.

172 **What happened next was not expected.**] These events are described in *History of Woman Suffrage*, Vol. III, 1876–1885, eds. Elizabeth Cady Stanton, Susan B. Anthony, and Matilda Joslyn Gage (Rochester, NY: Susan B. Anthony and Charles Mann), 27–31.

176 **"we will not hold ourselves bound to obey . . . representation,"**] From Abigail Adams's famous "Remember the Ladies" letter (March 31, 1776) to her husband John Adams, then serving in the Continental Congress: "Do not put such unlimited power into the hands of the Husbands. Remember all Men would be tyrants if they could. If perticuliar care and attention is not paid to the Laidies we are determined to foment a Rebelion, and will not hold ourselves bound by any Laws in which we have no voice, or Representation." *Abigail Adams: Letters*, ed. Edith Gelles (New York: Library of America, 2016), 91.

177 **John Bright . . . after the defeat of the Confederacy.**] https://www.abrahamlincoln.org/lincoln-speaks/important-lincoln-supporter-britain/index.html.

The idea for the Statue of Liberty . . . spread around the world.] Don H. Doyle, *The Cause of All Nations: An International History of the Civil War* (New York: Basic Books, 2014), 311.

178 **President Grover Cleveland gave . . . "the open gates of America."**] *Inauguration of the Statue of Liberty Enlightening the World by the President of the United States, on Bedlow's Island, New York, Thursday, October 28, 1886* (New York: D. Appleton and Company, 1887), 32.

Farther south . . . nor judicial construction can prevent."] For background on the *Plessy* decision, see Thomas J. Davis, *Plessy v. Ferguson* (Santa Barbara, CA: Greenwood, 2012), 7, 189; Williamjames Hull Hoffer, *Plessy v. Ferguson: Race and Inequality in Jim Crow America* (Lawrence: University Press of Kansas, 2012), 95; Harvey Fireside, *Separate and Unequal: Homer Plessy and the Supreme Court Decision That Legalized Racism* (New York: Carroll & Graf, 2003), 196–97.

"the equality before the law of all citizens . . . without regard to race."] For Justice Harlan's dissent see *Plessy v. Ferguson* (1896) https://supreme.justia.com/cases/federal/us/163/537/.

180 **His speech went well . . . you will become President of the United States."**] David McCullough, *Mornings on Horseback: The Story of an Extraordinary Family, a Vanished Way of Life and the Unique Child Who Became Theodore Roosevelt* (New York: Simon & Schuster, 1982), 348–50.

183 **"one more step . . . Army in actual practice."**] "To William Wirt Kimball," November 19, 1897, *Theodore Roosevelt: Letters and Speeches*, ed. Louis Auchincloss (New York: Library of America, 2004), 123.

184 **Egregious**] Used here in the now archaic sense of *distinguished*.

General Blanco at the instigation of the Archbishop] Ramón Blanco, 1st Marquess of Peña Plata (1833–1906), the Spanish governor general of the Philippines, often worked in concert with Bernardino Nozaleda y Villa (1844–1927), the Spanish Archbishop of Manila.

188 **"All the world is my country, and all mankind are my countrymen."**] In the December 15, 1837, issue of *The Liberator*, Garrison wrote that "our country is the world—our countrymen are all mankind."

"Where liberty is . . . that is my country."] In a January 2, 1804, letter from surveyor Isaac Briggs to President Thomas Jefferson, Briggs writes of the Mississippi Territory that "of all countries which I have seen, I think this would be my choice as a residence, were it not for the sanction given to slavery—'Where liberty is, there is my Country.'" This quotation was in common circulation, often misattributed to Benjamin Franklin and, as Debs does here with two variants, to Jefferson himself and to Thomas Paine. https://founders.archives.gov/documents/Jefferson/01-42-02-0203.

189 **Jno. Rockefeller]** John D. Rockefeller, Jr. (1874–1960), only son and principal heir of his father, John Senior, who was a cofounder of Standard Oil. Soon after graduating college, he became a director in J. P. Morgan's newly established U.S. Steel, which would involve him in the mining business for many years to come.

190 **"I wanted the American eagle . . . to conquer, not to redeem."]** From an interview in the New York *Herald*, October 15, 1900.

192 **it was an English judge]** Twain alludes to the famous 1772 *Somerset v. Stewart* case in England in which the judge, William Murray, 1st Earl of Mansfield, issued a writ of habeas corpus for James Somerset, an enslaved man who had been brought to England from North America in 1769, and who had then run away and been recaptured. Mansfield ruled that slavery could exist only where supported by positive law, and that since such was not the case in Great Britain, Somerset was free upon his arrival there.

199 **Three years later . . . claiming independence for his people.]** A. Scott Berg, *Wilson* (New York: G. P. Putnam's Sons, 2013), 422; Erez Manela, *The Wilsonian Moment: Self-Determination and the International Origins of Anti-Colonial Nationalism* (New York: Oxford University Press, 2007), 35–53; Margaret Macmillan, *Paris 1919: Six Months That Changed the World* (New York: Random House, 2001), 233.

"This is the most tremendous . . . to all the world."] The full text of Wilson's Fourth of July address was reprinted in the July 9, 1919, edition of *The New York Times*.

201 ***made impossible by the Espionage act*]** Passed during World War I, the Espionage Act of 1917 and the Sedition Act of 1918 criminalized dissenting speech, including speech abusive of the U.S. government, the flag, the Constitution, and the military.

***And this is Better Speech Week.*]** For over a decade, beginning in 1918, Better American Speech Week was observed in schools throughout the country, a wartime initiative that equated patriotism with good grammar and proper pronunciation.

***the American Legion, the Ku Klux Klan and other patriotic societies*]** The American Legion was chartered by Congress in 1919. A racist terror group originally founded in the South in the aftermath of the Civil War, the Klu Klux Klan was resuscitated in 1915 and became an organization with national reach and significant political clout.

202 **I. W. W.s]** Referring to the Industrial Workers of the World, a consolidated union organization formed in Chicago in 1905, whose members were sometimes called Wobblies.

214 **family wealth of around $5,000]** Roughly $120,000 in 2026 dollars.

215 **the "Four Freedoms" speech]** There are several important works on this crucial speech: Elizabeth Borgwardt, *A New Deal for the World: America's Vision for Human Rights* (Cambridge, MA: Harvard University Press, 2005); Jeffrey Engel, *The Four Freedoms: Franklin D. Roosevelt and the Evolution of an American Idea* (New York: Oxford University Press, 2016); Harvey Kaye, *The Fight for the Four Freedoms: What Made FDR and the Greatest Generation Truly Great* (New York: Simon & Schuster, 2014).

221 **Fortuitously, that was also . . . *The Evolution of the Text*).]** Bidwell, *The Declaration in Script and Print*, 13.

But so great was the . . . this Declaration stand for."] Stephen Puleo, "The Secret Plan to Protect America's Founding Documents During WWII," *Politico*, September 25, 2016, https://www.politico.com/magazine/story/2016/09/world-war-two-protect-national-archives-214257/;

John Y. Cole, "The Library and the Declaration," *Library of Congress Information Bulletin* (August 1997), https://www.loc.gov/loc/lcib/9708/declare.html.

224 **"a just and solid republican government . . . over a great portion of the globe."]** *Thomas Jefferson: Writings*, 1084–85.

"there are to-day no truer exponents . . . than the American Negroes."] *W.E.B. Du Bois: Writings*, ed. Nathan Huggins (New York: Library of America, 1986), 370.

225 **No one stops to ask how or why or if it be true.]** Riots erupted in Harlem on August 1 and 2, 1943, after a white policeman, James Collins, shot and wounded Robert Bandy, a Black soldier. As Bethune suggests, rumors circulated in the Black community that Bandy had been killed, leading to retaliatory strikes against white-owned property in Harlem. Six people were killed and more than six hundred were injured over the course of the two days of unrest.

226 **Others look about them to remember riots in Detroit and Los Angeles and Beaumont.]** The disorder in Harlem marked the culmination of a long summer of racial unrest in 1943, including riots in Mobile, Alabama (May 25), Los Angeles, California (June 3–8), Beaumont, Texas (June 15), and Detroit, Michigan (June 20–22).

"groping of the long inert masses."] Quoting from Wendell L. Willkie, *One World* (New York: Simon & Schuster, 1943), 22.

227 **as hard and resistant as the walls of the ghettos of Warsaw.]** Beginning in 1939, German authorities concentrated Poland's large Jewish population into a small section of the capital city of Warsaw. Bethune's reference here would have struck a powerful chord with her readers because of events that had recently occurred in Warsaw when, after twenty-nine days of heroic resistance, from April 19 to May 16, 1943, the Jewish ghetto was systematically destroyed by German forces.

229 **he joins in demanding the ballot for the District of Columbia]** Residents of the nation's capital district—which always had a large Black population—would not gain the right to vote in presidential elections until ratification of the Twenty-Third Amendment on March 21, 1961.

"white primary"] So-called white primaries were racially restricted Democratic Party elections that effectively disenfranchised Black voters. They were ruled unconstitutional by the Supreme Court in 1944.

230 **"one as the hand and separate as the fingers,"]** Bethune paraphrased a line from Booker T. Washington's famous Atlanta Exposition speech, delivered on September 18, 1895, which amounted to a tacit acceptance of segregation: "As we have proved our loyalty to you in the past, in nursing your children, watching by the sick-bed of your mothers and fathers, and often following them with tear-dimmed eyes to their graves, so in the future, in our humble way, we shall stand by you with a devotion that no foreigner can approach, ready to lay down our lives, if need be, in defense of yours, interlacing our industrial, commercial, civil, and religious life with yours in a way that shall make the interests of both races one. In all things that are purely social we can be as separate as the fingers, yet one as the hand in all things essential to mutual progress."

PART V

232 **I have a communication . . . in memory of my husband on this important day.]** Brazil honored the memory of Franklin Roosevelt, who had died on April 12, 1945, by awarding Mrs. Roosevelt the Ordem do Cruzeiro do Sul (The National Order of the Southern Cross), in the degree of "Commander." According to a State Department release the presentation ceremony "took place in the headquarters of the Brazilian Press Association" and "was regarded by the press as one of the highlights of the wide-spread ceremonies in Brazil celebrating the anniversary of American independence."

234 **Martin Luther King, Jr., would call Americans "strange liberators,"]** In a speech delivered at Riverside Church in New York City on April 4, 1967, entitled "Beyond Vietnam—A Time to Break Silence": "They must see Americans as strange liberators. The Vietnamese people proclaimed their own independence in 1954—in 1945 rather—after a combined French and

Japanese occupation and before the communist revolution in China. They were led by Ho Chi Minh. Even though they quoted the American Declaration of Independence in their own document of freedom, we refused to recognize them. Instead, we decided to support France in its reconquest of her former colony. Our government felt then that the Vietnamese people were not ready for independence, and we again fell victim to the deadly Western arrogance that has poisoned the international atmosphere for so long. With that tragic decision we rejected a revolutionary government seeking self-determination." *American Speeches: Political Oratory from Abraham Lincoln to Bill Clinton*, ed. Ted Widmer (New York: Library of America, 2006), 656.

236 **On the 9th of March this year, the French troops were disarmed by the Japanese.**] In the waning months of the Pacific War, as Japanese forces were being driven back on many fronts, they launched Operation Bright Moon against French forces in Indochina, a coordinated series of attacks on colonial garrisons throughout the region. After the French were overrun and forced to retreat northward into China, the Japanese installed in Vietnam a puppet regime (the Empire of Vietnam) under Bảo Đại, the last emperor of the Nguyễn dynasty, which dated back to the early nineteenth century.

237 **the Teheran and San Francisco Conferences**] Allied leaders met in Tehran from November 28 to December 1, 1943, to coordinate strategy against the Axis powers in Europe. Ho may have meant the Yalta Conference, February 4–11, 1945, where the Allies committed to "the establishment of order in Europe and the rebuilding of national economic life . . . by processes which will enable the liberated peoples to destroy the last vestiges of Nazism and Fascism and to create democratic institutions of their own choice." San Francisco was the site of the first United Nations Conference (April 25–June 26, 1945), at which the organization's charter was framed and promulgated. Its preamble begins "WE THE PEOPLES OF THE UNITED NATIONS DETERMINED to save succeeding generations from the scourge of war, which twice in our lifetime has brought untold sorrow to mankind, and to reaffirm faith in fundamental human rights, in the dignity and worth of the human person, in the equal rights of men and women and of nations large and small."

244 **Truman sent signals of agreement . . . on June 29, 1947.**] Speaking before the NAACP, Truman cautioned that "the way ahead is not easy. We shall need all the wisdom, imagination and courage we can muster. We must and shall guarantee the civil rights of all our citizens. Never before has the need been so urgent for skillful and vigorous action to bring us closer to our ideal. We can reach the goal. When past difficulties faced our Nation, we met the challenge with inspiring charters of human rights—the Declaration of Independence, the Constitution, the Bill of Rights and the Emancipation Proclamation. Today our representatives, and those of other liberty-loving countries on the United Nations Commission on Human Rights, are preparing an International Bill of Rights. We can be confident that it will be a great landmark in man's long search for freedom since its members consist of such distinguished citizens of the world as Mrs. Franklin D. Roosevelt." (Transcript courtesy of the Truman Library Institute, https://www.trumanlibraryinstitute.org/historic-speeches-naacp/).

250 **On December 13, 1952, the transfer was finally effected.**] See Cheryl Fox, "The Shrine at the Library of Congress, 1924–1952," https://blogs.loc.gov/manuscripts/2022/06/the-shrine-at-the-library-of-congress-1924-1952/.

"We are enshrining . . . the wit of modern man can devise."] Quoted in Milton O. Gustafson, "The Empty Shrine: The Transfer of the Declaration of Independence and the Constitution to the National Archives," *American Archivist* (July 1976): 272.

254 **Ralph Bunche, Marian Anderson, Jackie Robinson**] Three distinguished Black Americans, each a trailblazer: diplomat and civil rights activist Ralph Bunche (1904–1971), the first Nobel laureate of African descent; singer and activist Marian Anderson (1897–1993), the first African American to perform at the Metropolitan Opera; and athlete Jackie Robinson (1919–1972), who broke the color barrier in Major League Baseball in 1947.

256 **Among the many surprises . . . and embracing a delusion."]** Hannah Arendt, "Action and the 'Pursuit of Happiness,'" *Thinking Without a Banister: Essays in Understanding 1953–1975* (New York: Schocken Books, 2018), 211.

258 **"felicity of the pen"]** Arendt alludes here to a famous observation by John Adams, from an August 6, 1822, letter to Timothy Pickering: "Mr Jefferson came into Congress in June 1775 and brought with him a reputation for literature, science, and a happy talent at composition. Writings of his were handed about remarkable for the peculiar felicity of expression." https://founders.archives.gov/documents/Adams/99-02-02-7674.

259 **"private rights and public happiness" (James Madison)]** From *The Federalist*, No. 14. *The Debate on the Constitution: Federalist and Antifederalist Speeches, Articles, and Letters During the Struggle over Ratification, Part One*, ed. Bernard Bailyn (New York: Library of America, 1991), 436.

in John Adams's phrase] From *Discourse on Davila*, No. 2 (1790): "There is in human nature, it is true, simple *Benevolence,* or an affection for the good of others; but alone it is not a balance for the selfish affections. Nature then has kindly added to benevolence, the desire of reputation, in order to make us good members of society. *Spectemur agendo* expresses the great principle of activity for the good of others. Nature has sanctioned the law of self-preservation by rewards and punishments. The rewards of selfish activity are life and health; the punishments of negligence and indolence are want, disease, and death. Each individual, it is true, should consider, that nature has enjoined the same law on his neighbor, and therefore a respect for the authority of nature would oblige him to respect the rights of others as much as his own." *The Works of John Adams*, Vol. VI, ed. Charles Francis Adams (Boston: Charles C. Little and James Brown, 1851), 234.

"exclusively to their personal interests" (Cooper)] From James Fenimore Cooper, *The American Democrat, or, Hints on the Social and Civic Relations of the United States of America* (Cooperstown, NY: H. & E. Phinney, 1838), 58: "In a monarchy, men are ruled without their own agency, and as their time is not required for the supervision or choice of the public agents, or the enactment of laws, their attention may be exclusively given to their personal interests. Could this advantage be enjoyed without the abuses of such a state of things, it would alone suffice to render this form of government preferable to all others, since contact with the affairs of state is one of the most corrupting of the influences to which men are exposed."

Tocqueville reports how widespread the "taste" and the "passion for public freedom" was] In the second part of *Democracy in America* (1840): "I think that democratic peoples have a natural taste for liberty. Left to themselves, they seek it out, love it, and suffer if deprived of it. For equality, however, they feel an ardent, insatiable, eternal, invincible passion. They want equality in liberty, and if they cannot have it, they want it still in slavery. They will suffer poverty, servitude, and barbarity, but they will not suffer aristocracy." *Alexis de Tocqueville: Democracy in America*, trans. Arthur Goldhammer, ed. Olivier Zunz (New York: Library of America, 2004), 584.

260 **an unfriendly historian . . . upon this side of an otherwise grim business.]** Edmund Burke, in his *Reflections on the Revolution in France* (1790), portrays the French Revolution as a tragicomedy on the grandest scale, its main actors as simultaneously frauds and dupes.

as Tocqueville pointed out] In *L'ancien régime et la révolution* (1856): "But of all the strange phenomena of these times, the strangest to us, who have seen so many revolutions, is the absence of any thought of revolution from the mind of our ancestors. No such thing was discussed, because no such thing had been conceived. In free communities, constant vibrations keep men's minds alive to the possibility of a general earthquake, and hold governments in check; but in the old French society that was soon to topple over, there was not the least symptom of unsteadiness." Alexis de Tocqueville, *The Old Regime and the Revolution*, trans. John Bonner (New York: Harper & Brothers, 1856), 175–76.

"the world of public affairs was not only hardly known to them but was invisible" (Tocqueville)] Ibid., 173: "There being no approach toward political liberty, the business of government was not only ill understood, it was not understood at all. Having no share in it themselves, and seeing nothing that was done by those who had, these writers lacked the superficial education which the habit of political freedom imparts even to those who take no part in politics."

261 **Tocqueville once rightly remarked that "of all ideas . . . the first ones to disappear."]** Ibid., 192: "It is noteworthy that of all the ideas and feelings which prepared the Revolution, the idea of political liberty, properly so called, was the last to make its appearance, and the desire for it was the first to vanish."

262 **Robespierre's theory of revolution]** Presented to the National Convention of October 10, 1793, in his "Report on the Principles of a Revolutionary Government." *Speeches of Maximilien Robespierre*, trans. anonymous (New York: International Publishers, 1927), 62.

Jefferson's insistence on some "ward system,"] As detailed in his July 12, 1816, letter to Samuel Kercheval: "The true foundation of republican government is the equal right of every citizen, in his person and property, and in their management . . . Divide the counties into wards of such size as that every citizen can attend, when called on, and act in person. Ascribe to them the government of their wards in all things relating to themselves exclusively. . . . by making every citizen an acting member of the government, and in the offices nearest and most interesting to him, will attach him by his strongest feelings to the independence of his country, and its republican constitution." *Thomas Jefferson: Writings*, 1398–99.

265 **George Washington declared . . . to the hands of the American people."]** In his First Inaugural Address, delivered on April 30, 1789. *George Washington: Writings*, ed. John Rhodehamel (New York: Library of America, 1997), 733.

Jefferson's phrase . . . gave us liberty at the same time."] From his *Summary View of the Rights of British America*. See page 18 in this volume.

266 **that which Jefferson called "the disease of liberty"]** In a December 26, 1820, letter to the Marquis de Lafayette, https://founders.archives.gov/documents/Jefferson/03-16-02-0400.

The nations of Western Europe . . . are today joining together] In 1957, six European countries, including France, Italy, and West Germany, signed the Treaty of Rome, creating the European Economic Community, a trade pact and customs union. Four years later, in 1961, the compact was extended into the Organisation for Economic Co-operation and Development, expanding its membership and paving the way for the creation, three decades later, of the European Union.

267 **insure its domestic tranquility . . . and our posterity.]** Kennedy quotes from the preamble to the U.S. Constitution.

271 **justice rolls . . . stream.]** Cf. Amos 5:24.

272 **its governor]** George Wallace (1919–1998) was the Democratic governor of Alabama, 1963–67, 1971–79, and 1983–87.

every valley . . . it together.] Cf. Isaiah 40:4–5.

My country . . . let freedom ring!] In his peroration King interlaces lyrics from the song "America" (1832) by Samuel F. Smith (1808–1895).

274 **Malcolm X . . . the privileges of an independent people."]** Remarks at the University of Berkeley, October 11, 1963, https://www.icit-digital.org/articles/malcolm-x-at-uc-berkeley-october-11-1963.

276 **the slaughter of over 50,000,000 black people]** This is "50,000" in the original, an evident printer's error.

278 ***the coming of the Wasicus*]** Using the Sioux, or Lakota/Dakota, term for a non-Indigenous person.

280 **the Fort Laramie Treaty of 1868]** Signed on April 28, 1868, this treaty created the Great Sioux Reservation, a large tract that encompassed much of the western half of what is now the

state of South Dakota, including the Black Hills. In 1874, General George A. Custer led U.S. Army troops into the Black Hills, accompanying miners searching for gold. Three years later the federal government confiscated the land, less than a decade after it had recognized Sioux sovereignty.

281 **the continued refusal to sign the United Nations 1948 Treaty on Genocide.**] The United States voted with the rest of the UN General Assembly in support of the Genocide Convention in 1948, but the U.S. Senate would not formally ratify the treaty until 1988.

287 **read "The Madness of the Day," by Maurice Blanchot.**] Maurice Blanchot, *The Madness of the Day* (*La Folie du Jour*), trans. Lydia Davis (Barrytown, NY: Station Hill, 1981).

290 **"Miss Liberty is still . . . live together as one."**] Ronald Reagan, "Remarks at the Opening Ceremonies of the Statue of Liberty Centennial Celebration in New York," New York, July 3, 1986, https://www.reaganlibrary.gov/archives/speech/remarks-opening-ceremonies-statue-liberty-centennial-celebration-new-york-new-york.

293 **"to the times when . . . we rowed through the storm with heart and hand. . . ."**] Thomas Jefferson to John Adams, January 21, 1812, *Thomas Jefferson: Writings*, 1259.

297 **one of the most abused documents in the history of preservation."**] Verner Clapp, "The Declaration of Independence: A Case Study in Preservation," *Special Libraries,* Vol. 62 (December 1971): 503.

300 **"transformational change"**] The Tea Party arose during, and in opposition to, the administration of Barack Obama, and this was a phrase he was known to use, for example, in these remarks delivered in Strasbourg, France, on July 11, 2009: "We know that transformational change is possible. We know this because of three reasons: First, because, for all our differences, there are certain values that bind us together and reveal our common humanity: the universal longing to live a life free from fear, and free from want; a life marked by dignity and respect and simple justice. Our two republics were founded in service of these ideals. In America, it is written into our founding documents as 'life, liberty, and the pursuit of happiness.' In France: 'Liberté'—(applause)—absolutely—'egalité, fraternité.' (Applause.) Our moral authority is derived from the fact that generations of our citizens have fought and bled to uphold these values in our nations and others." "Remarks by President Obama at Strasbourg Town Hall", https://obamawhitehouse.archives.gov/the-press-office/remarks-president-obama-strasbourg-town-hall.

301 **which echoed the final sentence of John F. Kennedy's lone inaugural,**] "With a good conscience our only sure reward, with history the final judge of our deeds, let us go forth to lead the land we love, asking His blessing and His help, but knowing that here on earth God's work must truly be our own." John F. Kennedy, Inaugural Address, Washington, D.C., January 20, 1961, *American Speeches: Political Oratory from Abraham Lincoln to Bill Clinton*, 538.

302 **who had mentioned the Stonewall riot . . . in his second inaugural**] "We, the people, declare today that the most evident of truths—that all of us are created equal—is the star that guides us still; just as it guided our forebears through Seneca Falls, and Selma, and Stonewall; just as it guided all those men and women, sung and unsung, who left footprints along this great Mall, to hear a preacher say that we cannot walk alone; to hear a King proclaim that our individual freedom is inextricably bound to the freedom of every soul on Earth. (Applause.)" "Inaugural Address by President Barack Obama," January 21, 2013, https://obamawhitehouse.archives.gov/the-press-office/2013/01/21/inaugural-address-president-barack-obama.

303 **the so-called Defense of Marriage Act**] The Defense of Marriage Act, or DOMA, was signed into law by President Bill Clinton in 1996. It defined marriage for federal purposes as the union of one man and one woman, enabling states to refuse recognition of same-sex marriages from other states. The act was declared unconstitutional by the Supreme Court in *United States v. Windsor* (2013).

"Don't Ask, Don't Tell."] Another Clinton-era policy, "Don't Ask, Don't Tell," allowed LGBTQ+ individuals to serve in the U.S. military if they kept their orientation private. At the same time it prohibited the military from inquiring in the first place, or otherwise engaging in discrimination. It was in effect from February 28, 1994, until September 20, 2011.

EPILOGUE

307 **"A profound silence . . . something deeply felt and truly great.**] *Alexis de Tocqueville and Gustave de Beaumont in America: Their Friendship and Their Travels*, ed. Olivier Zunz, trans. Arthur Goldhammer (Charlottesville: University of Virginia Press, 2010), 79.

308 **"twenty-five years of age . . . a Mulatto and a Black."**] Eric Slauter, "The Declaration of Independence and the New Nation," in *The Cambridge Companion to Thomas Jefferson*, ed. Frank Shuffelton (New York: Cambridge University Press, 2009), 12.

"Be true to what you said on paper."] Martin Luther King, Jr., Speech at Mason Temple, Memphis, April 3, 1968, *American Speeches: Political Oratory from Abraham Lincoln to Bill Clinton*, 685.

309 **"It was the lot . . . of working out of it."**] Thomas Jefferson to John Adams, March 25, 1826, https://founders.archives.gov/documents/Jefferson/98-01-02-5983.

"rebuke and a stumbling-block"] Letter to Henry L. Pierce and Others, April 6, 1859, *Abraham Lincoln: Speeches & Writings 1859–1865*, 19.

"The Declaration of Independence makes a difference."] To Evert A. Duyckinck, March 28, 1849, *The Letters of Herman Melville*, eds. Merrell R. Davis and William H. Gilman (New Haven, CT: Yale University Press, 1960), 81.

SOURCES & PERMISSIONS

TEXTS

INTRODUCTION

The Declaration of Independence, engrossed text. https://www.archives.gov/founding-docs/declaration-transcript.

PART I

"An Act declareing the Rights and Liberties of the Subject and Setleing the Succession of the Crowne." 1688 c.2 (Regnal. 1_Will_and_Mar_Sess_2), https://legislation.gov.uk.

An essay concerning the true original extent and end of civil government. By the late learned John Locke, Esq. (Boston: Re-printed and sold by Edes and Gill, in Queen-Street, 1773), 115–21.

[Thomas Jefferson], *A Summary View of the Rights of British America.* Williamsburg [VA]: Printed by Clementina Rind [August 1774]. *The American Revolution: Writings from the Pamphlet Debate, II: 1773–1776*, ed. Gordon S. Wood (New York: Library of America, 2015), 91–93, 106–8.

Declaration and Resolves of the First Continental Congress. *Extracts from the Votes and Proceedings of the American Continental Congress, Held at Philadelphia, on the Fifth of September, 1774. Published by Order of the Congress.* (London: Reprinted for J. Almon, opposite Burlington House, Piccadilly, 1774), 1–9. *Journal of the Proceedings of the Congress Held at Philadelphia, September 5th, 1774.* (London: Reprinted for J. Almon, opposite Burlington House, Piccadilly, 1775), 47–48.

A Declaration by the Representatives of the United Colonies of North-America, Now Met in General Congress at Philadelphia, Setting forth the Causes and Necessity of their taking up Arms. (Watertown [MA]: Re-printed and Sold by Benjamin Edes, 1775), 5–8, 13–15.

[Thomas Paine], *Common Sense; Addressed to the Inhabitants of America, . . . A New Edition, with Several Additions in the Body of the Work.* (Philadelphia: Printed and sold by W[illiam] and T[homas] Bradford [February 1776].) *The American Revolution: Writings from the Pamphlet Debate, II: 1773–1776*, ed. Gordon S. Wood (New York: Library of America, 2015), 653–56, 690–91.

[John Adams], *Thoughts on Government: Applicable to the Present State of the American Colonies. In a Letter from a Gentleman to his Friend.* (Philadelphia: Printed. Boston: Re-printed and sold by John Gill, in Queen-Street.) *John Adams: Revolutionary Writings 1776–1783*, ed. Gordon S. Wood (New York: Library of America, 2011), 49–51, 53, 55–56.

"III. Third Draft by Jefferson, [before June 1776]." Founders Online, National Archives, https://founders.archives.gov/documents/Jefferson/01-01-02-0161-0004. (Original source: *The Papers of Thomas Jefferson, vol. 1, 1760–1776*, ed. Julian P. Boyd. Princeton, NJ: Princeton University Press, 1950, 356–365.)

The Virginia Declaration of Rights. *The Articles of Confederation, the Declaration of Rights, the Constitution of this Commonwealth, and the Articles of the definitive treaty between Great-Britain and the United States of America / published by order of the General Assembly.* (Richmond, VA: Printed by Dixon and Holt, 1784.)

"Natick, Massachusetts, June 20, 1776." *American Archives*, ed. Peter Force, 4th Series, Vol. VI (Washington, D.C.: 1833–1846), 703.

"A Declaration by the Representatives of the United States of America, in General Congress Assembled." *Thomas Jefferson: Writings*, ed. Merrill D. Peterson (New York: Library of America, 1984), 19–24.

PART II

[Thomas Hutchinson], *Strictures upon the Declaration of the Congress at Philadelphia; in a Letter to a Noble Lord, &c.* (London: Printed in the year 1776.) *The American Revolution: Writings from the Pamphlet Debate, II: 1773–1776*, ed. Gordon S. Wood (New York: Library of America, 2015), 775, 780–82, 790, 799–800.

"Petition of 547 loyalists from New York City, November 28, 1776." https://nyheritage.contentdm.oclc.org/digital/collection/p16124coll1/id/32899.

Lemuel Haynes, "Liberty Further Extended. Or Free thoughts on the illegality of Slave-keeping; wherein those arguments that are used in its vindication are plainly confuted. Together with an humble address to such as are Concerned in the practise." *Black Writers of the Founding Era: A Library of America Anthology, 1760–1800*, eds. James G. Basker and Nicole Seary (New York: Library of America, 2023), 132–34.

Lancaster Hill, Peter Bess, Brister Slenser, Prince Hall, and Others, "The Petition of a great number of Negroes who are detained in a state of Slavery." *Black Writers of the Founding Era: A Library of America Anthology, 1760–1800*, eds. James G. Basker and Nicole Seary (New York: Library of America, 2023), 152–54.

The Declaration of the Rights of Man and of the Citizen (Déclaration des droits de l'homme et du citoyen). https://www.elysee.fr/en/french-presidency/the-declaration-of-the-rights-of-man-and-of-the-citizen.

Samuel Adams, Address to the Massachusetts Legislature, January 17, 1794. *The Writings of Samuel Adams*, ed. Harry Alonzo Cushing (New York: G. Putnam's Sons, 1908), IV. 354–59.

Noah Webster, *An Oration on the Anniversary of the Declaration of Independence* (New Haven, CT: William W. Morse, 1802), 14–18.

Haitian Declarations of Independence. Marcus Rainsford, *An Historical Account of the Black Empire of Hayti: Comprehending a View of the Principal Transactions in the Revolution of Saint Domingo; with its Antient and Modern State* (London: Albion Press, 1805), 439–46.

Venezuelan Act of Independence. *Interesting Official Documents Relating to the United Provinces of Venezuela, Viz. Preliminary Remarks, the Act of Independence, Proclamation, Manifesto to the World of the Causes which have Impelled the Said Provinces to Separate from the Mother Country; Together with the Constitution Framed for the Administration of their Government. In Spanish and English.* (London: Longman and Co., 1812), 3–5, 15–19.

The Mecklenburg Declaration of Independence, April 30, 1819. William Henry Hoyt, *The Mecklenburg Declaration of Independence: A Study of Evidence Showing that the Alleged Early Declaration of Independence by Mecklenburg County, North Carolina, on May 20th, 1775, is Spurious* (New York: G. P. Putnam's Sons, 1907), 4–5.

John Quincy Adams, *An Address delivered At the request of a Committee of the Citizens of Washington on the occasion of reading the Declaration of Independence, on the Fourth of July, 1821* (Washington, D.C.: Davis and Force, 1821.) *John Quincy Adams: Speeches & Writings*, ed. David Waldstreicher (New York: Library of America, 2025), 223–31.

John Adams and Thomas Jefferson Letters, June 1826. John Adams to John Whitney, June 7, 1826, *John Adams: Writings from the New Nation 1784–1826*, ed. Gordon S. Wood (New York: Library of America, 2016), 674–75. Thomas Jefferson to Roger C. Wightman, June 24, 1826, *Thomas Jefferson: Writings*, ed. Merrill D. Peterson (New York: Library of America, 1984), 1516–17.

Daniel Webster, *A Discourse in Commemoration of the Lives and Services of John Adams and Thomas Jefferson, delivered in Faneuil Hall, Boston, August 2, 1826* (Boston: Cummings, Hilliard and Company, 1826), 36–43.

PART III

Frances Wright, Fourth of July Address, New Harmony, Indiana, July 4, 1828. *American Speeches: Political Oratory from the Revolution to the Civil War*, ed. Ted Widmer (New York: Library of America, 2006), 168–72.

William Lloyd Garrison, "Dangers of the Nation: An Address." *National Philanthropist and Investigator*, Boston, MA, July 22, 1829, page 1, columns 5–6; July 29,1829, page 1, columns 1–3.

"The Working Men's Declaration of Independence." *Mechanic's Free Press*, Philadelphia, PA, December 26, 1829, page 2, columns 2–3.

John Quincy Adams, *An Oration addressed to the Citizens of the Town of Quincy on the Fourth of July, 1831, the Fifty-fifth Anniversary of the Independence of the United States of America* (Boston: Richardson, Lord and Holbrook, 1831). *John Quincy Adams: Speeches & Writings*, ed. David Waldstreicher (New York: Library of America, 2025), 307–14.

Texas Declaration of Independence, March 2, 1836. *Unanimous Declaration of Independence, by the Delegates of the People of Texas, in General Convention, at the Town of Washington, on the Second Day of March, 1836* (San Felipe de Austin: [Joseph] Baker and [Gail] Borden [Jr.], 1836), broadside. Archives and Information Services Division, Texas State Library and Archives Commission.

Liberian Declaration of Independence, July 26, 1847. *The Independent Republic of Liberia; Its Constitution and Declaration; Address of the Colonists to the Free People of Color in the United States, with Other Documents; Issued Chiefly for the Use of the Free people of Color* (Philadelphia: William F. Geddes, 1848), 8–9.

Speech of Mr. Calhoun, of South Carolina, on the Oregon Bill. Delivered in the Senate of the United States, June 27, 1848 (Washington, D.C.: [John T.] Towers, 1848), 14–16.

"Declaration of Sentiments and Resolutions." *Report of the Woman's Rights Convention. Held at Seneca Falls, N.Y., July 19th and 20th, 1848* (Rochester, NY: John Dick at the North Star Office, 1848), 4–12. *American Women's Suffrage: Voices from the Long Struggle for the Vote 1776–1965*, ed. Susan Ware (Library of America, 2020), 36–40.

What to the Slave Is the Fourth of July? An Address, July 5, 1852. *Frederick Douglass: Speeches & Writings*, ed. David Blight (New York: Library of America, 2022), 174–78.

Abraham Lincoln, Speech at Independence Hall, February 22, 1861. *Abraham Lincoln: Speeches & Writings 1859–1865*, ed. Don E. Fehrenbacher (New York: Library of America, 1989), 213–14.

Abraham Lincoln, Response to Serenade, Washington, D.C., July 7, 1863. Ibid., 475–76.

Abraham Lincoln, Address at Gettysburg, Pennsylvania, November 19, 1863. Ibid., 536.

PART IV

Charles Sumner to John Bright, March 13, 1865. *The Civil War: The Final Year Told by Those Who Lived It*, ed. Aaron Sheehan-Dean (New York: Library of America, 2014), 629–31. *The Selected Letters of Charles Sumner*, Vol. II, ed. Beverly Wilson Palmer (Boston: Northeastern University Press, 1990), 273–74. Copyright © 1990 by Beverly Wilson Palmer; copyright © 1990 by University Press of New England, Lebanon, NH. Used by permission.

Declaration of Rights of the Women of the United States. *History of Woman Suffrage*, Vol. III, 1876–1885, eds. Elizabeth Cady Stanton, Susan B. Anthony, and Matilda Joslyn Gage (Rochester, NY: Susan B. Anthony and Charles Mann), 31–34.

Theodore Roosevelt, Speech in Dickinson, Dakota Territory. "A Rancher Speaks to His Neighbors," *Theodore Roosevelt Association Journal*, Library of Congress Manuscript Division. https://www.theodorerooseveltcenter.org/digital-library/o305809. Theodore Roosevelt Digital Library. Dickinson State University.

Declaration of Philippine Independence. *The Laws of the First Philippine Republic (The Laws of Malolos) 1898–1899*, comp. and ed. Sulpicio Guevara (Manila, Philippines: National Historical Commission, 1982), 203–6. Used by permission.

"Eugene V. Debs' Speech at Chicago July Fourth: The Mission of Socialism is as Wide as the World." *Social Democrat Herald*, Chicago, IL, July 13, 1901, 1, 4.

Mark Twain, "The Day We Celebrate." *Mark Twain: Collected Tales, Sketches, Speeches, & Essays 1891–1910*, ed. Louis J. Budd (New York: Library of America, 1992), 820–22.

Emma Goldman, "A New Declaration of Independence." *Mother Earth, Monthly Magazine Devoted to Social Science and Literature* IV.5 (July 1909): 137–38.

Woodrow Wilson, "The Meaning of Liberty." Address at Independence Hall, Philadelphia, July 4, 1914, *President Wilson's Addresses*, ed. George McLean Harper (New York: Henry Holt & Company, 1918), 85–86, 88–89, 93–94.

H. L. Mencken, "Essay in American." *The Evening Sun*, Baltimore, MD, November 7, 1921, 10.

Calvin Coolidge, "The Inspiration of the Declaration." Calvin Coolidge, *Foundations of the Republic: Speeches and Addresses* (New York: Charles Scribner's Sons, 1926), 441–42, 449–54.

Huey Long, "Every Man a King." *American Speeches: Political Oratory from Abraham Lincoln to Bill Clinton*, ed. Ted Widmer (New York: Library of America, 2006), 403–4, 409–10.

Franklin Delano Roosevelt, Eighth Annual Address to Congress. Ibid., 444–46.

Franklin Delano Roosevelt, Address to the Nation. Michael S. Bell, PhD. "July 4, 1941: FDR's Address to the Nation." Published July 4, 2024. https://www.nationalww2museum.org/war/articles/july-4-1941-fdrs-address-nation.

Declaration by United Nations, January 1, 1942.

Mary McLeod Bethune, "Certain Unalienable Rights." *What the Negro Wants*, ed. Rayford Whittingham Logan (Chapel Hill: University of North Carolina Press, 1944), 248–55. Copyright ©1944 by the University of North Carolina Press, renewed 1972 by Rayford W. Logan. Used by permission of the publisher.

PART V

Eleanor Roosevelt, "My Day, July 4, 1945." *The Eleanor Roosevelt Papers Digital Edition* (2017), https://www2.gwu.edu/~erpapers/myday/displaydoc.cfm?_y=1945&_f=md000067. Used by the permission of the Estate of Eleanor Roosevelt.

Declaration of Independence of the Democratic Republic of Viet Nam. Ho Chi Minh, *Selected Works*, Vol. 3 (Hanoi: Foreign Languages Publishing House, 1960–62, 1977), 53–56. Used by permission of Thế Giới Publishers.

The Universal Declaration of Human Rights. https://www.un.org/en/about-us/universal-declaration-of-human-rights.

To Secure These Rights: The Report of the President's Committee on Civil Rights. (New York: Simon & Schuster, 1947), 3–10.

Thurgood Marshall, The Edwin R. Embree Memorial Lecture, February 1954. *Supreme Justice: Speeches and Writings*, ed. J. Clay Smith, Jr. (Philadelphia: University of Pennsylvania Press, 2003), 78–79, 82–83, 88. Used by permission.

W.E.B. Du Bois, A Proposed Declaration of Independence for the People of Africa. Special Collections and University Archives, University of Massachusetts Amherst Libraries, https://credo.library.umass.edu/view/full/mums312-b144-i345. Used by permission of The Du Bois Literary Estates, Odell Murry, Trustee.

Hannah Arendt, "Action and the 'Pursuit of Happiness.'" *Thinking Without a Banister: Essays in Understanding 1953–1975* (New York: Schocken Books, 2018), 211–17. Copyright ©2018 by The Literary Trust of Hannah Arendt and Jerome Kohn. Used by permission.

John F. Kennedy, Address at Independence Hall. Courtesy of the John F. Kennedy Presidential Library and Museum. https://www.jfklibrary.org/learn/about-jfk/historic-speeches/address-at-independence-hall.

Martin Luther King, Jr., Address to the March on Washington, August 28, 1963. *American Speeches: Political Oratory from Abraham Lincoln to Bill Clinton*, ed. Ted Widmer (New York: Library of America, 2006), 556–60. Copyright ©2000 The Heirs to the Estate of Martin Luther King, Jr. Reprinted by arrangement with the Estate of Martin Luther King, Jr., c/o Writers House as agent for proprietor, New York, NY.

"Black Panther Platform." *Helix* (Seattle, WA), Vol. 3, no. 7. (May 9, 1968): 13.

Declaration of Continuing Independence by the First International Indian Treaty Council, at Standing Rock Indian Country, June 8–16, 1974. https://www.iitc.org/wp-content/uploads/DECLARATION-OF-CONTINUING-INDEPENDENCE-1974-FIN.pdf.

Jacques Derrida, "Declarations of Independence," trans. by Tom Keenan and Tom Pepper, *New Political Science* vol. 7, no. 1 (15): 7–15. English translation copyright ©1986, Caucus for a New Political Science. All rights reserved. Republished by permission of the copyright holder and the publisher.

Ronald Reagan, Address to the Nation on Independence Day, July 4, 1986. Courtesy of the Ronald Reagan Presidential Library & Museum. https://www.reaganlibrary.gov/archives/speech/address-nation-independence-day.

John Perry Barlow, A Declaration of the Independence of Cyberspace, Davos Switzerland, February 8, 1996. Courtesy of the Electronic Frontier Foundation. https://www.eff.org/cyberspace-independence.

Declaration of Tea Party Independence. Tea Party Patriots in Nassau County, NY. https://nassautea.wordpress.com/2010/02/24/declaration-of-tea-party-independence/.

Barack Obama, Remarks on the Supreme Court Decision on Marriage Equality. https://obamawhitehouse.archives.gov/the-press-office/2015/06/26/remarks-president-supreme-court-decision-marriage-equality.

ILLUSTRATIONS

INTRODUCTION

Figure 1: Fourth of July banners hang from the Constitution Avenue side of the National Archives Building in Washington, D.C., on June 30, 2016, in preparation for the upcoming Fourth of July weekend. Photo by Brogan Jackson. Courtesy of the National Archives and Records Administration.

Figure 2: A facsimile image from the third printing from the 1823 William Stone copperplate engraving of the Declaration of Independence, carried out by the Bureau of Engraving and Printing in 1976. Courtesy of the National Archives and Records Administration.

Figure 3: "In Congress, July 4, 1776, A Declaration by the Representatives of the United States of America in General Congress Assembled." Broadside by John Dunlap, printer to Congress, printed in Philadelphia, July 4, 1776. Courtesy of the National Archives and Records Administration.

Figure 4: Cover of the *Baltimore Almanack*, 1783. Courtesy of the John Carter Brown Library at Brown University.

Figure 5: John Trumbull, *The Declaration of Independence, July 4, 1776* (1818). Rotunda of the U.S. Capitol. Courtesy of Wikimedia Commons.

Figures 6 and 7: Thomas Jefferson. Draft of Declaration of Independence, 1776. Manuscript. Courtesy of the Library of Congress, Manuscript Division.

PART I

Figure 8: "The Bill of Rights ratified at the Revolution by King William, and Queen Mary, previous to their Coronation." Engraving by John Cary after a drawing by Samuel Wale, from Edward Barnard, *The New, Comprehensive and Complete History of England* (London: A. Hogg, 1783). Courtesy of the Library of Congress, Prints and Photographs Division.

Figure 9: Title page, *An Essay Concerning the True Original Extent and End of Civil Government. By the Late Learned John Locke, Esq.* (Boston: Re-printed and sold by Edes and Gill, in Queen-Street, 1773). Courtesy of the John Carter Brown Library.

Figure 10: *King George III in Coronation Robes.* Portrait (1765) by Allan Ramsay. Courtesy of the Royal Collection Trust.

Figure 11: *The Bostonians in Distress.* Engraving attributed to Philip Dawe. London: Robert Sayer and John Bennett, 1774. Courtesy of the Metropolitan Museum of Art.

Figure 12: *The Battle of Lexington, April 1775. Plate I.* Engraving by Amos Doolittle. Courtesy of the Library of Congress.

Figure 13: Thomas Paine (incorrectly "Edward Payne, Esq."), 1783. Mezzotint by James Watson after a portrait by Charles Willson Peale. Courtesy of the National Portrait Gallery, Smithsonian Museum.

Figure 14: John Adams. Engraving by Stephen Alonzo Schoff after a 1766 portrait by Benjamin Blyth. From Charles Francis Adams, ed., *The Works of John Adams*, Vol. II Boston: Charles C. Little and James Brown, 1850). Courtesy of University of Michigan Library.

Figure 15: Thomas Jefferson. Portrait (1791–93) by Charles Willson Peale. Courtesy of Independence National Historical Park.

Figure 16: George Mason. Etching by Albert Rosenthal, 1888, after a 1750 portrait by John Hesselius. Courtesy of Independence National Historical Park.

Figure 17: Illustration for John Trumbull's 1776 mock epic *M[c] Fingal: A Modern Epic Poem. Or, The Town-meeting*: "As thus he spake, our squire M[c] Fingal / gave to his partizans a signal. . . . The Tories set up a gen'ral rout in chorus." Engraving by Asaph Willard after a drawing by Elkanah Tisdale, from *The Poetical Works of John Trumbull, LL. D.*, Vol. I Hartford: Samuel G. Goodrich, 1820). Courtesy of Princeton University Library.

Figure 18: "House where Jefferson wrote the Declaration of Independence, s.w. cor 7th & Market St. 1776." Watercolor by Benjamin Ridgeway Evans, 1889. Courtesy of the Library Company of Philadelphia.

Figure 19: "The Manner in which the American Colonies Declared themselves Independant of the King of England, throughout the different Provinces, on July 4, 1776." Engraving by George Noble after a painting by William Hamilton, from Edward Barnard, *The New, Comprehensive and Complete History of England* (London: A. Hogg, 1783). Courtesy of the Library of Congress, Prints and Photographs Division.

PART II

Figure 20: "The wicked Statesman, or the Traitor to his Country, at the Hour of Death." Engraving by Paul Revere, 1774, featured on the cover of *The Massachusetts Calendar; or An Almanack for the Year of our Lord Christ 1774.* Courtesy of the American Antiquarian Society.

Figure 21: "The Bostonians Paying the Excise-man, or Tarring and Feathering." Mezzotint attributed to Philip Dawe, 1774, and printed for Robert Sayer and John Bennett, 53 Fleet Street, London. Courtesy of the John Carter Brown Library.

Figure 22: "Rev. Lemuel Haynes, A.M." Engraving by Daggett, Hinman & Co. From Timothy Mather Cooley, *Sketches of the Life and Character of the Rev. Lemuel Haynes, A.M.* (New York: Harper & Brothers, 1837). Courtesy of Wikimedia Commons.

PART III

PART IV

Figure 46: Charles Sumner. Daguerreotype (1865) from the Brady-Handy Collection. Courtesy of the Library of Congress, Prints and Photographs Division.

Figure 47: "The Statue of 'The Freed Slave' in Memorial Hall." Illustration by Fernando Miranda from *Frank Leslie's Illustrated Newspaper*, August 5, 1876. Courtesy of Wikimedia Commons.

Figure 48: Declaration of Rights of the Women of the United States by the National Woman Suffrage Association. July 4th, 1876. Courtesy of the Library of Congress, Rare Books and Special Collections Division.

Figure 49: The tablet of the Statue of Liberty. Courtesy of Wikimedia Commons.

Figure 50: "A new declaration of independence in the year 1885." Chromolithograph by Berhard Gillam, published by Keppler and Schwarzmann, New York, July 1, 1885. Courtesy of the Library of Congress, Prints and Photographs Division.

Figure 51: Theodore Roosevelt. Photograph (1884) from the New York World-Telegram and the Sun Newspaper Photograph Collection. Courtesy of the Library of Congress, Prints and Photographs Division.

Figure 52: Acta de la Proclamacion de Independencia del Pueblo Filipino, June 12, 1898. Courtesy of the National Library of the Philippines Digital Collection.

Figure 53: Eugene V. Debs, portrayed in a cartoon from *Lincoln Socialist-Labor*, Saturday, June 8, 1895. Courtesy of Marxists Internet Archive.

Figure 54: Mark Twain. Photograph (1908) by Alvin Langdon Coburn. Courtesy of Click Americana.

Figure 55: Front page of *Mother Earth*. IV.4, June 1909. Courtesy of Internet Archive.

Figure 56: Front page of *The Philadelphia Inquirer*. 171.5, Sunday, July 5, 1914. Courtesy of Newspapers .com.

Figure 57: Publicity photo of H. L. Mencken. Published by Alfred A. Knopf in 1920. Courtesy of Wikimedia Commons.

Figure 58: "The Shrine of the Declaration of Independence and the Constitution, Washington, D.C." Undated postcard produced by B. S. Reynolds Co., Washington, D.C.

Figure 59: Huey Long. Photograph (1935) by Harris & Ewing Inc. Courtesy of the Library of Congress, Prints and Photographs Division.

Figure 60: Franklin Delano Roosevelt addresses a joint session of Congress, January 6, 1941. AP file photo. Image courtesy of and copyright ©1941 The Associated Press.

Figure 61: Fourth of July Declaration by the President, 1941. Courtesy of the National Archives at College Park, NAID: 514323.

Figure 62: The Declaration of Independence photographed in 1903 and 1940. Courtesy of the National Archives and Records Administration.

Figure 63: Declaration by United Nations, January 1, 1942. Courtesy of the United Nations.

Figure 64: Mary McLeod Bethune, Daytona, Florida, January 1943. Photograph by Gordon Parks. Courtesy of and copyright ©1943 The Gordon Parks Foundation.

PART V

Figure 65: "Rome. 7/24/45—July Fourth in Oslo—U.S. troops and vehicles parade down the main street of Oslo, capital of Norway, during celebrations observing the American Independence Day, July 4, 1945.—Signal Corps Photo through Rome OWI—Approved by appropriate military authority (B List out). 7190-A." Courtesy of the Digital Collections of the National WWII Museum.

Figure 66: Bản Tuyên ngôn độc lập của nước Việt Nam Dân chủ Cộng hòa (The Declaration of Independence of the Democratic Republic of Vietnam). Courtesy of Wikimedia Commons.

Figure 67: Eleanor Roosevelt displays the Universal Declaration of Human Rights. Courtesy of the Franklin Delano Roosevelt Presidential Library and Museum.

Figure 68: Illustration from *To Secure These Rights: The Report of the President's Committee on Civil Rights* (New York: Simon & Schuster, 1947), 7.

Figure 69: Transfer of Charters of Freedom to the National Archives, December 13, 1952. Courtesy of the National Archives.

Figure 70: Thurgood Marshall outside the Supreme Court, August 22, 1958. Image courtesy of and copyright ©2017 The Associated Press.

Figure 71: W.E.B. Du Bois, Mary McLeod Bethune, and NAACP Executive Secretary Walter White at the first meeting of the United Nations, 1945. Courtesy of the National Archives for Black Women's History.

Figure 72: Hannah Arendt at the first Congress of Cultural Critics, 1958. Photograph by Barbara Niggl Radloff. Courtesy of the Munich City Museum, Photography Collection, Barbara Niggl Radloff Archive.

Figure 73: President John F. Kennedy Delivers Address at Independence Hall, Philadelphia. Photograph by Cecil Stoughton, July 4, 1962. Courtesy of the John F. Kennedy Presidential Library and Museum.

Figure 74: Dr. Martin Luther King Jr. Delivers Address to the March on Washington, August 28, 1963. Photograph © Bob Adelman. Courtesy of the Library of Congress, Prints and Photographs Division. (Permission to feature Dr. King's likeness courtesy of Writers House.)

Figure 75: Black Panther Party poster, 1968. Lithograph on paper. Collection of Merrill C. Berman. Courtesy of Universal History Archive/Getty Images.

Figure 76: American Indian Movement "Longest Walk" protest, July 11, 1978. Courtesy of the Library of Congress, Prints and Photographs Division.

Figure 77: Four advertisements: Monsanto Chemicals and Plastics (1952), Rath Black Hawk Bacon (1960), Kraft American Cheese (1966), Pontiac Grand Prix (1976). All images courtesy of eBay.

Figure 78: Jacques Derrida, 1980. Courtesy of Liberation Next.

Figure 79: President Ronald Reagan and First Lady Nancy Reagan watch the Statue of Liberty as she is surrounded by bursts of fireworks, July 4, 1986. President and Mrs. Reagan watch from the deck of the aircraft carrier U.S.S. *John F. Kennedy*. AP Photo/Bob Daugherty. Image courtesy of and copyright ©1986 The Associated Press.

Figure 80: An image from the world's first eBook, published on July 4, 1971. Courtesy of Project Gutenberg.

Figure 81: Detail of 1940 photograph of the Declaration of Independence. Courtesy of the National Archives and Records Administration.

Figure 82: Tea Party Protest in Dallas, Texas, April 15, 2009. Photograph by Matthew T. Rader. Courtesy of Wikimedia Commons.

Figure 83: President Barack Obama walks toward the podium before speaking in the Rose Garden of the White House in Washington, Friday, June 26, 2015, after the Supreme Court declared that same-sex couples have the right to marry anywhere in the U.S. AP Photo/Pablo Martinex Monsivais. Image courtesy of and copyright ©2015 The Associated Press.

Great care has been taken to locate and acknowledge all owners of copyright material included in this book. If any such owner has inadvertently been omitted, acknowledgment will gladly be made in future printings.

INDEX

The text of this book is set in Garamond Premier, a new interpretation of a hand-cut typeface created in the mid-1500s by Claude Garamond. Designed by Robert Slimbach and released in 2004 by Adobe Systems, it was hailed by typography expert Thomas Phinney as "a more directly authentic revival" than the previously released Adobe Garamond.

The paper is acid-free and exceeds the requirements for permanence established by the American National Standards Institute. Text design and composition by Westchester Publishing Services, Danbury, CT. Printing and binding by Sheridan, Chelsea, MI. Jacket printing by Phoenix Color, a division of Lakeside Book Company.